Building Virtual Communities

Building Virtual Communities examines how learning and cognitive change are fostered by online communities. Contributors to this volume explore this question by drawing on their different theoretical backgrounds, methodologies, and personal experience with virtual communities. Each chapter explores the different meanings of the terms "community," "learning," and "change." Case studies are included for further clarification. Together, these chapters describe the building out of virtual communities in terms that are relevant to theorists, researchers, and practitioners. The chapters provide a basis for thinking about the dynamics of Internet community building. Consideration is given to the role of the self or individual as a participant in a virtual community and to the design and refinement of technology as the conduit for extending and enhancing the possibilities of community building in cyberspace. *Building Virtual Communities* will interest educators, psychologists, sociologists, and researchers in human-computer interaction.

K. Ann Renninger is a developmental and educational psychologist at Swarthmore College. She conducts research for the Math Forum (www.mathforum.org), a virtual resource center for mathematics education. Other volumes she has co-edited include *The Handbook of Child Psychology*, Volume 4, *Child Psychology and Practice*, Fifth Edition (1998); *Interest and Learning* (1998); *Change and Development: Issues of Theory, Method, and Application* (1997); *The Development and Meaning of Psychological Distance* (1993); and *The Role of Interest in Learning and Development* (1992).

Wesley Shumar is a cultural anthropologist at Drexel University and an ethnographic evaluator for the Math Forum (www.mathforum.org). He is the author of *College for Sale: A Critique of the Commodification of Higher Education* (1997) and co-author of the forthcoming *Culture, Subject, Psyche: Anthropology, Psychoanalysis and Social Theory*.

Learning in Doing: Social, Cognitive, and Computational Perspectives

Founding Editor
JOHN SEELY BROWN, *Xerox Palo Alto Research Center*

General Editors
ROY PEA, *SRI International, Center for Technology in Learning*
CHRISTIAN HEATH, *The Management Centre, King's College, London*
LUCY A. SUCHMAN, *Centre for Science Studies and Department of Sociology, Lancaster University*

Continued on page following the Index

Building Virtual Communities

Learning and Change in Cyberspace

Edited by

K. ANN RENNINGER
Swarthmore College

WESLEY SHUMAR
Drexel University

CAMBRIDGE
UNIVERSITY PRESS

PUBLISHED BY THE PRESS SYNDICATE OF THE UNIVERSITY OF CAMBRIDGE
The Pitt Building, Trumpington Street, Cambridge, United Kingdom

CAMBRIDGE UNIVERSITY PRESS
The Edinburgh Building, Cambridge CB2 2RU, UK
40 West 20th Street, New York, NY 10011-4211, USA
477 Williamstown Road, Port Melbourne, VIC 3207, Australia
Ruiz de Alarcón 13, 28014 Madrid, Spain
Dock House, The Waterfront, Cape Town 8001, South Africa

http://www.cambridge.org

First published 2002

Printed in the United States of America

Typefaces Janson Text 10.5/13 pt.   *System* LaTeX 2_ε [TB]

A catalog record for this book is available from the British Library.

Library of Congress Cataloging in Publication Data

Building virtual communities : learning and change in cyberspace / edited by
K. Ann Renninger, Wesley Shumar.
    p. cm.
  Includes bibliographical references and index.
  ISBN 0-521-78075-6 – ISBN 0-521-78558-8 (pb.)
  1. Electronic villiages (Computer networks)   2. Internet – Social aspects.
3. Computer networks – Social aspects.   I. Renninger, K. Ann.   II. Shumar, Wesley.
TK5105.83 .B85   2002
004.67–dc21   2001052485

ISBN 0 521 78075 6 hardback
ISBN 0 521 78558 8 paperback

Contents

List of Tables and Figures

Tables

Figures

Contributors

Amy S. Bruckman
Georgia Institute of Technology
College of Computing
801 Atlantic Drive
Atlanta, GA 30332-0280
asb@cc.gatech.edu

Roger J. Burrows
University of York Centre for
Housing Policy
Heslington, York YO10 5DD
United Kingdom
rjb7@york.ac.uk

Raoul Cervantes
Momoyama Gakuin University
(St. Andrew's University)
1-1 Manabino
Izumi, Osaka,
Japan 594-1198
ksakui@hotmail.com

Douglas B. Clark
University of California
at Berkeley
Education in Mathematics, Science &
Technology (EMST)
4523 Tolman Hall
Berkeley, CA 94720-1670
clark@socrates.berkeley.edu

Michael Cole
University of California, San Diego
Laboratory of Human Cognition
La Jolla, CA 92093-0092
mcole@ucsd.edu

Richard Coyne
University of Edinburgh
Department of Architecture
20 Chambers Street
Edinburgh EH1 1JZ United Kingdom
Richard.Coyne@ed.ac.uk

Alex J. Cuthbert
University of California at Berkeley
Education in Mathematics, Science &
Technology (EMST)
4523 Tolman Hall
Berkeley CA 94720-1670
alx@socrates.berkeley.edu

Ann Locke Davidson
Educational Connections, LLC
1012 S.W. King Avenue, Suite 301
Portland, OR 97205
davidson@educationalconnections.com

Judith Fusco
SRI International
333 Ravenswood Avenue
Menlo Park, CA 94025
jfusco@unix.sri.com

David Hakken
SUNY Institute of Technology
PO Box 3050
Utica, NY 13504-3050
hakken@sunyit.edu

Christopher Hoadley
SRI International and Stanford
    University
333 Ravenswood Avenue BN271
Menlo Park, CA 94025
tophe@ciltkn.org

Caroline Haythornthwaite
University of Illinois at
    Urbana–Champaign
Graduate School of Library and
    Information Science
501 East Daniel Street
Champaign, IL 61820
haythorn@uiuc.edu

Beverly Hunter
Piedmont Research Institute
130 Mossie Lane
Amissville, VA 20106
bev_hunter@piedmontresearch.org

Carlos Jensen
Georgia Institute of Technology
    College of Computing
801 Atlantic Drive
Atlanta, GA 30332-0280
carlosj@cc.gatech.edu

Steven G. Jones
University of Illinois
Department of Communication
    (m/c 132)
1007 W. Harrison, Room 1140
Chicago, IL 60607
sjones@uic.edu

James A. Levin
University of Illinois Department
    of Educational Psychology
220 Education Building
1310 S. 6th Street
Champaign, IL 61820
j-levin@uiuc.edu

Marcia C. Linn
University of California
    at Berkeley
Graduate School of Education
4523 Tolman Hall

Berkeley, CA 94720-1670
mclinn@socrates.berkeley.edu

Sarah Nettleton
University of York Department
    of Social Policy and Social Work
Heslington, York YO10 5DD
United Kingdom
sjn2@york.ac.uk

Jason Nolan
University of Toronto
252 Bloor Street West
Toronto, Ontario M5S1V6
Canada
jason.nolan@utoronto.ca

Roy D. Pea
Stanford University
Institute for Learning Sciences
    and Technologies
School of Education
Cubberly Hall
Stanford, CA 94305
roypea@stanford.edu

K. Ann Renninger
Swarthmore College
Program in Education
500 College Avenue
Swarthmore, PA 19081-1397
krennin1@swarthmore.edu

Patricia K. Schank
SRI International
333 Ravenswood Avenue
Menlo Park, CA 94025
schank@unix.sri.com

Mark S. Schlager
SRI International
333 Ravenswood Avenue
Menlo Park, CA 94025
schlager@unix.sri.com

Janet Ward Schofield
University of Pittsburgh
517 LRDC
3939 O'Hara Street
Pittsburgh, PA 15260-5159
schof@pitt.edu

Wesley Shumar
Drexel University
Department of Culture and
  Communication
3141 Chestnut Street
Philadelphia, PA 19104
wes@drexel.edu

Joel Weiss
Ontario Institute for Studies in
  Education of the University
  of Toronto
CTL Dept, 11 South

252 Bloor Street West
Toronto, Ontario M5S1V6
Canada
weiss@oise.utoronto.ca

Dorian Wiszniewski
University of Edinburgh
Department of Architecture
20 Chambers Street
Edinburgh EH1 1JZ
United Kingdom
Dorian.Wiszniewski@ed.ac.uk

Series Foreword

This series for Cambridge University Press is becoming widely known as an international forum for studies of situated learning and cognition.

Innovative contributions are being made by anthropology; by cognitive, developmental, and cultural psychology; by computer science; by education; and by social theory. These contributions are providing the basis for new ways of understanding the social, historical, and contextual nature of learning, thinking, and practice that emerges from human activity. The empirical settings of these research inquiries range from the classroom to the workplace, to the high-technology office and to learning in the streets and in other communities of practice.

The situated nature of learning and remembering through activity is a central fact. It may appear obvious that human minds develop in social situations and extend their sphere of activity and communicative competencies. But cognitive theories of knowledge representation and learning alone have not provided sufficient insight into these relationships.

This series was born of the conviction that new and exciting interdisciplinary syntheses are underway as scholars and practitioners from diverse fields seek to develop theory and empirical investigations adequate for characterizing the complex relations of social and mental life and for understanding successful learning wherever it occurs. The series invites contributions that advance our understanding of these seminal issues.

Roy Pea
Christian Heath
Lucy Suchman

Preface and Acknowledgments

This volume is unique in its focus on the learning and change that takes place in the building of communities in cyberspace. Knowledge and resources for knowledge building are central to both virtual and physical communities. Members, or participants, in any community are engaged in learning that is critical to the survival and reproduction of that community. This learning may be even more true for virtual communities than it is for physical communities. For those concerned with building virtual communities and those who are working to understand the impact of virtual communities on participants, clarity about the nature of learning and change that is enabled by the Internet is of particular importance.

At first glance, identifying the nature of learning and change that takes place as a virtual community builds out may seem a straightforward-enough proposition. A dearth of literature has supported the importance of community to learners of all ages (Barab & Duffy, 2000; Bellah et al., 1985; Bransford, Brown & Cocking, 1999; Brown & Campione, 1994; Lave, 1993; Wellman & Gulia, 1999; Wenger, 1999). Through community participation, learners find and acquire models and have the opportunity themselves to be models and apprentices. In community participation, activities such as asking questions and providing the person with whom one is talking with background information are both supported and socialized.

The task of identifying what to watch (the indicators to be studied) in building an online community is not at all straightforward, however. There are many potential indicators but no clarity about which apply to all communities. Moreover, studies of community, learning, and/or change typically draw on different fields of specialization. Community, for example, can be studied in terms of its design, who its members are, how learning is facilitated, whether learning occurs, why learning occurs, and so forth. A further complication is the wide range of computer-mediated formats being used to enable community development. These formats range from complex organizations that have budgets for programmers, project staff, and Web persons to build out a community in response to participants' needs; to MOOs that have an anarchistic form of community in which people come, "hang out," and leave; to discussion lists that have designated leaders and focus on a specific agenda or topic.

At present, there tend to be two types of conversations about building community online. One conversation is occurring among those in the learning sciences, including those trained as educational psychologists, educational technologists, computer scientists, and cognitive scientists. This discussion focuses on the design of communities and the ways in which users or participants work with and learn from the experience of community participation. Another conversation is taking place among sociologists, anthropologists, and linguists. This discussion focuses on the nature of participants' collective imagination and feelings of identity as a tool for understanding belonging and attachment to particular virtual communities. It also details the social interaction necessary to describe communication and sociability. Presumably because these groups do not tend to ask the same questions, they do not attend each other's conferences, nor do they tend to cite each other's work.

The present volume extends both of these conversations by engaging the reader in examining the interdependence of the forms, structure, and possibilities for facilitating the building-out of communities in cyberspace. Contributors to this volume include a widely divergent group of authors, all of whom are working to understand and build out communities online. They vary in the questions on which they have focused, theoretical backgrounds, methodology, and computer-based format with which they have worked.

The opening chapter traces the use of the term "community" to describe physical and virtual space. It suggests that computer-mediated formats in particular may enable what might better be understood as the myth of community to be realized by community participants. The chapters that follow have been assigned to one of three sections: types of community, structure of community, and possibilities for community. Like all typologies, the chapters in each section could also have been included in each of the other sections. The chapters are juxtaposed to highlight the tension between differences of theoretical and methodological perspectives on the situated and universal aspects of learning enabled by and in the development of online communities.

In "Types of Community," the first section, learning and change are described as being contingent on the kind of virtual community that has been constructed, its purposes, its fluidity, and its given informational resources (e.g., conversations among professionals, archives, etc.). In "Structure and Community," the second section, learning and change is understood to be enabled by both the design features of particular communities and theories about how people learn. The communities described highlight the relation between community structure and identity. The structure of community can be seen as both a constraining and an enabling possibility. In "Possibilities for Community," the third section, opportunities for learning and change are described as emerging from the existing type and structure of community. The possibilities for a community may not be predictable.

Thinking across theoretical and methodological differences such as those represented by the range of chapters included here involves work but should offset the limitations of any particular world view (Cole, 1996). To assist the reader, definitions of community, learning, and change are included in each, and case examples are provided as illustration. Conversations that arise from this volume might take numerous directions. A volume such as this is expected to hold a different meaning for each reader. In fact, each reader is likely to find his or her own favorite or most useful chapters, and these might be expected to differ from those of the next reader.

Together these chapters describe the building-out of virtual communities in terms that are relevant to theorists, researchers, and practitioners. The theoretical and methodological differences reflected in the chapters suggest a need for a common language and conceptual context for describing learning and change as part of community building. No grand theory is offered, however.

The chapters provide readers with a basis for thinking about the dynamics of Internet community building across a variety of computer-based contexts. This includes consideration of the role(s) of the self or individual as participants in virtual community, and the design and refinement of technology as the conduit for extending and enhancing the possibilities of community building in cyberspace.

K. Ann Renninger
Wesley Shumar

Acknowledgments

Jan Hawkins was one of the earliest champions of this volume, and her backing in its early stages is gratefully acknowledged. The encouragement of Julia Hough and Philip Laughlin, our editors at Cambridge University Press, throughout the various stages of this project is most appreciated. They recognized the possibilities that a volume such as this represented for opening a conversation among researchers and practitioners. We thank Scott Price for his help in creating a cover that reflects the range of computer-mediated communities included in the volume. Finally, we recognize the National Science Foundation's efforts to encourage its grantees to evaluate their work. Collaboration on this volume stemmed from the effort to identify indicators that could be used to study participant learning and change at The Math Forum (NSF grant #9618223). Any opinions, findings, and conclusions or recommendations expressed in this volume however, are those of the author(s) and do not necessarily reflect the views of the National Science Foundation.

References

Cole, M. (1996). *Cultural psychology: A once and future discipline*. Cambridge, MA: Harvard University Press.

Barab, S. A., & Duffy, T. (2000). From practice fields to communities of practice. In D. Jonassen & S. M. Land (Eds.), *Theoretical foundations of learning environments* (pp. 25–56). Mahwah, NJ: Lawrence Erlbaum.

Bellah, R. N., Madsen, R., Sullran, W. M., Swidler, A., & Tipton, S. M. (1985). *Habits of the heart: Individualism and commitment in American life*. Berkeley: University of California Press.

Bransford, J. D., Brown, A. L., & Cocking, R. R. (1999). *How people learn: Brain, mind, experience, and school*. Washington, DC: National Academy Press.

Brown, L., & Campione, J. C. (1994). Guided discovery in a community of learners. In K. McGilly (Ed.), *Classroom lessons* (pp. 229–70). Cambridge, MA: MIT Press.

Lave, J. (1993). *Understanding practice*. New York: Cambridge University Press.

Wellman, B., & Gulia, M. (1999). Net surfers don't ride alone: Virtual communities as communities. In M. Smith and P. Kollack, (Eds.), *Communities in cyberspace*. New York: Routledge.

Wenger, E. (1999). *Communities of practice*. New York: Cambridge University.

Foreword

Virtual Communities for Learning and Development – A Look to the Past and Some Glimpses into the Future

Michael Cole

The reader is in for a treat in the highly knowledgeable and varied chapters that follow. The volume includes authors from a wide range of disciplinary and theoretical perspectives, all of whom have experience working directly with computer-mediated communication and community building. Each chapter provides a different perspective on the many ways that human interactions are being mediated in some fashion by the Internet. Each chapter also makes suggestions about the implications of this new set of technological capacities for the social organization of learning and development in contemporary society. This vast territory is unusually well explored in this volume.

As the comments of several of the authors indicate, memories of becoming involved in computer-mediated communication (CMC) as a medium of intellectual communication have something of a "flashbulb" character to them. Not unlike my memory of where I was when John Kennedy was shot, I remember the conditions that led to my use of CMC and my discovery that it could be a resource for community building.

The year was 1978. I had just moved to the University of California at San Diego (UCSD) with a joint appointment in Psychology and Communication. These two academic units were located on different parts of the campus. To complicate matters, my major research project was the study of classroom lessons in a school located approximately 20 miles from the campus, but my research laboratory was part of an organized research unit located near the psychology department. Burdened with heavy administrative duties in Communication, I found it very difficult to coordinate with my research team on the one hand and my colleagues in Psychology and the Center for Human Information Processing (CHIP) on the other.

Luckily for me, Jim Levin, whose work appears in this volume, joined our laboratory. Jim had been a graduate student in Psychology and had worked with faculty members in CHIP. He introduced our lab to the idea that we could have terminals connected to an electronic network that would store and forward messages from one account to another and would create a common message space where we could coordinate as a group. Our lab was quickly outfitted with the needed terminals (the first PC was still three years over the horizon) and we began to use them with a view toward coordinating our movement in time and space.

It did not take long for us to learn that sprinkled among our instrumental coordinating messages, various academic ideas began to make their appearance. Moreover, since graduate students and postgraduate students involved in our research were part of the network, it was not long before our communications served the multiple functions of coordinating meetings in time/space and engaging in CMC education/research online.

Our curiosity was also attracted by the potential uses of CMC for opening up classrooms to the outside world. Jim Levin took the lead in this effort, setting up connections between San Diego and Alaska using satellite-based telecommunications facilities that were filtering into the public sector from the military. Physical separation, we discovered, could, under propitious conditions, lead to promising reorganization of children's writing during the school day.

Nor did it take long for us to begin using the computer-to-computer store-and-forward systems that grew out of the Advanced Research Projects Administration (ARPA) net to extend our own intellectual activities beyond UCSD. Our laboratory has long been a place where scholars from different parts of the United States and different countries spend a year or two, engaging with us in our research and introducing us to new perspectives. Once habituated to easy online discussions while they were living near UCSD and attending our weekly lab meetings, those who remained behind, as well as those who moved on, began exploiting a combination of telephone-line-based and satellite-based CMC to continue our discussions. Thus it came about that, in the early 1980s we began what later came to be known as a list serve, which continues to this day (see www.lchc.ucsd.edu/mca for the history and current state of this activity).

As the Internet expanded to become the World Wide Web and graphic capabilities became common, the use of computers and telecommunications networks became an increasingly pervasive focus of our research attention. They served to organize educational activities that link our university with its surrounding communities, enabled the formation of distributed consortia of researchers, and changed the way we teach our university courses. As I am sure is true of many, my daily activities have been transformed by the new technologies of communication, for better and for worse.

It is from this experiential background and a long-standing interest in issues of learning and development as processes of joint, mediated, human activity, I approach the task of writing a foreword to this volume. In particular, I focus on a few broad themes that this volume has enabled me to reflect on.

First, I am reminded by many of the authors that any discussion of virtual communities, whether organized in the service of education or for any of the other myriad uses to which they are put, is helped enormously by viewing our current conceptual understandings in terms of their histories. This general orientation applies with special force to the concept of community, which came into the English language relatively recently in its history and has been changing rather rapidly in the past 150 or so years.

Williams (1973) notes in his analysis of the history of the concept of community that the term "community" entered the English language in the fourteenth century from Latin by way of French. "Community" referred primarily to a geographically localized group of people until approximately the seventeenth century (the terms *commune* in French and *Gemeinde* in German retain this meaning to the present day). But beginning between the seventeenth and nineteenth centuries, "community" expanded to include the idea of a group of people who hold something in common (as in community of interests) or who share a common sense of identity even if they do not live in a single locale. This expansion of meanings was accompanied by a self-conscious separation between the idea of a community and the idea of a society. As Shumar and Renninger note in their introductory chapter, "On Conceptualizing Community," the distinction between community and society has come down to us from the work of the German sociologist, Tonnies (1887/1940), as a contrast between a more direct, more total, and more emotionally charged set of relationships (community/gemeinschaft) and the more formal, abstract, and instrumental relationships associated with the idea of society (gesselschaft), which in turn is closely related to the concept of nation state and its bureaucratically mediated institutions.

The conceptual differentiation of community and society in the nineteenth century coincided with, and was enabled by, a series of changes in technologies in general and technologies of communication in particular. At the beginning of the century, most people lived on the land in small communities and grew or made by hand the vast majority of their worldly goods. Schooling was nowhere a general social phenomenon. The fastest mode of transportation was on water. By the end of the century, there was, in many parts of the world, a major shift in modes of living away from the land and residence in small communities toward manufacturing and residence in ever-growing cities. Schooling was made mandatory. Railroad networks became extensive, and electricity was brought under control to enable telegraphy and telephony, as well as skyscrapers and mass production. People viewed escape from the confining circumstances of small communities with their absence of choice and privacy to the bright lights of large cities as liberating. An old German proverb captures this eagerness to escape the intrusive nature of small town life quite nicely: "Stadtluft Mach Frei" (City air sets you free). With these social changes, it appeared that the ideology of the Enlightenment, with its emphasis on reason and individual initiative, was attainable as a general condition of life.

This generally "upbeat" characterization of historical change had, of course, its dark underside. Not only were cities liberating, but they were also alienating. Additionally, they were, until public health innovations of the late nineteenth century, dangerous to one's health, either from disease or violent crime. Moreover, whatever virtues these demographic/lifestyle changes had, their virtues were by no means equally distributed. The technological have-nots were subjected to levels of political and economic exploitation that were previously impossible on a mass scale. In addition, the technological marvels of the new modes of life were evenly matched by technologically mediated mayhem. At the very time that the European powers succeeded in dividing up control over the rest of the world, and Tonnies was formulating the distinction between community and society, these same European powers began to turn on each other with a murderous efficiency that depended critically on just those technologies that made the new modes of life possible. By the mid-twentieth century the world had witnessed a level of human carnage never before seen, and, with the advent of control over atomic energy, humanity literally reached the threshold of annihilation by its own hands. The formally colonized countries of the world had won their de jure independence, but their de facto dependence on their former masters remained. By the end of the twentieth century, those countries that had taken literally the idea that enlightened human reason could create a scientifically guided, bountiful, and just society had crumbled, leaving a return to religious fundamentalism or the invisible hand of the free market as the leading ideological and political economic world views.

It is fascinating to me that as the mid-century form of modernism that I grew up with seemed to be collapsing all around me, a new form of technology arose that promised to undo the mischief of its predecessors. The previous technological toolkit and its associated patterns of life promoted mass society and a countervailing individualism, with its loss of personal community and alienation. The new forms of technology promised to re-form and remediate human activity, restoring the lost sense of community that was ever more frequently commented upon.

This vision was not new. Consider, for example, the following early promise of a return to community through new technologies which would make the

Nation a neighborhood.... The electric wire, the iron pipe, the streetrailroad, the daily newspaper, the telephone...have made us all one body....There are no outlanders. It is possible for men to understand one another....Indeed, it is but the dawn of a spiritual awakening. (William Allen White, 1910, quoted in Putnam, 2000, p. 376)

Rheingold, initiator of the Well, an early and famous virtual community, illustrates this new form of personal/community regeneration when he writes,

My flesh-and-blood family long ago grew accustomed to the way I sit in my home office early in the morning and late at night, chuckling and cursing, sometimes crying, about words I read on the computer screen. It might have looked to my daughter as if I were alone at my desk the night she caught me chortling online, but from my point of view I was in living contact with old and new friends, strangers and colleagues. (Rheingold, 1994)

It is a salutary characteristic of the chapters in this volume that, without denying the transformative affordances of CMC, they do a thorough job of deconstructing the one-sided, techno-optimism of the promoters of a brave, new world in the World Wide Web. Yes, there are potentials for creating community using the Internet, but achieving that potential is not automatic, easy, or necessarily enduring. Like freedom, it is a fragile accomplishment that must be constantly worked at and watched over.

I will have more to say about the real complexities of community mediated by CMC with respect to the chapters of this book shortly. But first, here are a few words about the term "virtual," which also has a history. Curiously, "virtual" came into the English language from Latin and French about the same time as did "community." Initially it referred to things that had special and effective physical capacities, linking it closely to our ideas of virtuous. But in the seventeenth and eighteenth centuries, like "community," the meaning of "virtual" underwent changes. *The Complete Oxford English Dictionary* (1971) identifies this new meaning as something "That is so in essence or effect, although not formally or actually, admitting of being called by the name so far as the effect or result is concerned" (p. 3639). At the same time, virtuality became associated with optics, referring to an apparent image created by refraction upon rays of light.

Rheingold, who appears to have coined the term "virtual community," provides a definition that accords reasonably well with the "so in essence or effect" of virtual in extending the term to apply to communities when he wrote, ". . . People in virtual communities do just about everything people do in real life, but we leave our bodies behind. You can't kiss anybody and nobody can punch you in the nose, but a lot can happen within those boundaries" (Rheingold, 1994).

Ekblad (1998), who studied the virtual academic community that my colleagues and I initiated in the early 1980s, captures the "existing in effect, but not in actuality" sense of virtualness that appears to apply to this kind of community. She wrote that the community linking participants is "most obviously virtual in nature" when it displays the characteristics of "being transient, recurrently emerging and distributed over the network of the system." Here the "being so in essence" and the "apparent image" notions of virtual come together in a propitious way that seems to capture what is required to create and sustain computer-mediated communities and, perhaps, given the nature of contemporary societies, communities of all kinds (see hem.fyristorg.com/evaek/index.html).

When we combine the special characteristics of community in the mobile, distributed, electronically mediated, and globalized conditions of modern life with the particular characteristics of virtualness that enable and constrain these characteristics, one of the most striking features of virtual communities, even that subset of virtual communities that is self-consciously designed to promote learning and development, is their enormous heterogeneity.

This heterogeneity stands out clearly even within the relatively restricted projects focused on learning and development described in this book. I think it is fair to say that while every one of the projects the authors describe contains a "virtual" component, each is unique in the combination of institutional arrangements, educational content, forms of Internet communication, and participant goals that it embodies. For example, the initiators of MediaMOO had exploration of new media environments for education as their topic; several years of intense interest and involvement were followed by fractionation and gradual disintegration. They conclude their hunt for a lost community with some strong hunches about factors that builders of virtual communities need to take into account, including focus on continued shared goals and continuity of leadership (see Bruckman & Jenson, this volume). To take a different example, the initiators of an online forum for elementary school children demonstrate that when girls' interests are highlighted, they are as interested as boys (in this case, more interested) in using computers as a medium of communication. But the students' community is almost as much mediated by face-to-face interactions as it is by their computer-mediated interactions (see Davidson & Shofield, this volume). To take yet another example, sustainability remains an open questions for a site on which teachers of mathematics are given access to expertise and ready-to-hand high-class curricular materials that produce real advances in teaching and learning (see Renninger & Shumar, this volume).

Hunter (this volume), who has more experience than most in seeking to use the Internet to promote learning and development, makes the essential point that the success of such efforts depends crucially upon the institutional frameworks of the face-to-face communities where people are physically located. While the Internet has the *potential* to create a sense of global community among American children of military personnel scattered around a large air force base in northern Italy, that potential is not realizable owing to such debilitating facts as that all communication in the schools which are in locus sites of communication are subject to military surveillance.

Of course, nonmilitary school children in regular schools are also subject to surveillance, and their access to the "freedom" of the Internet is circumscribed by software and social injunctions to prevent their minds from being virtually polluted by material deemed inappropriate. Nonetheless, so long as the materials they can access are made sufficiently interesting, and their teachers are willing to create and maintain a virtual community of Internet-using educators, the relative isolation of the classroom can be broken, and projects that draw them into authentic, developmentally productive learning can be arranged, as Levin and his colleagues have been showing for years. Yet one should not expect such activities to be constantly running at a high pitch. Rather, they are (as a rule) enrichment activities that require planning and much maintenance work. Like the MediaMOO, they have a typical rhythm of growth, activity, and decay. But, unlike the MediaMOO, which did not have a larger network of participants for whom joint activities that break the isolation of the class-room are an ongoing source of educational and professional enhance-ment, the larger "virtual community" of teachers in the case of Levin and Cervantes (this volume) make the regeneration of new activities a constant resource for sustaining virtual interaction. Some of these inter-actions will be more productive than others, and all of them hold out hope based on the experience of repeated success despite the knowledge that some projects die in their early stages.

I urge the reader to pay as close attention to the failures reported here as to the successes. Despite the enormous hype attached to the World Wide Web as the harbinger of a new educational/world order, we know far too little about the various hybrids of Web-mediated, book-mediated, institutionally constructed and constrained forms of interaction that are talked about in terms of virtual community and that promise (or it is threaten?) to become the norm in the decades to come.

Questions on which I am still thinking include:

- Are we entering an era in which communities of interest/choice will come to dominate modern life?
- Will threats to the environment from current living patterns force a disaggregation of human living patterns back into smaller communities, trading virtual travel for the real thing?
- Will the decentralizing, democratizing affordances of the Internet win out, or will it result in new forms of centralized, top-down control?
- And finally, with respect to learning and development, will a rising tide of Web-mediated learning and development bring about productive forms of deschooling or serve, instead, as a tool for high-class, inquiry-based learning for a small class of knowledge haves, and the realization of some form of Aldous Huxley's distopian nightmares for a brave new world?

If contemporary social theorists are correct, the modern era faces us with unprecedented new ways of being in the world and, with it, new dangers, new opportunities, and new forms of community in which we, along with others, will face those challenges. Human interaction has al-ways been, in some measure, virtual. That successive waves of technolog-ical innovation increase the density of mediation between individuals and groups can be expected to remain one of the major sources of changes in human life and, along with it, changes in the nature of learning and development. The pages to follow offer the reader a variety of glimpses into that uncharted future.

References

Ekblad, E. (1998). *Contact, community and multilogue: Electronic communication in the practice of scholarship*. Paper presented at The Fourth Congress of the International Society for Cultural Research and Activity Theory (ISCRAT), Aarhus University, Denmark, 7–11 June 1998. Available: hem.fyristorg.com/evaek/writings.html.

The Complete Oxford English Dictionary. (1971). Oxford: Oxford University Press.

Putnam, R. D. (2000). *Bowling alone: The collapse and revival of American community*. Putnam. New York: Simon & Schuster.

Rheingold, H. (1994). *The virtual community*. Available at http://www.rheingold.com/vc/book/ [1 March 2000].

Tönnies, F. (1887/1940). *Community and society*. C. P. Loomis. (Trans.) New York: American Book Company.

Williams, R. (1973). *Keywords*. Oxford: Oxford University Press.

Building Virtual Communities

Introduction

On Conceptualizing Community

Wesley Shumar and K. Ann Renninger

At the very moment that there is talk about the loss of "real" community, many theorists, researchers, and practitioners – groups who don't typically "speak" to one another – all appear to share a common interest in the community enabled by the Internet (Jones, 1995, 1998; Kiesler, 1997; Loader, 1997; Mitchell, 1995; Rheingold, 1993; Shields, 1996; Smith & Kollack, 1999). These discussions range from the need to redefine community, based on the dynamic and seemingly elusive qualities of virtual community; to concern for appropriate indices and measures for describing a community in the process of rapid change; to efforts to identify the nature of users, how they are interacting, and their needs.

Several features of the virtual world contribute to the recent proliferation of references to, and the self-referencing of particular sites as, virtual communities. These features include: (a) an image of a community to which a core of users/participants returns over time, with whom a community might be built out (providing feedback, lending a volunteer hand, contributing to discussions and activity, etc.); (b) distinctions between physical and virtual communities in terms of temporal and spatial possibilities; and (c) the multilayered quality of communicative space that allows for the mingling of different conversations, the linking of conversations across Web sites, and the archiving of discussions, information, and the like, that permits social exchange around site resources at a future time.

In this chapter, we explore the ways individuals and groups are using the Internet to build communities.* *Virtual communities* involve a combination

---

* Of course, it is not possible to take an "objective" position on these issues. We have a Constructivist impulse to help bring virtual community into existence. We have been working with groups who seek to expand the realm of social possibility through the Internet, and this is reflected in our discourse (Bourdieu, 1991).

1

of physical and virtual interaction, social imagination, and identity. They may be distinguished from *physical communities* in that virtual communities can extend the range of community, and individuals can tailor their personal communities (Bauman, 2000; Wellman, 2001).

The archiving of online interactions makes possible forms of interaction that can be both more flexible and more durable than face-to-face interactions. The ongoing availability of resources positions participants to revise their images of themselves, as well as the range of interactions in which participants engage. In addition, new and more subtle shifts in identity are made possible. While many of the early discussions of virtual community focused on large identity shifts (e.g., men could masquerade as women) more recent work has shown that these kinds of shifts are perhaps not that important (Herring, 1994, 1995, 1996; O'Brien, 1999). The ability to come to identify with a group online, and support to do so, actually provides a scaffold for a different and enhanced sense of possibility for individuals (see Renninger & Shumar, this volume).

The discourse of virtual community that often comes from some core Internet users and technological enthusiasts, however, has been branded potentially exclusionary by some. This discourse has been labeled potentially racist and classist contributing to a digital divide (www.pbs.org/digitaldivide/). Further, to construe community in terms of interest is considered socially naïve.

The need to counter elitism is one for which we have a great deal of sympathy. This need, in itself, is not an argument against the existence of communities in the virtual world. The Internet provides advantages to those who question the existing power structure and offers counterexamples to discussions of community imagination (Anderson, 1991). Imagining community involves a discursive process of defining terrain and boundaries of community. The terrain and boundaries are constrained by differences of power among individuals. Nevertheless, the future of the Internet requires that those in positions of power be able to effect policy changes that will ensure a landscape that is not dominated by the elite (www.digitaldividenetwork.org/content/sections/index.cfm).

The critique that interest is too narrow a basis for defining community is more complex. This argument implies that communities have essential qualities: shared sets of physical resources and needs; mutual interdependence; and complex social organization including kinship, political, economic, and administrative layers. Since these qualities are only seen in small measure in virtual environments that are nothing like "real communities," the Internet and the Web could instead be understood as interesting technologies for advanced telecommunication. This critique suggests that the term "community" is being used to denote so many concepts that it no longer holds any meaning.

Certainly every commercial Web site appears to have added an interactive layer to attract more traffic. Several software organizations are currently trying to leverage users by promoting community to support costs – users can answer each other's questions rather than taking up valuable company time and phone lines. On the other hand, to assume that there is an essential set of criteria that defines community and social interaction is unnecessarily limiting. Clearly there is a great deal of diversity in the ways people are using the Internet and the range of online social interaction that occurs (Kling, 2000). Despite the wide range of types of social groupings on the Internet and the interaction they make possible, each type is organized in a way that reflects the particular forms of interaction it makes possible (Hakken, 1999). Such principles of organization are idiosyncratic because they are socially constructed. The forms of interaction that evolve, furthermore, might best be understood as both symbols of and participants' internalized images of possibilities for community (Renninger & Shumar, this volume).

In the context of different sets of social arrangements and different personal needs, the individuals and the groups described in this volume strategize ways in which the Internet can enhance their collective needs. The Internet can also provide new resources that are both reliable and usable. These new groups and strategies are part of the spatial and temporal transformation of social life in contemporary societies.

Community As Symbol and Activity

Implicit in the current debate about whether the Web enables virtual community are some classic sociological assumptions about community. Efforts to define community typically assume a Tönniesian opposition of gemeinschaft and gesellschaft. Gemeinschaft for Tönnies (1887/1957) is the coherent community in which culture and family are intact, and social life is whole because of this. This is a central concept for modern sociology. The contemporary sociological assumption is that modernity results in a loss of traditional community values and structures and replaces them with impersonal relationships and fragmented cultural values that constitute gesellschaft.

Cohen (1985) showed that this assumption of traditional communities being replaced by modern society is part of the larger Durkheimian (and perhaps Marxian and Weberian) tradition in sociology. Durkheim (1984) posed two main forms of social organization: mechanical and organic solidarity. Mechanical solidarity describes communities built on close ties among kin groups where reciprocity binds the group together. Organic solidarity describes modern institutions that replaced the traditional forms of organization. He argued that mechanical and organic solidarity can exist side by side in the same society at the same time, although the larger tradition turns them into alternative moments in the historical development of society (Cohen, 1985). In the Durkheimian scheme, an ethnic neighborhood in a large city, for example, might be a pocket of mechanical solidarity within the most advanced and organically organized city. It was not necessarily Durkheim's intent to posit that history reflects movement toward increased individual autonomy and impersonal institutional structures that replace the functions of traditional kith and kin and away from mechanical solidarity and close personal attachments. Such a definition of community would be tautological.

Cohen (1985) suggested that community tends to be defined by social scientists as that which we have lost to modernity. They create a kind of fiction about the relation of time and historical movement that does not apply to many specific locales. This type of fiction has an impact upon how we are positioned to think about the building of virtual communities even if we are unfamiliar with the assumptions that discussions of community imply. The definition of community informs the image held, the words used to describe community, and the sets of expectations concerning what community can be. The definition is further complicated since, as mentioned earlier, so many companies are trying to use the term "community" to do everything from building brand awareness to trying to get users to provide free technical support. We must recognize that there are many strategies and diverse goals in the uses of the term "community" and in the efforts to build community online.

In the context of the larger public narrative about the loss of community, another narrative that stems from a long history of nostalgia for the spirit of community has developed (Oldenburg, 1989; Putnam, 2000). This narrative focuses on recapturing community. Anderson (1991) points out that all communities – with the possible exception of foraging bands – are imagined. The image of the loving, close family and community emerges from a collective past but is, in fact, a thoroughly modern myth that meets current needs. Traditional communities were organized according to a system of power in which the church, kinship, and kingship could be quite brutal. Traditional communities were not based on intimate personal relationships and bonds of caring. Furthermore, Anderson suggests that nationalism could supplant the older imaginings of organization, religion, and the dynastic realm only when specific cultural conceptions of antiquity "lost their axiomatic grip on men's minds" (Anderson, 1991). Likewise, we would argue that the rise of the virtual comes at a moment when the organization of community has become more individualized and less structured by larger social forces of class, work, geographic location, and the like (Bauman, 2000; Castells, 1996, 1999; Wellman, 2001). Interestingly, it appears that virtual communities have led us to a discourse and potential reality of what in the past had only been a utopian version of community.

For example, efforts to construct small towns and utopian communities throughout the United States starting in the eighteenth century were considered to be experiments in modernity. In the present era, these experiments are now construed as exemplars of the "traditional communities" of family, kin, shared values, and greater intimacy when at one time they were suspect and ridiculed. Online communities are the most recent inheritors of this mantle of experimentation. It is not surprising that the discourse of community is ubiquitous and distinctions between traditional and modern are once again being used to explore the new postmodern utopia – the high-tech social form that can return us to so-called traditional values and intimate personal relationships. This is the language we have for describing our present experience.

Posing ideal categories of gemeinschaft and gesellschaft simply because they are comfortable and feel right, however, may keep us from recognizing forces that structure social relationships and, specifically for our current purposes, the forms of social relationships that are being enacted in computer-mediated communication. The categories are not necessarily reflections of the realities of community. Interaction over the Web, for example, is fluid and dynamic. It does not easily fit former static images of community. The process of community building holds the potential for mapping onto ideals associated with community that previously could only be described as mythic.

Physical and Virtual Communities

Differences of spatial and temporal organization contribute to the tendency to see physical communities as more organic, where contents of interest are shared in shared space, while virtual communities by necessity have a greater level of intentionality. In fact, physical communities are generally understood to exist in contiguous space and to be temporally synchronous. On the basis of spatial and temporal dimensions, people in physical communities share concerns, resources, quality of life, help, and so forth. Internet communities are more typically conceptualized as electronic town halls (Mitchell, 1995; Rheingold, 1993), lifestyle enclaves (Renninger & Shumar, this volume; see also Bellah et al., 1985), or lifestyle groups (Burrows & Nettleton, this volume) that are spatially and temporally dislocated.

The ways in which land, water, and other resources can be divided up carry with them material dimensions that lends substance to the symbolic boundaries of physical communities. In virtual communities, spatial and temporal boundaries are entirely symbolic. Resources themselves are symbols. Symbolic boundaries and resources are all fodder for the imagination of what a given community consists of and can be, as well as the kinds of interaction that this new type of engagement reflects.

As a result, groups who cast the Internet as a creative new social medium typically describe the lurker, or noncontributor, as someone who is shirking social responsibility. Concerns about lurking exist precisely because the virtual world has no physical presence, and interaction in this world becomes more highlighted (Smith, 1999). Yet, it is also the case that in virtual communities, just as in physical communities, not everyone is an active participant in all things, all the time (Zhu, 1998). In fact, people can take up different roles, and they can change their conceptions about their possibilities as a function of their activity with a site over time (Renninger & Shumar, this volume). In this way, the lurker could be construed as a potentially productive participant who is not ready to make a contribution, is reflecting on follow-up to previous contents, and so forth. Participants are in different stages of "legitimate peripheral participation" (Lave & Wenger, 1991).

In the virtual community, relationship is typically defined not by proximity but by contents of individual interest – classes of objects, ideas, or events about which participants have differing levels of both stored knowledge and stored value (see discussion in Renninger, 2000). The fact that virtual communities are defined by contents for which community has an interest is one of the reasons that critics tend to see virtual communities as something other than community. Participants' connections to community are both cognitive and affective, rather than simply spatial and temporal.

A specificity of connection to virtual communities is qualitatively different than the connection participants typically have for physical communities. The connection to virtual communities is supported by affordances (Gibson, 1966) that invoke imagination about and identification with a site, such as autonomy, time, space, choice, opportunity, support, and depth of content. Furthermore, the learning that is undertaken as participants work with a site has an agency and opportunity for changed understanding of self (see Renninger & Shumar, this volume). This opportunity also appears to differ from the range of opportunities available in physical communities.

As a symbolic construction, any community, whether physical or virtual, depends upon the images that its participants hold. Further, all communities depend upon how participants enact the ideas they have. Any given participant's community (or status therein) is often the result of actions that are both intended and unintended. Thus, participants' conceptions of community are highly fluid and multifaceted. Not only does a given community have the potential to be understood in different ways by its participants, but this same community also is likely to differ for the same participant as a function of circumstance.

Barth (1981) suggested that anthropologists have had a tendency to describe a group in terms of homogeneous culture. He argues that a group can be described in terms of how members imagine the community's boundaries. As such, he suggests that a similar culture emerges from the experience of boundedness, rather than as the cause of boundedness. Likewise, Cohen (1985) described the boundaries between groups as complex symbolic matter, meaning that the simple boundaries seen by outsiders are not the most important distinctions for insiders. The boundaries for insiders are often overlapping and involve finer and finer distinctions that eventually point to basic units of interaction. The United States as a boundary is significant to those outside the United States, for example, but for its citizens its boundary is rarely thought about, except in connection to outsiders. The more significant boundaries for U.S. citizens are states, cities, counties, neighborhoods, and street blocks. One could also then consider the boundedness of social groups that cut across some of these smaller geographic boundaries and result in additional groupings (e.g., a gay and lesbian community alliance, an environmental organization).

Communities on the Internet underscore points made by both Cohen and Barth about the symbolic nature of community. Rather than assuming that a community is one-dimensional and can, therefore, be identified from the outside, it is important to consider what a virtual community means, what it offers, what it affords its participants, and what its boundaries are. Individuals can become known across discussion groups and several related use net groups (Smith, 1999). A list such as alt.postmodern may, in fact, be part of a complex weave of community over the Internet for those who contribute to it, even though discussion lists might not immediately appear to fit our working definition of community.

An ideal of community apparently leads people to invest themselves in the Internet and the sets of imagined and desired interactions the Internet affords. In fact, wholly to embracing or rejecting discussions of virtual community building is logically difficult. It is only possible to trace the effects of these discussions on groups and individuals as they work to produce a discourse about community in the process of their interactions. Building-out a virtual community that harnesses the potential of interaction entails a vision of connections between the community and its participants. Social imagination for both groups is enabled and constrained by norms (e.g., a protocol for interaction) that in turn provide the basis for an imagination about what is possible (for an example, see Renninger & Shumar, this volume).

The boundary between physical and virtual communities is permeable, however, making it difficult to conceptualize either form of community as a completely separate entity. Even though the utopian vision of the physical community recasting itself as a virtual community can backfire (e.g., virtual communication is reduced to an online public opinion poll), the risk of not realizing the potential of virtual communication exists for more established communities on the Web.

Thus, for those working to encourage community development, the relation between physical and virtual community can be quite explicit. For example, a physical community can re-imagine itself and its informational resources as a virtual community to solicit opinion, to provide information and resources, and, as such, to expand upon dreams of a more democratic polity.

The relation between physical and virtual communities can also be more implicit. If a teacher in a school can engage a separate set of colleagues who are part of that teacher's "virtual community," this contributes to how that teacher is seen and the ways he or she interacts with in-school colleagues. In a real way, both sets of colleagues may be part of the teacher's "community," but making the distinction (or sometimes erasing the distinction) between physical and virtual community may have significant implications for the teacher's work life. It seems that virtual communities can also be characterized by the complexity of making and unmaking boundaries. These boundaries signal community for participants who enact these visions within overlapping fields of political and economic constraint.

Although the interplay of community is a complex weave of participants' desires and strategies, community over the Web is often reduced to written communication that may be supplemented with sound and images. Like the telephone, computer-mediated communication facilitates communication between people. Like the radio and television, it also has facilitated the dissemination of sound and images to a broad constituency. The Internet, however, has produced dislocations of time and space in the process of offering new means for communicating. As such, the Internet has led to the bonding of people as a hallmark of the modern community. The fluidity of boundaries and flexibility of how community is defined make it possible for participants to enact forms of community in the virtual world and extend the definition of community as a function of social imagination.

As international email conversations become quick and easy, and chat rooms eliminate spatial barriers and make long-distance sociability instantaneous, many researchers studying computer-mediated communication and the virtual world have had to grapple with the potential for communication technologies to compress time and space as well (Harvey, 1990). This compression not only has had profound consequences for the organization of work and the movement of labor, capital, and goods (Harvey, 1990), but it has also had profound consequences for the individuals who interact with one another over these vast distances and for their local culture. These consequences have led to what Turkle (1995) called an "identity crisis," wherein the sense of self in virtual spaces becomes multiple as a function of diverse relationships and social arenas.

It is the case that time and space can be expanded as well as compressed, however. Email correspondences are quicker than the mail (hence the term "snail mail") but much slower than face-to-face conversations. Further, email interactions tend to have aspects of each of these modes of communication; email interactions are a little like letters and a little like conversations. Depending on the form of communicative interaction they are compared to, email can be faster or slower than the forms of communicative interaction to which a person is accustomed. Many people email simple requests because it is less invasive than a phone call and hence seen as more polite. In this instance, the individual is willing to wait longer for the interaction to unfold than it would over the phone. As such, communicative interaction is stretched out. These more stretched-out conversations have become a part of daily life in many social arenas.

Virtual interaction can also be thought of as creating more space for social interaction and hence as expanding space. Online components to physical interactions in college courses (Polin, 2000) provide a virtual space in addition to the physical space for class meetings. These virtual spaces may have many "rooms" where there are discussion boards, live chat rooms, or even a virtual space with avatars in which to interact (see Schlager et al., this volume).

All virtual groups, whether they are electronic town halls or interest groups, are positioned to take advantage of the space–time flexibility of the Internet. The quality of compressing or expanding space–time contributes to making online interaction appealing to people. Wellman and his colleagues (Chmielewski & Wellman, 2000) suggest that, even though new users of the Internet may initially substitute online "weak" social relationships for physically close "strong" social relationships (e.g., Kraut et al., 1998; Nie & Erbring, 2000), over time this effect disappears. In fact, long-term users of the Internet are more likely to maintain contact with those they are close to, including those in close physical proximity, with the result of stronger ties between colleagues, family, and so forth.

Transformations of time and space and the new forms of interaction facilitated by the Internet and information technologies have required individuals to reconsider their understanding of the possibilities for ways in which they and others elect to come together. Transformations also affect the implications of these possibilities for what individuals had previously imagined community to be (Anderson, 1991; Jones, 1997). These participants have a sense of belonging that influences their interactions, whether they are reflectively aware of it or not. The participants are involved in evaluating who belongs. This evaluative process influences the language participants use to describe their activity. It also defines relationships of power or the shape of a community (national boundaries rather than kin or religious affiliation) and participants' imagination about themselves and possibilities (Markus & Nurius, 1986) in this social reality (Anderson, 1991).

The process of imagination that characterizes belonging may involve overlapping groups of people and be differently construed in various contexts. The process is a necessary component of community building, regardless of whether a community is a physical community. On the Web, however, tools (e.g., email chat rooms, instant messaging [IM]) allow synchronous or asynchronous interaction at a distance or next door. These tools allow a certain number of tasks to be automated and enable the individual to multitask, facilitating the individual's constructions of community. These tools invoke profound temporal and spatial dislocations that also open up new ways for participants to contribute to the building-out of communities. In turn, communities also provide participants with opportunities to develop their understanding (Scarmedalia & Bereiter, 1997) and expand their sense of self (Lifton, 1993).

How a community is built out appears also to have a reciprocal relation to purpose. If an electronic town hall (Mitchell, 1995; Rheingold, 1993) is designed for the purpose of reducing costs, in addition to creating a democratic public sphere, then it is likely to focus on a narrow range of issues and to be a thin replacement for more robust human interaction (Bellah et al., 1985; Jones, 1995, 1997; Kiesler, 1997; Smith & Kollack, 1999).

The Internet undoubtedly creates possibilities for interaction that people did not have before (Cherny, 1999; Davis & Brewer, 1997; Herring, 1996). Such interaction leads to the enacting of networks, and often the traces (e.g., emails, Web pages, archived material) of these interactions remain as influences on social relationships, the distribution of social goods, and the structure of work (Wellman et al., 1996; Wellman & Gulia, 1999).

Internet communication, like the telephone and the telegraph, is less personal and allows for fewer forms of communication than do interactions in real space. There is no voice intonation or facial expression nor are there other extralinguistic cues. However, Internet communication is also cheap (once it is in place) and instantaneous. It allows people to communicate over great distances, and they may share pictures, diagrams, and so forth. Further, such exchanges can be posted on Web pages and archived, meaning that it is possible for participants to share information, ideas, and the like, long after the information and ideas were compiled (Kollack, 1999; Smith & Kollack, 1999).

The availability of stored resources and information, coupled with the flexibility in the time and space of usage, may well account for the attributions of utopian possibilities for community via the Internet. From the beginning, the Internet has been seen as supporting a special kind of generalized reciprocity since archived exchanges, information, and so on, continue to be useful over time. This reciprocity may also account for the unusual levels of intimacy people have been able to reach online, in contrast to the types of relationships these same people have in physical communities. Reciprocity has led to a complexity of discourse not found in physical communities (e.g., discussions that build out of previous discussions, links between sites, and concurrent discussion formats such as IM and Web-based synchronous discussion).

Community As Multilayered Communicative Space

On the Internet, verbal interactions and text can both be part of the same social interaction. The communicative space is multilayered and allows for the mingling of different conversations that have an infinitely renewable life. Whether spoken or written, however, such interactions modify former interactions and vice versa. In their writing, Bakhtin, Holquist and Emerson (1986) suggested that utterances always obtain meaning within some specific social interaction, and that meaning is always shifting as the interaction shifts. Applied to the Internet, every utterance or each interaction is understood to be articulated with intention and, through inference, is based on available knowledge that may be in an archive, as well as individual interest. This process not only constantly redefines more traditional notions of the individual but also the meaning of what individuals say and the work that they do together.

Harré and his colleagues (Davies & Harré, 1990; Harré & Van Langenhove, 1991) used the term "positioning" to denote the way power works through discourse processes. Positioning is inherently a dynamic and dialectic approach to conversation and interaction. It describes the process of constituting and reconstituting subjects that characterizes the redefinition of the individual. Unlike the static notion of social role, positioning describes the dynamic aspects of discursive interactions in a specific context, in which the subject is not a fixed entity but is always in the process of defining who he or she is. Individual interaction can be understood as an ongoing construction and revision of narratives about other participants and the extent of their shared understanding of norms and structures (Davies & Harré, 1990). As such, power needs to be recognized as part of any interaction. It also reflects the social structure and norms of interaction in the social spaces (physical and virtual) of participants.

Online, it is an option to craft these social spaces by making norms more explicit. Across interactions, the comments of a speaker can be said to position the listener and can imply a hierarchical relationship with the listener such as that in a work relationship. In a virtual social field, however, the listener can exit the social space without others being aware of the exit, draw upon resources from other locations, and reposition the relationship through his or her response. The listener is not liberated from the hierarchical structure, but, with resources upon which to draw and both time and space within which to do so, he or she is positioned to change the interaction. Only the participants' understanding of possible selves (Markus & Nurius, 1986; Markus & Wurf, 1987) constrains their potential repositioning of the relationship, and even this understanding stands to be adjusted.

Clearly, the ability to circumvent hierarchical positioning might be very important for an individual's ability to learn and grow. It might also help the individual to find other like-minded individuals who want to escape such interactions. An essential part of the discussion around the virtual community has focused on the self and its transformation through the objects and spaces brought together by computers. The claim is that because we cannot see each other or hear each other's voices over the Internet, a virtual body can replace the real body. Initially, a virtual body was accomplished with text through description, but now it can be accomplished through the use of images. This renders the Internet a rather dream-like existence where identities can be re-imagined at will and can be condensed or diffused by images of other identities, where one can become other to oneself or more than one really is.

The sense of community that once held is undergoing change as a function of technological developments. The casting of oneself in terms of lifestyle and more surface forms of association, such as Gergen's (1991) description of "the saturated self" and Lifton's (1993) notion of "Proteanism," reflects the zeitgeist of the virtual community. Casting of oneself also suggests changed notions about imagination, identity, and the structure of community that render Durkheim's distinction between mechanical and organic solidarity irrelevant and herald a more dynamic conceptualization of community.

In their work with the Internet, individuals accrue knowledge about possibilities for community participation that differs radically from what they once understood the components of community (e.g., group, boundaries, participation, identity) to include. As a result, individuals are positioned to change themselves and their communities. In fact, because of the permeability of the virtual and physical worlds, even those who are not participants in virtual communities are impacted by changed ideas about and experiences of community.

The forms of interaction, sociability, and community available on the Internet have revised our imagination about self and community. There is the potential for plasticity, in that participants can try out different roles and styles of interaction. Even more important, however, the role of context is de-emphasized in the virtual world because of the affective and cognitive character of the individual's connections to it. In the physical world, context tends to ground a person in one reality (view of the past, sense of self, ideas of group, etc.). In contrast to the physical world, the lack of context in the virtual world enables imagination, identity, and the kind of valuing that deepens interest and enables knowledge building.

Imagination is critical for understanding the ways in which individuals strategically seek out social life and their changed thinking about themselves and others. Such changed possibility can be reflected in content, such as when individuals at a distance are positioned to avail themselves of regular interaction rather than being limited to one conference or meeting a year. It also provides validation and support for individuals, as in the case of those isolated from others by disease who online can discuss symptoms, treatments, new research information, and so forth.

The Internet has altered our sense of boundaries, participation, and identity. It allows for the recasting of both self and community, meaning that through the Internet a person or group can revise his or her sense of possibilities. Rather than asking whether there is a virtual community, it seems more appropriate to consider how we might effectively describe evolving conceptualizations of community and their implications for building-out virtual communities.

Acknowledgments

We acknowledge the many individuals including our students, fellow researchers, and participants in The Math Forum (mathforum.org) community who have influenced our thinking about community. We particularly appreciate discussions with Gene Klotz and Steve Weimar who struggled with us as we attempted to understand the possibilities for building community using the Internet and other informational technologies. We benefited from many long conversations with Marc Smith and Doug Porpora about the nature of community and community research in both physical and virtual environments. We also learned from Jonathan Church who read through an early draft of this chapter and helped to guide us through the anthropological literature on community.

We also thank Melissa Kobelin, Jill Ratzan, and Jonathan Shaw who helped us to prepare this chapter for publication. Finally, we recognize funding received from Swarthmore College's Faculty Research Fund and the National Science Foundation to The Math Forum (# 9618223), although the conclusions described in this chapter do not necessarily reflect the views of these funders.

References

Anderson, B. R. O. G. (1991). *Imagined communities: Reflections on the origin and spread of nationalism* (Rev. and extended ed.). London/New York: Verso.

Bakhtin, M. M., Holquist, M., & Emerson, C. (1986). *Speech genres and other late essays* (1st ed.). (V. W. Mcfee: Trans.). Austin: University of Texas Press.

Barth, F. (1981). *Process and form in social life*. London/Boston: Routledge & Kegan Paul.

Bauman, Z. (2000). *Liquid modernity*. Cambridge, England/Malden, MA: Polity Press/Blackwell Press.

Bellah, R. N. Madsen, R., Sullivan, W. M., Swidler, A., & Tipton, S. M. (1985). *Habits of the heart: Individualism and commitment in American life*. Berkeley: University of California Press.

Bourdieu, P. (1991). *Language and symbolic power*. Cambridge, MA: Harvard University Press.

Castells, M. (1996). *The rise of the network society*. Cambridge, MA: Blackwell Publishers.

(1999). *Critical education in the new information age*. Lanham, MD: Rowman & Littlefield.

Cherny, L. (1999). *Conversation and community: Chat in a virtual world*. Stanford, CA: CSLI Publications.

Chmielewski, T., & Wellman, B. (2000). Tracking Geekus Unixus: An explorers' report from the National Geographic Website. *SIGGROUP Bulletin, 21*(1).

Cohen, A. P. (1985). *The symbolic construction of community*. Chichester/London/New York: E. Horwood and Tavistock Publications.

Davies, B., & Harré, R. (1990). Positioning: The discursive production of selves. *Journal for the Theory of Social Behavior, 20*(1), 43–63.

Davis, B. H., & Brewer, J. (1997). *Electronic discourse: Linguistic individuals in virtual space*. Albany: State University of New York Press.

Durkheim, E. (1984). *The division of labour in society*. Basingstoke, Hampshire, England: Macmillan.

Gergen, K. J. (1991). *The saturated self: Dilemmas of identity in contemporary life*. New York: Basic Books.

Gibson, J. J. (1966). *The senses considered as perceptual systems*. Boston: Houghton Mifflin.

Hakken, D. (1999). *Cyborgs@cyberspace?: An ethnographer looks to the future*. New York: Routledge.

Harré, R., & Van Langenhove, L. (1991). Varieties of positioning. *Journal for the Theory of Social Behavior, 21*(4), 393–407.

Harvey, D. (1990). *The condition of postmodernity: An enquiry into the origins of cultural change*. Oxford England/Cambridge, MA: B. Blackwell.

Herring, S. (1994). *Politeness in computer culture: Why women thank and men flame.* Cultural Performances: Proceedings of the Third Berkeley Women and Language Conference (278–94). Berkeley, CA: Berkley Women and Language Group.

(1995). *Men's language on the Internet.* Paper presented at the Papers from the 2nd Nordic Language and Gender Conference (Nordlyd), Tromso, Norway.

(1996). Posting in a different voice: Gender and ethics in computer-mediated communication. In C. Ess (Ed.), *Philosophical approaches to computer-mediated communication* (pp. 115–45). Albany: SUNY Press.

Jones, S. G. (1995). *CyberSociety: Computer-mediated communication and community.* Thousand Oaks, CA: Sage.

(1997). *Virtual culture: Identity and communication in cybersociety.* London/Thousand Oaks, CA: Sage.

(1998). *CyberSociety 2.0: Revisiting computer-mediated communication and community.* Thousand Oaks, CA: Sage.

Kiesler, S. (1997). *Culture of the Internet.* Mahwah, NJ: Lawrence Erlbaum.

Kling, R. (2000). *Systematic studies of social behavior that involve the Internet: A social informatics perspective.* Paper presented at the Keynote Talk for Internet Research 1.0: The State of the Interdiscipline The First Conference of the Associate of Internet Researchers, University of Kansas.

Kollack, P. (1999). The economies of online cooperation: Gifts and public goods in cyberspace. In M. A. Smith & P. Kollack (Eds.), *Communities in cyberspace.* London/New York: Routledge, pp. 220–39.

Kraut, R., Lundmark, V., Patterson, M., Kiesler, S., Mukopadhyay, T., & Scherlis, W. (1998). Internet paradox: A social technology that reduces social involvement and psychological well-being? *American Psychologist, 53* (9), 1017–31.

Lave, J., & Wenger, E. (1991). *Situated learning: Legitimate peripheral participation.* New York: Cambridge University Press.

Lifton, R. J. (1993). *The protean self: Human resilience in an age of fragmentation.* New York: Basic Books.

Loader, B. (1997). *The governance of cyberspace: Politics, technology and global restructuring.* London/New York: Routledge.

Markus, H., & Nurius, P. (1986). Possible selves. *American Psychologist, 4*(9), 954–69.

Markus, H., & Wurf, E. (1987). The dynamic self concept: A social psychological perspective. *Annual Review of Psychology, 38,* 299–337.

Mitchell, W. J. (1995). *City of bits: Space, place, and the infobahn.* Cambridge, MA: MIT Press.

Nie, N. H., & Erbring, L. (2000). *Internet and society: A preliminary report.* Stanford, CA: Stanford Institute for the Quantitative Study of Society.

O'Brien, J. (1999). Writing in the body: Gender (re)production in online interaction. In M. A. Smith & P. Kollack (Eds.), *Communities in cyberspace.* London/New York: Routledge, pp. 76–104.

Oldenburg, R. (1989). *The great good place: Cafés, coffee shops, community centers, beauty parlors, general stores, bars, hangouts, and how they get you through the day* (1st ed.). New York: Paragon House.

Polin, L. (2000). *Symbiotic transformation in virtual communities.* Paper presented at the International Conference of the Learning Sciences, Ann Arbor, MI, as part of the symposium Individual Change and Cultural Process: Their Role in Virtual Community Building.

Putnam, R. D. (2000). *Bowling alone: The collapse and revival of American community.* New York: Simon & Schuster.

Renninger, K. A. (2000). Individual interest and its implications for understanding intrinsic motivation. In C. Sansone & J. M. Harackiewicz (Eds.), *Intrinsic and extrinsic motivation: The search for optimal motivation and performance* (pp. 373–404). New York: Academic.

Rheingold, H. (1993). *The virtual community: Homesteading on the electronic frontier.* Reading, MA: Addison-Wesley.

Scardamalia, M., & Bereiter, C. (1997). Adaptation and understanding: A case for new cultures of schooling. In S. Vosniadou, E. D. Corte, R. Glaser & H. Mandl (Eds.), *International perspectives on the psychological foundations of technology-based learning environments* (pp. 14–26). Mahwah, NJ: Lawrence Erlbaum.

Shields, R. (1996). *Cultures of Internet: Virtual spaces, real histories, living bodies.* London/Thousand Oaks, CA: Sage.

Smith, M. A. (1999). Invisible crowds in cyberspace: Mapping the social structure of the Usenet. In M. A. Smith & P. Kollack (Eds.), *Communities in cyberspace.* London/New York: Routledge.

Smith, M. A., & Kollock, P., Eds. (1999). *Communities in cyberspace.* London: Routledge.

Tönnies, F. (1887/1957). *Community & society (gemeinschaft und gesellschaft).* East Lansing: Michigan State University Press.

Turkle, S. (1995). *Life on the screen: Identity in the age of the Internet.* New York: Simon & Schuster.

Wellman, B. (2001). Physical place and cyberplace: The rise of personalized networking. *International Journal of Urban and Regional Research, 25*(2), 227–52.

Wellman, B., & Gulia, M. (1999). Net surfers don't ride alone: Virtual communities as communities. In M. A. Smith & P. Kollack (Eds.), *Communities in cyberspace.* New York: Routledge, 167–94.

Wellman, B., Salaff, J., Dimitrova, D., Garton, L., Gulia, M., & Haythornthwaite, C. (1996). Computer networks as social networks: Collaborative work, telework, and virtual community. *Annual Review of Sociology, 22*, 213–38.

Zhu, E. (1998). Learning and mentoring: Electronic discussion in a distance learning course. In C. J. Bonk & K. S. King (Eds.), *Electronic collaborators: Learner-centered technologies for literacy, apprenticeship, and discourse* (pp. 233–59). Mahwah, NJ: Lawrence Erlbaum.

Part One

Types of Community

1   The Mystery of the Death of MediaMOO

Seven Years of Evolution of an Online Community

Amy Bruckman and Carlos Jensen

What Happened to MediaMOO?

A typical Tuesday evening, 1993–1996: In the online cafe, writing teachers begin to arrive. Twenty-five teachers will spend an hour discussing how to handle inappropriate student behavior in electronic environments. Afterwards, a few will stay for a game of Scrabble^T and good conversation. Some will also attend the poetry reading on Wednesday. In a virtual hallway, an anthropologist stops to chat with a computer programmer about some recently released software. A communications professor in Seattle, Washington, meets with a graduate student in Queensland, Australia, to discuss a survey of online behavior they are developing together. More than one thousand people from thirty-four countries are active members.

A typical Tuesday evening, 1999: The space is empty. The writing teachers found another place to meet years ago. The communications professor drops by, finds no one else connected, and immediately leaves.

The "place" is MediaMOO, a text-based virtual reality environment (multiuser domain or MUD) designed to be a professional community for media researchers (Bruckman & Resnick, 1995). MediaMOO was founded in 1992 by Amy Bruckman as a place where people doing research on new media could share ideas, collaborate, and network. MediaMOO's environment was designed to recreate the informal atmosphere and social interaction of a conference reception. Members came from a wide variety of disciplines, creating a diverse environment that fostered interdisciplinary research and learning.

MediaMOO reached its peak of activity in the mid-1990s but had fallen into disuse by 1998. What caused MediaMOO's decline? Could it have been avoided? Is this a story of failure, or is change inevitable and

21

desirable? What broader lessons about the design of online communities can we draw from this experience?

Methodology

To explore these questions, we began by holding a public forum. We chose the topic "The Future of MediaMOO: Autopsy and Redesign" for discussion at MediaMOO's annual birthday celebration on 20 January 1999. Sixty members participated. Attendees included many former leading members of the community who are now less active.

After the forum, we conducted a series of interviews. First, we interviewed five former MediaMOO regulars. We tried to understand how their perspective had changed over time: What brought them to MediaMOO initially? Why did they chose to invest their free time in this community? Why do they no longer participate? Initial telephone interviews were complimented with follow-up email conversations with both interviewees and several other key members of the community.

To understand whether our observations are part of a broader trend, we also interviewed the leaders of three similar communities: Diversity University (DU), Tapped In, and Meridian. A combination of telephone, email, and MUD interaction were used for these interviews. We also corresponded with the founders of The Netoric Project, BioMOO, and CollegeTown.

With this work we hope to contribute both to our understanding of a particular historical moment in the evolution of the Internet, and more broadly to our understanding of online communities as not static but rather continually evolving entities.

Defining Success

Many people obsess about the definition of "community." The word is often used in a value-laden way. If your group qualifies as a community, then it has almost magical properties; if it does not earn this sacred term, then it is debased. We believe these arguments are a waste of time. Instead, we use the word "community" in the loosest possible, value-neutral fashion: a community is a group of people interacting with one another in some fashion. This definition frees us to address the more important underlying question: what value does a given group bring to its members? What are our criteria for "success" of the community/group?

These questions have no easy, objective answers. Most simply, one can say that a community is successful to the extent that it meets the needs of its members. In geographic communities and other communities where participation is either required or difficult to change, the degree of activity in the community may not be closely correlated with its degree of success. The fact that the residents are still present may not mean that they are happy – they may simply be trapped. In online communities in which participation is genuinely voluntary, success is somewhat easier to judge. If people chose to participate, they likely think that they are benefiting from the experience in some way. If this were not the case, they would not spend their valuable time participating in the online community. (This, of course, assumes that people are good judges of how to spend their own time, a statement that many would dispute.) In the case of voluntary participation communities like MediaMOO, level of activity is a useful measure of the success of the community.

By the simple metric of degree of activity, MediaMOO was a grand success from its inception through roughly 1996; then it began to decline. Through our research, we have identified these factors as contributing to its decline:

- Splintering off of subgroups
- Technical obsolescence
- Historical change in the history of the Internet
- Choice of target audience/population model
- Lowered enthusiasm of the leadership

In the rest of this paper, we will discuss each of these factors and then conclude by outlining our plans to redesign MediaMOO based on what we have learned.

Splintering Off of Subgroups: A Victim of Success

MediaMOO was designed as a place for researchers involved in some aspect of media studies to meet, share ideas, and explore the Internet as a social space. In a time before the Web, when the Internet was just starting to become a popular phenomenon, MediaMOO provided a space for researchers to "discover" online communities and their potential. In this role, MediaMOO succeeded admirably, spawning dozens of new research projects and online communities. In some ways, MediaMOO's success led to its decline, as large groups of its core members "graduated" to form their own online communities.

The original goal of the MediaMOO project was to explore the application of the constructionist theory of education (Papert, 1991) to the design of online communities (Bruckman & Resnick, 1995). Constructionist theory argues that learning by doing, learning through design and construction activities, is better than learning through passive receipt of information. A professional community is a kind of learning community. To increase users' involvement with MediaMOO, we decided to encourage them to build the virtual space themselves. Through this process, they would make the virtual world reflect their interests and needs better than we could ever anticipate those needs for them. The act of construction of the world also provided opportunities for professional networking, community building, and learning about programming and online community design.

The approach was largely successful: one group built The Netoric Center for writing teachers. Inside Netoric, they built The Tuesday Cafe for their weekly Tuesday-night seminars on how to use the Internet in their research and teaching. A graduate student built the Science, Technology, and Society Center. Special places were created for poetry readings and Scrabble^T games. Employees of Apple Computer built a model of their offices, complete with a robotic front desk guard mimicking the friendly personality of its real-world counterpart.

However, as time progressed, some of these subcommunities splintered off to become full-fledged independent communities. MediaMOO in effect served as an incubator where fledgling groups began, grew, and eventually chose to go off on their own. Tari Fanderclai and Greg Siering founded The Netoric Project, the largest subgroup to emerge on MediaMOO. We estimate that more than a third of MediaMOO members at one time were Netoric affiliates. Fanderclai gives this account of the evolution of Netoric and The Tuesday Cafe:

We – the computers and writing community – found MediaMOO because Eric Crump and Michael Day found it and started encouraging people to join. Soon Greg and I started to get some ideas about organized activities there. We organized a big discussion as a sort of special event. Paul Bowers and Glenn Mayer helped us a lot in the beginning, too. That worked pretty well; then some people started talking about how it would be nice if we had a regular discussion time, and so Greg and I built the Netoric Headquarters and the four of us started organizing Tuesday Cafe discussions. Eventually Paul B. and Glenn dropped out, but Greg and I kept going. MediaMOO happily accepted all the computers and writing people who wanted to join, and we also got some regular members (some of whom are still with us) who weren't computers and writing folks per se, but who were interested in a lot of our topics. Although the computers and writing crew was pretty much ripe for whatever kind of online synchronous forum got invented, the multidisciplinary community at MediaMOO contributed a lot to our initial growth, and we got a lot smarter about all sorts of technological developments and other topics a lot faster because of all the people we had access to there.

Eventually we moved to Connections for several reasons. I administrate Connections, and it's much easier for us to say to just write us for characters than to have them go through the whole application process on someone else's MOO. Also, Connections has a realm system that makes it super easy for a whole bunch of people to collaborate on a space, and so we were able to have the community participate in Connections, without having to get room owners to deal with exit permissions and such every time they want to connect a room. That's been a nice community builder, as we had hoped it would be.

The main reason, though, is that the Netoric Project members spend a lot of time talking about using MOOs in classes. It was frustrating for people to learn all about MediaMOO only to find out they couldn't bring their classes there. We wanted to be on a MOO that people who got excited about could use for their classes, and we also wanted to take advantage of the presence of classes on the MOO to be able to get students to come to Netoric events such as the Tuesday Cafe. That's turned out to be a great resource; Connections and the Netoric Project have really contributed to each other's growth. (Fanderclai, personal communication; quoted with permission)

MediaMOO was intended as a space for professional researchers to network. A short application was required to join. While anyone could visit as a guest, only those who were doing some kind of media research could become full members. This requirement was essential to creating the kind of atmosphere that made MediaMOO successful – more like meeting colleagues gathered for a professional conference than like meeting random people on a street corner. Consequently, while writing teachers exploring how to use the Internet in their classes qualify for membership, their writing students do not. This MediaMOO policy is fundamental to what made the environment a successful professional community, but it was ultimately problematic for Netoric Project writing teachers.

The same policy issue affected the splintering off of another subgroup, CollegeTown. CollegeTown was founded by Professor Ken Schweller of Buena Vista University in Storm Lake, Iowa. Schweller writes:

College Town was founded in January 1994 as part of a class project in a class I was teaching called "Living and Learning in CyberSpace." My first MOO experience was on LambdaMOO where I learned to program MOO code and made a huge set of annoying objects such as MOO Brew and MOOtercycles. I quickly tired of the "gee whiz" aspect of one-upmanship MOO coding and became very interested in how this amazing and versatile platform might be applied in a useful educational setting. That's when I discovered MediaMOO. I liked it at once because of its serious purpose, its restricted admissions and its deemphasis on role playing. I set up a TV studio and built cameras, TVs, tapes, and VCRs to allow users to record

MOO events for later playback and distribution. I have always felt that archives were an essential element for sustaining community and this seemed like a fun way to enable that.

I eventually became a wizard on MediaMOO and gained experience in MOO management and administration. Eventually, however, I decided that I needed to develop a new MOO more in line with my own personal goals. I wanted a MOO where classes could be held and teachers could meet to collaborate and do research. I wanted a place where undergraduates could experiment with MOO coding and the creation of serious virtual environments without the distraction of anonymous identities and D and D type role-playing. I saw a MOO as an excellent instrument for teaching my computer science students the elements of object oriented programming. And so I worked together with my CyberSpace class to create CollegeTown. We worked together to plan the layout, basically a Campus, a Town, and a Wilderness Area. We insisted on users using their real names and connecting all rooms to existing rooms using a graphic layout. We disabled teleporting and encouraged everyone to walk about. As a result of my experiences on MM we were able to create CollegeTown in a very short time in a remarkably smooth manner. (Schweller, personal communication; quoted with permission)

When Schweller left MediaMOO to start CollegeTown, MediaMOO lost one of its most energetic and dedicated leaders. When Fanderclai and Siering left MediaMOO to move to Connections, MediaMOO lost their leadership as well as a third to one half of MediaMOO's active population. The departure of The Tuesday Cafe was the single biggest factor in MediaMOO's decline.

Nevertheless, it's impossible to view these departures as "failures." MediaMOO played a crucial role in the development of The Netoric Project, CollegeTown, BayMOO, BioMOO, and others. As the subgroups matured, they grew to a point where establishing their own separate community was appropriate and necessary. The problem, then, is not that subgroups splintered off but that new subgroups were not present on MediaMOO in earlier stages of development.

One solution to the problem of splintering subgroups is to adopt a distributed architecture that allows subgroups independence while maintaining connection and affiliation with the parent group. This solution has the added advantage of supporting scalability.

We can explain the concept of a distributed architecture with an analogy. Imagine trying to show a new movie to as many people as possible. One approach would be to build the biggest movie theatre you can possibly build. You might be able to make one the size of a large football stadium where 100,000 can see a movie at the same time; however, there will be traffic problems as everyone tries to arrive and leave for the show. It would be impossible to construct a theatre for 1,000,000 people. Instead, imagine that you show the movie in 10,000 separate theatres. It would be easy to show the movie to millions of people at once, with no traffic tie ups. This is analogous to a distributed architecture.

Affiliated groups and subgroups may chose to share policies. While the theatres are separate, they might agree to show the same movie, sell popcorn for the same price, and prohibit smoking during the show.

Not every subgroup needs to adopt the same policies. To continue the analogy, suppose that, in the single large theatre model, some people want to prohibit advertisements before the show, but the majority want to show ads to subsidize the cost of the event. The minority is out of luck. However, in the distributed, multiple-theatre model, one theatre can easily decide not to show ads and instead charge a higher admission. They do not necessarily need to renounce all affiliation with the federation of theatres to make this local policy change. Or to return to The Netoric Group on MediaMOO, a distributed architecture would allow this subgroup to let students participate in their subcommunity without affecting the greater community of which they form part.

A hierarchy of groups and subgroups with separate computers and separate leadership at each level can comfortably grow to a much larger size than one unified group for both technical and social/policy reasons. We plan to design and implement a distributed system for the next version of MediaMOO.

Many of MediaMOO's fragmentation problems could have been addressed through a distributed architecture. However, the problem was not just that subgroups were splintering off, but rather that new subgroups were not forming to take their place. Why were there no new subgroups forming on MediaMOO? Two intertwined answers concern history and technology.

A Historical/Technical Moment

Development on MediaMOO began in the fall of 1992, and MediaMOO's official opening party was held on 20 January 1993. MediaMOO predates the World Wide Web as we know it. Tim Berners-Lee had the original idea of a World Wide Web in 1989, but the real beginning of the Web can be traced to the release of the first web browser, NCSA Mosaic, in September 1993.

MediaMOO is a text-only system and is based on the MOO software developed by Curtis and White (Curtis, 1992). A MOO, or Multiuser Object Oriented environment, is a kind of a MUD – MOO stands for

MUD Object Oriented. MUDs are text-based virtual worlds that were originally invented in the late 1970s as Dungeons and Dragons games (Bartle, 1990); however, they have been adapted for a wide variety of applications since then. Users can connect from any computer with an Internet connection using a simple Telnet program. These minimal hardware and software requirements made participation possible for a wide range of people.

Though it is hard to imagine now, in 1993 the real-time communication afforded by the MOO software was cutting-edge technology. In general, MUDs were on the technological forefront, and Curtis and White's MOO software was particularly strong in its support for end-user programming. Other MUD languages either are accessible only to professional programmers (e.g., LPC) or have only very limited capabilities (e.g., MUSE and MUSH). MOO was the first system to make a full-featured programming language accessible to naïve users. In 1990, Curtis used MOO to start a recreational community called LambdaMOO. LambdaMOO members displayed an astonishing amount of creativity and dedication in building the virtual world. However, as Schweller noted, the recreational nature of LambdaMOO did not make it suitable for more serious pursuits. Together with astrophysicist David Van Buren, Curtis planned to start AstroVR, a MOO designed to be a professional community for astrophysicists. AstroVR itself never became a thriving community; however, it did inspire Bruckman to create MediaMOO.

In 1993, the Internet was about to explode in popularity. Many people in both industry and academia understood that this was about to happen. Few could have predicted the magnitude of the growth of the Internet, but many sensed that something significant was coming. Those people came to MediaMOO. They came to MediaMOO to try to understand this emerging medium first hand. At the time, MediaMOO was the latest hot new technology. In this environment, they planned their future involvement with Internet research and business, and networked with others similarly inclined.

Three to five years later, MOO technology was out of date. At the simplest level, a plain text environment with no fonts, graphics, or links is awkward compared to the World Wide Web. It's clear that MediaMOO would be improved if it supported at least Web-style graphics and links. This has already been implemented by a number of developers by creating a Java-based Web front end to access the virtual world (a particularly good example is Tapped In, a community for teacher professional development, www.tappedin.org).

Some argue that it would be desirable to have a two- or three-dimensional dynamic representation of objects within the virtual world. This is more problematic. Although such environments are visually appealing, they may actually impede human communication. In a text-based world, users have access to a full range of body language and emotion, limited only by their writing ability and imagination. It is possible in text for a user to raise an eyebrow skeptically, wiggle their nose mischievously, or lean against a wall exhaustedly. Graphical avatars are generally limited to a short list of basic gestures explicitly implemented by the developers, such as nodding and smiling. Researchers like Vilhjalmsson are exploring solutions to these problems, but for now they remain unsolved (Vilhjalmsson & Cassell, 1998). The higher production values of such environments currently make them much less expressive and less user-extensible. The use of these techniques may be viable in the future, but they are not yet mature enough for widespread use.

We believe that technological improvements are necessary but not sufficient to revive the community. Something subtler than mere lack of desirable software features is at the root of the problem. In the early years of MediaMOO, its form and content were intertwined: it was both a place to meet people interested in new media and a participatory exploration of a new media form. The former remains, but the latter does not. By 1997, MOO was old technology and of little interest in itself.

To stay on the cutting edge of technology, MediaMOO would have to reinvent itself not once but continually. This requirement is unfortunately so labor intensive that it is impractical. It leaves a question: to what extent is there a need for a place for media researchers to network using well-understood technology that is not inherently interesting? Our answer is that the need remains but for a different population than MediaMOO's original audience.

Changing Population Models

Throughout our lives, we form a part of many different communities. Most of these affiliations are transitory. An individual may move from being a member of a kindergarten class, to a college fraternity, to a homeowners' association, to a retirement home. Even if each individual is only part of a group for a short period of their life, that group may have a stable population: seniors leave the fraternity, but new freshmen arrive to take their place.

Groups in which membership is lifelong are increasingly rare. Individuals may chose to remain in the same geographic or religious community for a lifetime; however, even this is becoming less and less common in many industrialized societies. Kim points out that many online community designers fail to understand the difference between "stage-of-life" and "lifelong" population models (Kim, personal communication; quoted with permission).

MediaMOO's initial design assumed that most members would join and continue to participate indefinitely. If a few left, more would hear about the community by word of mouth. From 1993 through 1996, the population was stable at roughly 1,000 active members.

In 1993, professionals in the "multimedia" industry came to Media-MOO to gain a first-hand understanding of the next big thing, the Internet. By 1997, professionals in the industry already understood the Internet and were too busy with their research and corporate positions to have time for the kind of casual networking MediaMOO affords.

We believe that the solution to this problem is to change both our population model and our target audience. The group of people who have a compelling need to make new professional contacts in this field and who would most benefit from what MediaMOO has to offer are young professionals and graduate students in media-related fields. These people are unlikely to participate indefinitely. In our redesign of MediaMOO, we need to assume a "stage of life" population model. To replenish the ranks of the established members who opt to leave, we need to constantly attract new professionals.

On Leadership

The decline in the level of activity on MediaMOO coincided with a decline in the activity level of the community's founder and lead administrator, Amy Bruckman. It is likely that the two are related.

Bruckman began MediaMOO in the fall of 1992. In October 1995, she launched MOOSE Crossing, an online community designed to be a constructionist learning environment for children and the subject of her PhD dissertation (Bruckman, 1997, 1998). As time went on, she spent increasingly less time greeting new MediaMOO members, answering questions, organizing events, and encouraging users to begin new projects.

MediaMOO's waning is in contrast to the increasing success of Tapped In, a community designed to support teacher professional development

(Schlager, Fusco & Schank, 1998, this volume). Visitors to Tapped In are almost always greeted enthusiastically and cheerfully by volunteers or paid staff immediately on arrival. Four to seven organized community events typically happen per week, of which roughly half are usually organized by staff and half by volunteers. Part of what makes this possible is that Tapped In has five paid staff members. (They devote different percentages of their time to the community, adding up to approximately 2.5 full-time paid positions.) The paid staff in turn encourage and organize a volunteer staff of ten to twenty. With this amount of energy invested in leadership, Tapped In is a lively and growing community with 4500 members at the time of this writing, growing at a rate of 200 per month (Schlager, personal communication; quoted with permission).

Similarly, Diversity University (DU) has a much more active leadership than MediaMOO and also has stayed more active as a community. DU's founder Jeanne McWhorter agrees that leadership is a factor in their success:

> As you alluded to, there is considerably more wizard/manager presence on DU [than MediaMOO]. From the very beginning I have spent every available waking hour online or semi-accessible. One thing I have always emphasized for our administrative (as opposed to just programming) wizards/managers is personal attention. . . . I really do think this has a lot to do with ongoing population. Despite how we might feel, there is a certain celebrity status to being a wizard or manager, and when people log onto a world, they like to see us there and interacting. . . . People hate logging onto an empty world too, so regardless why the admins or users are there, it is a draw (McWhorter, personal communication).

As McWhorter indicates, leaders fill not just a practical but also a symbolic function. When that role is left vacant, the community suffers.

Looking Forward

The essential idea of an online professional community for media researchers still seems to have promise. Based on this research, we plan the following changes to MediaMOO:

- Introduce a distributed architecture that will allow subgroups to retain some connection to the parent group while growing in autonomy.
- Add static two-dimensional Web-like graphics and links (but NOT dynamic or three-dimensional graphics).
- Emphasize graduate students and young professionals as the target audience with a "stage of life" population model.

- Develop a new leadership staff (led by Carlos Jensen) with more time and enthusiasm for MediaMOO and its future.

Designers of online communities might find these lessons more broadly applicable:

- It's important to be aware that there are multiple population models (ie., stage of life, life long), and to make sure to chose the right population model for a given community.
- Subgroups will inevitably form, and may splinter off. Community managers should anticipate this, and may adopt strategies such as fostering the growth of new subgroups, and giving mature subgroups a degree of autonomy while maintaining connection to the parent group.
- Enthusiasm of the leadership of the group is essential. If original leaders become too busy or tire of playing that role, they must be replaced with new, enthusiastic leaders, or possibly supported behind the scenes in maintaining a public presence in the group.

In this paper, we have tried to summarize some of the changes that occurred over MediaMOO's seven-year history. We hope that the lessons learned will be of interest to other community designers and will contribute to our understanding of the delicate interactions of technology, policy, and leadership, which create online culture.

Acknowledgments

The authors thank all the members of MediaMOO and leaders of other online communities who shared their thoughts and insights with us. Special thanks to B. J. Berquist, Isabel Danforth, Tari Fanderclai, Judith Fusco, Gustavo Glusman, Richard Godard, Amy Jo Kim, Jeanne McWhorter, Daniel Rose, Mark Schlager, Ken Schweller, and Greg Siering.

References

Bartle, R. (1990). *Interactive multi-user computer games* [World Wide Web page]. Available: ftp.lambda.moo.mud.org/pub/MOO/papers/mudreport.txt [1 May 1991].

Bruckman, A. (1997). *MOOSE crossing: Construction, community, and learning in a networked virtual world for kids*. PhD dissertation, MIT, Cambridge, MA.

Bruckman, A. (1998). Community support for constructionist learning. *Computer Supported Cooperative Work*, 7, 47–86.

Bruckman, A., & Resnick, M. (1995). The MediaMOO project: Constructionism and professional community. *Convergence*, *1*(1), 94–109.

Curtis, P. (1992). Mudding: Social phenomena in text-based virtual realities. *Proceedings of the Conference on Directions and Implications in Advanced Computing.* Berkeley, CA: Computer Professionals for Social Responsibility.

Papert, S. (1991). Situating constructionism. In I. Harel & S. Papert (Eds.), *Constructionism* (pp. 1–11). Norwood, NJ: Ablex Publishing.

Schlager, M., Fusco, J., & Schank, P. (1998). Cornerstones for an On-line Community of Education Professionals. *IEEE Technology and Society, 17*(4), 15–21, 40.

Vilhjalmsson, H., & Cassell, J. (1998). BodyChat: Autonomous communicative behaviors in avatars. In *Autonomous agents* (pp. 269–76). Minneapolis: ACM.

2   Female Voices in Virtual Reality

Drawing Young Girls into an Online World

Ann Locke Davidson and Janet Ward Schofield

Popular media, prominent politicians, and technology enthusiasts convey rich imagery about the transformative educational potential of the Internet. Compelling visions are epitomized in a speech given by U.S. President Clinton:

children in urban, suburban and rural districts, rich, poor, middle class – for the first time in the history of America, because of these [Internet]* connections, we can make available the same learning from all over the world at the same level of quality and the same time to all our children. It will revolutionize education. (Sioux Falls, SD: 1996)

Indeed, there is little argument about the fact that universal Internet connections would provide many students with access to a vast array of information as well as to potentially enriching opportunities to interact with distant others who would not otherwise be available.

However, it is less certain that Internet access in and of itself will end up making available the same learning for all school age children; strong evidence indicates that existing attitudes toward, interest in, and use of technology are clearly related to variables such as gender and race. For example, gender and race have been shown to predict Internet use even when financial barriers to access are removed, with young, European American males dominating (Kraut et al., 1996). Boys are more likely than girls to use computers during discretionary time (Durndell & Lightbody, 1993; Hess & Miura, 1985; Hoyles, 1988; Schofield, 1995) to enroll in computer science courses, particularly as the required level of expertise increases, and to earn computer science degrees (Hoyles, 1988; National

---

* Brackets here and later in the paper indicate text that the authors have inserted for the purpose of clarification. Brackets surrounding ellipses ([. . .]) indicate that some portion of the text has been removed, again for the purpose of clarification.

Center for Education Statistics, 1997; Schofield, 1995). Boys also tend to like computers more than girls and to express more confidence about their ability to learn and use computers (American Association of University Women, 1998; Sutton, 1991; Whitley, 1997).

Such findings suggest that girls may end up participating less extensively in the rich virtual community provided by the Internet than may boys. This has some troubling implications. First, to the extent that the Internet lives up to its potential as a valuable educational resource (Cummins & Sayers, 1995; Hunter, 1993), this would seem undesirable. Second, since technological expertise, including expertise in Internet-based applications, opens up promising career paths with relatively high salaries and many opportunities (Chandrasekaran, 1998; Steinberg, 1997; Veneri, 1988), already existing male/female disparities in earnings might be exacerbated. Third, such a situation would hardly be conducive to expanding the cadre of highly trained individuals available to fill demanding computer-related jobs in this country – the dearth of which is already posing a potential problem for our nation's economy (Bronner, 1998; Harmon, 1998). With impending demographic changes indicating that an increasingly small proportion of the workforce will be white males in the coming century (Fullerton, 1997), finding ways to increase the interest of female and minority group students in computing is an urgent undertaking.

One factor that suggests that progress in this area is possible is the recognition that interests and feelings of competence are potentially malleable. Specifically, the form and strength of interests are influenced by experiences in a variety of social settings (Krapp & Fink, 1992; Renninger, 1992). Likewise, feelings of competence can also change markedly with changes in the social aspects of an instructional situation (Steele & Aronson, 1995). Thus, changes in the nature of the situation in which girls typically encounter computers or changes in the nature of computer-based interaction and communication have the potential to enhance both girls' interest in computing and their technical skills.

In this chapter, we focus on three types of change: alterations in interest, alterations in attitude, and alterations in competence. We also relate these changes to the social context in which they occur. Specifically, we present a case study of third-grade (ages 8–9) girls, describing how they responded to a rather unusual virtual community-based learning environment: a "MOO." A MOO, or Multiuser Object Oriented, environment is an online, text-based environment that offers opportunities for communication and interaction. In a MOO, multiple individuals can log on simultaneously. The users share access to a database of "rooms," "exits," and other objects. Users take on "character" roles, manipulate objects in the environment, move from room to room, and engage in conversations with other MOO users.* Over time, the girls working in this environment became a community of users; they interacted frequently in mutually supportive ways and began identifying themselves as a clear social group with a strong common interest and special expertise in using technology to communicate with others.

The case illustrates that this experience changed these girls in important ways. Specifically, the experience enhanced existing levels of interest in technology, built technical confidence, and increased technical skills. The case study also demonstrates that technology does not act in isolation but rather interacts with instructional setting and social variables to bring about unanticipated as well as intended effects.

Gender: A Social Construct with Behavioral Implications

The literature concerned with the production and implications of gender differences provides a useful introduction to some of the issues addressed in the case study presented here. There is much to indicate, for example, that gendered behaviors and attitudes described as typical may vary according to situation (Epstein, 1997; James, 1997; Lott, 1997). For example, women may act as aggressively as men under conditions of anonymity, although they often act less aggressively in other contexts (Lott, 1997). Further, many stereotypical expressions of gender disappear when work status is held constant (James, 1997). Also, membership in varied ethnic, racial, and social class communities affects both the experience and expression of gender (Fordham, 1996; Hurtado, 1997; Raissiguier, 1994). This literature suggests that women may behave quite differently when working individually or among female peers than when working among male counterparts.

While differences in the expression of gender are shaped by and vary with social circumstances, certain common orientations and patterns of behavior have been observed. Women, especially European-American ones, are somewhat more relational than men – that is, more likely to ap-

---

* The girls' reaction to this particular type of virtual community is especially relevant in that MOOs historically (along with chat rooms and other interactive domains) have been dominated by males who engage in fantasy-based competitive games (Gender Wars in Cyberspace, 1995; Turkle, 1995).

proach the world as an individual within a social network, more likely to acquire skills relevant to developing and sustaining personal connections, and more likely to seek out situations and develop behaviors that foster relationships (Gilligan, 1982, 1993; Miller, 1986; Tannen, 1990). This literature suggests that technological contexts that offer opportunities to develop relationships as well as to practice skills relevant to building and sustaining them may prove engaging for females because they build on preexisting interests. Consistent with this observation, there is evidence that girls prefer software with expressive or relational themes and may perform better on tasks that involve such (Lepper & Cordova, 1992; Light & Littleton, 1997; Sanders, 1985). Further, girls appear to benefit from collaborative approaches to programming and computer-supported work (Huber & Schofield, 1998; Johnson, Johnson & Stanne, 1985; Sutherland & Hoyles, 1988).

Study Participants and Methods

The data for this case were gathered in the context of a broader study of a National Science Foundation-funded effort to implement and institutionalize Internet use in a large, urban school district. As part of this research, we collected a large corpus of interview, field note, email, and student work product data from several schools. One of these schools was Independence Elementary, the site of this case study.

The MOO project carried out at Independence involved a group of third-grade students aged 8 to 9. In all, ten girls and two boys participated. Eight of the girls were European-Americans and two were African-Americans. They came to the activity with some technical experience but little exposure to the Internet. For example, eight reported having a computer at home, which they used principally for word processing, producing and saving things, and entertainment. However, just one had Internet access, and none had worked previously on a MOO. Also important, these girls manifested attitudes and visions of technology like those expressed by other females in the literature. First, almost to a person, they reported initial anxiety about working in a new technological environment,* a finding discussed at length later in this paper. Second, as a group, these girls emphasized tool-like and pragmatic purposes (e.g., work, typing) rather

---

* Reviews of the literature indicate that females of all ages tend to express more fear and less confidence about their ability to learn and use computers than males (American Association of University Women, 1998; Huber & Schofield, 1998; Sutton, 1991).

than play* when describing their initial conceptions of computer uses. Third, almost half of the girls expressed some doubt about whether they would want to work with computers in the future.

The students worked in two groups that met weekly on different days of the week. Four girls worked together on one day and six girls and the two boys worked together on a second. Therefore, we observed two MOO classroom sessions each week for most of the school year. In addition to taking extensive and detailed field notes, the research team collected copies of messages students left for the public on the MOO's electronic "bulletin board" and the messages students sent to other MOO users.

Near the end of the academic year, the research team carried out audiotaped interviews with the teacher and MOO students. Nine of the ten girls chose to participate – all eight European-American girls and one African-American girl. The interviews were conducted individually, in a private setting, and it was emphasized that all information gathered would be reported anonymously. Open-ended and semistructured in nature, the interviews were used to collect information about participants' attitudes toward the project as well as their ideas about various features of the instructional context and the relationship between gender and computing. In addition, participants responded to a set of closed-ended questions designed to measure with Likert scale response options their interest, confidence, and worry about computer use at the beginning and end of their MOO experiences.

Thematic categories were applied to the field notes and interviews (Miles & Huberman, 1994; Strauss & Corbin, 1990). We also took great care to "triangulate" – that is, to look across all data sources in analyzing student outcomes as well as their responses to various instructional features. Finally, we analyzed closed-ended student interview questions statistically.

The Learning Environment: Self-Expression and Relationship Building in a Collaborative Instructional Setting

To provide the reader with some sense of what the girls encountered as they worked online, we briefly describe both the MOO and the social nature of the instructional setting.

---

* Some studies indicate that even when computer experience is equivalent, women more often than males envision computers as a practical tool, while males speak of the computer in intimate, personal terms and view computers as instruments for tinkering and play (Hall & Cooper, 1991; Nolan, McKinnon & Soler, 1992).

The MOO: A Place for Self-Expression and Social Exchange

The MOO was designed by Ms. Ebert, Independence Elementary's librarian. Her goal was to engage students more actively in reading and to enhance their reading and writing skills. Thus, the MOO she developed consists of several "rooms," each populated by storytellers or an interactive object of some type. Visitors – as characters – can "sit" in chairs and hammocks, read about a room's furnishing and decorations, and interact with programmed storytellers or others also logged on at the time. Students enter commands to "wake up" programmed storytellers who tell a variety of stories. Visitors can also access virtual reality "bulletin boards" to read notes left by others or to leave messages of their own. Typically, these notes are responses and comments about the stories read. Finally, visitors can access a mail utility that allows them to send electronic letters to others met at the MOO.

The MOO elicits visions of engaging in conversation in a safe, comforting, and relaxed domestic space. For example, visitors entering one area read the following screen:

You have stepped onto a balcony. A wide stone railing surrounds it. Stone benches line either end. Large pots of brightly colored geraniums sit on the wide railing. More pots of flowers hang down from the ceiling. [. . .]
   Ebbie [Ms. Ebert's character] is sitting sideways on a bench, her legs propped up on the bench, her back leaning against the tower wall, drinking a cup of cocoa. Gumby [a visitor's character] is stretched out in a hammock swinging high overhead. She sips from a can of Sprite.

In other areas, the text invites visitors to express personal thoughts and experiences. For example, in one room there is a virtual reality "bulletin board" focused on stuffed animals. During the year we observed, its greeting read:

January 26, 1996, is Stuffed Animal Day at Independence School. As part of the celebration we are asking you to leave a message on this bulletin board about your stuffed animal. Maybe a story about how you got one or how you named one. Maybe something that happened to one.

Here, visitors find a place to talk about a topic conducive to self-revelation and expression, as children often name their animals, tell them secrets, and imbue them with personalities and emotions.

While working at the MOO, students engaged in expressive and interactive tasks – responding to the stories they read and corresponding with other users they had met while working online. Ms. Ebert encouraged the girls to go beyond simple description to express their opinions or feelings about the texts read.

In addition, the girls took advantage of the opportunities for spatial and temporal flexibility the Internet affords to craft a virtual community. Specifically, over several months, they built a relationship with a blind user, Mr. Tims, who happened to visit the MOO from his computer located across the country. After Mr. Tims posted a message to the stuffed animal bulletin board, Ms. Ebert encouraged the girls to respond and a rich correspondence evolved. (See Murphy et al., 1997, for a detailed description.) Defining features of this relationship included regular contact and an emphasis on exchanging personal details. Over the course of several weeks, Ms. Ebert and Mr. Tims encouraged the girls to ask him questions and to tell him things about themselves. Further, Ms. Ebert endeavored to instruct the girls on the social niceties of doing so, as in the following field note segment:

Ms. Ebert suggests that in her response to Mr. Tims, Robyn might start out by saying, "Hi, how are you?," and then ask questions. She also tells Robyn that she thinks in addition [she might write] "I read your letter with Ms. Ebert." She explained to Robyn that it's nice to begin a letter with an introduction instead of just mailing a bunch of questions back.

It is worthwhile to note that learning to elicit and exchange personal details has been described as a skill highly relevant to building female friendships (Tannen, 1990).

Collaborative Nature of the Instructional Setting

The students met once each week to work in the school library at a bank of four computers lined along the back wall.* Four to eight students worked at a time, in pairs or an occasional group of three, chatting as they worked. Ms. Ebert worked in the students' midst, moving from pair to pair when necessary.

In this instructional environment, Ms. Ebert clearly expected mutually supportive behavior. She encouraged and at times required students to help others, to allow partners to state what they would like to do, to

* Four girls worked on one day, while six girls and two boys worked on another day. The girls typically worked with the same female partner, although at time girls interested in a similar activity exchanged seats. The boys worked together on the days we observed. Occasionally, a female joined them – often in order to provide guidance and assistance.

consider a partner's wishes when making work plans, and to share the keyboard. Her preferences were especially apparent when she chastised girls who drifted toward more self-centered behaviors. In the following note, for example, she directs one girl to "help" her partner:

Sarah [looking away from her partner, who is typing a message to leave at the MOO] said to Ms. Ebert, "You sure are enjoying that," [referring to Ms. Ebert's preparation to send an e-mail letter] [...] Ms. Ebert, hearing Sarah [and noticing that she has stopped working with her partner], says to Sarah, "Be a good helper. Don't leave her out there typing alone."

In short, organizational structure as well as teacher behavior combined to communicate that this was a collaborative instructional environment. In accord with these expectations, the girls tended to converse frequently about stories they were reading, to work together and discuss ideas when writing messages, and to discuss letters they were composing.

The relationships that evolved between Ms Ebert and her students were also different from those found in more conventional classroom settings, where teachers tend to function as experts presenting information to large groups of students (Goodlad, 1984). For example, Ms. Ebert revealed personal feelings and perspectives characteristic of a friend rather than those typical of traditional teacher–student interactions, as demonstrated in the following field note excerpt:

The room was incredibly loud at this moment, and suddenly in the midst of it, Ms. Ebert exclaimed, "Oh, this is not my day!" Danielle turned sharply toward Mike and said, "Don't yell! She's having a hard time. She might erase everything." Ms. Ebert was kneeling on the floor with her elbows on the table that the computers were sitting on, and she hung her head and ran her fingers through her hair. It turned out she had erased, or she believed that she had erased, all of the letters that she had highlighted instead of moving them. She said a couple of times, "I just can't believe this. I can't believe this." Danielle began to pat her back soothingly, as if to reassure her.

Over the course of the year, it became clear that this was an instructional environment in which the students and Ms. Ebert came to know one another well. As Ms. Ebert noted, "you're much closer to the kids you've worked with on the Net, because you get to do them in a small group. And not only that, when they start commenting about stories, or when they have e-mail with somebody, you start learning how they feel as people [...] they're more of a little human being, and you're more of a human being to them."

Girls' Responses: Increased Technical Interest, Decreased Technical Anxiety, and Evolving Technical Competence

Having described features of the MOO-based learning environment, we turn to consider how the girls responded. Uniformly the data indicate important consequences of their involvement in this project. We summarize these within three general categories: increased technical interest, decreased technical anxiety, and evolving technical competence. We discuss these three outcomes separately, in spite of the fact that interconnections between them are quite likely (see Prenzel, 1992), because they appear to be conceptually distinct enough to warrant separate treatment.

Increased Technical Interest

A number of indicators suggest that the girls' interest in technology increased markedly over the year. First, as is apparent in Table 2.1, at the end of the year the girls described themselves as more certain that they wanted to use a computer in their future work than they had been at the beginning. Second, they said they were more confident that working in a MOO would be something they would choose to do in their free time. Third and finally, during interviews, all the girls reported that if they had the opportunity at home to read and respond to stories at the MOO they would do so.

Table 2.1. *Interest in Computer and MOO Use*

Question Stem	Pre*	Post	t	df
1. How sure want to use a computer in work when older?	3.78	4.68	$-2.83^{†}$	8
2. How sure that work on MOO is something you would do for fun in your free time if you could?	4.13	5.00	$-2.97^{†}$	7

* All answers are on a five point scale from 1 = not at all sure to 5 = very sure.
† $p < .02$.

Consistent with the girls' self-reports of increased interest, field notes reveal that as time went on the girls began to memorize technical commands and addresses that would allow them to get to and move around the MOO with increasing efficiency, though they were not required to do so. In the segment from field notes presented next, for example, Ms. Ebert is surprised to find that a student has learned a command that she had not focused upon in her teaching:

Ms. Ebert helps the girls exit and gets them to the command line in Unix. Robyn, seeing this, says, "What?" and then asks, "Now do we telnet?" Ms. Ebert looks at the girls and says, "You don't know telnet." Then Robyn and Fiona say, "Yes we do! Yes we do!" and then they recite [the instructions necessary to] telnet to the MOO.

Field notes show also that in spite of their early reservations, the girls came to actively strive to find ways to increase the time they spent working at the MOO. For example, they frequently asked for permission to go to the library to work during their lunch period when they could have been socializing with friends. And, on seven different occasions, girls were observed asking to work past the bell signaling the end of their work period, another clear indicator of their interest in this activity. In some instances, they actively negotiated for more time, as in the following field observation segment:

The bell rings as the girls are just beginning [to read] their [on-line] story. They continue to read and pay no attention to the bell [...] Ms. Ebert comments, "That was the bell. Was anybody aware of that?" [The students continue to read for a couple of minutes past the bell.] Ms. Ebert says, "You know what? You really have to go." Robyn says in protest "We're almost done!" Ms. Ebert replies, "No, I don't think so." Then she comments that [Robyn's regular classroom] teacher is going to kill her. Fiona says, "We'll tell the teacher we lost track of time. We didn't hear the bell." Sarah then says from the other side of the room, "We'll tell her we were all in the bathroom, and there were fifth graders in there, and we couldn't hear the bell."

When interviewed, Ms. Ebert noted that "there's a big increase in the amount of enthusiasm [now as compared to at the beginning of the year]. In the beginning they were enthusiastic, but now they're even more because they just really liked it. . . . They just keep *nagging* me about going to the MOO." Interestingly, the girls' enthusiasm manifested itself despite the fact that their online activities were not graded.

Decreased Technical Anxiety, Increased Technical Confidence

Samantha: What I say is girls can ... women can do anything that men can do, and sometimes even better. Because I know I can work better on the MOO than Frank can or Mike.

The preceding statement, made during an interview at the conclusion of the MOO project by one of the girls involved, radiates confidence. It is especially striking because Samantha said she was quite worried, prior to project involvement, about working on the computer. We saw this same pattern of decreased technical anxiety and increased technical competence among other respondents. Overall, the girls reported that they, like their peers in the literature, were initially anxious about working with computers. But at the project's end, the girls asserted that they were no longer worried about working on the computer and that they were confident that they could learn what was required of them there. Moreover, as Table 2.2 illustrates, they perceived themselves as having become less anxious and more confident over time.

Table 2.2. *Anxiety and Confidence Concerning Computer*

Question Stem	Pre*	Post	t	df
1. How worried or nervous about working on the computer?	2.56	1.0	3.78[†]	8
2. How sure you can learn what Ms. Ebert wants you to learn on the computer?	3.44	4.67	−3.77[†]	8
3. How sure you can teach other kids to use the MOO?	3.78	4.44	−2.87[‡]	8
4. How sure you can teach your parents or other adults how to use the MOO?	2.88	3.75	−2.97[‡]	7

* Answers for the question concerning anxiety are on a five point scale, with the 1 indicating less anxiety (1 = not at all worried to 5 = very worried). Answers for the rest are on a five point scale, but in this case higher means indicate increased confidence (1 to 5 = very sure).
[†] $p < .005$.
[‡] $p < .02$.

When asked to rate how worried or anxious they felt about working on the computer when the project began, for example, all but two girls expressed some worry. Their elaborations on this closed-ended question suggest that, initially, they were especially concerned about somehow damaging or harming equipment and were also anxious about whether their previous computer experience had adequately prepared them for what was to come:

> *Kristina:* Oh . . . worried or nervous? Very nervous! [. . .] That I would probably type something . . . push a wrong button and mess up the computers. That was one of the things I was *really* scared of.
>
> *Samantha:* Well, I was worried about messing up . . . like I didn't know what to do, and I was worried I'd mess up the computer because there's all that stuff over there on the side of the room, and I'm thinking, "Well, what if I do something wrong?"
>
> *Robyn:* Like, it was my first time, because we just got our computer [at home] like about – last June or something [. . .] And so I didn't really know about computers, and I was nervous – like, "Oh, what am I gonna' do on the computer?"

Our field notes from early in the year also captured manifestations of this self-reported anxiety:

[The girls are composing a reply that they will post about a story they have read.] The girls then type, "I would like to know what a wongie is." Then one of the girls hits return, and one of the other girls calls, "Wait!! We're not done posting yet" in a very concerned tone. Ms. Ebert looks over to see what's going on, and she calms them down and shows them that they've done their return correctly, and the girls say, "Oh, okay, that's how you do it."

The majority of the girls interviewed also said that they were not completely sure they would be able to learn what Ms. Ebert wanted them to learn on the computer (see Table 2).

Over the course of the school year, the girls' worry about using computers decreased, and there was an increase in their technical confidence (see Table 2). We were particularly struck by the fact that, when asked to rate how worried or nervous they felt about working on the computer at the time of their year-end interview, each of the girls said that she was not at all worried. There were similar increases in the confidence the girls expressed about their ability to learn what their teacher wanted them to learn on the computer, their ability to teach other students how to work on the MOO, and their ability to teach adults to work on the MOO.

Our field notes corroborate the girls' perceptions. As time went on, we observed the girls confidently offering help to classmates and engaging in self-correcting, troubleshooting behaviors on their own:

MOO classroom session: Frank and Mike were trying to read a story. They were frustrated, with Frank saying, "It's not working!" They keep typing the command "say alligator." [. . .] Ms. Ebert comes over and asks the boys whether or not they have the name of the story correct and they say yes. [Ms. Ebert leaves.] Samantha goes back to look at the top of the screen to see the different story choices the boys have [available to them] and finds out that, in fact, they do not have the name of the story right. She checked this by typing "wake lute" [by entering a command that allows her to see all of the stories available from a given electronic storyteller] and then commented, "There is no alligator."

Also, during year-end interviews, the girls asserted vigorously that females are as competent as males with computers. It is perhaps relevant to note that although girls were observed assisting the two boys who also participated in these MOO activities, we never observed these boys assisting the girls.

Perhaps because her focus was reading and writing, Ms. Ebert had not perceived any initial reticence on the girls' part and did not note changes in anxiety and confidence over the course of the year as a result. In fact, she remarked instead that the girls "weren't nervous and they still aren't nervous." These data do not triangulate perfectly, but the preponderance of evidence supports the conclusion that the girls' anxiety decreased and their confidence increased over the year. Not only did they report this themselves in an interview situation carefully structured to foster honesty, but parallel indications of this change appear in our field notes.

Increased Technological Competence

[Samantha sits in front of a computer next to Ms. Ebert. Both are moving around the MOO as characters.] Samantha asks, "How do you hide?" and Ms. Ebert tells her the command [that will enable her to hide her character]. Samantha also asks, "Well, if I know how to hide, how do you find other people?"

[After class, Ms. Ebert comments that Samantha has read all the material available in this MOO and is becoming frustrated.] "If Samantha wants to stay committed to this project next year, then I think what we'll really have to do is make a change so that she can be a builder on her own," says Ms. Ebert. "And we can just give her projects to build on her own, because she really has the [technical] skills."

Our data suggest that the girls acquired an introductory understanding of virtual reality environments and expanded their visions of technology use as a result of their participation in this activity. By spring, for example, all could interact as characters with features of the MOO environment – for example, wake interactive storytellers by entering commands, direct a storyteller to read a particular story, and place a note or piece of writing on various MOO bulletin boards. The girls also could move through the MOO with ease.

Consistent with the interviews and our field notes, Ms. Ebert also observed a significant improvement in the girls' technical competence: "at the end of last school year they were definitely moderately to extremely skilled. They were getting really good at the MOO. [. . .] [T]hey went from a beginner who didn't know anything about using the MOO to just being almost independent."

At least three girls took the initiative to acquire more sophisticated understanding about characters and the nature of virtual reality environments. These girls, for example, experimented with various sorts of character movement as well as acquired commands that would enable their characters to do a greater variety of things – for example, hide as well as move.

These types of understanding were not goals for the teacher; again, she was more interested in engaging the girls in reading. Nevertheless, because some girls became sufficiently interested, they pursued and acquired knowledge about these aspects of virtual reality independent of any urging from their teacher.

These data also suggest that, over the course of the year, the girls broadened their conceptions of the uses to which computers can be put. Before working at the MOO, six of the nine girls reported that they did not realize that computers could be used to communicate and interact. They generally associated computers with work, mentioning the following uses: adult work, typing, "hard things," learning, finding things, and games. After working on the MOO, the same girls reported that they realized computers could be used for communication, interaction, and publication. Specifically, they mentioned such uses as listening to stories, writing to people across the United States, listening to people, getting in contact, seeing things about other people, and publishing stories.

Understanding Girls' Responses

In the preceding section, we see girls responding with increasing and persistent interest to a novel use of the Internet. In some cases, they go beyond their teachers' expectations to seek out new technical knowledge.

At the same time, as they participate in this activity, their technical anxiety decreases, and confidence and competence increase.

To demonstrate that the girls experienced change, however, does not explain why they did so. In this section, we present data that highlight the instructional and social features that appear to have supported the girls' evolving interest and enthusiasm, lessened their day-to-day anxieties, increased their confidence about working in this instructional setting, and fostered technical competence.

Specifically, we argue that one important factor contributing to the girls enjoyment of their work at the MOO was that working at the MOO enabled them to practice and develop knowledge relevant to sustaining personal connections and social networks, or what Gilligan calls relational knowledge (1982, 1993). The girls appeared to be particularly interested in the relational aspect of community enabled by the spatial and temporal flexibility of the Internet. Second, we show that the girls were extremely comfortable in this setting because they knew that they could find and depend upon technical assistance from their peers and teacher. The girls derived confidence and experienced less anxiety because of this. Third, as we will discuss at length in the following section, the girls had female role models that they could observe in this environment – this fact likely also helped lessen their initial sense of technical anxiety. In addition, both the second and third factors likely encouraged girls to participate in technical experimentation and exploration, which, in turn, contributed to the acquisition of new technical knowledge not required by their teacher.

Before presenting data specific to these arguments, we note briefly that the opportunity to build relational skills was not the only reason that MOO activities proved enjoyable. Consistent with previous studies of technology and intrinsic motivation (Lepper & Malone, 1987; Schofield, 1995), some of the girls emphasized the increased choice and sense of control they experienced when explaining why they preferred work at the MOO to that of their classroom. (Recall that the MOO allowed many choices: students could opt to visit various MOO "rooms"; choose among storytellers that offered stories of different types; write something for a bulletin board, or read notes written by other visitors, among other activities.) Further, the MOO encouraged fantasy, which can be very motivating (Lepper & Malone, 1987). In addition, one girl appeared to derive as much intrinsic enjoyment from technical play as she did from interaction with others. Nonetheless, overall, the relational opportunities provided by the MOO seemed to be important.

Thus, we turn now to illustrate our argument that girls derived enjoyment from the relational opportunities this MOO provided, experienced comfort in this instructional setting, and benefited from their observations of female technical competence while working there.

Expressing Feelings and Perspectives

Drawing on studies of talk among females, scholars have noted that females enjoy sharing their daily experiences, as well as describing their thoughts and feelings about these experiences (Tannen, 1990; Treichler & Kramarae, 1983). Tannen (1990) noted that even though male friends frequently talk about activities, female friends enjoy verbalizing thoughts and feelings about their problems and experiences, a difference also noted by Schofield (1989) in her study of middle-school-aged children. For women, "the essence of friendship is talk, telling each other what they're thinking and feeling, and what happened that day: who was at the bus stop, who called, what they said, how that made them feel" (Tannen, 1990, p. 80). Such talk allows females to display similarities and matching experiences, and thereby to further relationships and establish connections (Tannen, 1990).

As mentioned in the description of the instructional setting, girls had an opportunity to comment on what they read while they worked. During interviews, several girls made it clear that they greatly enjoyed the opportunity this gave to share thoughts and feelings and to read those expressed by classmates:

> *Interviewer:* What have you liked best about working at the MOO?
>
> *Karen:* Mostly I like telling how I like the stories and everything, and I love typing. [. . .] I like to tell how I like it, and what I liked about it, and if it was funny or anything.
>
> *Fiona:* . . . [W]e get to read other people's posts – we get to learn how people feel about the story.

The girls' actions also reveal their orientation toward exploring and expressing thoughts and feelings. While working, a good many took advantage of the opportunity to verbalize and publicize personal experiences and feelings by posting at the MOO. A response to a story about

Paddington Bear, and a response to a story about a character who reveals a secret, provide examples of this:

> *Sarah:* I have had a bear almost all my life, his name is Babby. He has had his name all his life just like his place in my heart. He got his name in a very strange way. Let me tell you about it. One day I was sitting in my house when the lady across the street came over she had a bear in her arms – it was for me! I rushed up to her. I yelled BABBY! I think I was one so I have no idea why I yelled that but the name stuck. [MOO excerpt edited for spelling, punctuation and capitalization errors]
>
> *Mia:* The queen said some secrets are better if they are told. I think this is true. Sometimes if you have a secret you go around feeling sad.

Both Sarah and Mia reveal feelings, as Sarah tells her reader about her love for a teddy bear treasured since childhood and Mia tells her reader how she feels when she is burdened with a difficult secret.

Developing Relational Skills, Building New Relationships

The MOO also offered the girls an opportunity to develop relationships with new individuals, such as Mr. Tims the blind user. The girls, as previously mentioned, developed this relationship by posing questions that enabled them to better understand Mr. Tims' situation and his feelings about his situation. Question asking has been associated with women's general orientation toward developing relationships and interconnections with others, since questions communicate interest in and provide information relevant to understanding others (Lyons, 1990; Tannen, 1990; Treichler & Kramarae, 1983).

It was apparent that the chance to develop a new relationship and practice friendship-building skills was very engaging for the girls. When asked what they liked best about working on the MOO, the girls who exchanged mail with Mr. Tims spoke about the chance to develop that relationship. As one put it, "I like typing to [him] because I know then when I get an answer and I ask him questions, I know more about him." Asked whether they would prefer to meet Mr. Tims just once, in person, or to write to him regularly by computer (without ever meeting him), all but one of the girls said she would prefer to continue writing by computer, explaining that correspondence over time allows one to ask more questions and thereby to continue developing a relationship.

*Deriving Enjoyment and Confidence from the Presence
of Familiar Others*

Fiona: I wouldn't feel as good as I do now [if I worked in the library
alone] because . . . nobody that I know except maybe Ms. Ebert and
maybe some people that I know from the other grades at the library
would be there – not Robyn and Kristina and Sarah

Sarah: [. . .] If Ms. Ebert were busy with something else, and they
weren't there, and I wanted to do something and I didn't know how to
get to it, then I wouldn't be able to do it.

In this instructional environment, participants have ample opportunities to interact with peers and their teacher. Because the computers are
side by side, participants can see and hear what most of their peers are
doing. Since students work in pairs and because they are encouraged to
collaborate, they also have ample opportunity to speak with one another.
It is clear that the girls valued this aspect of their instructional environment; when asked how they would feel if they were to continue working
at the MOO next year, but coming to the library and working alone, eight
of the nine responded negatively to the idea of losing the social interaction. The girls said also that they would prefer to work with their familiar
teacher, with seven of nine expressing a clear preference for Ms. Ebert
when asked how they would feel if they were to work on the MOO with
a different unspecified teacher the following year.

In explaining their preferences for working with peers and a familiar
teacher, the girls said first that they enjoyed the opportunity to spend
time with their friends. As one put it, "when I work with my friends
I feel more happier and more like . . . company. Why would I want to
go by myself?" And, asserted another, "we all should be able to work
together, because then we all know what's going on [. . .] it's lots of fun."
The girls also enjoyed Ms. Ebert's close proximity and the friend-like
persona she presented while working among them. As one explained,
"I like that now we became friends with her, and I think that's cool." To the
girls, Ms. Ebert appeared more relaxed, more readily accessible for help,
and less agitated than in a whole class situation, and they preferred this.
Working in an environment perceived as highly enjoyable seems likely to
have contributed importantly to the girls' growing interest in computing,
as prior research suggests, interest is associated with enjoyable experience
(Prenzel, 1992).

In addition to experiencing enjoyment, the girls also derived comfort
and confidence from the presence of friends and a familiar teacher and

clearly believed that they could depend on these individuals for assistance when and if necessary. Further, some linked the presence of supportive friends and a supportive teacher directly to a decreased sense of anxiety, as do the following respondents:

> *Leslie:* I'd feel probably... I think I'd feel kind of nervous [if I was alone] because if I was supposed to know something and I didn't know it, I'd be nervous that I was supposed to go to this room and I didn't know how to get there. I would ask Ms. Ebert, but I would also like somebody – one of my friends or a kid in my class – to work with me.
>
> *Danielle:* [Another] teacher might not know a lot about computers, and I would feel more confident with Ms. Ebert around [...] [S]he mostly knows about computers because she goes on the computers a lot. So like if someone messes up, she knows what to do.

Studies of individuals entering environments where members of their social group have traditionally been underrepresented indicate that socially isolated individuals may experience discomfort and even crises in confidence (Davidson, 1996; Pettigrew & Martin, 1987; Schofield, 1995; Steele & Aronson, 1995). Further, these individuals may be hesitant to turn to socially different peers for help (Davidson, 1996). Recall that these females entered a novel technological setting with initial anxiety. We believe that the presence of socially similar others was helpful for promoting active participation as well as lessened anxiety about technical learning. This, in turn, likely contributed to increased technological learning more generally.

Observing a Technically Proficient Female Role Model

In considering girls' tentative relation with technology, many scholars have expressed concern about the paucity of available female role models (Huber & Schofield, 1998; Pelgrum, 1992). Guided by a female who herself created the MOO-based classrooms where they worked, the girls in our study were exposed to a role model quite different from those typically portrayed in computer magazines.

As Ms. Ebert worked, she presented a blended technical identity that incorporated various orientations toward technology. On the one hand, she displayed a mastery orientation like that displayed by typically male technophiles (Turkle, 1984). She spoke with enthusiasm about her interest in programming, demonstrated a willingness to experiment with the technology at hand, and confronted intruders who interrupted her or her students' work in their MOO classroom. At the same time, and in contrast to images of the solo male hacker and confrontational male virtual reality buff, Ms. Ebert promoted and demonstrated collaborative approaches to obtaining technical knowledge and nonconfrontational approaches to dealing with other MOO users.

In the following excerpt from field notes, Ms. Ebert asserts this blended technical identity. She reveals intrinsic interest in both programming and technical play, but she also appears comfortable about having turned to someone else for help:

Ms. Ebert then said to the girls, "You know what? I got the kooshes to work." [. . .] In virtual reality, the girls [characters] had been juggling these things [ball-like objects] called "kooshes." [. . .] Ms. Ebert [during a previous classroom session] had tried [unsuccessfully] to put in a command so that when one of the girl's characters in the MOO came to juggle the koosh, the pronoun referring to that individual would be correct [in gender] [. . .] Mia asked, "Well, how did you find out?" [how to do this] and Ms. Ebert explained to Mia that she was presently taking a programming course, and that another woman at the course had managed to put pronouns in her program. [. . .] Ms. Ebert looked at her program and found out how she did it. So, Ms. Ebert said to the girls, "We shared."

Similarly, Ms. Ebert modeled both confrontational and nonconfrontational approaches to intrusions to the MOO by uninvited visiting characters. For example, when a visitor failed to respond to requests to stop interrupting her students' work, Ms. Ebert removed the visitor by disabling part of the virtual reality environment. But at another time, when a visitor did not appear to intend to disturb classroom activity, Ms. Ebert simply moved the girls to another MOO "room" where they could work uninterrupted.

Some of the meanings that the girls derived from observing Ms. Ebert emerged when we asked them to comment on the view that males are more competent than females on computers. Five of the girls refuted this by referring to Ms. Ebert among other female role models. As one explained, "Ms. Ebert and Miss Gerard [this student's classroom teacher] have taught me about computers, and mostly more things about computers than males." Here, it is important to note that although eight girls reported that their mothers used a computer either at work or at home and six said that their mothers did so fairly regularly, just one referred to her mother and a second to an older sister when citing evidence of female competence. Perhaps this is because many of the uses girls reported for their mothers did not challenge gender stereotypes. Specifically, girls reported that their mothers generally worked with computers for practical reasons, using word processing programs to make school notices, type work schedules, write letters, and so forth. In watching and working with

Ms. Ebert, it is likely that the girls received either explicit or implicit messages that they too could be simultaneously technically competent, relational, and collaborative.

Conclusion

We describe a technological realm and an instructional setting that encourage social interaction, expression of feelings and perspectives, and collaboration. In addition, aspects of this environment highlight female technical competence. Young girls working here responded by building on- and off-line relationships and by practicing relationally oriented skills and behaviors – things they have likely been socialized to value as females.

For these girls, several important yet unanticipated changes occurred as a result of this experience. First, they expressed increasing interest in technology; second, they showed decreased technical anxiety and increased technical confidence; and third, they developed new technical skills in a setting traditionally dominated by males, a MOO. The fact that these findings were significant across all closed-ended questions despite the small sample size indicates a rather robust effect. The case study certainly suggests that attitudes toward and interest in technology are not fixed but rather evolve as users interact with unique instructional and technological environments. Moreover, changes in interest, anxiety, and confidence might well lead to increased learning regarding computers in both the short and long term. First, increased interest, increased confidence, and decreased anxiety may encourage and enable girls to pay more attention to the technical task at hand. If this attention is appropriately directed, this is likely to lead to increased technical learning.

Second, it is not possible to determine the long-term consequences of this experience; however, it seems probable that the findings of increased technical interest and decreased technical anxiety could change these students' motivation to further their technical knowledge. This attitude might affect future course selections and even career choices, which, in turn, might lead to increased learning. Such speculation is supported by the work of Eccles and her colleagues (Eccles, 1983), as is the finding that over the course of the year the girls perceived themselves as more certain that they would want to use a computer in their work as adults.

One question that might be asked is whether these girls would show the same changes in technological interest, confidence, and competence if they were working in a less relational environment or with a male teacher. We cannot answer this question definitively. However, we do know that the girls linked their enjoyment of this learning situation directly to its relational qualities – the opportunities it provided to build new relationships and to further those that previously existed. Further, we also know that the girls derived comfort and confidence from their observations of a technically proficient female teacher and their proximity to familiar female peers. Therefore, we suspect that specific elements of the learning environment mattered importantly in the outcomes we observed.

A second question that could be asked is whether boys would respond as or even more positively to this type of instructional environment. The fact that just two boys participated in the MOO experience strongly limits what can be said about this. However, according to Ms. Ebert, who worked with additional boys during other class periods, males were markedly less enthused and it was difficult to keep them involved in the project. She observed, "[T]hey [the boys] have never shown any interest [in] the MOO this year. [...] They wanted to touch the keyboard and play with the computers. They didn't want to have to think about stories and writing answers [...] [I]t's strange." Consistent with Ms. Ebert's description, the two boys we observed were markedly less enthused than their female peers. Perhaps, as Ms. Ebert's observation implies, the kinds of relational opportunities offered at this MOO were not as interesting and engaging for the males. This is consistent with arguments made in the gender-difference literature (Gilligan, 1982, 1993; Tannen, 1990).

Finally, one might consider how the opportunity to develop an Internet-based social relationship enhanced the sense of community experienced by the girls and Ms. Ebert. Certainly, the opportunity to interact with Mr. Tims over time, on a regular basis, and about topics of common interest furthered the girls' sense of themselves as a social group. The temporal and spatial flexibility of the Internet – specifically the opportunities the Internet provides users to bridge spatial boundaries at virtually any time if users are willing – helped make this possible. (One might argue that it is possible for students to develop this type of relationship with a community member off-line, but in fact it is rare for a community member to meet regularly with a small group of students during the school day. In Mr. Tims' case, weekly visits would be almost impossible given his physical location across the country.)

It is important to note that the changes we describe were not the changes initially predicted or sought by the designer of this technological instructional setting. Recall that Ms. Ebert was primarily interested in improving students' reading and writing abilities; thus, she created a MOO that offered students many opportunities to practice these types of skills. As this case reveals, technology does not act in isolation but rather interacts with the specific instructional setting and particular social variables to bring about unanticipated as well as intended effects.

A broadened approach to the MOO-based activities such as that described in this paper might encourage and empower females not just to participate but also to shape and potentially redefine a domain long dominated by males. It is important to note and acknowledge that even as aspects of this instructional environment engaged the girls with technology, it did not achieve another potentially important outcome. The girls used technology here primarily as a tool to build relationships and express feelings, rather than to attain programming skills. Developing the ability to manipulate their MOO-based environment or their characters was not part of their teacher's agenda, though the girls were at least able to observe Ms. Ebert doing so and did develop basic capabilities in these areas. In the long run, we believe girls would benefit from instruction that emphasizes development of these skills as well. MOOs offer users the chance not just to interact but also to enter into a more personalized relationship with technology; users can attribute characteristics to their user-characters and acquire technical language that allows them to manipulate aspects of the MOO environment itself.

Acknowledgments

The research reported here was funded by Contract No. RED-9253452 with the National Science Foundation and a grant from the Spencer Foundation. All opinions expressed herein are solely those of the authors and no endorsement of the conclusions by NSF or the Spencer Foundation is implied or intended.

References

American Association of University Women (1998). *Gender gaps: Where schools still fail our children.* New York: Marlowe & Company.

Bronner, E. (1998, June 25). Voracious computers are siphoning talent from academia. *The New York Times,* A1.

Chandrasekaran, R. (1998, January 12). U.S. to train workers for tech jobs. *The Washington Post,* A1.

Cummins, J., & Sayers, D. (1995). *Brave new schools: Challenging cultural illiteracy through global learning networks.* New York: St. Martin's Press.

Davidson, A. L. (1996). *Making and molding identity in schools: Student narratives on race, gender and academic engagement.* Albany: State University of New York Press.

Durndell, A., & Lightbody, P. (1993). Gender and computing: Change over time? *Computers in Education, 21,* 331–6.

Eccles, J. (1983). Expectancies, values and academic behaviors. In J. T. Spence (Ed.), *Achievement and achievement motives* (pp. 75–146). San Francisco: W. H. Freeman.

Epstein, C. F. (1997). The multiple realities of sameness and difference: Ideology and practice. *Journal of Social Issues, 53,* 259–78.

Fordham, S. (1996). *Blacked out: Dilemmas of race, identity and success at Capital High.* Chicago: University of Chicago Press.

Fullerton, H. N., Jr. (1997). Labor force 2006: Slowing down and changing composition. *Monthly Labor Review, 120,* 23–38.

Gender Wars in Cyberspace (1995, March 8). *The Boston Globe,* pp. 29, 32.

Gilligan, C. (1982). *In a different voice: Psychological theory and women's development.* Cambridge, MA: Harvard University Press.

(1993). Joining the resistance: Psychology, politics, girls, and women. In L. Weis & M. Fine (Eds.), *Beyond silenced voices: Class, race and gender in United States schools* (pp. 143–68). Albany: State University of New York Press.

Goodlad, J. I. (1984). *A place called school: Prospects for the future.* New York: McGraw-Hill.

Hall, J., & Cooper, J. (1991). Gender, experience and attributions to the computer. *Journal of Educational Computing Research, 7,* 51–60.

Harmon, A. (1998, January 13). Software jobs go begging and threaten high technology boom. *The New York Times,* p. A1.

Hess, R. D., & Miura, I. T. (1985). Gender differences in enrollment in computer camps and classes. *Sex Roles, 13,* 193–203.

Hoyles, C. (1988). Review of the literature. In C. Hoyles (Ed.), *Girls and computers* (pp. 5–12). London: Institute of Education.

Huber, B. R., & Schofield, J. W. (1998). Gender and the sociocultural context of computing in Costa Rica. In H. Bromley & M. W. Apple (Eds.), *Education/technology/power: Educational computing as a social practice* (pp. 103–131). Albany: State University of New York Press.

Hunter, B. (1993). Internetworking: Coordinating technology for systemic reform. *Communications, 36,* 42–6.

Hurtado, A. (1997). Understanding multiple group identities: Inserting women into cultural transformations. *Journal of Social Issues, 53,* 299–328.

James, J. B. (1997). What are the social issues involved in focusing on difference in gender? *Journal of Social Issues, 53,* 213–32.

Johnson, R. T., Johnson, D. W., & Stanne, M. B. (1985). Effects of cooperative, competitive and individualistic goal structures on computer-assisted instruction. *Journal of Educational Psychology, 77,* 668–77.

Krapp, A., & Fink, B. (1992). The development and function of interests during the critical transition from home to preschool. In K. A. Renninger, S. Hidi, & A. Krapp (Eds.), *The role of interest in learning and development* (pp. 397–429). Hillsdale, NJ: Erlbaum.

Kraut, R., Scherlis, W., Mukhopadhyay, T., Manning, J., & Kiesler, S. (1996). HomeNet: A field trial of residential Internet services. *Communications of the ACM, 39*, 55–63.

Lepper, M. R., & Cordova, D. I. (1992). A desire to be taught: Instructional consequences of intrinsic motivation. *Motivation and Emotion, 16*(3), 187–208.

Lepper, M. R., & Malone, T. W. (1987). Intrinsic motivation and instructional effectiveness in computer-based education. In R. E. Snow & M. J. Farr (Eds.), *Aptitude, learning, and instruction*, Vol. 3: *Conative and affective process analyses* (pp. 255–96). Hillsdale, NJ: Erlbaum.

Light, P., & Littleton, K. (1997). Situational effects in computer-based problem solving. In L. Resnick, R. Saljo, C. Pontecorvo & B. Burge (Eds.), *Discourse' tools' and reasoning: Situated cognition and technologically supported environments.* Heidelberg: Springer-Verlag, pp. 224–39.

Lott, B. (1997). The personal and social correlates of a gender difference ideology. *Journal of Social Issues, 53*, 279–98.

Lyons, N. (1990). Listening to voices we have not heard. In C. Gilligan, N. P. Lyons & T. J. Hanmer (Eds.), *Making connections: The relational worlds of adolescent girls at Emma Willard School* (pp. 30–72). Cambridge, MA: Harvard University Press.

Miles, M. B., & Huberman, A. M. (1994). *Qualitative data analysis: An expanded source book.* Thousand Oaks, CA: Sage.

Miller, J. B. (1986). *Toward a new psychology of women* (2nd ed.). Boston: Beacon Press.

Murphy, K., Naples, L., Schofield, J., Davidson, A. L., & Stocks, J. (1997). *Difference blindness/blindness difference: Student explorations of "disability" over the Internet.* Paper presented at the meeting of the American Educational Research Association, Chicago.

National Center for Education Statistics (1997). *Digest of education statistics.* Washington, DC: National Center for Education Statistics, Office of Educational Research and Improvement.

Nolan, P. C., McKinnon, D. H., & Soler, J. (1992). Computers in education: Achieving equitable access and use. *Journal of Research in Computing in Education, 24*, 299–314.

Pelgrum, W. J. (1992). International research on computers in education. *Prospects, 22*(3), 341–9.

Pettigrew, T. F., & Martin, J. (1987). Shaping the organizational context for black American inclusion. *Journal of Social Issues, 43*, 41–78.

Prenzel, M. (1992). The selective persistence of interest. In K. A. Renninger, S. Hidi, & A. Krapp (Eds.), *The role of interest in learning and development* (pp. 71–98). Hillsdale, NJ: Erlbaum.

Raissiguier, C. (1994). *Becoming women, becoming workers: Identity formation in a French vocational school.* Albany: State University of New York Press.

Renninger, K. (1992). Individual interest and development: Implications for theory and practice. In K. A. Renninger, S. Hidi, & A. Krapp (Eds.), *The role of interest in learning and development* (pp. 361–95). Hillsdale, NJ: Erlbaum.

Sanders, J. S. (1985). Making the computer neuter. *The Computing Teacher, 12*, 23–7.

Schofield, J. W. (1989). *Black and white in school.* New York London: Teachers College Press.

(1995). *Computers and classroom culture.* New York: Cambridge University Press.

Steele, C. M., & Aronson, J. (1995). Stereotype threat and the intellectual test performance of African Americans. *Journal of Personality and Social Psychology, 69,* 797–811.

Steinberg, J. (1997). Jobs associated with the Internet. *Occupational Outlook Quarterly, 41,* 2–9.

Strauss, A., & Corbin, J. (1990). *Basics of qualitative research.* Newbury Park, CA: Sage.

Sutherland, R., & Hoyles, C. (1988). Gender perspectives on Logo programming in the mathematics curriculum. In C. Hoyles (Ed.), *Girls and computers* (pp. 40–63). London: Institute of Education.

Sutton, R. E. (1991). Equity and computers in the schools. *Review of Educational Research, 61,* 475–503.

Tannen, D. (1990). *You just don't understand: Men and women in conversation.* New York: William Morrow.

Treichler, P. A., & Kramarae, C. (1983). Women's talk in the ivory tower. *Communication Quarterly, 31*(2), 118–32.

Turkle, S. (1984). *The second self: Computers and the human spirit.* New York: Simon & Schuster.

(1995). *Life on the screen: Identity in the age of the Internet.* New York: Simon & Schuster.

Veneri, C. (1988). Here today, jobs of tomorrow: Opportunities in information technology. *Occupational Outlook Quarterly, 42,* 44.

Whitley, B., Jr. (1997). Gender differences in computer-related attitudes and behavior: A meta-analysis. *Computers in Human Behavior, 13,* 1–2.

3 Community Building with and for Teachers at The Math Forum

K. Ann Renninger and Wesley Shumar

This chapter addresses the way in which the Internet forms the core of an intentional, online community by promoting communication between interested parties. The Math Forum (mathforum.org) is a unique group of individuals who are committed to using computers and the Internet to enhance what they know about learning, teaching, and doing mathematics. The Math Forum includes programmers, project and service staff, Web persons, and an ever-expanding number of teachers, students, and other individuals (i.e., parents, software developers, mathematicians). Thus, community building for The Math Forum staff includes work with teachers, with partners (National Council of the Teachers of Mathematics, Mathematics Association of America, and so on), and with specific services developed by The Math Forum staff that enable teachers and students to come together to pose and seek solutions to problems.

The Math Forum uses the Internet to provide interactive services that foster mathematical thinking and discussion. These services include Ask Dr. Math and several Problems of the Week (PoWs); a teacher discussion format called Teacher to Teacher (T2T); an archive of problems, participant contributions (e.g., lesson plans), and past discussions; and an Internet newsletter. Within four years, with no explicit efforts to garner promotion or publicity, the site grew to include 1,600,000 Web pages and to attract 3.5 million accesses and over 800,000 visitors per month – a third of which constitutes sticky traffic ranging from world-famous mathematicians to elementary school children.

Participants, including The Math Forum staff, hold an image of The Math Forum as a community and have done so since its inception.* For

---

* The Math Forum has built out its services both with participants and in response to participants' strengths and needs. Its initial funding came from a succession of grants from

a person who logs on for the first time, however, The Math Forum may appear to be simply an online collection of resources or services. Based on in-depth, structured interviews with participants, online questionnaires, and notes to the Webmaster and staff, however, it seems that the community of The Math Forum develops through participant interactions with The Math Forum services, staff, and other participants who facilitate their thinking about the kinds of questions, issues, and solutions that participants bring to the site.

The Math Forum community is not simply lodged in its participants, but rather in the particular interactions of its participants, which include The Math Forum staff. The participants interact around the services and resources participants generate together. These interactions provide a basis for participant knowledge building about mathematics, pedagogy, and/or technology. The interactions also contribute to what might be described as a Math Forum culture that encourages collaboration on problem posing and problem solving. Participants' work together is facilitated by the design of Math Forum services and the particular affordances of the Internet.

Students who submit solutions to the PoWs,[†] for example, receive individualized feedback in the form of questions, observations, and/or

the National Science Foundation (NSF), beginning with The Visual Geometry Project (1986–92) in which *The Geometer's Sketchpad* was developed. Now a commercial product, this software was developed to enable geometers to depict the patterns and relations on which geometers were working. In response to users of Sketchpad, who sought to exchange figures with other users, the Geometry Forum (1992–5) was established. Its central goals included support of geometry education and the facilitation of communication about geometry.

The advent of the Web coincided with NSF's urging that The Geometry Forum expand to encompass mathematics more generally. The Geometry Forum became The Math Forum in 1996. This change extended its goals to include support of mathematics education, structuring of services to facilitate mathematical thinking, and examination of the contribution that technology can make to learning and instruction.

In 2000, The Math Forum partnered with WebCT, a business that sells, supports, and develops the use of the WebCT course tool for organizing courses that teachers and professors create for their classes online. It was expected that the Forum could serve as a model for learning communities. With the downturn in the economy, WebCT decided to focus on core services and sold The Math Forum to Drexel University. Both WebCT and Drexel University partnerships met NSF mandates for its projects to attain sustainability for their infrastructure. While The Math Forum continues to include projects and partnerships sponsored by the NSF, Math Forum staff and services are endeavoring to meet the increased need to scale services.

[†] Presently there are seven Problems of the Week posted each week: an elementary problem (ElemPoW), a middle school problem (MidPoW), an algebra problem (AlgPoW), a geometry problem (GeoPoW), a discrete problem (DmPoW), a calculus problem (CalPoW), and a component-enhanced problem (ESCOTPoW).

suggestions that push them to make connections between what a particular student understands a problem to ask and what he or she already
understands. The feedback students receive from this service, like that of
other Math Forum services, encourages them to reflect on their problem
solving, including the connections they have made and the strategies they
have used. This feedback does not tell students what the next step is but
rather poses questions that provide the kind of support that students need
to work effectively with problem demands.

Interaction on a site such as The Math Forum can take several forms.
Interaction is a design feature of each service. Interaction also characterizes participant engagement with The Math Forum. In many schools,
talking about either math or teaching math is considered taboo, even if
you teach it. For teachers feeling the press of these settings, interaction
can be participant-driven with individuals seeking collegiality or friends
with whom to talk about math. Interaction also can be private, in the sense
that The Math Forum is a safe community in which one can review feedback, talk about concerns, and seek answers to problems. One teacher, for
example, told us that he would never admit to his colleagues that he had
not had geometry since high school. He used The Math Forum archives
to learn the geometry he needed to teach. At present, he uses the archives,
Web units, and lessons that others have posted on the site.

As a richly textured virtual space, The Math Forum represents opportunities for its participants to deepen and consolidate their understanding
of mathematics, technology, and/or pedagogy (Lave & Wenger, 1991).
However, it also exists in a reciprocal relation to its participants. Participants help to define and refine its services through their responses to
Forum-generated questionnaires, interviews, Web-page comments, and
informal exchanges.

In this sense then, The Math Forum "community" can be thought of
as a reference group with whom one shares information and interests that
extend beyond the kind of physical connection one might hope for in a
neighborhood. The Math Forum has no requirements or expectations
like those one may encounter when one moves into a new neighborhood
(that one will mow the grass when it is a certain length, lend sugar, etc.).
Of importance to Math Forum participants is its provision of autonomy
(Krapp & Lewalter, 2001; Ryan & Deci, 2000) – participants use as much
or as little of the site as they choose, when and where they decide to do
so, and may or may not choose to tell others about their work.

Autonomy appears to engender both intellectual and emotional
connections between the participants and The Math Forum because

site services are interactive and, as such, supports knowledge building. Students, for example, develop connections to the folks with whom they are working online when, for example, they are asked what they understand a math word problem to be asking, given a chance to rethink the decisions they made, or encouraged to resubmit a solution to a problem. Furthermore, being acknowledged as having gotten a start on a problem is quite different from being told an answer is incorrect. In fact, relationships with staff are reinforced by features of the services that recognize students as individuals, for example, when the mentor "remembers" what the student did the week before and acknowledges this. (In actuality, the mentor may well remember what a given student did in working with a problem, but, given the volume of student submissions to The Math Forum site, this also may not be the case. Built into the design of the PoW services, for example, is the ability for mentors to draw on information about a student's previous submissions and prior responses to these. This allows the mentor to tailor his or her response to the student's solution in terms of that student's strengths and needs.)

Teachers develop a connection to The Math Forum that is similar to that of the students. Teachers, too, work to understand and ask questions about math, teaching math, and so forth. This kind of use or connection to The Math Forum is reinforced by Math Forum protocol for responding to participants. This protocol emphasizes the importance of welcoming and listening to participants, confirming an understanding of the question(s), and providing links to necessary information without judgment.

Despite the fact that several types of interactions provide the basis for community on The Math Forum site, interaction is not a sufficient condition for participant re-engagement. Interaction is the vehicle that allows the kind of reflection that is critical for the development of mathematical thinking (Schoenfeld, 1992). Interaction on The Math Forum site is a structural feature that enables participants to increase their knowledge, and because of the opportunity to build knowledge, participants come to identify with The Math Forum as a community. The Math Forum community supports participant learning and enables participants to grow as mathematical thinkers.

The Math Forum's services and resources support knowledge building much as the highly successful instructional technique called cross-age tutoring does. Findings from research on this method of grouping students for instruction uniformly suggest that both tutors and tutees benefit (Renninger, 1998). Students involved in cross-aged tutoring deepen their understanding of topics, improve their social skills, and improve their attitudes toward school.

Like cross-aged tutoring, the interactive qualities of The Math Forum's services provide a participant with tutors or tutees, as needed. The content of the services enable users to develop their understanding of mathematics and pedagogy further. The content of The Math Forum's resources is the "stuff" around which interactions occur. This kind of knowledge construction enhances participants' feelings of competence (Renninger, 2000; White, 1959) and enables them to identify remaining questions, in turn leading them to reengage The Math Forum in search of answers.

On The Math Forum site, community and the learning that it affords are considered to be in a continuous process of evolution. The present chapter focuses on the experience of building community with and for teachers at the Forum. Descriptive information about Math Forum Teachers is provided – and the cases of three teachers are detailed – to illustrate the kinds of opportunities for learning and changed practice that an interactive, service-oriented site can afford. Following this, discussion centers on the roles of imagination and identity in the development of a community where there is a reciprocal relation between the staff's design of services and the strengths and needs of site participants as learners. Finally, discussion turns to opportunities for knowledge building as catalysts for community participation.

Forum Teachers

The National Council of Teachers of Mathematics' *Principles and Standards for School Mathematics* (2000) has charged teachers with the need to enhance the mathematical thinking of their students by using reform-based practices including technology in their teaching. For teacher participants, the kind of mathematical, pedagogical, and technological resources available at The Math Forum site are all potentially useful.

Not all teachers use the site, but those who do range from being technology explorers to those who are technologically proficient; the teachers also range in their levels of expertise in both mathematics and pedagogy. Based on responses to The Math Forum's 1999 Internet Questionnaire,*

---

* The Math Forum Internet Questionnaire was posted to all participant (students, researchers, parents, mathematicians, teachers, etc.) who opened the home page or any of sixteen Math Forum services during the third week in May each year between 1996 and 1999. The questionnaire consisted of forced-choice and open-ended questions that were used both to provide descriptive data about users and feedback to staff about service development. A total of 814 teachers responded to the questionnaire in 1999.

for example, teachers using The Math Forum are likely to have been using the Internet for two or more years and are equally likely to:

- Hail from diverse backgrounds (rural, suburban, or urban);
- Vary from having a well-developed interest for mathematics to having a less well-developed interest for mathematics;
- Use a variety of resources for the purposes of lesson planning and self-education;
- Have found out about The Math Forum from a range of sources, most frequently by surfing the Web, doing a search, or responding to a recommendation from a colleague;
- Contribute to The Math Forum by telling others about it, sharing the resources they find, helping students to mentor PoWs, and developing materials;
- Describe The Math Forum as an important – or even an absolutely essential – part of their Internet activity.

Patterns of teacher usage of The Math Forum in 1996 indicated that teachers were initially using the site primarily for planning lessons and recreation. By 1997, teachers began to be more likely to use the site for finding resources and planning lessons. This pattern held through 1998 and 1999. Low on the set of reasons for using the site were opportunities for discussion. Although the opportunity to discuss geometry had been a raison d'être for building out The Math Forum, Forum teachers more typically make use of the site's interactive services, including the archives.

The next section of this chapter focus on characterizing the context within which teachers pursue particular resources on the site. The cases of three Math Forum teacher participants are described, followed by a description of the larger sample of teachers interviewed as part of this study.

Case Descriptions of Three Teachers

Sonia Leach (pseudonym), Bob Nelson (pseudonym), and Alecia Smith (pseudonym) are teachers who use The Math Forum. The three teachers differ in their levels of knowledge about mathematics, pedagogy, and technology. They also vary in their initial intentions for using The Math Forum, interest for the site, levels of students they teach, and types of schools in which they work. Their cases are drawn from a sample of forty-two Forum teachers who were interviewed once a year over the three-year period, 1997 through 1999.

These case descriptions are informed by in-depth structured interviews, the Internet questionnaires conducted with all Math Forum participants each year, service-specific questionnaires, participant observation during workshops, participant observation in Math Forum staff meetings including focus groups used to discuss service design and facilitation, and regular meetings with Math Forum staff between 1997 and 1999.

Sonia Leach

Sonia Leach began using The Math Forum site when she was a first-grade teacher in a public school in a densely populated suburb. The school in which she taught had approximately 350 students and was 60 percent minority. It was a special-needs school. It had also just been named a model tech school and was in the process of getting wired for Internet use. She had one computer connected to the Internet in her classroom and access to a lab. She talked about technology as a resource for her students since they came from less-advantaged backgrounds.

Sonia initially used The Math Forum as an enrichment activity in her class of fifteen to sixteen students because she needed to be using technology in some way. She downloaded The Math Forum's Elementary Problem of the Week (ElemPoW) and had the students take it home to complete. Sonia liked the process of having parents working with their children on the ElemPoW because it involved the parents in their children's education. In fact, she reported that several of the families developed an interest in the PoW problems and were drawn to explore The Math Forum on their own. A few times that first year, Sonia worked in class with her students on the ElemPoW because problem solving was a whole-school focus.

By the end of her first year of work with The Math Forum, Sonia was thinking about how she could integrate work with the site in her classes the next year. She was looking forward to taking a computer home from school over the summer and was working on getting an Internet connection at home. She said she wanted to be able to have time to work with The Math Forum resources herself. Although she indicated that she was not strong in math, she said that her husband was, and he would be interested in The Math Forum, too.

Following a year of intermittent Math Forum use and its positive reception by her students and their parents, it appears that Sonia began to take the kind of risks necessary to engage mathematics more directly. She sought out resources in the form of an Internet connection so that she could work with the site and continue to develop her knowledge of mathematics; in addition, The Math Forum was something that she could share with her family.

When asked about why she started to use The Math Forum, Sonia talked at first about her son, who had started using The Math Forum in his middle school class for extra credit and then began doing it for pleasure. She was very excited about sharing the changes that had taken place in her son's attitude about math. She said he had never been a hard worker before, but The Math Forum and particularly the Middle School PoW (MidPoW) piqued his interest. She mentioned that the comments Mrs. B (the MidPoW mentor) sent her son were very supportive and challenging at the same time. Sonia said he was "really touched by her. It's almost as if he knows her." This experience clearly moved both Sonia and her son; it appears to have had an impact on her teaching, the parents of her students, and her colleagues.

For Sonia, The Math Forum represented a very personal form of interaction online through the personality of Mrs. B. She saw how powerful simply recognizing what a child was able to do and encouraging him could be. This, she felt, had turned her son into a math student. This experience gave her confidence as a teacher. As she explained, "if The Math Forum could help my son so much, it could do a lot for me and my students' parents, and even help with my own math ability." Over time, Sonia began to become more innovative about how to get computer equipment and how to use The Math Forum in her class. Her interest and enthusiasm grew as she began to use the ElemPoW more regularly in her class. Sonia also began to talk with her peers about what she was learning and what they might be able to do using Math Forum resources with their students.

Mrs. B.'s responses to Sonia's son had modeled possibilities for working with students that Sonia then used with her own students. This modeling also appears to have inspired Sonia to overcome her fear of technology and the need to use it in her classes. By the second wave of interviews, Sonia had became highly motivated around computing questions. Rather than being fearful, her concerns had shifted to pragmatic problems to be solved.

Sonia now teaches in a nearby tech school for 900 gifted and talented students. Although she continues to work with a significant group of English as Second Language students in this new school, she describes its population as being upper middle class. She notes that she has four networked computers in her class, in addition to having access to a computer lab. She says that at least half of the students in her class have computers at home. The availability of computers has greatly enhanced her ability to use technology with her students.

Sonia reports that once she moved to her new setting, she began using computers a lot and began teaching in more varied ways: she introduced her students to using the computer for research and has the students working on projects in various grouping arrangements. Currently, she is reading about how to help students to develop their own Web pages. She also continues to use the Forum in her classes.

From the outset, Sonia repeatedly said how much she liked the responses the ElemPoW mentors gave her students. She likes the fact that they encouraged the students to think carefully about problems and to explain their decision making. She continues to think that The Math Forum provides her students with more challenging math than she could provide for them. She reports that she "uses anything on The Forum that I can find." She has also been encouraging her more accelerated students to send questions in to the Ask Dr. Math service.

Sonia's situation is typical of many of the teachers interviewed. At the first interview, Sonia, like the other teachers, did not have her own computer or Internet access at home. She expressed concern about her knowledge of mathematics and was reluctant to move in the direction of using more technology out of a fear that it would be beyond her. By the second interview, Sonia had begun to express an interest in the possibilities that computers held and was using some Math Forum resources in her class. She still expressed some trepidation about getting a system set up and connected to the Internet from home, however. By the third interview, Sonia had integrated Math Forum materials into her curriculum and was leading others in their efforts to develop Internet-based resources for her grade level. The Internet was fully a part of her home and school life. It had also afforded her an opportunity to change jobs and to work in a school that had more resources.

Sonia's experience is emblematic of the way The Math Forum as an organization can provide support for teachers and students. The Math Forum staff (and the many who volunteer as mentors, etc.) have a set of cultural assumptions that at first rarely match those of the teachers (the parents, or the students) with whom they work. The staff loves math – seeing in it its sheer elegance, challenge, and depth. They enjoy the process of problem solving and are interested in sharing this with others. They find challenging the need to identify exactly what it is that a child (teacher, etc.) does not know and how to work with them to figure it out. For the staff, this is just another "problem" to be solved. The staff believes that it is possible for all people to work with math. They are not inclined to "give" answers but to ask questions to facilitate learning. Their approach is what Cobb (1995) would label both indirect and multivocal. It is the kind of exchange that empowers because it is gauged to meet the individual where he or she is and in this process also stretches their understanding (Schoenfeld, 1992).

The staff, along with other Math Forum participants, helped to develop and facilitate the services that Sonia found useful. Sonia's recognition of their usefulness was based on her understanding of the power that talking and thinking about math with another person could have. Her son had been so changed in his attitude about math that he provided her with a very personal object lesson in the ways that people can be influenced by others even if those others are physically removed and only have the ability to share text over the Internet. She saw in her son's experience implications for her own students and the parents of her students who at that point were often starved for resources. Unlike some who readily see the math possibilities afforded by The Math Forum, Sonia at first focused on the relational possibilities and support that mentorship on the site provides.

In the course of working with The Math Forum, Sonia began problem solving in ways that were different than those she had been using prior to her work with The Math Forum. She began figuring out how to use site resources such as the PoW and Dr. Math in her classes even though they were not technically part of the curriculum. This method eventually led her to explore instructional approaches that enhanced the learning that she could provide for her students. Sonia also began to think about how she could get a computer at home so she would have a chance to familiarize herself with its possibilities. This decision then led her to explore other parts of the site. Her interest for technology had shifted from being something she had to engage in to something that she wanted to master. It has an impact on her instructional practice, including her feelings about herself as a teacher of mathematics.

Bob Nelson

At the time of his first interview, Bob Nelson was teaching in a middle school in one of the poorest cities in the United States. The school had 750 students and class sizes of approximately thirty-two students. He had taught there for six years. By the time of the third interview, he had taken a teaching position in a progressive private school. Bob is sure that it was his technological expertise, as reflected in the work he had been doing with his students on the Forum site, that enabled him to get the new job. In the new school, he uses the PoW as a core component of his curriculum. He has classes of seventeen to twenty-three students and several computers that have Internet hook-ups right in his room.

Initially, Bob's use of The Math Forum centered on the MidPoW. He liked the nonroutine challenge problems that were posted each week. He also liked the fact that the students had to develop their abilities to use and explain mathematical terms when they wrote out their answers. He began using the MidPoW with his sixth-grade pre-algebra students. He figured that by the time they got to eighth grade, they would have three years of work with The Math Forum and would have learned its "problem-solving approach."

Because most of his students did not have computers at home or an Internet connection, and because Internet connections were scarce at the school, Bob downloaded the PoW each week on his own computer, worked on it with his class during the week, and then wrote up the work they had done in class and sent this to The Math Forum for the class. He described the different ways his students had solved the problem, as well as the answers that they had gotten. One of the MidPoW mentors noted that Bob's work with his class was a model of how teachers might orient students to mathematical thinking.

As soon as he found the site, Bob began using the PoW in all his classes. He said that the PoW helps him to model summarizing and explanation for his students. He also said that the PoW gives students practice with skills that complement his curriculum. He likes the way that the MidPoW mentors push students to reexamine their assumptions and to explain their ideas more fully. Bob said that the mentors' work with his students makes him feel that he has an ally. It also establishes a bar for the students that is tangible and demanding and is not so easily dismissed as his idiosyncratic idea about what mathematics involves. He reports that his students consider the PoW a personal challenge and look forward to doing it each week.

Several aspects of Bob's situation are noteworthy. Like a number of the people who found The Math Forum just surfing around on the Internet, Bob is interested in both math and technology. When working on his Masters' degree in statistics, for example, Bob found a business site that compiled all the data he needed for his project. Bob developed a relationship with an editor at the site and eventually sent him a copy of his paper, had some good discussions about it, and so forth. Sharing ideas with others over the Internet so inspired Bob that he sought money from the state and matching money from his district so that he could provide better and more immediate access to the Internet for his students. Bob also tutored online for America Online (AOL) in exchange for free hours of online time when AOL still charged by the hour. In this way, Bob first accessed the PoWs and began doing them with his students. For Bob, the PoW represented "another way to involve my students in math."

In his new school, Bob teaches seventh-grade math using the PoW as a core component of the curriculum. Every Monday he prints off the new MidPoW because it is one of the stations that he will have all of the students do. He talks about the problems as important to student learning because they require students to draw on all the math that they know. If the content of the week's problem maps onto the content they are covering, then this is part of their regular assignment; if the problem covers content that they have not reached yet, then they receive bonus credits.

He feels that students need to keep working with math – all kinds of math – and he works to build this into his curriculum. His students do have access to a computer lab and have the option of submitting their PoW solutions directly to The Math Forum using the Web. Some students simply write out their answers and submit them to him, and he submits them to The Math Forum. Bob also meets once a week after school with students, and they tackle PoWs that they have not done as part of class (i.e., the ElemPoW, the AlgPoW, the GeoPoW, and/or the DmPoW). He says he loves working with the students on problem solving and thinks that "The Math Forum problems are the best around." Bob says that there are two real advantages to using The Math Forum PoWs as part of the curriculum: the PoWs make it possible for all his students to connect to math, and all of his students make progress. He commented that he currently is not only using The Math Forum for his students, but also finds himself drawn to Math Forum resources because they allow him to "keep learning," too.

In the former school, Bob had helped students become part of The Math Forum community by downloading the problems and working with the students to figure out what the problems asked them to do and to decide how they might be addressed. He also submitted solutions for them and reviewed the mentors' comments on their solutions. In his new school, he can leave most of the submission and review efforts to his students, but he continues to help them identify with The Math Forum community by working alongside them, providing face-to-face experience of and support for working with the PoW and other online services such as Ask Dr. Math when this is needed.

Bob likes the fact that the math on The Math Forum is challenging and deep. He has been talking about his use of the PoW in his classes to his other colleagues. One of his colleagues has started to use some of the PoW problems when she can make them work in her class. Another colleague is new this year. He has been talking with both the new colleague and the eighth-grade team about The Math Forum in the hopes of encouraging them to give it a try, too. His goal is to see that the MidPoW becomes a regular part of the middle school curriculum in his district.

Although Sonia and Bob both report on their own developing interest for The Math Forum and encourage their colleagues to check it out, Bob's case provides a contrast to Sonia's. Bob considers himself to be a mathematician and was comfortable with technology when he was first interviewed. Bob seized on the PoW as a tool for enhancing his students' abilities to problem solve, whereas Sonia had tentatively begun her work with the PoWs as enrichment for her students. Perhaps because Bob is working with older students – but more likely because of his confidence in his mathematical abilities – Bob had his students begin working with The Math Forum's problems as an extension of their class work as soon as possible.

Bob, like Sonia, continues to grow through his interaction with The Math Forum staff and his use of Math Forum resources. Whereas Sonia connected to The Math Forum because of the relational opportunity it afforded her son and her students, Bob was drawn to The Math Forum's challenging content and the possibilities it offered both his students and himself. Like Sonia's increased use of The Math Forum in her classes and for her own exploration, Bob's use of The Math Forum also shifted. He began work with the site by having his students work with the MidPoW, and now has them working with the MidPoW in addition to other PoWs. He also has been using the archives, the frequently asked questions (FAQs), the discussion groups, and Dr. Math.

The proximity of the different services on the site to other services has led him to explore and expand his use of The Math Forum. This is partly because he is a seeker and partly, as he says, because having found the quality of the PoWs to be good, he is keenly interested in exploring other Math Forum services. "They are all," as he points out, "right there."

Alecia Smith

Alecia Smith attended one of The Math Forum's first summer workshops and, following it, began designing her own pages for the Web.

Alecia teaches mathematics and computers to at-risk seventh graders in a suburban Title 1 school that is racially mixed: 54 percent Hispanic, 30 percent African-American, and 16 percent white and other.

Alecia also recently arranged to lessen her teaching load so that she could assume more responsibilities for computers in the school. She says that she loves working with mathematics and computers and training students to use them. As she commented, "You don't dwell on what you don't have, you maximize what you have. I always tell the kids . . . we have 20 great computers."

At first, Alecia explored how she could use technology to enhance curricular materials she had already developed. She did not know any html. She had written her lessons in ClarisWorks and was interested in synchronizing MathWeb and Mosaic. Alecia would write up a preliminary html page and send it to one of The Math Forum staff members. The Math Forum staff person would correct it and put it up. Every time Alecia got help of this sort, she figured out what the staff member had just done and integrated this into the next pages she made. As Alecia completed each of the pages, she used them in her classes, posted them on The Math Forum for others to use, and found herself engaged in online conversations about them.

For example, referring to some work Alecia had posted on the Web, one teacher asked her about the difference between a tessellation and a fractal. Alecia responded with an answer over email but then began to respond over the Web. As the conversation developed, Alecia began to link it to other sites about fractals. Alecia also archived the conversation for those who might have a use for it in the future. During the conversation, another teacher joined them and began to ask about the relation between fractals and kaleidoscopes. Alecia and these two other teachers then began to design lessons together and to link these to the work of mathematicians on the site who were working on the same issues.

Alecia first found out about The Math Forum from a professor friend who gave her information about a workshop the staff were planning to hold. Even though Alecia was teaching middle school and the call for workshop participants was directed to those teaching geometry, she decided to apply. Alecia attended the workshop but seemed to some of the staff to have little if any interest in the discussions taking place. One of them asked Alecia what was wrong. Alecia told her that she just was not that interested in the different ways that the Internet could be used. She mentioned that the Internet would be interesting if it could be more personal or dynamic. The staff member responded that the Internet could be anything Alecia wanted it to be and offered to help her do the things she wanted to do, such as writing html so that she could make Web pages out of her lessons.

Over the years, Alecia primarily stayed in touch with one staff member because "she knows me, values me, and works with me. That feeling of support needs to be there for someone to give their time to something that is not monetarily rewarding. Also, there needs to be a way that it completely ties into their own work... not adding in something extra, but offering a different method of presentation or tool."

Alecia continues to be interested in integrating technology into the fabric of her classes and most recently has been working to integrate the PoWs into her curriculum. She has assumed a leadership role in thinking about how these problems might be enhanced so that they meet student needs even more effectively. Alecia also continues to seek help for proofreading, using include statements on the Web pages she develops, and so forth. In addition, Alecia has begun to work with a number of different staff members because the basis of her involvement with the site has broadened from producing pages for classes to including mentoring teachers as part of the T2T service and using the PoWs in her classes.

Like Bob, Alecia came to The Math Forum with a solid background in mathematics and almost immediately started integrating her work with The Math Forum into her classes. Instead of pursuing the use of services on the site, however, Alecia sought ways to use technology to enhance her work with her students. Alecia contributed these Web units and lessons to the site, and conversations that have built on these contributions have helped both her and others to stretch their thinking. Like Sonia, Alecia appreciated the relational opportunities the site provided, in addition to the support The Math Forum provides for extending what she was already doing as a teacher and as a student of math.

Like Sonia, Alecia also saw in The Math Forum an opportunity to enhance her knowledge of technology. While both women were drawn to the relational quality of support provided by the mentors and staff on the site, the risks the two women assumed differed. Because Sonia had a weaker background in mathematics, she used the PoW to enhance her students' exposure to math. Sonia tentatively began learning about the possibilities that technology afforded both her and her students as she experimented with one of its services. In contrast, Alecia's strength and confidence in her mathematical abilities appear to have led Alecia to put up and share lessons with others almost immediately. Once Alecia had support for developing her lessons into pages that she could use with her students, she sought feedback, made revisions, and began making links between her work and that of other teachers and mathematicians on the site.

Exploration of site resources and the possibilities for using the site in their classes enabled Sonia, Bob, and Alecia to "own," or personalize their uses of The Math Forum – to make it whatever they wanted it or needed it to be. All three of these teachers developed an individual interest in the site that was supported by both the resources *and* the interaction they found. Moreover, each teacher worked to create opportunities that allowed his or her interest to continue to develop. It is notable that all three teachers changed their professional status over the three-year-period during which we talked with them. In each case, the change was facilitated by the work they had begun on The Math Forum site and their changed perceptions of possibilities for themselves as teachers using technology to work with their students.

The Larger Sample of Interviewed Teachers

The case descriptions of Sonia, Bob, and Alecia are drawn from a sample of forty-two teachers whose participation in The Math Forum was studied using in-depth phone interviews and follow-up email exchanges between 1997 and 1999. Some of these teachers were participants in Math Forum workshops, some were teachers in the Urban Systemic Initiative* with whom The Math Forum worked through its grant support from the National Science Foundation, and finally some were teachers who had just begun using the site when the sample of teachers we would interview was being identified. Teachers were selected for interview study by grade level (twenty-one elementary and twenty-one middle and secondary school teachers), experience with technology (twenty-one more, twenty-one less), gender (fourteen male, twenty-eight female), and experience teaching (fourteen less than five years, twenty-eight who had been teaching five years or more).

Most of the teachers interviewed shared characteristics with Sonia, Bob, and Alecia.[†] They had begun working with some aspect of the

---

* The Urban Systemic Initiative (USI) is an NSF block grant to urban school systems for the purpose of facilitating large-scale systemic reform. The Math Forum worked with USIs in two cities.

[†] Six of the forty-two teachers (14 percent) interviewed began but did not work continuously with The Math Forum over time. Like Sonia when she first began using the site, these tended to be teachers who were required to use technology and thought that The Math Forum might be a resource. Over the three-year period, some did return to The Math Forum when they had a particular need. Most of them either found resources on other sites

site – an aspect that mapped onto either an individual strength (i.e., mathematics, teaching mathematics) or a need (i.e., mathematics, teaching mathematics). Over time most of them began to find ways to integrate one or more of The Math Forum services into their teaching and to explore the use of other resources on the site. They also either explicitly or implicitly grew to identify the site as a resource for their own professional learning. In fact, like Sonia, Bob, and Alecia, they all moved into positions that they considered exciting and challenging largely because of their work with The Math Forum.[‡]

It appears that teachers use The Math Forum when there is support for their efforts to connect to it (e.g., the enthusiasm of Sonia's students and their parents, help from Math Forum staff such as that provided to Alecia), or when teachers can make The Math Forum meet their immediate needs (e.g., Sonia's need to use technology in her classes, Bob's interest in helping his students become problem solvers; Alecia's desire to put her course materials up on the Web). In fact, teachers who continue to use The Math Forum over time tend to offer one of three reasons for doing so. They describe The Math Forum as offering: (a) opportunities to talk, think, and share resources with others about mathematics, technology, and/or pedagogy; (b) interactions with expert-others who model and provide support for problem posing and problem solving; and (c) a wide and ever-deepening range of quality content about mathematics, technology, and pedagogy.

The teachers interviewed were likely to connect first to a somewhat idiosyncratic and individually specified sense of community (Castells, 1999; Wellman, 2001). The teachers engage as much or as little of The Math Forum's resources in their teaching and professional learning as they

---

that met their needs or simply did not use technology. They each described their changed senses of connection to The Math Forum in terms of time. None of these teachers appeared to have had a concrete vision of the possibilities Forum services afforded them beyond the odd answer to a question, and they never seemed to realize the sense of "community" at The Math Forum to which the others referred. As one teacher observed, "For teachers in this school to make good use of The Math Forum, they would need to have it be a school goal and built into in-services."

[‡] Each of the teachers whose case is described began work in schools serving lower socioeconomic status (SES) students and, with the exception of Alecia (whose advancement occurred within school), moved into more technology-rich and affluent schools because of the professional learning they did with The Math Forum. This type of professional advancement also characterized teachers in the larger sample. Data from the Internet questionnaires also suggest that teachers in lower SES schools are increasingly finding and using The Math Forum with their students. These data further suggest that even though The Math Forum is serving as a resource for for teacher advancement and might be considered responsible for teachers leaving schools that serve populations of lower SES, no fewer students in these settings are benefiting from the resources that The Math Forum provides.

choose, and over time their readiness for these services changes (Lave & Wenger, 1991). Their use of Math Forum services typically deepens in the areas that were their initial points of contact with The Math Forum. Their use also expands and becomes more exploratory with respect to other aspects of the site and the contents of mathematics, technology, and pedagogy more generally.

For teachers who come to think of The Math Forum as a community, the site engages them in expanding their roles as teachers, colleagues, and members of the broader community of educators, much like Little and McLaughlin's (1993) description of substantial models of teacher professional development. Unlike more traditional forms of teacher professional development, however, The Math Forum provides services for teachers and opportunities to interact around these services; it does not specify what teachers need to do (see discussion in Renninger, Weimar & Klotz, 1998). It provides an inquiry-oriented (Bruner, 1966) extension for the mathematics classroom, as well as a "forum" through which teachers can explore and actively personalize their work with topics related to mathematics and its use.

Building Community with and for Teachers

In earlier sections of this chapter, we link interactive resources with participant knowledge building on The Math Forum site and suggest that interactive resources enable participants to deepen their use of The Math Forum over time. Discussions in the literature on virtual communities have more typically focused on participants, participants' capacity for imagination about community, and identity and leadership as keys to community survival. In this section of the chapter, each of these aspects of virtual community building is considered in relation to virtual community as it exists in a richly textured site such as that of The Math Forum. Participants' capacities for imagination and identity are viewed as essential but not sufficient for the development of virtual community. Instead, interactive services and multiple avenues of communication are thought to provide critical support for participants' images of, and identification with, a site.

Imagination

The development of the Internet and the forms of interaction that it makes possible has led to discussion of virtual communities as requiring cultural imagination (Jones, 1998). In this form of community, a person carries an image of real-time community into their virtual interaction with others. Weise (1996), for example, describes her own discovery of the Internet and her feelings about the sense of community it gave her:

In a way [it] was like being given the gift of an extended family, something I had never experienced. Suddenly, every night I had family dinner, could sit back and nibble at my food while aunts and uncles and cousins argued and told stories about people I had never met, but whose experiences enriched me. (p. xii)

She likens the experience of being online to "a backyard fence, a coffee shop, a favorite hangout, a weekly support group" (p. xv). Echoing the power of belonging described by Weise and highlighting the importance of a shared sense of norms to feelings of community (Oldenburg, 1989; Putnam, 2000), one teacher recently said of The Math Forum's Teacher2Teacher (T2T) question and answer service:

the best part about this Forum for me . . . [is] the chance to "chat" about math ed with educators who aren't out to find fault with the rest of the posters. . . . [and] the chance to ask questions without fear of getting my head snapped off.

Despite the fact that The Math Forum technically is a set of resources, the image of The Math Forum as a community appears to be reinforced by its responsiveness to participants, its interactive services, and the depth and breadth of the learning it enables participants to acquire. The resources that The Math Forum provides for participants are limitless. Careful attention has been paid to archiving on the site since its inception, and the quality of its ask-an-expert services and challenge problems continue to "feed" The Math Forum's archives. In this sense, The Math Forum enables a kind of generalized reciprocity because one can use the resources that The Math Forum provides without keeping someone else from doing so. Furthermore, contributions to the site help Math Forum staff to continue to build it out in ways that meet personal needs (Kollack, 1999).

The Math Forum As a Context for Imagination

Several features of Math Forum practice reinforce the perception of The Math Forum as a community where everyone can think about math: (a) the staff – including volunteers – are trained to be responsive to users, (b) questionnaires and queries to the site are perceived as an information exchange, and (c) site resources are edited and built out as a response to users' strengths and needs. This Math Forum culture is a shared understanding of all participants. For staff, Math Forum culture translates as ongoing thinking about the kind of support and resources participants need to use services well. Participants talk about coming to identify with The Math Forum and feeling that the site is responsive to them.

A largely invisible scaffold, or protocol, for responding to participants ensures that the "voice" identified with each of The Math Forum services reflects a value for learning. PoW mentors, Dr. Math volunteers, T2T teacher mentors, and the like, welcome participants and ask questions as a means for clarifying their understanding of participants' submissions, questions, and so forth.

Volunteer mentors and new staff in each of the services are trained in using this scaffold in their response to participants as part of a tenuring process. In the Dr. Math service, for example, the tenuring process ensures that the math doctors work with (as opposed to simply answering) participants who submit questions. Mentors' questions provide background information about the efforts a participant has made to address the question and the type of resources he or she has examined (i.e., the Dr. Math archive). The Dr. Math service is not intended to provide homework help or a ready-answer service. Rather, Dr. Math is designed to allow participants of all ages to think about math.

The staff regularly consults participants about their needs and updates them on site developments. The questionnaires are presented as information gathering for site support. The questionnaire addresses two types of information: information that the staff genuinely want to know to continue to build out services (e.g., Do users mind being pointed to a FAQ, rather than receiving an answer to a question for which there already is an archived answer on the site?) and information that the staff think participants need to continue to use the site effectively (e.g., information that the PoW would be shifting to Web-based submissions to more effectively provide information to teachers about their students' submissions). The questionnaires include both forced-choice and open-ended questions and are used to inform staff work plans. A complaint on one of the open-ended questionnaires, for example, said that the PoWs do not fit the Australian curriculum. The staff thought about this in terms of the needs of that user to understand the PoW as an extension of curriculum, rather than as a replacement for curriculum. In response to the complaint, pages were developed so that teachers could share the ways in which they use the PoW to extend and complement their curriculum. The staff felt that if one person needed this information, others were likely to need it as well.

In addition to scaffolding user knowledge, all answers to Dr. Math, the math library annotations, Web pages, and so forth are scanned as a control on flaming and spamming. This permits correction of spelling, punctuation, and grammatical errors on all archived materials. As Anderson (1996) suggested, scanning for correction of errors signals respect for participants. Edited materials also shift the readers' attention to the content of participant questions, source of information, and so forth, rather than issues of presentation.

The Math Forum staff is also responsive to what they see as perceived participant needs, even though participants may not be aware of them. The T2T service, for example, was developed in response to questions being submitted to Ask Dr. Math that were not specifically about the patterns and relations between symbols but addressed the process of learning, mathematics learning, or teaching. T2T includes questions about philosophies of learning, general issues in pedagogy (tracking, management, etc.), math pedagogy, specific information about resources and lessons or mathematics information, and professional development. While topics such as these might have fit what others have called topic drift, Math Forum staff identified the topics as participant needs. With help from the U.S. Presidential Awards for Excellence in Science and Mathematics Teaching Program, The Math Forum staff established T2T.

The T2T service was patterned on the Ask Dr. Math service. T2T is also designed to permit discussions to develop off of archived questions, which means that participants reading the archives can reactivate discussions of topics. Teacher mentors for the service include a Forum staff member and volunteer mentors. Because the Forum staff member had worked with the Dr. Math service previously, she modeled its approach to users in her responses to the teachers and the T2T mentors (the Presidential Awardees). She also developed a tenuring process that paralleled that of the Ask Dr. Math service for the mentors. This protocol led T2T mentors to hear and check out their understanding of questions before replying to them. She also provided feedback to the mentors about tone and structure (i.e., greeting, separating ideas in paragraphs to improve readability) of their responses and the usefulness of incorporating links to other services and resources on the site.

As one mentor commented on a recent questionnaire sent to the teacher mentors:

Mentoring [in] the Teacher2Teacher service is great fun but also it stimulates my thinking on a variety of subjects. I think it might be more valuable to the mentors than it is for those who write in!

Similar to the reciprocal quality of other Forum services, T2T mentors learn through their participation in this service. Those who participate in the discussions that accompany the T2T responses and those who read through the logs are afforded additional opportunities to learn from it as well.

Staff members for each of the services also continue to learn and to provide a model of how they learn for their users. As one said in summarizing the solutions submitted for the *Find the Area of this Square Problem* (mathforum.com/geopow/solutions/solution.ehtml?puzzle=46):

One thing that I kind of messed up was that I worded the problem poorly. I asked, "Can you find the area of the square?" That implies that there is only one possible answer, which isn't true. Usually when I say **the** answer, I mean **all the possible answers** – keep that in mind! But here I should have asked you to find **an** answer, since in fact there are infinitely many answers to this problem. I'll try to be more careful with my wording in the future.

I also drew a picture that was too accurate – it looked sort of like it might look, when in fact you should never rely on a picture to give you clues about what's longer than what. You can only go by the facts you're given in the problem.

This type of commentary helps students (teachers and participants, more generally) to cut through the notion that learning is a discrete process or that doing math is only about getting the right answer (Schoenfeld, 1992). Such intellectual honesty also helps to make explicit the culture of the Forum and distinguishes it from what many users who come to the site have previously understood mathematical thinking to involve – that math is about being right or wrong. Intellectual honesty also establishes The Math Forum as a community of practice, where participation by the novice is accepted (Lave & Wenger, 1991; Schlager et al., this volume).

Several working assumptions inform the staff's work with participants. The staff assume that the topics of math, technology, and pedagogy provide interesting and worthwhile challenges and tools. The staff believe that people of all ages and educational backgrounds can think about these challenges. Finally, the staff design the software and invisible scaffolding of participants' queries so that they can engage in thinking with participants by listening well and asking questions to inform and clarify. The staff's assumptions about how to work with participants also provide a basis for participants' perceptions of The Math Forum as a community.

The Math Forum staff understand themselves to be offering users a vision of Internet communication and community, in addition to being a conduit to connect people, store resources, and make those resources readily available to others. The staff's cultivation of community is intended to enable quality mathematical interaction and, as such, the exchange of high-quality mathematical content. Math Forum participants have a stake in learning together and sharing their skills and ideas with each other (see similar discussions of real-time discourse communities in Ball, 1993; McLaughlin & Talbert, 1993; Putnam & Borko, 2000; Wineburg & Grossman, 1998). Staff and participants appear to expect (or come to understand) that collaboration yields more than the kind of thinking that any one person can produce for him- or herself.

Participants also have more specific, or individual, images of The Math Forum. These images vary as a function of participants' knowledge about possibilities for themselves on the site, the needs of participants' students, participants' purposes for visiting the site, and so forth. Thus, for example, Sonia might talk about The Math Forum community in terms of the mentors' work with her students, Alecia might refer to support for her classroom teaching, and a staff member might talk about the range of materials now in the archive and how they are being used, the classification of problem types, and the needs of teachers working with students at different levels of instruction.

The Math Forum As Virtual Community

The Math Forum can be characterized as a virtual community because it engenders feelings of belonging and purpose (Anderson, 1991; Jones, 1997). Even though participants do not come to the site with similar levels of knowledge about mathematics, technology, and/or pedagogy, participants share a vision of the site as a community where people of all different levels of experience go to do, think, and be challenged in math. Several characteristics of the site contribute to the shared sense of The Math Forum as a community. These include the consistency of the type of interaction participants have with the different service, the quality and depth of resources that are available, and the responsiveness of the site to the strengths and needs of its participants.

The Math Forum is both similar to and different from two types of virtual communities often identified in the literature: lifestyle enclaves and electronic town halls. The Math Forum might be said to fit Bellah et al.'s (1985) description of a lifestyle enclave in that the Forum is a kind of taste and/or recreational interest group (see also Jones, 1995, 1998; Kiesler, 1997; Smith & Kollack, 1999). Bellah et al.'s work suggests that lifestyle enclaves are becoming places where individuals can express their identities, sharing and interacting with like-minded people in an otherwise consumer-based society. Instead of real-time neighborhood gatherings (i.e., town functions such as picnics), a lifestyle community enables people to share their interests. Bellah et al. point out, however, that the downside of this kind of community is that interactions often are one-dimensional and foster identities that have a thin veneer. On the Web, these one-dimensional interactions typically take the form of a discussion of one interest (i.e., cat owners talking and sharing information) or a larger set of shared needs and interest (i.e., a writers' discussion group).

While to some extent fitting the description of a lifestyle enclave, The Math Forum is also unique. Its commitment to community allows for multiple goals, and its activities are designed to enable users to meet their strengths and needs. Participants are expected to change and be enabled to assume various leadership roles (e.g., helping a colleague to use the PoWs or mentoring for the PoWs, Ask Dr. Math, or T2T). It is not simply taste or recreation oriented. The range of possible options for engagement that The Math Forum site offers is much broader than that offered by most recreational communities. The Math Forum has intentionally proliferated the ways people can interact on the site (e.g., discussion groups, question-and-answer services, PoWs) by providing multiple points of access, more channels of communication, and opportunities for sustained interaction. Such interaction, for teachers, has a recreational function but also serves as a source of professional learning. The combination of opportunities to build knowledge and the autonomy within which to do so appears to have engendered interest for The Math Forum and a willingness to contribute to its resources.

The Math Forum also could be said to fit the description of the electronic town hall (Mitchell, 1995; Rheingold, 1993), wherein the virtual community serves as an extension of the physical community. Electronic town halls have been described as enabling the development of democratic communities not possible in the physical world because of temporal and spatial flexibility (one can participate when participation fits into one's schedule wherever one logs in). The Math Forum is more limited than a town hall in that it is only focused on mathematics and mathematics learning. On the other hand, those who choose to focus on mathematics have the opportunity to do so at The Math Forum, regardless of affiliation, location, and so on. Furthermore, Math Forum resources and services are considered to be extensions of possibilities afforded in classrooms, not replacements for them. The "democratic" possibilities of The Math Forum may be even more explicit than the more generic town hall. Teachers in many types of classrooms are using Math Forum services with students, many of whom would not necessarily have the access or support for such access at home. In addition, teachers and students interact with others from different backgrounds and occupations on the site who think with them as mentors, provide resources, and so forth.

Lifestyle enclaves and electronic town halls hold the potential for people to participate. At The Math Forum, having a broader set of services provides a basis for participants to continue to build knowledge. Participants tend to grow through work with one service and move on to check out or work with other services. As such, the participants' sense of The Math Forum as community evolves and continues to shift as their vision of possibilities develops. With time, The Math Forum comes to be experienced as a community that has a dynamic set of resources. This perception of community differs from the more static sense of community that characterizes a lifestyle enclave or an electronic town hall. Such static communities constrain imagination about what is possible on such a site, leading users to be takers. A more dynamic community such as The Math Forum allows participants to challenge what they know through interaction and resource development with others.

Participants like Sonia, Bob, and Alecia made a particular connection to The Math Forum and from there began to explore the site and deal with its enormity. Rather than being overwhelmed by its size, they accommodated to it. The Math Forum site enables them to feel connected because the site continues to grow in a reciprocal relation to them. Importantly, it offers participants most of what they need, or they have learned to make requests.

Identity

If a person is to participate in a virtual community, he or she needs to have both an image of what a virtual community is and a feeling of connection to, or identification with, that community. Identification with a community suggests that a participant has found points of overlap between who she or he is and the activity of the community. For example, participants in The Math Forum, like Bob, know that they can learn from participation and in this process contribute to shaping The Math Forum to meet their needs and serve those of others. Participants like Sonia and Alecia can be supported to identify with the community, and in working with the community expand their sense of possible selves (Markus & Nurius, 1986).

In online discussion groups, people check others out, looking at email addresses, signature styles, and phrasing that marks their membership in a group (Donath, 1999). Achieving recognition, or becoming known by name, is a goal for many discussion list participants (Baym, 2000). On The Math Forum site, this kind of identity exists. At least theoretically, there also is support for the possibility of changing identity because a richly textured site on the Web affords anonymity. Participants do not need to use their real voices or pictures of themselves in their responses, for example. On Web pages, they can use fantasy substitutes. This makes their Internet identity dream-like, where identities can be re-imagined at will and can be either condensed or diffused images of other identities (Turkle, 1995; see also Kirkley, Savery & Grabner-Hagen, 1998).

Participants who continue to grow their knowledge as they work with a site (exploring other services on the site, integrating a service such as a PoW into their work with their students, etc.) begin to shift their identities, and this is internalized into their physical personas. Sonia's enthusiasm for her son's changed attitude about mathematics following work with and support from Mrs. B. on the PoW, for example, is paralleled by both her own shifting attitudes about technology and teaching math. Her son began thinking of himself as a person who could do mathematics, and she sought more opportunities to work with technology and expanded her usage of The Math Forum in her classes.

Once a person connects to The Math Forum site (e.g., has explored it enough to know something of its potential), he or she has a role in its development and grows through this role to take on other roles. Teachers take on all kinds of roles on The Math Forum site. They tell others about it; share resources that they have downloaded with other teachers; involve their students in using the PoW(s), Ask Dr. Math, and the archives; help students to mentor the PoW; develop, share, and comment on materials; participate in Math Forum discussion groups; supervise students who mentor a PoW; use Math Forum software as a template to run their own PoW; involve preservice teachers in Math Forum projects; act as support cavalry for a PoW; offer math education resources in a language other than English; serve as a T2T mentor; serve as a math doctor; contribute Web units or other resources; provide feedback and comments on pages; and so forth. Given that these roles are also archived as contributions, they continue to be resources that are available to others over time.

Each of the roles teachers assume on the site involves knowledge building (Scardamalia & Bereiter, 1997). The roles require reflection on the question posed or problem submitted, restatement of service goals and applications, and so forth. In assuming these roles, teachers act on the knowledge they have and organize, restate, or develop it so that they can think with others. Teachers both identify with the site through these roles and continue to reengage the site because it provides opportunities to extend their knowledge in ways that they continue to value – by helping them answer their questions, challenging them to think in new ways, and so forth.

On a site such as The Math Forum where users move between services that provide different opportunities for engagement, all the roles teachers assume can be thought of as forms of site leadership. Site participation is a form of leadership since it helps to stretch the thinking of other participants (in discussion, because it is archived, etc.). Teachers like Sonia, Bob, and Alecia maintain roles and extend themselves to assume new ones. Math Forum teachers (and staff) typically move into new roles as the challenge piques their interest. This means that the teachers (or staff) carry what they have learned about working with other services to any new context. It also means that they are in a position to suggest needed adjustments and the like.

The continuity and overturn of leadership on The Math Forum site is an important feature of the site and one that distinguishes it from most other sites. In discussion groups, for example, leaders represent a small fraction of the users, and many of them cross-post to other sites (Smith, 1999). For less dimensional sites, leadership is typically a cause of anxiety because it is considered important to both maintaining and building this type of virtual community, and it is not known what exactly is needed for existing leaders to continue to lead.

Shifting between leadership opportunities on The Math Forum site is a natural part of participant learning. It might also be expected to lead to fragmentation, or what Gergen (1991) called the saturated self, since a person invests him- or herself into many different situations (Little & McLauglin, 1993). On the Web, there is no expectation that one could see all that another is doing. Saturation appears to ensure a sense of belonging. Many of the teachers interviewed, for example, reported that they had been lonely in their schools and had few if any colleagues who shared their interests. Meeting like-minded teachers (researchers, staff, etc.) through The Math Forum and being able to stay connected with them provides teachers with an extended professional community. In the cases of both Sonia and Bob, participation in The Math Forum community actually enabled them to join real-time communities in new school settings that included support for their interests and equipment and expectations that allowed them to further develop these interests.

Another teacher whom we interviewed uses the site with his students and also volunteers as a mentor (math doctor) for Ask Dr. Math. He told us about a particularly difficult meeting his math department had about curriculum issues. He said he took some of the key questions they had been raising in their meetings to one of the math discussion groups on The Math Forum Web site. In talking through the issues with his Math Forum colleagues, he found himself able to think fully about their complexity, and this experience enabled him to revisit the issues differently at their next meeting. It seems that teachers using The Math Forum identify with the site through the roles that they can assume. The teachers continue to reengage The Math Forum because they find others who provide them with opportunities to extend their knowledge in ways that they continue to value – by helping them to answer questions, challenging them to think in new ways, and so forth.

The Math Forum also identifies for its participants that participation and contribution to the site is not only their right but that this right makes the site the resource that it is. Participants have opportunities to comment on all pages, the Webmaster is in touch with participants about their comments and inquiries, and questionnaires are regularly posted on the site that both solicit participant opinions regarding possible directions for The Math Forum and intentionally provide note of anticipated changes on the site. Thus, participants who return to the site over time come to understand the community as one that is open to and in a process of change, as well as one that is responsive to their needs.

Knowledge Building and Change

As Jones and Spiro (1995) pointed out, it is not sufficient to assume that providing sources of information such as facts, statistics, lists, visual data, and so forth on the Web will necessarily lead a participant to thinking about their meaning. Data from the interviews described suggest that teachers who continue to engage interactive services on The Math Forum site are enabled to use such resources and positioned to help others find meaning in their use. Furthermore, many teachers do not come to The Math Forum site with the ability to effectively use Web resources in their teaching, or for their own edification, but develop this ability through work with the site.

At The Math Forum, there is a reciprocal relation between the design of services and the strengths and needs of participants as learners. The balance of services and support that individual participants need from the site varies, however. The cases of Sonia, Bob, and Alecia represent three types of teacher participants. There are (a) those like Sonia when she first found the site *who need a reason to engage and need support to continue this effort*; (b) those like Alecia when she first joined The Math Forum workshop *who see in The Math Forum an opportunity but need support* to make it work; and (c) those like Bob *who immediately begin to change what they have been doing* to be able to take advantage of the opportunities they have found.

When she first came to the site, Sonia exemplified *the teacher who needs a reason to engage and needs support to continue this effort*. The community she found at The Math Forum was initially lodged in one of the PoW mentors. Mrs. B was the person who, in responding to Sonia's son's PoW submission, helped him to change his attitude about mathematics. Mrs. B modeled the unstated but clear premise of site culture, that a person can and will learn over time. The model of Mrs. B's interactions enabled Sonia to imagine what the community of The Math Forum could mean for her students and for her. Sonia's efforts to make her connection to The Math Forum work were also supported by the demands of her school, which had recently become a model tech school; the mentors who responded to her students; her students' parents' enthusiasm for doing the PoW; and her students' positive response to working with PoW problems. Sonia received what may appear to be a tremendous amount of support. She continued to need support even after she had moved on to seeing more of the opportunities The Math Forum afforded, much as Alecia had when she first found the site. Sonia's need for support shifted, however. Because Sonia saw opportunities, she developed an interest in how she could use these opportunities in her teaching and in her own professional learning.

For teachers like Alecia and Bob, the community found at The Math Forum was easily traversed from the first visit. They were comfortable with mathematics and were excited to find a resource that enabled them to stretch their students. Alecia, when we first met her at The Math Forum teacher workshop, represented *the teacher who sees opportunity but needs support* to be able to use it in her work with her students. Like Sonia, Alecia needed the connection to a Math Forum staff person who enabled her to master html, insert graphics into her pages, and so forth. Support from Math Forum staff enabled her to begin putting her own lessons on the Web; with time she linked these to other resources, and so forth. She talked about the support she received from The Math Forum as making a difference in her participation, and she was clear that the rewards for her participation were reaped from the professional learning that work with The Math Forum staff afforded her. Over the three years that we talked with her, Alecia shifted from needing support and drawing on one Math Forum staff member for this support to working with multiple Math Forum services and providing support to other users. She moved from being able to see opportunity and needing support to being able to make use of it, creating opportunities for herself and others including her students on the site.

When he started his work with The Math Forum, Bob exemplified *the teacher who immediately begins to change* what he was doing in order to use Math Forum resources in his classes. He put in substantial effort to take advantage of the opportunities he found for himself and his students. Bob was more interested in the quality of the responses received and the level of mathematics which The Math Forum offered his students. He too had begun his use of the Web in a more individualized relationship with an editor at a business site. By the time he found The Math Forum, he had been socialized to think about sharing as one of the "great opportunities'" of work on the Web. During the three years in which he was interviewed, he continued to expand the number of services on The Math Forum site that he explored and used. He built The Math Forum into his curriculum and in his new job modeled this integration for his colleagues. Bob intends that The Math Forum PoWs will be an established component of all middle school mathematics courses in his district. Like Math Forum staff who model approaches to thinking mathematically in the design of services and in their mentoring, Bob is working to support his school colleagues' use of The Math Forum. In fact, he commented that he hoped to end up with colleagues that are challenged and students coming into his classes who think about mathematics as problem solving.

Over the three year period that we talked with the teachers, each teacher changed in the amount of support he or she needed to check out site resources and figure out how to make use of them. At the end of three years, Sonia's needs for support began to share characteristics of Alecia's needs when Alecia first found The Math Forum, and Alecia's need for support had begun to share characteristics with Bob's needs. In fact, by the third year of the study, all three of the teachers were working with others to use The Math Forum and were learning more about their practice because of this experience.

Not surprisingly, shifts in the teachers' usage of the site were accompanied by changes in their description of The Math Forum as a community.

The teachers shifted from first identifying their community at The Math Forum with a particular person or service to recognizing that the community included groups of individuals, contributions to the site on which they could confer, and a host of resources that they had yet to explore. It appears that making meaning (and use) of available resources could not have taken place for the Sonias and Alecias, in particular, unless they felt individually supported in their questioning, solutions, comments, and so forth. Furthermore, it was important to both Sonia and Alecia that they were able to grow through support and become supportive of others' learning. This allowed them to recognize their changed sense of possible selves (Markus & Nurius, 1986).

The Math Forum's experience of building out a community with and for teachers suggests the importance of opportunities for knowledge building and changed participation to the sticky traffic that characterizes the site. Site participants do vary, and much like the success of cross-aged tutoring as a pedagogical tool (see Renninger, 1998), Math Forum staff have seized on participant differences as a strength. They facilitate the match of persona who have a particular form of knowledge with others who need to understand it, are willing to teach another about it, and so forth. Math Forum staff assume that participants range in their knowledge about mathematics, technology, pedagogy, and the like, and that the way to figure something out is to look in the archives or ask a question. Moreover, as descriptions of site resources suggest, the staff also work with participants to learn how to ask questions. The staff request participants to provide some background about how they have approached a question. They are interested in the dead-ends encountered, and so forth, because this information enables them to take up a more useful conversation with the participant.

In addition to facilitating knowledge seeking, the need to scale services with limited numbers of staff* have necessitated the voluntary support of participants in answering other participants' questions, responding to student submissions, helping to provide support for teachers, and so forth. Usefully, activities such as these involve reflection about what is understood and the kind of thinking with others that enables participant volunteers to continue to build knowledge (Scardamalia & Bereiter, 1997; see also discussion in Bransford, Brown, & Cocking, 1999). The

---

* The GeoPoW alone went from receiving 60 questions a week to 1,400 questions a week over the three-year period of NSF funding. One staff member and volunteers provide the individualized responses to these students.

opportunity to continue to grow understanding in ways for which one is ready provides autonomy (Ryan & Deci, 2000), as well as a basis for the kind of valuing that characterizes the asking of follow-up questions and the development of individual interest (Renninger, 2000). Site engagement in this sense then is intrinsically motivating and might be expected to be self-perpetuating.*

Several characteristics appear to have enabled the site to build out and the community that is The Math Forum to continue to evolve. These include support for learning that enables participant value to develop. The Math Forum provides for different forms of support and types of participation. The Math Forum staff expect that participant change will occur and that knowledge building based on interactive services will provide a catalyst for community participation. However, there is little expectation about what the particular methods to be employed are or which questions need to be asked when. The staff works with teachers and other participants as learners in much the same way as the literature on student learning suggests that students be instructed (Bransford et al., 1999). The staff start with what a participant does understand and works together with the participant to figure out what he or she does not understand.

The staff's goal is to provide participants with the kind of support that enables changed understanding to occur. They do this through scaffolding, modeling, and apprenticeship (Collins, Brown & Newman, 1989). As the cases of Sonia, Alecia, and Bob suggest, supporting other participants enables teachers to help themselves. While it is legitimate to participate peripherally on The Math Forum site, and many do, only the teachers who were not supported in their use of site resources remained

---

* One challenge for The Math Forum has been the NSF requirement that the infrastructure for ongoing projects such as The Math Forum become sustainable outside of funded NSF research and development projects on the site. In addition to figuring out how to develop online a sticky community that enables its participants to grow their knowledge, this NSF requirement also necessitates that staff dedicate time to both scaling (because of the success of what they have been able to accomplish, they have a rapidly increasing number of participants) and sustainability of the services.

The Math Forum staff view themselves not only as providing an infrastructure for building out The Math Forum community but also as being of the community in the sense that they engage and work with participants. Their discourse about community and how it develops has informed both the scaffolding that they provide and the design of the services. A critical dimension of The Math Forum's facilitation of participants' possibilities for knowledge building and changed participation in the site has been its support first by the NSF, then by WebCT and, more recently, by Drexel University. One can discuss the building out of community with and for teachers provided that the infrastructure for the site is supported.

peripheral participants of The Math Forum community over time. In this sense then, Forum participants are a community of learners whose participation evolves (Lave & Wenger, 1991). The community is dynamic and responsive to participants as individuals.

In fact, once identified as a site for classroom use and professional learning, The Math Forum is more than a set of interactive resources, and participants can capitalize on the time and space afforded by the Web as they work with it (Duffy, Dueber & Hawley, 1998). Teachers can use as much or as little of Math Forum resources as they want to, when and where they choose. Importantly, it is The Math Forum's interactive resources on which teachers continue to draw. Interactive resources provide models and opportunities for apprenticeship for teachers as well as their students. Instead of heralding the disappearance of community (Oldenburg, 1989; Putnam, 2000), The Math Forum's richly textured site appears to be extended and enriched by its participants. They continue to grow in their understanding of what the possibilities for themselves as users of the site include. It is the mix of interactive opportunities that appears to have enabled The Math Forum to build out its site with and for teachers.

Acknowledgments

We acknowledge the many contributions that our students, fellow researchers, and participants in The Math Forum community have made to our thinking about the nature of community online, and the specific roles of participant learning and change in community development. In particular, we appreciate the assistance of Kimberly Corbette, Liza Ewen, Annie Fetter, Kristina Lasher, Eve Manz, Melissa Running, Richard Tchen, Jody Underwood, and Roya Salehi in compiling data reported in this chapter. We also would like to thank Melissa Kobelin and Jill Ratzan for their help in reviewing the literature, and Sarah Seastone and Jonathan Shaw for their contributions to preparing this chapter for publication. Finally, we gratefully acknowledge support from Swarthmore College's Faculty Research Fund and National Science Foundation funding to The Math Forum (# 9618223). The findings and conclusions reported here, however, do not necessarily reflect those of the funders.

References

Anderson, B. R. O. G. (1991). *Imagined communities: Reflections on the origin and spread of nationalism* (Rev. and extended ed.). New York: Verso.

Anderson, J. (1996). Not for the faint of heart: Contemplations on Usenet (virtual community). In L. Cherny & E. R. Weise (Eds.), *Wired women: Gender and new realities in cyberspace* (pp. 126–38). Seattle: Seal.

Ball, D. (1993). With an eye on the mathematical horizon: Dilemmas of teaching elementary school mathematics. *The Elementary School Journal, 93*(4), 373–97.

Baym, N. K. (2000). *Tune in, log on: Soaps, fandom, and online community.* Thousand Oaks, CA: Sage.

Bellah, R. N., Madsen, R., Sullivan, W. M., Swidler, A., & Tipton, S. M. (1985). *Habits of the heart: Individualism and commitment in American life.* Berkeley: University of California Press.

Bransford, J. D., Brown, A. L., & Cocking, R. R. (1999). *How people learn: Brain, mind, experience, and school.* Washington, DC: National Academy Press.

Bruner, J. S. (1966). *Toward a theory of instruction.* (120) Cambridge, MA: Harvard University Press.

Castells, M. (1999). *Critical education in the new information age.* Lanham, MD: Rowman & Littlefield.

Cobb, P. (1995). Mathematical learning and small-group interaction: Four case studies. In P. Cobb & H. Bauersfeld (Ed.), *The emergence of mathematical meaning: Interaction in classroom cultures* (pp. 25–129). Hillsdale, NJ: Lawrence Erlbaum.

Collins, A., Brown, J. S., & Newman, S. E. (1989). Cognitive apprenticeship: Teaching the crafts of reading, writing, and mathematics. In L. B. Resnick (Ed.), *Knowing, learning, and instruction: Essays in honor of Robert Glaser.* (pp. 453–94). Hillsdale, NJ: Lawrence Erlbaum.

Donath, J. S. (1999). Identity and deception in the virtual community. In M. A. Smith & P. Kollack (Eds.), *Communities in cyberspace.* London: Routledge.

Duffy, T. M., Dueber, B., & Hawley, C. L. (1998). Critical thinking in a distributed environment: A pedagogical base for the design of conferencing systems. In C. J. Bonk & K. S. King (Eds.), *Electronic collaborators: Learning-centered technologies for apprenticeship, and discourse* (pp. 51–78). Mahwah, NJ: Lawrence Erlbaum.

Gergen, K. J. (1991). *The saturated self: Dilemmas of identity in contemporary life.* New York: Basic Books.

Jones, S. G. (1995). *CyberSociety: Computer-mediated communication and community.* Thousand Oaks, CA: Sage.

(1997). *Virtual culture: Identity and communication in CyberSociety.* London/ Thousand Oaks, CA: Sage.

(1998). *CyberSociety 2.0: Revisiting computer-mediated communication and community.* Thousand Oaks, CA.: Sage.

Jones, S. G., & Spiro, R. (1995). Contextualization, cognitive flexibility, and hypertext: The convergence of interpretive theory, cognitive psychology, and advanced information technologies. In S. L. Star (Ed.), *The cultures of computing* (pp. 146–57). Cambridge, UK: Blackwell.

Kiesler, S. (1997). *Culture of the Internet.* Mahwah, NJ: Lawrence Erlbaum.

Kirkley, S. E., Savery, J. R., & Grabner-Hagen, M. M. (1998). Electronic teaching: Extending classroom dialogue and assistance through e-mail communication. In C. J. Bonk & K. S. King (Eds.), *Electronic collaborators: Learner-centered technologies for literacy, apprenticeship, and discourse* (pp. 209–32). Mahwah, NJ: Lawrence Erlbaum.

Kollack, P. (1999). The economics of online cooperation: Gifts and public goods in cyberspace. In M. A. Smith & P. Kollack (Eds.), *Communities in cyberspace.* London/New York: Routledge, pp. 220–39.

Krapp, A., & Lewalter, D. (2001). Development of interests and interest-based motivational orientations: A longitudinal study in vocational school and work settings. In S. Volet & S. Järvelä (Eds.), *Motivation in learning contexts: Theoretical and methodological implications* (pp. 201–32). London: Elsevier.

Lave, J., & Wenger, E. (1991). *Situated learning: Legitimate peripheral participation.* New York: Cambridge University Press.

Little, J. W., & McLaughlin, M. W. (1993). *Teachers' work: Individuals, colleagues, and contexts.* New York: Teachers College Press.

Loader, B. (1997). *The governance of cyberspace: Politics, technology and global restructuring.* London/New York: Routledge.

Markus, H., & Nurius, P. (1986). Possible selves. *American Psychologist, 4*(9), 954–69.

McLaughlin, M. W., & Talbert, J. (1993). Introduction: New visions of teaching. In D. K. Cohen, M. W. McLaughlin, and J. E. Talbert (Eds.), *Teaching for understanding: Challenges for policy and practice* (pp. 1–12). San Francisco: Jossey-Bass.

Mitchell, W. J. (1995). *City of bits: Space, place, and the infobahn.* Cambridge, MA: MIT Press.

National Council of Teachers of Mathematics (2000). *Principles and standards for school mathematics.* Alexandria, VA: NCTM.

Oldenburg, R. (1989). *The great good place: Cafés, coffee shops, community centers, beauty parlors, general stores, bars, hangouts, and how they get you through the day* (1st ed.). New York: Paragon House.

Putnam, R. D. (2000). *Bowling alone: The collapse and revival of American community.* New York: Simon & Schuster.

Putnam, R. T., & Borko, H. (2000). What do new views of knowledge and thinking have to say about research on teacher learning? *Educational Researcher, 29*(1), 4–15.

Renninger, K. A. (1998). Developmental psychology and instruction: Issues from and for practice. In I. E.. Sigel & K. A. Renninger (Eds.), *Handbook of child psychology,* Vol. 4: *Child Psychology in Practice,* 5th ed. (pp. 211–74). New York: John Wiley.

(2000). Individual interest and its implications for understanding intrinsic motivation. In C. Sansone & J. M. Harackiewicz (Eds.), *Intrinsic and extrinsic motivation: The search for optimal motivation and performance* (pp. 375–404). New York: Academic.

Renninger, K. A., Welmar, S. A., & Klotz, E. A. (1998). Teachers and students investigating and communicating about geometry: The Math Forum. In R. Lehrer & D. Chazen (Eds.), *Designing learning environments for developing understanding of geometry and space* (pp. 465–87). Mahwah, NJ: Lawerence Erlbaum.

Rheingold, H. (1993). *The virtual community: Homesteading on the electronic frontier.* Reading, MA: Addison-Wesley.

Ryan, R., & Deci, E. (2000). When rewards compete with nature: The undermining of intrinsic motivation and self-regulation. In C. Sansone & J. M. Harackiewicz (Eds.), *Intrinsic and extrinsic motivation: The search for optimal motivation and performance* (pp. 14–56). New York: Academic.

Scardamalia, M., & Bereiter, C. (1997). Adaptation and understanding: A case for new cultures of schooling. In S. Vosniadov, E. DeCorte, R. Glaser, & H. Mandl (Eds.), *International perspectives on the psychological foundations of technology-based learning environments* (pp. 149–63). Mahwah, NJ: Lawrence Erlbaum.

Schoenfeld, A. (1992). Learning to think mathematically: Problem solving, metacognition, and sense making in mathematics. In D. A. Grouws (Ed.), *Handbook of research on mathematics teaching and learning: A project of the National Council of Teachers of Mathematics* (pp. 334–70). New York: Macmillan.

Smith, M. A. (1999). Invisible crowds in cyberspace: Mapping the social structure of the Usenet. In M. A. Smith & P. Kollack (Eds.), *Communities in cyberspace*. London/New York: Routledge.

Smith, M. A., & Kollock, P. (Eds.) (1999). *Communities in cyberspace*. London: Routledge, pp. 195–219.

Turkle, S. (1995). *Life on the screen: Identity in the age of the Internet*. New York: Simon & Schuster.

Weise, E. R. (1996). A thousand aunts with modems (Virtual Community). In L. Cherny & E. R. Weise (Eds.), *Wired women: Gender and new realities in cyberspace* (pp. vii–xv). Seattle: Seal.

Wellman, B. (2001). Physical place and CyberPlace: The rise of personalized networking. *International Journal of Urban and Regional Research, 25* (2), 227–52.

Wenger, E. (1999). *Communities of practice*. New York: Cambridge University Press.

White, R. (1959). Motivation reconsidered: The concept of confidence. *Psychological Review, 66*, 297–333.

Wineburg, S., & Grossman, P. (1998). Creating a community of learners among high school teachers. *Phi Delta Kappan, 79*, 350–3.

4 Learning in the Virtual Community Depends upon Changes in Local Communities

Beverly Hunter

In this chapter, a virtual community is defined as a group of people who interact with each other, learn from each others' work, and provide knowledge and information resources to the group related to certain agreed-upon topics of shared interest. A defining characteristic of a virtual community in this sense is that a person or institution must be a contributor to the evolving knowledge base of the group and not just a recipient or consumer of the group's services or knowledge base. Members and the community as a whole take advantage of information technologies and telecommunications for these purposes, in addition to face-to-face interactions they may have. The notion of learning as applied to a virtual community means that there is a mutual knowledge-building process taking place. Members learn both by teaching others and by applying to their own situations the information, tools, know-how, and experiences provided by others in the virtual community. In contrast, a local community is a group of people and organizations who have common interests, concerns, and mutual interdependence by virtue of their living and working in a geographic locality under a common government. In both of the case studies discussed in this chapter, efforts were made to strengthen local communities through applications of information technologies and telecommunications.

Learning and change in the virtual community is increasingly interdependent with learning and change in the participants' local institutions and local communities. This is a fundamental difference from earlier virtual communities. Educational virtual communities in the 1980s and early 1990s were pioneering efforts that attracted visionary innovators, teachers, and their students. More typical of future virtual communities, however, will be the need to engage a dramatically broader base of stakeholders from participating institutions. For educational reforms and innovations to take hold and become institutionalized, *all* learners and teachers and other stakeholders need to be able to participate. This shift in the purposes and participant base will require designers and facilitators of virtual communities to focus much more on changes in professional development practices and the culture and policies of educational institutions than was the case in the pioneering stage.* This chapter is based on the experience of the author as a designer, participant, researcher, or observer of dozens of virtual communities in education over the past two decades (e.g. BrownLAB, 1999; Spitzer et al., 1994; TEECH, 1997), as well as research on educational innovation within local school communities. In particular, the author draws upon experience and research from two projects funded by the U.S. National Science Foundation: the National School Network (NSN) 1993–7, and the Department of Defense Education Activity (DoDEA) Model Schools project 1995–8. The findings from these two cases are corroborated by recent large-scale surveys of U.S. schools and teachers (Becker, 1999).

National School Network: Collaboration and Learning Among Changing Networked School Communities

In 1993, the National School Network, funded by the U.S. National Science Foundation, posed the following question for communities in the United States:

Can we construct and manage communications networks and information services to support educational innovation on a local level in such a way that taxpayers, governments, and private industry will view their benefits as warranting the investment needed to support them on a large scale? (*Toward Universal Participation in the NII*, 1994, p. C5)

Between 1994 and 1998, over 450 local communities and institutions in the NSN were building local information infrastructure while inventing new roles and educational services that take advantage of the technologies (Hunter, 1994, 1995a, b, 1997a, 1998; Newman, Bernstein & Reese, 1992). Table 4.1 shows the kinds of NSN organizations. As is evident from the table, the organizers of the NSN sought to include a wide range of the kinds of institutions traditionally a part of the educational system.

---

* A useful conceptual framework for understanding these changes both in virtual communities and local educational institutions is the well-known "Technology Adoption Life Cycle" proposed by Geoffrey Moore in *Crossing the Chasm* (Moore, 1991).

Table 4.1. *Kinds of Organizations in NSN*

Organization Type	1995 Members	1997 Members
Schools	225	329
Intermediary institutions	115	145
State educational agency or network	6	5
Consortiums of schools/districts	9	9
School districts	24	37
Museums, science centers	8	8
Community organizations	8	8
Corporations/businesses	7	17
College/universities	21	17
R&D organizations/projects	40	40
Professional associations		4

NSN founders from these institutions had exciting visions of how they would use Internetworking* to change, restructure, and reform their institutions, curricula, teaching methods, assessment, collaborative measures across the local community, and economic development. Table 4.2 summarizes those motivations. Notice that nearly all of them imply the emergence of virtual communities.

NSN member institutions and local communities assist each other in their pioneering efforts by exchanging the knowledge they are gaining. In theory, every NSN member institution is both a consumer and a contributor – through the networks – of services, know-how, and content for the others. An NSN Exchange was set up on the World Wide Web to facilitate sharing and collaborative knowledge building among the members of this virtual community.

Dr. Henry Jay Becker of the University of California, Irvine, conducted the Baseline Survey of NSN schools in April 1995. This survey was designed to help build an initial picture of the schools for follow up as the project progressed (Becker, 1996b). Two years later in January 1997, survey booklets were mailed to 248 schools selected to represent the 300+

---

* Internetworking refers to the interaction of people and computers without concern for the boundaries of physical local area networks or organizations. See Hunter (1997b).

Table 4.2. *Reform Agendas of NSN Founders*

Reform Agenda 1994	Example Organizations
Create new kind of curriculum; implement new standards	Rosa Parks; Ralph Bunche; Mendocino; Allegheny, PA, schools partnership
Project-based learning with online teams	Glenview, IL school district
Integrate computational methods into curriculum	MDVirtual H.S.; Earth Systems Science Curriculum
Invent new methods for assessing student learning	Coalition of essential schools portfolio assessment
Collaborate beyond school walls	Exploratorium; Franklin Institute
Digitize, disseminate community resources, construct digital libraries	Patch H.S.; OCM Boces; Science Learning Network
Communitywide learning	Lexington; Mendocino
Home–school connections	Buddy System, Indiana
Connect scientists to schools	Earthwatch
Global collaborations	Global Lab
Economic development	Mendocino
School leadership in community	Gould Academy, ME; Sweetwater, WY
Teacher professional development	Boulder Valley; TeacherNet
Educational restructuring	Champlain Valley School District
Statewide educational reform	California; Texas
Expand educational market	Scholastic, PacBell
Aggregate educational resources	Geometry Forum

schools of the NSN (Becker & Ravitz, 1997). Separate booklets were identified for the School-Level Network Coordinator (a thirteen-page booklet with forty-seven questions, most with multiple subquestions), a five-page "Technical Supplement," and a four-page "Administrator Supplement." In addition, the "strongest Internet-using teachers" completed a thirteen-page, fifty-four-question booklet and randomly selected "other" teachers from each school completed a shorter fifteen-question survey. Data from these surveys enable us to examine many different indicators and perspectives regarding:

- The actual technical infrastructure that was built (who has access to the Internet within the schools),
- Participation in the construction of the local information infrastructure,

- The kinds of learning and teaching activities taking place and the extent of participation in those activities within a school, as well as between the school and its local community,
- The beliefs of teachers concerning the value and purposes of these activities and Internet in school generally, and
- Other conditions that might affect the nature of Internet use by teachers and students.

Two of the key findings from these surveys are that the technical infrastructure and user base grew rapidly in NSN schools and that the actual uses of that infrastructure differed from the original vision. In this chapter, we use some of the findings from this extensive survey in combination with qualitative information about and from NSN member institutions. This combination of broad-based systematic survey data and in-depth case study information enables us to understand not just the nature of learning and change in evolving organizational arrangements but also the stage of adoption of new practices within different groups in an institution.

Change in the Member Institutions Affects Learning in the NSN Virtual Community

As a virtual community, NSN sought an interaction of people, content, and tools that would require a modest effort on the part of any one participant but that would have a major payoff for all. It was expected that members could build upon each others' pioneering work and create a cumulative body of knowledge. The great challenge faced by the NSN was to invent one or more models for Exchange that would be

- Motivating enough to the potential participants that they would contribute information, experience, resources, and know-how to the other members of the Exchange;
- Educationally valid;
- Technically feasible across widely varying institutional infrastructures and skill sets;
- Evolving with the changing needs and interests of Internet users in the member institutions;
- Potentially replicable at any member site, and sustainable and scalable.

The NSN adapted, invented and tested several models and mechanisms for achieving its collaborative knowledge-building goals.

The primary constraint on the effectiveness of any of these mechanisms for collaboration was the extent to which stakeholders in the

NSN institutions and their local communities participated in the kinds of learning, teaching, and professional development activities envisioned by the founders of the NSN. Interestingly, the 1995 and 1997 survey data reveal a different pattern of Internet-use evolution in the participating schools than was envisioned by the founders. As indicated in Table 4.2, the visionaries saw the Internet as a tool for collaboration and participation in virtual communities. However, as the base of users of Internet grew within the participating institutions, the dominant vision changed.

Technical Infrastructure and User Base Grew Rapidly in NSN Schools

The survey data show that, in general, the schools in the NSN succeeded quickly in building the technical infrastructure needed to have people in schools participate in Internetworking. The participation rates within those schools grew rapidly. By 1997, the schools built a strong infrastructure of connectivity to the classroom level. Modems disappeared, and 96 percent of the schools had high-speed LAN-based Internet access. Fifty-one percent had T1 lines to the building. The typical NSN school had fifty simultaneous connections; the typical T1-connected school had seventy-three. In 57 percent of elementary schools, a majority of teachers had classroom Internet connections. Middle schools averaged fourteen connections per 100 students. In the high schools, 62 percent had T1 connections, and the mean number of connected computers was more than 100 (Becker, 1997). The tools became more widely accessible. Only 2 percent of respondents thought that the Internet was "too complicated to use," and only 13 percent said that Internet-connected computers were in an inconvenient location in the school.

The number of network users grew rapidly. Network coordinators in NSN schools reported rapid growth between 1996 and 1997 in terms of numbers of students and teachers using the Internet in their schools and the sophistication of their use. For example, two thirds of the schools reported a tripling of the number of students with some Internet experience, and nearly all the others reported doubling. Similarly, nearly half the schools reported a tripling of the number of teachers with Internet experience, and nearly all the others reported at least a doubling over the past school year. This is a strong indicator that the physical infrastructure built was accessible and usable by a rapidly growing proportion of the people in the schools. This growth in actual use is a necessary (but not sufficient) condition for Internetworking to be used in support of educational reform agendas.

Actual Uses Differs from the Original Vision

The spring 1997 survey of NSN schools reveals patterns of Internet participation and applications that differ from those envisioned by the founding members at the outset of the NSN in 1994. By far, the most common classroom use of the Internet by 1997 was to "search for specific information online" and to "look at sites on the World Wide Web." Ninety-four percent of the strongest Internet-using teachers reported having students perform this kind of activity. All other kinds of activities – those that involve online collaborations or knowledge building with adults and students outside of the school, for example – were reported far less frequently and involved far fewer students.

NSN School Practices Related to Student Email

Few schools in the NSN provided all students with email accounts. The 1997 survey of NSN schools found that relatively few of the NSN schools had distributed individual email accounts widely to students (Hunter, 1997a). At only 21 percent of the schools did half or more students have or use their own email accounts. More than one third of the NSN schools (35 percent) did not give individual email accounts to any students, and at another third (33 percent), only "a few" students had that privilege.

Agendas and Values Changed

A move toward project-based learning and related changes in instructional methods was frequently cited among the reform agendas described by NSN participants in 1994. However, the school network coordinators who responded to the 1995 survey viewed the Internet's value as a "huge and easily accessible library of information" to be much more important than publishing student work or communication and collaboration for students and teachers. By 1997, information retrieval was seen more universally among network coordinators as the Internet's most important value. Similarly, when asked in 1997 to rank order five possible values of the Internet, Internet-using teachers ranked "access to a huge variety of curriculum relevant information for teachers and students" far higher than any of the other choices which all relate to collaboration, communication, and participation in projects and products.

These survey results suggest that during the short period of three years (1994–7) there was rapid implementation of technology and a broadening of the base of users within the schools but imperceptible change in terms of the kinds of reforms sought by the initiators of these efforts. Using the Internet as a library resource requires minimal change in the fundamental culture and way of life of a school, in comparison with the other kinds of agendas listed in Table 4.2.

With the benefit of the survey data and a period of analysis and reflection, we can, in retrospect, see what the organizers of the NSN could not have understood at the time. They faced two major challenges that were not then understood or even formulated. First, the NSN sought to facilitate learning about emerging new modes of teaching, learning, professional development, and community interactions that are made possible through Internetworking. An assumption was made that since the innovators and early adopters of telecommunications networks in education had been involved in virtual communities, such practices would become widespread across a school once the enabling technical infrastructure was built and more users came on board. However, the majority of the people newly adopting the use of the Internet in the member institutions were not (yet) very much interested in these educational innovations. In other words, the nature of change within member institutions was different from the predicted changes. Second, the NSN sought to facilitate learning and collaboration across institutions through a virtual community. However, the majority of the people in the member institutions were not (yet) participating in *any* virtual communities. Therefore, as the use of the technology moved beyond the innovators and early adopters to the majority, it became less likely that these new users would contribute their voices, agendas, and experiences to the learning collaborative of the NSN.

Interdependence of NSN Virtual Community and School/Community Projects

Our claim of interdependence between NSN as a virtual community and the changing practices in its member institutions and communities is most clearly demonstrated by the relationship between NSN participation and schools' involvement in local community projects. A school's use of the Internet to foster closer linkages with its local community was a high priority for the NSN because of the original question (see earlier) that was posed about local taxpayers' perceptions of the benefits of communication networks for education. Using the 1997 NSN survey data, Becker attempted to predict "school use of its network resources to support its local community" (SUNRSLC) from sixteen diverse variables including demographics, school organization and climate, network infrastructure, teachers' skill and knowledge, teachers' use of the Internet, and participation in the NSN. School size, type, and demographics did not affect the likelihood of school–community projects, and none of the network infrastructure variables made a significant difference. In other words, the extent and nature of the technical infrastructure did not predict a school's use of its Internet resources to support the local community. The more district support and principal leadership, the more likely schools were to use their network facilities to support their local community.

The percent of teachers within a school that were knowledgeable Internet users and leaders (defined by *many* different survey items) was a strong predictor: the schools with Internet-knowledgeable teachers are the ones that were opening their resources to the community. However, mere broadening of participation in the Internet across teachers and subjects did not make any difference at all. Moreover, with the percent of knowledgeable/skilled Internet teachers in the equation, the district support and principal leadership variables drop out (i.e., their influence on SUNRSLC comes by affecting the spread of knowledgeable/skilled teachers). A significant predictor was how active the school was in the NSN activities and how tuned in they were to other NSN organizations. The more involved schools were in the NSN, the more likely they were to use their network resources for the benefit of their local community.

It is interesting now in light of these understandings to examine the methods used by the NSN to support learning in a virtual community in relation to the kinds of changes taking place within the local communities and member institutions.

Collaborative Exchange Models Tested by the NSN

The NSN used a variety of mechanisms to foster collaborations among member institutions in support of the reform agendas of its founders (Hunter, 1997a). These devices included, for example, a members database to make it easy for members of the NSN to become aware of each others' work and contact each other. The mechanisms for exchange also included:

- Case studies of member school–community projects,
- Online real-time "events" in partnership with members,
- Telementoring initiatives,
- Professional development initiatives,
- Moderated Exchange Desks,
- Face-to-face workshops,
- Monthly electronic newsletter,
- Monthly partner profiles,
- Technical and curriculum assistance at member schools.

The following describes some of these efforts and their relationships to the changing practices at member institutions.

NSN Case Studies of School–Community Projects

The NSN helped participating institutions exchange information concerning creative ways in which the schools and their local communities were working together and taking advantage of the evolving information infrastructure. (Goldman & Laserna 1997; Becker 1996a). Based on the experiences reported by NSN members, case studies and project vignettes were organized in the following categories: project-based learning with the community as an audience and resource, school-to-work experience, tutoring and mentoring including telementoring, community volunteers in schools, community service learning for students, community leadership roles for schools, community education, and family–school connection.

The collection of school–community projects information on the NSN Exchange was one of the most extensive such collections to be found in any one place. The hope was that communities would be inspired by these stories to initiate or strengthen their own community-based programs. Furthermore, analyses of the cases enabled insight into the processes by which school–community programs get initiated and institutionalized.

However, as compelling as these leading-edge examples are, such practices require a kind and level of school restructuring and curriculum reform that had not yet taken place on a widespread basis by 1997. In 1995, 28 percent of all NSN schools at the time reported at least one type of organization that was the beneficiary of students' Internet-related community service. For instance, a social studies class might learn about local government by building Web pages for the local government departments. Or a local business might donate equipment in exchange for having school students train the company's employees in the use of Internet tools. That percentage of schools was seen as fairly substantial in 1995. However, this aspect of student–school community leadership did not spread very fast. In 1997 only 33 percent of all NSN survey-responding schools involved students in an Internet-related community service activity, a mere five percentage points more than two years earlier. The most common target for service learning was local government agencies: 16 percent of NSN schools help there, while 11 percent helped local businesses. Middle schools are most likely to have students do Internet-related service learning (40 percent), somewhat more than high schools (34 percent) (Becker, 1997).

Similarly, only 14 percent of the *strongest* Internet-using teachers said that their students create Web pages as a service to others, such as community organizations, and the median number of students participating per teacher was only five. On the other hand, over half of the network coordinators reported that their school facilities were used to train parents or community members to use the Internet. Also, over half of the schools had "class or individual projects where the Internet was used to acquire information from community members or groups."

Online Real-Time "Events" in Partnership with Members

The NSN also organized over thirty-five live, online events, both text-based (Ichat, WWW chats) and video-based (CU-SeeMe computer videoconferencing), for schools in its network (Goldman, 1998). One goal for these events was to encourage students to be communicators and producers of knowledge and opinions rather than only recipients of information. These events also served as a catalyst for teacher and administrator understanding that the Internet could be used to open the classroom walls and to develop new forms of pedagogy. Another goal was to foster and strengthen partnerships among schools, businesses, and other organizations in local communities.

The live events involved adults and children in addressing local, national, scientific, and cultural issues. These events were then archived in the Exchange. In "Memphis Kids 'N Blues," student musicians presented original jazz compositions and talked with classrooms around the country. In science Events, students exhibited their science projects on topics ranging from environmental issues to medical breakthroughs. Working scientists contributed commentary to online conversations led by the students themselves. A modern composition, "Mahler in Blue Light," was broadcast from WGBH, an NSN partner. Music performance, appreciation, and curriculum merged as students listened and engaged in live conversation with composers and performers via the Internet. Children's Express presented an online chat and explored child labor conditions in Bangladesh. At the Earthwatch Annual Meeting, ground-breaking technology supported a "Virtual Expedition" project in Mexico, demonstrating the ability of teachers and students to communicate with researchers "in the field."

In general, these real-time events served as a bootstrapping activity to help mobilize local community collaborations around networking for education. For some school communities, participation in live NSN events by notables such as President Clinton, various Senators and congresspeople, children's authors, famous scientists and astronauts, and local experts called the attention of the local community to the potential of networking to enrich schooling. Net Day participants who helped build school networks were able to see educational applications of the technology. Through these events, NSN helped nonprofit organizations such as museums and science centers find ways to organize and deliver their valuable content to schools. Businesses and corporations having tools and technology to offer had opportunities to test educational applications of those tools and intellectual resources in schools. Their visibility in the NSN Exchange in turn attracted the interest of other corporations to participate. The number of corporations joining the NSN grew by ten in early 1997, and these have all been actively participating. Approximately fifty organizations contributed to the invention, delivery, and testing of new event-based and telementoring learning opportunities for students and teachers. Contributions are in the form of tools (e.g., Ichat, RealAudio, White Pine videoconferencing, Yahoo, Newsmaker), content (such as that provided by WGBH, CNN, Turner, EarthWatch, *Christian Science Monitor*, Children's Express, *Wall Street Journal*, Democratic National Committee, Cybersmith, and Parents Paper), and experts' time (e.g., Senators Edward Kennedy, Barbara Boxer, Lahey, NASA astronauts). In sum, real-time events were useful for helping diverse members of a local community to learn how to work together for mutual benefit, with each institution contributing its own unique resource to the activity and obtaining support from the others. Such collaborative efforts, if they were to become institutionalized, would constitute a major change in the educational system of a local community.

Unfortunately, the NSN and its member communities encountered technical and educational challenges in implementing these "events" and in ensuring their educational value. Even schools in the NSN – which have a robust technical infrastructure with Internet access for all – needed much technical assistance to enable classroom teachers to access and manage a real-time online event. Often the technical infrastructure was not adequate; for instance, inadequate bandwidth or the machines in the particular classroom are not powerful enough for the application. Bolt, Beranek, and Newman (BBN) as the intermediary institution had to supply a range of different kinds of technical, educational, and management expertise to make these events work. Teachers needed a long lead time for planning an educationally sound series of activities in preparation for such events, and in obtaining the support of their school's technical coordinator. Unless events coincided with planned curriculum, such activities were seen as supplemental, rather than integral to, the curriculum.

With respect to the events' effect on school practices, as indicated in Table 4.3, among teachers who used the Internet most frequently with their students, about 18 percent had their students participate in live events, with a median of twenty-three students. These results indicate

Table 4.3. *Internet-Using Teachers in NSN Schools Report on Students' Participation in Collaborative Learning Activities Online (Becker, 1997)*

Q-20   Below is a list of network learning activities. Indicate which of these activities you have had students participate in at school *since September*, and roughly how many students have participated.

Have you had students do this since September? If yes, how many students?

Instructional Activities:	% Yes	# Yes
c) On-going email exchanges between individual students (e.g., pen pals)	28	67
f) Collaborative math or science investigations	21	51
j) Follow scientists doing work around the world as they are doing it	21	49
l) Participate in live events, such as interviews, over Internet	18	43
d) On-going email exchanges between whole classes	15	36
k) Telementoring email exchanges between students and adult mentors	15	37
h) Be part of live chats involving students in different schools	14	32
n) Videoconferencing over the Internet	8	19
e) Collaborative writing projects with classes in other schools	7	17
o) Tutor or receive tutoring from other students via email	5	12

that it was the innovative and early adopter teachers who participated in this type of collaborative networked activity. This finding is consistent with our earlier observations about the nature of change in the NSN institutions during this period.

NSN Support for Telementoring

The NSN leadership in telementoring grew out of a motivation of some of the members who wanted their students to have opportunities to publish their work and get educationally useful feedback from audiences outside of school (Goldman, 1997). NSN hosted a conference for leaders of telementoring projects; organized extensive Web pages of information on existing telementoring programs; developed a Web-based tool called Mentor Center for managing telementoring relationships among a teacher, mentor, and mentee; and organized a number of telementoring projects. Examples of telementoring projects included the following: accomplished teachers mentored novice teachers to help them observe and analyze others' practice as a way to improve their own; graduate education students mentored high-school students in writing; lawyers in a law firm mentored sixth graders in writing; and bank employees mentored middle- and high-school students in a business-apprenticeship program.

In the 1997 NSN survey, out of the group of teachers who most often use the Internet with their students, 15 percent said they have their students participate in telementoring, with a median number of twelve students involved. Five percent of this teacher group have students tutoring or receiving tutoring from other students via email, with a median of seventeen students involved per teacher.

Although the extent of participation within schools was relatively small, telementoring emerged as one of the most educationally valuable and technically implementable models for collaboration at the early stage of telecommunications use in schools and communities. Within the NSN virtual community, a great deal was learned about telementoring as a result of the various experiments and collaborations on this topic. The following information was acquired: (a) telementoring is a meaningful and practical way to demonstrate the value of connectivity as it augments the resources available to the student, the classroom, and the teacher; (b) telementoring does not require as a prerequisite that major curriculum reforms have yet taken place; (c) industry recognizes that young people must be exposed to the skills they will need to perform productively in the workplace; (d) telementoring is a vehicle for exposing students to real-world experience and as a support for school-to-work programs;

(e) with telecommunications, mentors can be drawn from all segments of the community–local businesses, professionals, parents, and grandparents; (f) telementoring has low barriers to entry and does not require a large investment of time by a mentor to make a contribution; and finally (g) it can be adapted to work in a variety of settings – peer-to-peer, one mentor to a team, or one-to-one student to mentor.

NSN Support of Virtual Communities for Teacher Professional Development

One of the NSN visions for the use of the Internet was support of teachers' professional development. Innovations in teaching and implementation of new standards and curriculum often require that teachers learn to rethink their craft, their basic pedagogical teaching approach, and their goals for students. The founding members of the NSN thought that the Internet would help teachers to implement reforms by providing them with opportunities to collaborate and reflect with other teachers and experts outside their schools, obtain evaluations of educational materials, author new learning materials, and so forth.

The NSN model for professional development was aligned with its philosophy of fostering local capacity building through collaboration and knowledge building nationally. The Online Internet Institute (OII) was developed to help educators learn to use the Internet to shape curriculum and to connect them with local and national colleagues. The OII grew from the vision of two classroom teachers, Ferdi Serim and Bonnie Bracey, who saw involvement with the Internet community as an important part of professional development. OII stressed knowledge building – from offering mentoring to teachers in the use of the Internet to helping them develop curriculum with the resources they find online. Their experiences also carried over to having students in the classroom do similar work. The OII sought to build a virtual community in which teachers who learn Internet skills go on to mentor other teachers, offer constructive feedback on the projects they create, and share educational strategies online. The online component of OII occurred through an NSN server. Face-to-face workshops were essential for building local capacity. They were held at sites around the country and internationally.

In addition to its support for the OII, the NSN provided the underpinning for another national initiative in professional development led by Al Rogers. The acclaimed and corporate-supported CyberFair (Global SchoolNet, 1997a) educational contest was an outgrowth of NSN research, as acknowledged in the CDROM "Harnessing the Power of the

Web" (Global SchoolNet, 1997b). Rogers said, "This event could not have taken place without the research funding provided by the Testbed" (personal communication, August 1996). Thus, CyberFair is an example of how the NSN is being leveraged and amplified beyond the original scope.

However, few of even the strongest Internet-using teachers reported engaging in the OII sort of activity.* About 15 percent reported posting a message to a news group or electronic mailing list of educators daily or weekly. About 7 percent reported participating in a real-time chat about educational issues monthly or more. In fact, in the 1997 survey, Internet-using teachers were asked to rank the importance of possible reasons for using the Internet. These teachers ranked "life in a technological society" as the most important reason. Generally seen as unimportant were reasons like "new teaching practices," "reduce professional isolation," or "support school change."

Although school practices in professional development did not change significantly during this period, the innovators who did participate in this virtual community learned a great deal. The OII evaluation report (Ravitz & Serim, 1997) pointed to a growing area of interest – the creation of interactive teaching portfolios on the Web and the requirements for structuring the presentation of these for collaboration and evaluation by others. Syntheses of discussions and a focus on reflective dialogue (Spitzer, Wedding & DiMauro, 1994) is needed.

From the outset of the NSN, it seemed obvious that a major benefit of Internetworking for schools would be the creation of new opportunities for professional development of teachers. At a time when major new curriculum standards are being established and implemented in schools, districts, and states, the networks could enable new possibilities for teachers to learn about the standards and how to implement them. What happened instead was that Internetworking itself posed a new, additional set of requirements for teachers' development. Teachers needed to learn not only how to use the tools of Internetworking but also how to take advantage of these new information resources in their classrooms. Ravitz (1998) analyzed responses of Internet-using teachers to a series of questions concerning their own level of skill in performing Internet-related tasks such as using a search engine to find information, putting files on a server for others to access, and participating in an Internet Relay Chat (IRC)

---

* Although teachers did not report much direct use of the Internet for their own professional development, they did see themselves as changing their classroom practices in part as a consequence of their having their students use the Internet (Hunter, 1998).

discussion. He found a strong correlation between these responses and teachers' extent of use of Internet in their classrooms. This process turned out to be much slower than we originally expected, with the consequence that, in general, the major curriculum reforms and standards implementations have yet to take advantage of Internetworking in NSN schools.

NSN's Moderated Exchange Desks

Six Exchange Desks, similar to traditional Internet newsgroups, were established by the NSN. In these, members, with the assistance of a Desk moderator, exchanged information and ideas on major topics of relevance to the purpose of the NSN. The discussions created a Web-accessible archive of know-how and resources, with links to relevant member Web pages. The six Desks included: Local Information Infrastructure (LII); Professional Development; Standards, Evaluation, and Assessment; Curriculum and Instruction; Reference; and Dissemination.

As discussed earlier, in general only the innovators and early adopters within the schools contributed to knowledge exchanges like the Exchange Desks. However, they often served as intermediaries between the NSN virtual community and the more mainstream stakeholders within their local communities. For example, many NSN members responded to requests by administrators for information concerning their local Acceptable Use Policies for students.

NSN's Face-to-Face Workshops

People from 101 different NSN member organizations participated in face-to-face workshops, usually held in conjunction with national conferences. These meetings were essential for identifying common requirements and opportunities, providing professional recognition to members' accomplishments, and setting agendas for NSN work. The pioneering spirit and nature of members' work provided strong motivation to drive further collaborations among subgroups of the membership. For example, the telementoring initiatives were formulated as an outcome of a face-to-face meeting.

NSN's Monthly Electronic Newsletter

The newsletter contained articles by individual members, projects of the NSN, and news of general interest to members. The newsletter was sent electronically via email to about 450 members and listservs and is archived on the NSN Web page (nsn.bbn.com/news/newsletters/index.shtml). Members contributed or requested articles on particular issues facing decision makers, such as how leading-edge school communities have addressed issues about acceptable-use policies. The NSN newsletter was used by people within the member organizations for purposes such as informing others in their own institution about the nature and importance of their innovations. The high quality and authoritative character of the NSN provided innovators within a member institution with legitimacy; for example, some members used the NSN newsletter to achieve local and national recognition for their work. They reported receiving numerous contacts, both locally and nationally, based on their articles in the NSN newsletter.

NSN's Monthly Partner Profiles

Profiles championed the work of a member organization by putting a profile of its work at the top level of the NSN Web page. Profiles included Co-Vis, a National Science Foundation network for visualization of scientific phenomena; Science Learning Network, a collaborative of six science museums; Eisenhower National Clearinghouse, offering an extensive online collection of science and math resources and curricula; Madison, Wisconsin's Metropolitan School District, making history available online; The Sharing Place, an early childhood collaborative; Earthwatch, a scientific research institute; and the Hewlett-Packard E-mail Mentor Program connecting school-age students to HP employees around the world. The Partner Profiles proved to be an easily implemented method for bringing important, leading-edge work to the attention of the NSN members. Mechanisms like the community case studies, newsletters, and monthly partner profiles helped to create a sense of community across the NSN by helping the members to learn about the ways in which their colleagues in other institutions were addressing issues similar to the issues emerging in their own localities.

NSN Technical and Curriculum Assistance at Member Schools

The NSN in collaboration with The Math Forum (www.mathforum.org) conducted an experiment to find out what it will take for a school or school district to integrate Internet-based educational resources fully into their Local Information Infrastructure (NSN Newsletter #16,

1996). Supported by the National Science Foundation, The Math Forum is a comprehensive source of resources and learning activities in mathematics education. Staff members of both The Math Forum and the NSN conducted workshops in selected schools to facilitate teachers' use of the resources on The Math Forum. The schools were selected because at least a few teachers had indicated interest in instituting curricular change. Even in the NSN schools, which are more advanced than typical schools with regard to technical infrastructure, many teachers did not have ready access to the Internet in their classrooms. Even teachers who did have access needed the support of a technical person on a regular basis if they were attempting to do something new.

From a curriculum standpoint, the NSN and Math Forum staff members also encountered a "chicken-and-egg" scenario in which the Internet resources were perceived by math coordinators and teachers as being external to their own local curriculum. They were less than eager to invest the time needed to integrate those resources into their curriculum. Ironically, this was true even in a school where a new "investigations"-oriented math curriculum was being implemented. This experiment seems to indicate that there are more prerequisite "readiness" conditions to integral use of Internet-based resources in the curriculum than the pioneers originally anticipated.

Summary: Interdependence of Learning in the NSN Virtual Community and Change in NSN Members' Local Communities

The survey data from NSN member schools provide indicators of the extent and direction of changes that were taking place within these schools and their school communities with respect to Internet-working, teaching, learning, and school–community interactions. By reviewing the content and mechanisms employed by the NSN virtual community in relation to those changes in the local communities, we can gain insights into the NSN as a learning community – who was learning, what was being learned, and what mechanisms supported that learning. For those educational leaders who want to set up virtual communities that will serve the learning needs of the majority of people within their school or other institution (as opposed to the innovators and early adopters), some important lessons can be learned from the NSN experience. Certain kinds of changes need to take place in the local institution for the majority to benefit from the virtual community. In the next section, we will examine some of these interdependencies from the perspective of change (or the lack of it) within a local institution and school community.

Interdependence of Virtual Communities and Change in Educational Institutions: Examples from the DoDEA Model Schools Program

Our claim that learning in virtual communities is interdependent with the institutional context of the participants is reinforced by attempts to create virtual communities with teachers and students in the Department of Defense Dependents' Schools. In this section, we reverse perspective from the NSN case by looking at virtual community from the point of view of one local community, its context, and the local change factors that affected the ability of its teachers and students to learn in virtual communities.

Institutional Context: DoDEA and Aviano Air Base

The Department of Defense Education Activity is composed of the Department of Defense Dependents' Schools (DoDDS), serving dependents of U.S. military and civilian employees in foreign countries, and the Domestic Dependent Elementary and Secondary Schools (DDESS), serving military dependents in the United States and its territories. In the 1997–8 school year DoDDS served a total of about 81,000 students in 161 schools. DoDDS staff numbered 9,500 in fourteen countries around the world. DoDEA is a Department of Defense field activity operating under the direction, authority, and control of the Deputy Assistant Secretary of Defense for Personnel Support, Families, and Education. There are fourteen District Superintendents in DoDDS, reporting to a Europe Area Superintendent and a Pacific Area Superintendent, each of whom reports to the Director of DoDEA, located in Virginia. Decisions about school improvement priorities, budgets, curriculum standards, learning materials, school staffing, technology, and professional development are made at the headquarters in Virginia. Local schools do not have a local school board and have little or no control over budgets, technology plans, hiring, testing, school improvement priorities, or professional development strategies and opportunities. The school system annually publishes on the Internet and in news releases the standardized test scores for specific grade levels in each individual school (www.odedodea.edu/profiles).

School–Community Context: Aviano Air Base, 1995–1998

One of the DoDEA school communities is located at Aviano Air Base in northern Italy, about fifty miles north of Venice. Aviano is headquarters of the 16th Air Force and the base of the 31st Fighter Wing. Since 1994, military personnel stationed at Aviano have been engaged in a variety of high operations of the United States and NATO, such as peace enforcement operations in Bosnia-Herzegovina, northern Iraq, Albania, and Kosovo. Military parents often work long hours and extra shifts and are sent on temporary tours of duty away from home base, resulting in stress for families and children. There is no on-base housing for American military families in Aviano – families live in various Italian villages and towns spread over hundreds of square kilometers, resulting in many transportation issues and costs for families and the schools. Physical facilities on the base, including schools, are overcrowded and in a continual state of construction and redevelopment. Because of the Air Force's high state of operational readiness in Aviano, personnel mobility rates are very high. In the 1997–8 school year, the mobility rate of students of the elementary schools serving the air base exceeded 50 percent.*

Four schools serve the families of U.S. military and civilian employees of Aviano Air Base. Table 4.4 summarizes student population and teaching force of the schools at three locations, which are geographically separated by a twenty-minute drive.

As indicated in Table 4.4, the schools experience very high student mobility rates and had a very high rate of administrative turnover between 1995 and 1998. All the schools have different principals and assistant principals today than when the project began. Such high levels of administrative turnover make implementing administrative leadership for a schoolwide reform effort nearly impossible. The teachers in the Aviano Air Base schools are highly experienced. On average, those surveyed in the fall of 1996 reported 21.1 years of teaching experience. The school community situation of the Aviano Air Base and the DoDDS system results in stressful working conditions for teachers. Although the causes of

---

* The mobility rate refers to the percentage of students who transfer into or out of the school within a given school year.

Table 4.4. *DoDDS Schools Serving Aviano Air Base*

School	1995–6 # Students	1997–8 # Students	% Racial or language minority	1997–8 Student mobility rate	Admin turnover 1995–8	% Teacher > 10 years teaching
Aviano H.S. (7–12)	425	438	43	22%	300%	95
Aviano E.S. (preK–6)	532	650	40	49%	400%	80
Vajont E.S. (preK–6)	221	175	37	53%	200%	100
Pordenone E.S. (preK–6)	189	135	38	49%	0%	92

stress and workload in these schools may differ from those at schools in the United States, these working conditions are not unlike conditions in many other schools in the United States.

Model Schools Program and the Vanguard for Learning Project

In 1995, the Aviano schools applied and were selected by DoDEA to become part of the NSF-funded Vanguard for Learning project, one part of the DoDEA Model Schools program. The goal of the Vanguard project was to help the school community build the capacity to invent, implement, test, and evaluate innovations in learning and teaching that take advantage of technologies and to feed back the lessons learned to the larger school system. The overall Vanguard model and research questions are described elsewhere (Vanguard for learning, 1999). A central organizing structure of the Vanguard for learning project is the Team Action Project (TAP).

TAP Strategy and Resources for Learning and Change

The basic premise of the TAP structure and strategies is that a small group of teachers forms a project because the members share a common vision for how to improve learning and teaching of their students. Thus, the members of the TAP share a sense of ownership of the project. TAP is a structure for initiating, organizing, planning, implementing, evaluating, and communicating new ways of teaching, assessing, learning, collaborating, building knowledge, and organizing schoolwork. All teachers, administrators, and parents in the Aviano–Pordenone–Vajont school complex in the spring of 1996 were invited to create TAP teams based around their own shared visions for improving their teaching and better meeting students' and families' needs. TAPs were encouraged to incorporate the following elements into their projects:

- Have at least two leaders (i.e., cannot be an individual project),
- Address one or more of the DoDEA School Improvement Plan (SIP) benchmark priorities,
- Integrate subject matter across the curriculum or articulate curriculum across grade levels,
- Engage parents and other members of the local community in the learning and teaching process,
- Broaden student roles in the classroom and school community,
- Apply electronic technologies to the innovations.

Depending on the nature of the project, a TAP might include two or more teachers, a specialist, an administrator, parents, students, and outside experts. Teachers formulated and conducted their own investigations into the improvement of teaching and learning in a very concrete way. For instance, science teachers in grades 5 through 11 tried having high school students serve as cross-age peer teachers for elementary students, teaching them how to use microcomputer-based laboratory probes. Teachers and other TAP members identified areas of curricular and instructional needs, SIP priorities, and opportunities that may come from applications of new technologies. They investigated resources and methods that others have used to address similar needs. With various forms of support, they constructed innovative teaching practices and learning environments that they implemented with their students, tested and evaluated, and disseminated to other teachers and stakeholders in the local community and school system. Support included professional development opportunities, equipment and software, technical and educational consulting, assessment support, and help with dissemination.

Approximately fifty teachers from the four schools have participated or are currently participating in one or more of fifteen TAP teams. The participation rate is a little under half of all teachers in the four schools.

Table 4.5. *Percentage of Teachers Reporting Use of Certain Resources for Their Own Learning – TAP Vs. Non-TAP Participants*

Professional Development Resource	TAP % Using	Non-TAP % Using
Italy DSO workshops	50%	28%
Teachers in my school	82%	61%
Students in my school	77%	44%
Principal	41%	6%
Parents and base personnel	50%	28%
School computer teacher	55%	33%
SIP/SILT meetings	86%	47%
World Wide Web pages	77%	44%

As of Fall 1998, the elementary school TAPS were growing in teacher participation. TAP teachers made rapid strides in their own professional development, taking advantage of many different kinds of resources for learning. According to self-report surveys, TAP teachers went up from 60 percent "learning from teachers in my school" in January to 82 percent in May. They went from 46 percent "learning from students" in January to 77 percent in May. In contrast, only 44 percent of non-TAP teachers reported learning from students in May. Table 4.5 shows differences between TAP and non-TAP teachers in their reports of using some resources for their own learning.

The rapid learning and accomplishments of the TAPs is evidence that major changes can take place in a school community even under less-than-ideal conditions. However, even this high level of involvement and innovation was not sufficient to overcome institutional obstacles to learning in a *virtual* community.

Attempts To Create Virtual Community for Professional Development

As a part of the DoDEA Model Schools Vanguard for Learning project, researchers, teacher educators, educational technologists based in the United States attempted to form virtual communities with teachers in DoDDS schools in Italy. One mechanism developed for this purpose was a for-credit online course through California State University, San Marcos. Academic credit, paid for by the grant, was offered for teacher participation in these activities.

Even though the teachers involved in the TAPs developed and tested their innovations and grew professionally, efforts to create a virtual community were almost totally unsuccessful. The external research group originally expected far more use to be made of telecommunications networks, online collaborations, and student participation in online projects than occurred. This expectation was based on previous experience with teacher networks, the geographic isolation of the Aviano schools from other American schools in the United States, and the fact that DoDDS was making a major investment in telecommunications infrastructure for the schools.

Several reasons have been identified for teachers' unwillingness to take advantage of virtual communities for their own professional development. The first reason involved a problem of timing; the network infrastructure was unstable at the time the activities were initiated, so there were technical obstacles for those teachers who participated. However, as indicated in Table 4.5, 77 percent of TAP teachers did report using the World Wide Web for their own learning, so the technical infrastructure could not have been a major obstacle. Instead, the main obstacle was the culture of the schools. Teachers did not feel comfortable collaborating in an online medium. Several teachers expressed fears that their email was monitored by officials in DoDEA; therefore, they were afraid to engage in discussion and dialogue over the networks. One teacher observed:

DoDDS teachers are NOT used to sharing their thinking and being open to making BIG mistakes. They are so closely supervised and evaluated . . . that they are afraid to make major blunders or to think freely and perhaps support something that later turns out to be unpopular or against DoDDS policy.

Although these teachers had been using cc:mail for several years, most of them actually did not know how to send a message to an email address outside of the DoDDS cc:mail directory. Some believed DoDEA policy prohibited them from doing so. Figure 4.1 depicts the message that flashes across the screen when anyone in a DoDDS school logs on to a workstation connected to the LAN (i.e., when network services such as printing, Internet, and cc:mail are needed). The message is foreboding and a stark contrast to the collaborative spirit that the TAPs teams were building. To overcome the teachers' fears of online collaboration, the school system

---

*** W A R N I N G ***

THIS IS A DEPARTMENT OF DEFENSE (DoD) COMPUTER SYSTEM. ALL DoD COMPUTER SYSTEMS AND RELATED EQUIPMENT ARE INTENDED FOR THE EXPRESS USE OF COMMUNICATION, TRANSMISSION, PROCESSING, AND STORAGE OF OFFICIAL U.S. GOVERNMENT OR OTHER AUTHORIZED INFORMATION ONLY. ALL DoD COMPUTERS ARE SUBJECT TO MONITORING TO ENSURE COMPLIANCE WITH APPLICABLE REGULATIONS AND U.S. CODES, PROPER FUNCTIONING OF EQUIPMENT, TO PREVENT UNAUTHORIZED USE, DETERENCE OF CRIMINAL ACTIVITY, AND FOR OTHER SIMILAR PURPOSES. USE OF THIS EQUIPMENT CONSTITUTES CONSENT FOR THIS MONITORING. ALL USERS OF THIS DoD SYSTEM SHOULD BE AWARE THAT INFORMATION PLACED WITHIN IS SUBJECT TO REVIEW. IN ACCORDANCE WITH U.S. CODE, TITLE 18 AND AR 380-19 ANYONE FOUND IN VIOLATION OF SECURITY, COPYRIGHT, OR OTHER LAWS AND REGULATIONS ARE SUBJECT TO PROSECUTION OR APPROPRIATE DISCIPLINARY ACTION.

Figure 4.1. Warning message on DoDDS school computers.

would have to send a very concrete message through the chain of command that the policies had changed. Administrators and teachers would need more than statements that teachers were encouraged to take advantage of the networks for their professional development. They would need evidence, perhaps in the form of headquarters-sponsored online forums. For instance, the school system headquarters could put on their World Wide Web site a forum or threaded discussion group labeled and structured for particular groups of teachers across the system, such as a music teachers' forum. To change teachers' expectations and understandings of policy, the headquarters would need to further facilitate and reward participation by teachers in a very visible way. The point here is that the needed changes went beyond factors that could be changed by working only at the local level.

Where School Policies, Operations, Training, and Infrastructure Interact: The Case of the Writing Conference Partners Project

The Writing Conference Partners (WCP) project was one of the fifteen TAP projects. This team had a well-defined pedagogical innovation and a plan for testing it. Their idea was to have their students serve as writing conference partners for each other via email, rather than in the face-to-face classroom setting, as was their usual practice. Students would be paired with a student from one of the other two teachers' classrooms for the duration of a particular writing assignment. This TAP illustrates the reciprocal relationship between local and virtual community factors, in this case an attempted virtual community for students across three schools.

The initiators of the Writing Conference Partners project were three highly experienced teachers of writing in grades 4, 5, and 7 in three separate DoDDS school buildings in Italy. The lead teacher of this project was experienced with how students work as writing conference partners: in this pedagogical technique, students help each other in their individual writing process. In addition, the teachers had experience as teacher researchers and had previously conducted classroom research in this area. The teachers had also worked collaboratively. Finally, the technology application required for this experiment – email – was considered the easiest, simplest technology to apply. Indeed, the external research group viewed this project as a "quick win," one that could provide a role model of technology-based innovation teacher research. It was also an educationally sound innovation and would take advantage of the telecommunications and computer infrastructure to create virtual communities.

Over two school years, the efforts of the Writing Conference Partners and those attempting to support their work uncovered several interrelated systemic factors that are critical to the future and broader role of technologies in DoDDS. In two years of effort involving teachers, technologists, administrators, and outside experts, this team was not able to get all their students to send and receive electronic mail among three DoDDS schools. In theory and by general policy, "all DoDDS students have email accounts." However, the schools' cc:mail systems and servers were configured to send and receive students' email only internally within a school building and not outside of the local school. Some but not all students knew how to use their cc:mail accounts, and no systematic training was provided at any grade level. Technical support services were not prepared or assigned to provide support for maintaining student cc:mail accounts. Different staff and administrators had different beliefs concerning the policies and procedures for providing and maintaining student email accounts. For example, a plan to include the parent consent form for student cc:mail, in the school registration packet was not implemented due to lack of clarity on policies.

For this TAP project to work, several changes must take place both in the local school and in the school system. These changes include clear, detailed policies and the communication of policies throughout the school community, technical infrastructure aligned with policies, regularized training of all students in use of the technology, staff assignments for operating and maintaining the systems, and technical support for new applications of technology in the classroom.*

Implications for Future Virtual Communities and Educational Change

Internetworking provides us with new choices about the extent to which we merge activities, roles, and institutions previously separated in time and space – activities such as learning, teaching, working, playing, collaborating, and governing (Hunter, 1997b). With benefit of experience and data from testbed virtual community efforts of the past decade (Hunter 1992, 1993), we are now in a position to understand the interactions between learning in virtual communities on the one hand and changes in local communities on the other. Pioneering individuals (the innovators and early adopters of Moore's framework) can benefit from participating in virtual communities relevant to their learning needs, almost irrespective of the local conditions in which they live and work. By definition they are willing and able to overcome all sorts of obstacles to try out new practices that appear promising to them. If we are to place a high priority on offering these new learning opportunities to *all*, then local educational institutions and communities need to change along with the evolution of virtual communities. The culture and skills of

---

* The experience in the DoDDS schools helps to clarify the implications of the finding cited earlier about student email in NSN schools. Recall that few schools in the NSN provided all students with email accounts. But as the Writing Conference Partners illustrates, all students need to have and use email accounts if typical teachers will have them participating in email-based projects or virtual communities. This is another illustration of the challenge of "crossing the chasm." Innovator and early adopter teachers for over a decade have found ways to engage their students in networked learning communities and projects. They are willing to invest the extra time and effort needed to overcome the institutional technical and policy barriers to participation. More typical teachers believe it is beyond the scope of their job to teach students to use an email account, obtain permissions from parents, nag technical support staff to update student account records, and so forth. Typical teachers believe that if the school system wants students to participate in such activities, then the necessary infrastructure and student training will be made a regularized component of the school's operation. Hence, in the majority of NSN schools, and in the DoDDS schools, student participation in email-based projects was limited. This finding was at first a surprising since this genre of networked education project was one of the earliest kinds of network-based learning activities, hundreds or thousands of such projects exist, and many are free (Hunter, 1993).

collaboration that are the sine qua none of virtual communities need to be fostered within the local organization. This means that the designers and implementers of new virtual communities for learning need to work hand-in-hand with leaders in the local institutions that are the everyday worksite for the potential members of the virtual community. Some policies and procedures typical of traditional educational institutions must change if they are to cross the chasm between the early adopters and the majority. For instance, support and incentives for teachers' ongoing professional development need to be in place and regularized. Management and the allocation of time within a school must become more flexible to enable teacher collaborations locally as well as in the virtual community. Technology initiatives must be tied more closely to school improvement priorities and associated budget opportunities. Conversely, the virtual community needs to stay closely attuned to changing priorities, agendas, capacities, and participant groups from the local communities.

Designers and leaders of virtual communities must continue to provide appropriate social organization, technical tools for communication and information management, and content within the networked social space of a collaboratory. However, they must also help the local institutions and communities change in ways that benefit everyone.

Acknowledgments

This work was supported by National Science Foundation grant number RED9454769 and grant number REC9896243. The findings and conclusions reported here, however, do not necessarily reflect those of the funder.

References

Becker, H. (1996a). *The local community can become an important focus of school network activity*, [World Wide Web page]. Available: nsn.bbn.com/community/hb_sch_com/sch_com_toc.html [27 November 2001].

_____ (1996b). *National School Network Testbed Phase 2: Baseline survey of testbed-participating schools.* Report presented for the National School Network Workshop at the National Educational Computing Conference, Minneapolis, MN. Available: www.nsn.bbn.com/resources/research/overview.html [27 November 2001].

_____ (1997). *Two years of progress in the national school network schools.* Paper presented at TelEd*97, Austin, TX. Available: www.gse.uci.edu/Ravitz/becker_teled97/overheads_explained.html [27 November 2001].

Becker, H., & Ravitz, J. (1997). *The equity threat of promising innovations: The Internet in schools.* Paper presented as part of the Internet and Equity in Education

Symposium (Phillip Bowman, Chair) at the 1997 SPSSI Conference of the annual meeting of the American Psychological Association, Chicago. Available: www.gse.uci.edu/Ravitz/equity.html.

Becker, H. J. (1999). *Internet use by teachers* (Report No. 1). Irvine: University of California, Irvine, Teaching Learning & Computing study, Department of Education.

BrownLAB (1999). *Electronic collaboration: A practical guide for educators.* Providence, RI: Brown University, Northeast and Islands Regional Educational Laboratory.

Goldman, M. (1997). *School–community partnerships: Potential hero in today's transformation in two years of progress in the National School Network schools.* Paper presented at TelEd*97, Austin, TX. Available: www.gse.uci.edu/Ravitz/school_community_partner.html [27 November 2001].

—— (1998). *Telecommunications changes the relationship between schools and their communities.* Paper presented at Consortium for School Networking 3rd Annual Conference: K-12 School Networking on the Information Superhighway, Washington, DC. Available: www.gse.uci.edu/Ravitz/MGoldman_CoSN98.html [27 November 2001].

Goldman, M., & Laserna, C. (1997). Building school community relationships: National School Network testbed research [World Wide Web page]. Available: nsn.bbn.com/resources/research/buildsch_com.html [27 November 2001].

Hunter, B. (1992). Linking for learning: Computer-and-communications network support for nationwide innovation in education. *Journal of Science Education and Technology, 1*(1), 23–34.

—— (1993). NSF's networked testbeds inform innovation in science education. *T.H.E. Journal,* October.

—— (1994). Overview National School Network testbed [World Wide Web page]. Available: www.gse.uci.edu/Ravitz/overviewNSNT.html [27 November 2001].

—— (1995a). Learning and teaching on the Internet: Contributing to educational reform. In B. Kahin and J. Keller (Eds.), *Public access to the Internet.* Cambridge, MA: MIT Press, pp. 85–114.

—— (1995b). *Internetworking and educational reform: The National School Network testbed.* Paper presented at the 1995 INET Conference in Hawaii. Available: www.isoc.org/HMP/PAPER/065/html/paper.html.

—— (1997a). Fostering collaborative knowledge-building: Lessons learned from the National School Network testbed. In B. Collis & G. Knezek (Eds.), *Teaching & learning in the digital age: Research into practice with telecommunications in educational settings.* Eugene, OR: ISTE. Paper presented at the Annual Telecommunications in Education (TelEd) Conference, Austin, TX. Available: http://nsn.bbn.com/dissemination/docs/Hunter_TelEd97.html

—— (1997b). Learning in an internetworked world. In Institute for Information Studies (Eds.), *The Internet as paradigm.* Queenstown, MD: Institute for Information Studies.

—— (1998). Internetworking and educational reform: Are these different subjects? Paper presented at the annual meeting of the Committee on School Networking (CoSN), Washington, DC. Available: www.gse.uci.edu/Ravitz/cosn98.hunter/.

Math Forum. (1999). The Math Forum [World Wide Web page]. Available: www.mathforum.org [27 November 2001].

Moore, G. (1991). *Crossing the chasm: Marketing and selling high-tech products to the mainstream customers.* New York: Harper Collins Business.

Newman, D., Bernstein, S., & Reese, P. (1992). *Local infrastructures for school networking: Current models and prospects.* BBN Report No. 7726. Cambridge, MA: BBN Corporation.

NSN Newsletter 16, (1996), Available: nsn.bbn.com/news/newsletters/index.shtml [27 November 2001].

Ravitz, J. (1997). *What do Internet-using teachers say about their Internet use?* Paper presented at Tel*Ed97 in session titled Two Years of Progress in the National School Network Schools, Austin, TX. Available: nsn.bbn.com/ nsn_learnings/iut.html [27 November 2001].

(1998). *Conditions that facilitate teachers' Internet use in schools with high Internet connectivity: Preliminary findings.* Paper presented at the annual meeting of Association of Educational Communications and Technology, St. Louis. Available: www.gse.uci.edu/Ravitz/Ravitz_AECT98.html.

Ravitz, J. & Serim, F. (1997). *Summary of first year evaluation report for the Online Internet Institute.* Proceedings of the Edward F. Kelly Evaluation Conference, State University of New York, Albany. Available: copernicus.bbn.com/Ravitz/ oii_summary.html.

Spitzer, B., Wedding, K., and DiMauro, V. (1994). *Fostering reflective dialogues for teacher professional development.* Cambridge, MA: TERC. Available: www.terc.edu/papers/labnet/Guide/Fostering_Refl_Dialogues.html [27 November 2001].

TEECH (1997).Teacher Enhancement Electronic Communication Hall [World Wide Web page]. Available: teech.terc.edu [27 November 2001].

Toward universal participation in the NII: Phase 2 of a National School Network testbed. (1994). Proposal submitted to the Program on Networking Infrastructure for Education, NSF 94–5, National Science Foundation. BBN Proposal P94-STD-354, April 1994. Available: www.gse.uci.edu/Ravitz/TB2_proposal.pdf [27 November 2001].

Vanguard for Learning (1999). All Vanguard reports [World Wide Web page]. Available: learning.bc.edu/vanguard [27 November 2001].

Part Two

Structures and Community

5 Evolution of an Online Education Community of Practice

Mark S. Schlager, Judith Fusco, and Patricia Schank

[Teachers] have no time to work with or observe other teachers; they experience occasional hit-and-run workshops that are usually unconnected to their work and immediate problems of practice. [Effective professional development cannot] be adequately cultivated without the development of more substantial professional discourse and engagement in communities of practice.

–Darling-Hammond & Ball (1997)

One important role for technologies is as the backbone for an invigorated, vibrant professional community among educators. This will not happen, however, without considerable effort to design the technologies and the social structure of their use with this objective made explicit.

–Hawkins (1996)

The concept of *community of practice* has become a major theme of teacher professional development (TPD) research and practice. Advocates argue that communities of practice (CoPs) can be powerful catalysts for enabling teachers to improve their practice (Lieberman, 1996; Rényi, 1996). A growing body of TPD policy research (e.g., Loucks-Horsley et al., 1998; Darling-Hammond & Ball, 1997) is beginning to converge on a common set of effective professional development characteristics that stem largely from CoP concepts. For example, Lieberman's (1996; Lieberman & McLaughlin, 1992) research on teacher networks builds on CoP concepts of social networks (Wellman, 1997) and community gathering places (Oldenburg, 1997). Lieberman (1996) describes how informal retreats and dinner meetings help build professional relationships and socialize new members into the fold, thereby solidifying teachers' commitment to the community.

Professional development approaches that embody CoP characteristics (e.g., teacher collaboratives, subject-matter networks, professional

129

development schools, and school–university partnerships) have proven successful in local TPD reform projects (National Science Foundation, 1997; Stokes et al., 1997). Unfortunately, few local reform efforts have been able to sustain momentum beyond the life of the outside funding (Bush, 1997; McLaughlin, Mitra & Stokes, 1999) or to scale up to meet statewide needs (Corcoran, Shields & Zucker, 1998). Most TPD programs still take the form of traditional in-service days or workshops that do not reflect the characteristics and approaches of effective TPD suggested by research.

Although the TPD policy literature has not focused on technology's role in transforming, sustaining, or scaling up CoP-based TPD efforts, the studies cited earlier can be interpreted as providing a set of design requirements for developing a technology infrastructure to support TPD efforts that are transformative, sustainable, and scalable. State and local governments are spending hundreds of millions of dollars to install computers and network access in all classrooms and many more millions to train teachers to use the technology. Education technology research suggests that TPD and education reform programs can help leverage investments in school technology and the cultural incentives of "getting online" by employing Internet technology in the service of online CoPs for education professionals (Hawkins, 1996; PCAST, 1997; Becker, 1999; Pea, 1999). However, neither large investments in technology nor online TPD projects have reliably resulted in the kind of online community that is sustainable enough to support in-service teachers as they engage in the three- to five-year endeavor of classroom reform or scalable enough to support teachers as they enter the profession and grow professionally toward mastery (Corcoran, Shields & Zucker, 1998). We believe that this failure is due to the absence of effective models for both online professional development and online community.

In this chapter, we provide an overview of an online CoP model that is designed to match carefully Internet technology affordances (and constraints) with effective CoP-based community-building and professional development strategies. Our goal is to evolve a sustainable, scalable CoP for K–12 education professionals as they learn the ropes of their profession, implement new practices, and apply new content knowledge. We provide evidence of how our online CoP model supports both TPD providers and teachers as the community has grown and evolved over the past three years. We conclude with a discussion of attributes that lead to scalable, sustainable online education CoPs and of the roles such CoPs can play in systemic reform projects.

Taking Communities of Practice Concepts Online

Three years ago, we set out to establish an online TPD research testbed that could support thousands of teachers' professional activities while forging the kind of professional community that TPD policy researchers have found to undergird successful local school reform efforts (e.g., Little, 1994; Lieberman, 1996; Darling-Hammond & Ball, 1997; Loucks-Horsley et al., 1998). We have drawn many of our ideas and design guidelines from the CoP literature.

Brown and Gray (1995) define workplace CoPs as small groups of people held together by "a common sense of purpose and a real need to know what each other knows." George Pór (www.co-i-l.com/coil/knowledge-garden/cop/definitions.shtml) describes a CoP as "more than a 'community of learners,' a community of practice is also a 'community that learns.' Not merely peers exchanging ideas around the water cooler, sharing and benefiting from each other's expertise, but colleagues committed to jointly develop better practices." In the CoP literature, learning is viewed as a social activity that occurs as newcomers and journeymen move through an established community's professional hierarchy toward expertise (Lave & Wenger, 1991; Brown & Duguid, 1996; Wenger, 1998). Learning opportunities occur primarily through informal interaction among colleagues in the context of work. Newcomers gain access to the community's professional knowledge in authentic contexts through encounters with people, tools, tasks, and social norms. New practices and technologies are adopted by the CoP through the evolution of practice over time. Thus, a CoP can be an effective *hothouse* in which (a) new ideas germinate, (b) new methods and tools are developed, and (c) new communities are rooted. The CoP can help professionals gain access to, and facility with, ideas, methods, content, and colleagues; help novices learn about the profession through apprenticeship and peripheral participation; and enable journeymen to become valued resources and community leaders through informal mentoring and participation in multiple work groups.

On the surface, the characterization of CoPs as relatively small groups of people in a single workplace appears inconsistent with the goal of supporting large numbers of teachers engaged in learning new practices across grade levels, subjects, and organizations. We believe, however, that the two can be quite compatible. Members of a professional CoP often come from a larger network of colleagues spanning multiple organizations, drawn to one another for both social and professional reasons. A recent study by Andersen Consulting of online CoPs in several large corporations found that such CoPs work best as catalysts for innovation and learning when they exist outside the institutional controls and constraints of individual organizations (Cothrel & Williams, 1999). CoPs that cross organizational boundaries can grow and evolve over time as groups form and disband, projects begin and end, and individual members participate actively for a period of time, go dormant, and then find new opportunities to participate. Through organic growth, an online education CoP can achieve the economies of scale, diversity, and informal communication channels needed to spread innovation and become an ever-widening source of expertise.

Tapped In® Online Environment and Education CoP Model

In most workplaces, professionals have access to several computing and communications tools and workspaces that (a) support work practices of large numbers of different groups; (b) enable users to know whom they are interacting with and what is going on around them; (c) allow users to create, store, and share discourse objects (e.g., notes, overhead slides, Web page bookmarks); (d) communicate in real-time or asynchronously as the need arises; and (e) engage in group activities hosted by organizations as well as their own circle of colleagues. At the outset of our project, we recognized the challenge that the lack of technologies commonly available to CoPs in other professional fields presents for an education CoP. Telephones, fax machines, private offices and meeting rooms, document and enterprise servers, and videoconferencing are rare among teachers. However, just as professional CoPs outside of education are making more and more use of the Internet, intranets, and enterprise portals for communication (Constant, Sproull & Kiesler, 1997) and information management (Cothrel & Williams, 1999; Murray, 1999), so can education CoPs (e.g., Schofield et al., 1997). Access and bandwidth are still limiting factors, but they are no longer insurmountable barriers (Becker, 1999; CEO Forum on Education and Technology, 1999).

Our challenge was to instantiate the CoP affordances enumerated earlier as best we could within the constraints of most teachers' environment – no private offices, telephones, or high-bandwidth technologies, with only basic access to the Internet. The result is a work in progress called Tapped In® (TI). TI is an online education CoP where educators can attend activities hosted by a variety of education organizations, conduct their own online activities, or expand their circle of colleagues by participating in communitywide activities. The technology underlying TI is a platform-independent, Web-enhanced, multiuser virtual environment designed to support the needs of education professionals and TPD organizations over time (see Schlager & Schank, 1997, and Schank et al., 1999, for a more complete technical description). Activities occur (in real time or asynchronously) in virtual rooms that provide a basic set of communication mechanisms (speaking, whispering, paging, executing nonverbal actions) and support tools (e.g., virtual whiteboards, shareable text documents, Web page projection, transcript recorders).* As technology in schools advances, we add new capabilities.

In concert with our technology development, we have developed a two-pronged approach to cultivating an online CoP (described in more detail in Schlager, Fusco & Schank, 1998/1999). First, we invite organizations that serve teachers or other education professionals (e.g., school librarians, principals, district staff) to be *tenants* in the TI environment and use it to help accomplish their own TPD agendas. We recognize their expertise in TPD content and pedagogy, and they rely on our environment and online collaboration expertise. Second, because TI is not dedicated solely to one project or organization, we actively encourage any individual education professional or small group to join, help shape, and take ownership of the community. We host online communitywide activities to help acculturate nonaffiliated members to the community, and we provide services to help them create their own learning experiences.

Our current tenants include nationally recognized education organizations (e.g., Lawrence Hall of Science, Wiesenthal Museum of Tolerance, American Association of School Librarians), educational Web site hosts (e.g., The Math Forum, ED's Oasis), teacher preservice and master's degree programs (e.g., Pepperdine University, University of Illinois), and state and local education agencies (e.g., Kentucky Department of Education, Los Angeles County Office of Education, New Haven USD, Joint Venture: Silicon Valley Challenge 2000). By offering their TPD services in TI, the organizations enable their affiliated teachers to gain access to expertise, ideas, and resources (human *and* information) that no single organization could provide by itself. In return, the organizations receive support from the TI staff and from each other as they learn how to work effectively with teachers online. They also gain access to a cyber-ready pool of participants for their programs. Together, our members (more than 5,800 as of October 1999), tenant organizations (15 as of October 1999), and their activities make up the fabric of our CoP.

---

* The reader is encouraged to see www.tappedin.org/info/webtour.html for an illustration of the graphical user interface or to simply log in.

Consistent with CoP research, the primary catalyst for our growth is teachers' changing roles and contexts. For example, Pepperdine University School of Education students graduate and go into leadership positions in local and state education agencies. Lawrence Hall of Science summer institute attendees become resources for other science teachers in their districts. In these new roles, they bring more teachers into the community. Even a single workshop class visit to TI can result in a cadre of new members. One member describes his experience, which led to his introducing sixty-five of his colleagues to TI:

> This all started with my exposure to Tapped In in [professor's name] Instructional Technology classes at [name] University. . . . I did a one-credit independent study with [professor's name] as part of the course where I worked with a couple elementary science teachers for content support. In my work in these courses I would occasionally talk about Tapped In. Twice each month, throughout the school year, [name] our supervisor for library and information services in [school district], holds a countywide meeting for our school-based library media specialists (one for secondary and one for elementary). One day, [colleague's name] suggested that we should hold one of our countywide meetings in Tapped In. The January meetings were targeted. The rest is history.

In the three years since TI opened, we have seen many groups come and go without jeopardizing the growth of the community. Several of our early tenants have dropped out of TI, but each left behind a small proportion of affiliated teachers who have remained active and brought in new members in new contexts. For example, we recently received an email from a member who joined as part of a summer institute in 1997. She is now leading her own TPD project and is training a new cadre of teacher to use TI in the same suite of rooms that her old cadre used in 1997. She writes (edited):

> We've dedicated the [old room] in the [old project] suite to this project since we learned about TI to be able to do this [new] project. Folks on Saturday liked the idea of having a place of their own to meet. And that's not even counting their own virtual offices which they also relished. You do a real service to public school teachers by allowing them their own offices!
>
> We're using TI to continue to teach the solar astronomy of this project. Participants will work with staff at [university] to learn to operate [university's] telescope remotely. They'll have remote astronomy software running on the Web and will talk to staff on TI as they maneuver the telescope from their school. Since few have access to long-distance phone lines at school (and their principals would balk at the cost of the phone calls), but they all have Internet connections, TI makes the instruction possible.
>
> We'll also use TI to work on three-person investigations using a multimedia program called Astronomy Village. Each person takes an assigned role; TI will allow a group to confer about their progress and where the investigation will head

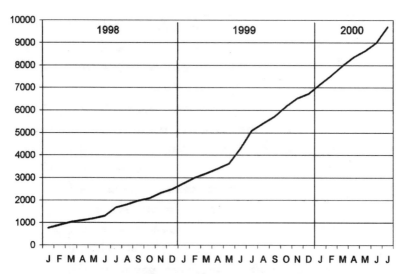

Figure 5.1. Tapped In® membership growth, January 1998 to July 2000.

next. I'm so psyched about this part that I'm going to participate in one of the groups.

And Thursday, I'm teaching my husband, dean and professor at [another university], how to use TI. I've been singing its praises and want him to see the possibilities. By the way, the help desk person Saturday and Sunday morning was awfully nice.

Another sign of TI's evolution as a CoP has been our growth both in number of members and in rate of participation since we began collecting data in February 1997.* During this period, our membership (Figure 5.1) and monthly log-in rate (Figure 5.2) have grown steadily in proportion to one another. Approximately 15 percent of the total membership log in per month, on average, no matter how large the community. TI members tend to be active for a period of time and then go dormant for some time before logging in again, as illustrated by the following email from a long-dormant member who wanted to attend an upcoming event:

I enrolled in Tapped In sometime last year. I received a character and a pw from TI, but then had a lot of work to do at school and haven't visited in probably 6 months.... When I visited this time, I couldn't access my character so went in as guest.... Could you please up-date my pw and give me any other updating info I might need.

---

* Although our grant funding, partnerships, and summer training workshops have been responsible for much of our growth, we must also acknowledge a wave of events and advances that we were fortunate enough to ride. These included ISPs offering free email accounts, Java-enabled browsers (which boosted our user interface capabilities), and rapid increases in processor speed and Internet access bandwidth in schools and at home.

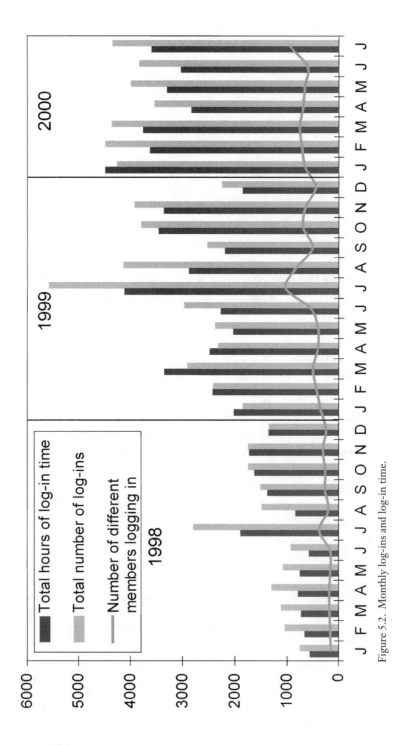

Figure 5.2. Monthly log-ins and log-in time.

136

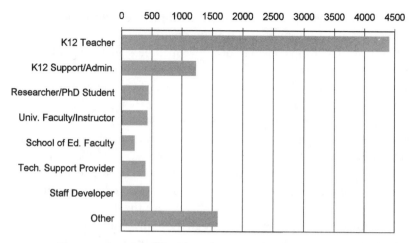

Figure 5.3. Tapped In® membership by occupation, July 2000 (n = 9,159).

Another indicator of CoP health is the ability to attract a population with diverse interests and expertise within the profession. Approximately half of our members describe themselves as K–12 teachers. The balance is composed of researchers and graduate students, university faculty, school of education faculty, technical support providers, staff developers, school support and administration staff, preservice teachers, and "other" (Figure 5.3). The proportions have remained relatively steady as the community has grown, indicating that we continue to attract a diverse range of new members as we grow. Below we provide additional evidence of the utility, sustainability, and scalability of the TI CoP model over the past three years.* We begin with a summary of some of the first data we collected in TI, data without which we could not proceed in growing the community.

Evolution of Group Discourse Norms and Skills

TI was founded on the basic premise that teachers could engage in professionally meaningful and productive discourse online. We, therefore, had to demonstrate not only that teachers could converse socially online (chat rooms are full of teachers) or post messages (teacher newsgroups and listservs abound) via text, but that they could achieve the same types of group objectives as they could in face-to-face meetings (e.g., brainstorming, decision making, informing, knowledge building).

---

* We do not address in this chapter the issues of financial sustainability or technical scalability, both of which we recognize as critical to the success of the model.

We began by experimenting on ourselves, using the environment as the primary means of communication among our research team.

Our research group consisted of twelve members, including TI developers with considerable experience in online synchronous communication and researchers who had not previously used TI or any similar system. Members of the group were widely dispersed geographically. Biweekly meetings occurred regularly throughout our first year. As with any newly formed multidisciplinary group, we had to learn each other's jargon and interpersonal styles. We also had to develop our own norms for interacting as a group. We were all used to the social constructs of face-to-face meetings – rapid-fire dialogue, long monologues, whispered side comments, topic shifts – and the skills needed to break into the dialogue at just the right moment or guide a meeting through the items on an agenda. We had to learn how to replicate these elements of meetings and group dynamics by expressing ourselves through a very narrow-bandwidth medium: typing lines of text.

An analysis of the transcripts from our meetings revealed many episodes of knowledge building, mentoring, and argumentation and resolution, all key characteristics of productive group work (see Derry et al., 2000). Our discourse was not without instances of miscommunication, confusion, and frustration at the pace of progress, but our ability to function more and more effectively over time as a team online suggested to us that staff developers and educators could also hold productive meetings online.

Discourse Analysis of Online TPD Meetings

To test our conjecture, we analyzed the online meeting discourse of participants in a TPD project designed to help high school and community college teachers learn new tools and strategies for teaching earth and space science. The TPD project began with two 2-week summer institutes in July and August 1997. Seven teams of two to four high school and/or community college teachers attended each institute to gain hands-on experience with software and techniques used in earth and space science. They received TI training on one morning of the institute. The teachers' objective during the institute was to begin to develop plans for inquiry-based learning projects that they would ultimately implement with their students. The project director decided to conduct periodic online meetings with the fourteen teams over the course of the school year to obtain updates on their progress in the classroom.

Project staff held three sets of real-time meetings in TI, in October 1997, January 1998, and May 1998. At least one representative from each of the fourteen teams was asked to log in and report on their progress, obstacles, and lessons that they wanted to share with other teams. Transcripts of all the meetings were collected via TI's automated transcript-logging mechanism and analyzed by research staff. The participants gave us permission to have their online meetings recorded for research purposes. The TPD project ended after the May sessions.

Our primary goal was to determine whether the cohort could conduct its business through online meetings and how the discourse evolved over time. We were also interested in how the dialogue might be affected by extraneous social conversation and by technology constraints, two factors that have led to criticism of text-based conversation in chat rooms. A coding scheme was developed to quantify the structure and flow of the online meetings, based, in part, on studies of face-to-face dialogue in collaborative design group meetings (Olson et al., 1992). We coded each utterance (and nonverbal action) as an instance of one of seven categories of discourse. The transcripts were read by two researchers, who applied the coding scheme independently and then came together to calibrate their findings. Differences between the two coders' ratings were resolved by a third reviewer. Here we summarize our findings from the four most frequent categories of discourse:

- Business focused – Comments related to a meeting agenda topic or other project-related point of discussion.
- Meeting management – Comments and actions related to the scheduling, meeting norms, meeting roles, follow-up, and structure of the meeting, including who is in attendance or absent or whose turn it is to speak.
- Technology related – Comments related to the use of TI or other online technology, including technology complaints and praise, questions, and answers to technology questions.
- Social – Social conversation not related to the specific business at hand, including greeting and exiting pleasantries, jokes, and digressions.

According to Olson et al. (1992), a typical face-to-face meeting consists of approximately 50 to 60 percent business-focused utterances supplemented by social and meeting management dialogue. Our data show that the online meetings approached this benchmark over time (see Figures 5.4 and 5.5). The relative proportion of business-focused entries increased from an average of 25 percent in October to about 50 percent in May.

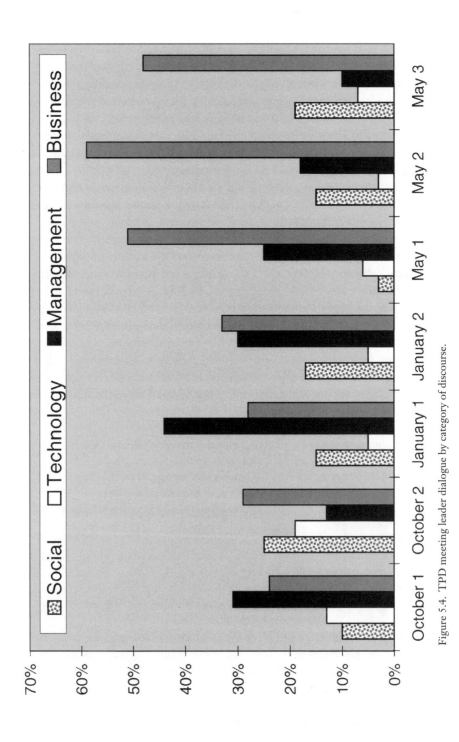

Figure 5.4. TPD meeting leader dialogue by category of discourse.

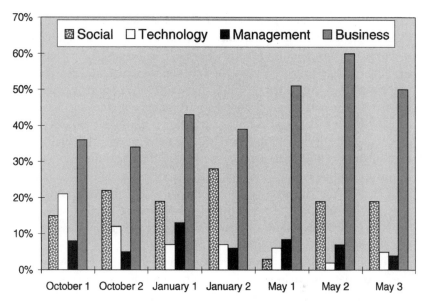

Figure 5.5. TPD meeting participant dialogue by category of discourse.

In the October and January meetings, the proportion of business-focused entries by meeting leaders as a function of their total entries was about 10 to 15 percent lower than the proportions of teachers' entries. By May, however, both leaders (Figure 5.4) and teachers (Figure 5.5) were devoting 50 to 60 percent of their entries to business-related topics, indicating that they were engaged in a balanced dialogue.

As expected, technology-related utterances were highest in October and declined in overall proportion to a steady rate of approximately 5 percent of all utterances as the users gained experience with the system. The transcripts show that technology-related entries did not decline further because new users attended the January and May meetings; they had to overcome some of the same difficulties that participants in October had already overcome. Figures 5.4 and 5.5 also show that leaders and teachers engaged in roughly equivalent proportions of social conversation across meetings, indicating that social conversation in the context of professional meetings is independent of familiarity with technology. As in face-to-face meetings, attendees greeted one another before the meeting was called to order, engaged in collegial banter, and often stayed behind at the end of a meeting to converse.

Finally, meeting management utterances were highest in the first set of meetings, when the professional development leaders were inexperienced at moderating an online meeting and the teachers were inexperienced in participating in one (much cross-talk was observed early on). A spike in meeting management utterances was observed in the first January meeting for the meeting leaders (Figure 5.4) because of a change in meeting management style introduced by the leaders to improve the flow of the meetings. After that meeting, the percentage of time leaders spent on meeting management declined to 10 percent in the final meeting, in accordance with patterns found by Olson et al. (1992) in face-to-face meetings. The decline in meeting management can be attributed to the development of (a) effective online meeting leadership skills and (b) group norms for online communication as the teachers became more familiar with each other, the style of communication, and the technology. We were particularly pleased to see that the proportional decline in meeting management by leaders was replaced by an increase in business-focused utterances.

The analysis showed that the meetings held in TI were in many ways similar to meetings held face to face. In both modes, meeting leaders attempt to keep the discussion on task to get through an agenda. Multiple threads of conversation emerge; some are carried through to conclusion, and others are not. Participants sit through presentations, holding whispered side conversations as they await their turn to present. New participants arrive late, disrupting the flow of conversation while they greet the others. In face-to-face meetings, presenters complain about computer and projection devices not working or traffic delays in getting to the meeting. In TI, participants complain that they lost their connection or their ISP is slow.

Face-to-face and online meetings also differ in important ways. For example, in face-to-face meetings, visual and auditory cues and social taboos prevent people from talking over one another, ignoring a question, or holding unrelated conversations. Such conventions must be relearned in online discourse, as illustrated in the following excerpt from one of the meetings. DonB is taking his turn presenting to the group. The meeting leader is Heather. Karla has been typing what she is going to say in her presentation and discovers that she does not know how to save what she has typed and participate in the current conversation without blurting out what she has typed to the group. She decides to barge in:

> *DonB*: I have used the internet for info on earthquakes, weather. . . . In fact my students successfully predicted the storm we are experiencing at the moment. We have also done several exercises using GPS.
>
> *FrancisB*: did you have the students work in groups or as individuals?

KarlaW: Can I barge in now? I finished typing something. And I don't know how to split it up with this request. Keep addressing Don if you want. I spent some time with the Tapped In folks in Menlo Park CA earlier this month as a representative from . . . [the utterance goes on for several more sentences]

HeatherU: Point of order . . . lets give Don feedback first, then we can move on to Karla's report which was projected. We'll give her a chance to "talk"; too. "presenters" let us know when you are done reporting out too. thanks.

Over time, the meeting leaders learned to orchestrate meetings effectively, and the teachers were shown how to queue up their presentations, resulting in organized, business-related discourse. Social banter that is characteristic of collegial groups was present but did not interfere with the meetings. Although the quality of discourse improved over several months, we believe that it could have improved much faster if the group had (a) begun meeting sooner following the summer institute, (b) met more frequently, or (c) had prior experience with online discourse. The lessons we learned from this experience have helped other groups in the community hold productive meetings more quickly. Moreover, TI members who have learned the ropes of online discourse in one context have been able to transfer those skills and group norms to new groups and contexts, making their initial investment more valuable over time.

Evolution of TI Community Services

Approximately half of our members and scores of small, local educator groups across the country have found TI through a Web search, listserv, newsgroup, or colleague's suggestion. TI enables these members (as well as those who are affiliated with a tenant) to derive value through community support services and activities that we and the members themselves organize. These activities not only enable members to receive assistance when needed but also enable members to serve as resources for other members. Through the process of acculturation to the community, online tools and practices become part of a teacher's palette of teaching and learning skills, and teachers gain the confidence to work collaboratively online.

We have developed several ways to scaffold members in that process, including our real-time Help Desk, After School Online discussions, and MeetMe mailing list. Our goal is to help users progress from novice to participant to leader in the community. Our key to achieving this goal is our Community Director, who devises the activities and services that keep people coming back to TI. The Community Director role includes event organization, volunteer recruitment, mentoring, and technical support (and, in our case, also research). The Community Director must continuously take the pulse of the community, plan new activities, and provide new services. We describe some of the Community Director's accomplishments.

Community Help Desk

Scores of guests and new members log into TI each week. Although some have been through TI training or are experienced enough in Internet environments to figure out how to communicate and get around within a few minutes, most are not. New members need to learn the ropes, and in our CoP model, more experienced members show them through their own example. The Help Desk is often the first helping hand that new members receive as they learn the ropes, as illustrated in the following email sent from a teacher in Cleveland to her colleagues after logging in to practice before her first online meeting:

I don't know if anyone has visited TAPPED IN yet. I spent my lunch hour today doing just that. Mostly, I was getting acquainted with how it worked. It was really neat that teachers from Kentucky, Pennsylvania, and Indiana were there with me. There was someone else online with us, BJB. He/she was someone designated to help new users and answer questions. My first visit was not only painless but enjoyable. The bell, ending my lunch period, seemed to ring too quickly. What was funny was, that as I was typing about how the bell had rung and I had to go . . . two other teachers typed the same thing! I had this picture of the whole Eastern United States changing classes at the same time!

We began the Help Desk by posting one of the TI staff in Reception (where people land by default when they log in) during business hours to answer questions, offer tutorials, and give tours. We soon found that (a) we were not able to sustain the service staffed only by the researchers *and* do any research, and (b) many members began to "hang out" with the Help Desk staffer in the reception area. Seeing an opportunity, we began to actively recruit veteran members of the community to volunteer as Help Desk staff. The volunteers "apprentice" to an experienced staffer for a period of time until they feel comfortable "holding down the fort" on their own. Help Desk staff often share tips, FAQs, and notes that they have written to answer common questions. The following (edited) transcript illustrates how a guest (Kathy) is greeted, in this case by a staff member (Marty), a volunteer (Charlie), and an apprentice (Carol):

> Marty waves hi to Kathy.
>
> *Marty* [to Kathy [guest]]: Can I answer any questions for you?
>
> *Kathy* [guest]: Do I have to be in a room ?
>
> *Marty* [to Kathy [guest]]: You ARE in a room called Reception.
>
> *Kathy* [guest]: Where is everyone and is anyone discussing University requirements for a FL?
>
> *Marty* [whispers, to Kathy [guest]]: Type WHO to see all the people who are currently logged in and their location.
>
> *Charlie*: FL?
>
> *Kathy* [guest]: Thanks Marty. Who are you?
>
> *Kathy* [guest]: Charlie – foreign language.
>
> *Charlie*: I'm Charlie xxxxxxx.
>
> *Marty* [to Kathy [guest]]: I work here at TAPPED IN. Charlie is a Spanish teacher.
>
> *Charlie*: I'm leading a group right now that is learning to use Tapped In. Hola.
>
> *Marty* [to Kathy [guest]]: Maybe Charlie can help answer your question.
>
> *Kathy* [guest]: Hola Charlie. Un amigo me dijo que hoy iba a tener una discusin entre maestros de español.
>
> *Kathy* [guest]: Id like to discuss what colleges are doing in the way of placement tests in Spanish. My darlings think they take two years and veg.
>
> *Marty* [to Kathy [guest]]: Right now, this is the place to be. Charlie is busy with 10 teachers of his own right now so he will take a while to answer you.
>
> *Charlie*: Kathy, I'd like to invite you to a discussion group at 2:30 p.m. about FL teaching.
>
> Charlie projects Agenda.

Foreign Language Discussion Group 11/18 Agenda
2:30 Welcome, introductions and ground rules.
3:00 Input on discussion topics for this group. Everyone is welcome to say what they want to discuss. Charlie will share material on Keypals and Project-based learning.
3:30 Coloquio en español para profesores

Kathy [guest]: I'd like to practice before then. What do I need to do?

Marty [to Kathy [guest]]: For the meeting, you only need to talk. we have a few ways to talk. Carol will help you learn them.

Carol [to Kathy [guest]]: I can help you with some of the basics before the meeting.

Carol [to Kathy [guest]]: "We can go to the After School Online room -just type aso"

Kathy [guest] says, "Thanks Marty. Hi Carol"

Kathy [guest] leaves for the ASO.

Carol leaves for the ASO.

Variations on this scenario are played out several times each day in TI, not only by staff and volunteers but by the members themselves. We believe that the Help Desk is one of the key factors in TI's success. Teachers tell us that we are the only resource on the Internet where they are greeted personally with an offer of assistance when they log in.

After-School Discussions

Another example of how we are scaffolding the community as it develops its own activities, social norms, and identity is our After School Online (ASO) discussion series. ASO is a weekly series of hour-long real-time discussions on topics suggested by the community and led by volunteers recruited from the community. Education organizations and independent consultants also hold ASO sessions to publicize their projects and interact with teachers. The topics for the month are announced to all TI members via an email newsletter and on a Web calendar. Those wishing to participate simply log in at the scheduled date and time. ASO is evolving into an important way to indoctrinate new members, a dissemination mechanism, and a way to help new or potential partner organizations learn how to use TI effectively.

ASO has no full-time discussion moderator; members of the community learn to conduct their own online sessions from participating and observing their peers. Each session begins with introductions. The leader prepares a series of notes about the topic (as is done in "brown-bag" seminars) in advance and projects them (like overheads) to the participants as conversational props. They are also able to project a Web page to the computer screens of others (who are using our TAPestry Java client) to lead a virtual Web tour.

Typically, sessions have attracted three to eight participants, a size that is manageable for a novice leader. In the first ten months of the program

(11/97 through 8/98), a total of 492 members and guests (181 unique people) attended eighty-six ASO sessions on over forty wide-ranging topics such as Internet Technologies, Connecting Cable TV, Literature, The Modern Presidency, and How to Lead Online Collaborative Projects. In the subsequent twelve months (9/98 through 8/99), a total of 731 participants (368 unique people) attended eighty-five topical ASO sessions (137 participants were guests). Many more attended ASO sessions that were new-member orientations (not included in the preceding counts). We are pleased not only that we have attracted a wide variety of participants (not the same small core of people), but also that a significant number of participants have found enough value in the sessions to return for other sessions. As one session leader summarized his ASO experience: "I may not get that big an audience for my After School Online talks but I have had some of the greatest conversations anywhere with the folks who do show up!"

We are also encouraged by the desire of education organizations to hold their own online events in TI. Having attempted to host their own chat rooms in the past, many groups now recognize the value of (a) our support services and (b) introducing their teacher affiliates to a community in which they can become a regular participant after the event. The following email announcement illustrates how an education organization blends asynchronous discussions on its own site with ASO sessions in TI:

You are invited to attend a FREE Online Event on: "Using Learning Styles to Improve Student Success", October 12–14, 1999, sponsored by the Distance Learning Resource Network (DLRN). Participants will have a chance to identify their students' preferred learning styles (as well as their own), and to discuss how integrating preferred modes of learning into their existing classes can improve the student learning experience.

Dr. Carla Lane, who has many years of experience in distance learning and applying learning styles, will moderate. Participants will ask questions, share comments, read background materials, and participate in both message forums (asynchronous) and a real time (synchronous) break out session. This is an ideal opportunity for both teachers and distance learning instructors interested in learning styles, multiple intelligences, assessment, and media selection.

Event Logistics:
Most activities will happen in the Online DLRN Interactive Learning Environment October 12–14. In addition, the real-time session will be part of the Tapped In's Community "After School Online" on Wednesday October 13 from 4.00–5.30 P.M. Pacific Time, or 7.00–8.30 P.M. Eastern Time.

The following email to our Contact Us email help line illustrates the reciprocal value such events have for the TI community. The sender indicates that he is going to introduce his class to TI. It is likely that some members of the class will become TI members:

I teach models of education and just beginning to relate to online learning. I hold a class Wednesday from 4PM to 7PM Colorado time. I would like to get familiar with your site and sign on ASAP before my class tomorrow. So we as a group can see the event "discovering learning styles" and interact with others, I will facilitate my group. I asked for a password today & this is my first experience with your organization.

Free Private Offices

Most teachers do not have offices in real life. Early on, we thought that having their own online *place* might motivate some teachers to experiment with online activities. We decided to offer free bare-bones offices (a room and a whiteboard) to any member who wanted one. We began with seventy-two offices and have over time added fourteen new floors. Offices have become one of our most popular features (even though we conjecture that most members rarely use their office). More than 600 of our 1,080 offices are now occupied by individual members or small groups. One preservice teacher discovered that if she kept her bookmarks in her TI office, they would always be available no matter where she logged in (a computer at home, one at a university, and another at her internship school). Other offices serve as a clubhouse for small groups of education professionals looking for an online venue to hold group meetings. Such groups rarely have the resources or expertise to set up an online collaboration environment of their own. However, they do often have innovative ideas and highly motivated members. We have developed formal partnerships with nine organizations that started out experimenting in TI with a single office.

Newsletters and Mailing Lists

Membership in TI can be thought of as similar to belonging to a professional society. Many of us belong to professional societies (e.g., ACM, IEEE, AERA) that we rarely if ever participate in actively, but we feel that we benefit from the association even if we only attend a conference or read the organization's periodical on occasion. In TI, we do not expect all members to log in all the time. Many log in regularly for a month or two and go dormant for months, only to surface again when a need or interesting event arises. To keep both active and inactive members connected to the community, we have established an electronic newsletter called *On the Tapis* (an old English phrase meaning under consideration) and a calendar of events that go out to all members monthly. Our intent is that, when members read about an activity, new tenant, or new feature that interests them, they will be motivated to check it out. The following email illustrates how the calendar mailing and ASO sessions go hand in hand to encourage member participation:

I would like to request a transcript of the Web Quests After School Online session with Bernie Dodge, scheduled to be held this Wed. p.m. Sept. 22. I'm going to try to attend the session online, but just in case I don't make the whole thing, a transcript of the meeting would be super. Thanks very much!

Many members (we estimate 30 to 40 percent) have not logged in past their first visit, and that is all right with us. Some log in after many months away; others never log in again but promote the community in other ways. The following email is from a project director wanting to publicize his project to teachers. He was told about TI by a colleague who had been in TI only once during a training session over 18 months ago. She had been receiving our monthly newsletter, *On the Tapis*, ever since:

Hello Tapped In! I am wondering if you can post this announcement ON THE TAPIS. One of your members, [SETI staff], referred me to your web-site. We are looking for high school science teachers in the San Francicso Bay Area to pilot test the SETI Institute's Voyages Through Time curriculum. For more info on this, please visit us at www.seti.org/education. and if you can post the following for us, many many thanks in advance. Contact me if any questions – [Email announcement to be forwarded follows.]

The MeetMe@tappedin.sri.com mailing list is a simple (low-tech) way for our members to find others with shared interests or needed expertise. The mailing list is described as follows on the Web site: "Post ideas you have for collaborative projects, tell the community a bit more about yourself, and set up meetings directly with your colleagues in TI through this list." Every email sent to the list is archived on the Web site (www.tappedin.sri.com/info/lists.html). New members can choose to subscribe to this list when they fill out the membership form. Approximately 250 members currently subscribe to the list. Since *MeetMe* was established in March 1998 through September 1999, 211 postings have been sent through the list by sixty-three different members. This volume of email traffic may seem low for a communitywide resource. However, rather than using the list as a public forum (thereby spamming uninterested subscribers), members respond to one another privately via email and telephone. The following emails are typical of the feedback we receive:

Just wanted you to know that I have receive half dozen or so responses to my inquiry about creating a web site! They have all been good suggestions, and most included links I can use or learn from! Thanks for your help!

Received some wonderful responses about my question on improving our inschool suspension. My post to this list was very fruitful. It resulted in a number of emails and three long distant phone calls. Many thanks.

University Classes and Teacher Workshops

Over a year ago, we began to notice groups of approximately 10 to 20 guests logging into TI at the same time. We began to inquire into the nature of the groups and found that they were most often university classes (graduate and undergraduate) studying education technology or inservice workshops designed to introduce teachers to the Internet. Over time, TI has become a regular Web stop for classes and workshops all across the country (and some foreign countries). During the June–July 1999 summer workshop season, tour groups logged in almost daily. Sometimes, the instructor or leader would log in days or weeks prior to the session (or email us) to ask whether the group could come in; we typically offer to give them a tour. The following email illustrates both how university faculty recommend TI to their students and how a long-dormant member becomes active:

I signed on to Tappedin a year or more ago; I have recommended that my graduate students (preparing to be school principals) sign on and use the site; however, other than receive the newsletter I have not yet used Tappedin. I tried to sign on today because I am interested in the topics for tomorrow evening and Tuesday, October 19, and would like to sign on for these sessions. Perhaps I have forgotten my password (If I selected it, I know what it would be; if you assigned one to me, I do not remember it). Please let me know what I should do to sign on and whether I can do this in time to sign on for the session tomorrow evening. I am interested in trying to set up a session for my technology class to meet and try the online discussion. I need to know how to go about doing this. Thanks. I do enjoy your newsletter. I have just not taken time to get familiar with the use of Tappedin. I think the idea is great.

We sent her the information she needed and, by coincidence, she logged in today and conversed with one of the authors of this paper. Many faculty return with new students each semester, and some have begun to incorporate TI visits in their class assignments. In the words of one professor, the sessions are "really eye-opening for them to see what was out there. The introduction to TI was a nice way to show them the type of support for teachers that they can expect to see in the future."

Hosting university classes and drop-in groups has helped us grasp the need to support teachers' growth from preservice teacher education and initial certification through master's and PhD programs for veteran teachers. TI has become a place where educators can be both professional colleagues *and* students of their profession. One relationship that formed this way has blossomed into a formal alliance between TI and Pepperdine University's Graduate School of Education and Psychology, which runs masters and doctoral programs that combine face-to-face and online courses. Pepperdine faculty and graduate students from around the country use TI daily to hold online study groups, seminars, and faculty office hours.

Why Online Education Communities Fail

We have demonstrated through TI that it is possible for a dedicated group of people to grow an education professional CoP of thousands of members by aggregating large education organizations and small groups, providing simple collaboration tools and continuous support, and hosting activities that foster relationship building. Despite our progress, we are not yet ready to claim success. To serve as an effective, sustainable catalyst for teacher learning, collaboration, and innovation, an online CoP must be given the time and resources to mature, develop social norms, grow leaders, and assimilate into the dominant local culture. At three years old, we consider TI to be approaching adolescence as a CoP – showing strong signs of maturity but still forming its own identity and not quite ready to sustain itself. As a nationwide testbed, TI has had to develop its own culture rather than fit any local culture. However, we are confident that our vision of a scalable, self-sustaining community of education professionals – a place in which new ideas germinate, new methods and tools are developed, novice educators can learn about the profession, and journeymen can become valued resources – is achievable within a regional context.

To help ensure the continued evolution of TI and inform the development of local education CoPs, we believe that it is important to understand why online education CoPs fail to sustain themselves or scale up to reach all who might benefit from them. Virtually all TPD and systemic reform projects now employ Internet tools (email, listservs, discussion boards, Web sites) to support their teachers. A handful of projects have been successful in establishing large-scale online education CoPs over several years. Some focus on a specific content area (notably the National Writing Project, Math Forum, and Access Excellence); others are geographically centered (Texas Education Network, Common Knowledge: Pittsburgh, Canada's SchoolNet, Denmark's SkoleKom). Unfortunately, most attempts have fallen short of needs and expectations, despite adequate funding, dedicated and enthusiastic staff, and advanced technology.

The reasons why some efforts succeed while others fail are complex and varied. A formal comparative analysis of the factors that contribute to the success or failure of large-scale online teacher communities would provide much-needed guidelines for the development of future online education CoPs. Here, we begin to help shape such an analysis by drawing on our understanding of the CoP literature and our own experience. For example, we and others have argued that traditional Internet tools are not designed to support the ebb and flow of discourse and collaboration that is characteristic of professional practice (Hardin & Ziebarth, 1996; Schlager & Schank, 1997; Cothrel & Williams, 1999). It is not that Web sites or discussion boards are inappropriate or unnecessary; they are simply insufficient to achieve the desired objectives of ongoing professional discourse – a listserv or newsgroup, no matter how well-trafficked, is not a community of practice.

TI, too, suffers from technological gaps and limitations, and we are working hard to integrate new capabilities into the environment (see Schank et al., 1999). However, we believe that lack of an appropriate technological infrastructure is only part of the problem. The more severe problems stem from a lack of understanding of how to employ online technology to achieve TPD goals and cultivate CoPs. We conjecture that misconceptions concerning the nature of online CoPs, how to cultivate them, and the role they can play in reform efforts have contributed to the disappointing outcomes.

One misconception is that layering online communication technology over a TPD organization's existing way of doing business (e.g., summer institutes or weekend workshops) will result in an online community that will support teachers back in the classroom. In many cases, project staff, who themselves have little experience planning or leading online activities, conduct an initial training and then wait to see whether teachers will use the technology before committing the time and resources needed to provide appropriate online activities, incentives, and support for teachers. Seeing no benefit to the technology *add-on*, the teachers are not motivated to use it; both staff and teachers feel overburdened by the technology, thereby reinforcing a negative perception of technology as a teaching and learning tool (Schlager et al., 1998/1999). To leverage the power of online communication technologies effectively, TPD staff must take the time to learn to conduct meaningful online activities and must provide incentives and tangible rewards for participation. Traditional TPD programs must be redesigned from the ground up (including organizational structure, budgets, and staffing) to integrate classroom-based online activities over extended periods of time.

We have heard several TPD project leaders who have tried to integrate online activities into their programs lament that they spend too much time and funding to train their staff and teachers to use online technology with too little benefit. They have fallen prey to a second misconception: the belief that TPD projects can simultaneously build an online community and provide content, training, and support through it. Corporations have learned the hard lesson that the adoption of new technologies is often "accompanied by an initial decrease in productivity, with benefits accruing only after the technology in question has been effectively assimilated, a process that often involves the introduction of significant structural changes within the adopting organization" (PCAST, 1997). Our own discourse study (described earlier) showed that both teachers and TPD providers must understand, and be proficient with, online technology *before* they can engage in productive activities online. We have found that both teachers and TPD staff can quickly learn to plan and engage in online activities through peripheral participation in the activities of other, more experienced members of a CoP. But if the project is new, where do the *more experienced* members come from? The answer must be: from outside the project in an already existing CoP.

Many TPD projects view an online CoP primarily as an outcome or by-product of their own efforts, rather than as a larger entity in which their efforts can take root, bloom, and propagate. This *project-centric* view of CoP (the project *is* the community) lacks (and in many cases conflicts with) essential elements stressed in both the CoP and education reform literatures. Over a career, teachers today are likely to participate in a succession of project-based communities with no connection or continuity among them. TPD organizations rarely work together or learn from one another. In many cases, an online community is established through insular, highly structured, top-down activities. Missing are the informal back channels of communication, information sharing, and trust building that are central to cooperation and the spread of innovation within a CoP. The resources, incentives, professional and social normative structures, and capacity to sustain and expand innovations throughout the education system must be in place *prior* to the infusion of reform practices (Elmore, 1996; Corcoran et al., 1998). Otherwise, even TPD reform projects that have been successful locally will be unable to sustain momentum beyond the outside funding or scale up to meet regional or statewide needs. This is the role of an online education CoP that exists outside of traditional institutional or project boundaries.

Toward Systemic Online Education CoPs

If individual projects should not build their own insular online community, then who should build it? Research on systemic education reform strategies that drive TPD (e.g., McDiarmid et al., 1997; Corcoran & Fuhrman, 1999; Lieberman & McLaughlin, 1999) suggests to us that building the capacity to leverage the combined power of (a) policy initiatives now driving reform in many states, (b) school-based teacher networks, and (c) innovative content-based TPD projects requires building both human and technological infrastructures systemwide to support sharing of information, communication, and collaboration across multiple stakeholder groups (e.g., policy makers, TPD providers, and local teacher collaboratives) – in essence, a *systemic* education CoP.

One function of a systemic online education CoP would be to build the capacity of, and provide incentives for, teachers to participate in a variety of teacher education, staff development, and self-motivated professional activities from their workplace via the Internet. A common online CoP infrastructure would enable teachers to become proficient with the tools and social norms that they will use in TPD activities through *informal* networking with colleagues, thereby reducing the burden on TPD providers, increasing participation, and allowing providers to focus on their core competencies.

A second role of a systemic CoP would be to build the capacity of TPD providers to offer via the Internet the kinds of TPD experiences that reflect research-based TPD strategies. Each provider should not have to learn by trial and error how to implement innovative TPD programs cost effectively. TPD projects must be designed and implemented within the context of an established CoP that enables innovation to spread through cooperation and division of labor among stakeholder groups and approaches. Cooperation among organizations within a CoP can enable organizations to avoid redundancy, identify and fill gaps in local TPD services, and focus on developing their core competencies to improve the quality of their TPD products and services. Large grant-funded university programs, local teacher education programs, teacher organizations, and private providers must all work together to support teachers as they gain proficiency with new content, tools, and pedagogy. District support staff and local master teachers must be provided with the means to identify and call in outside expertise to assist them when needed.

Finally, a systemic CoP would enable state education agencies to take on the role of organizer and host of an online CoP gathering place, planning and conducting regular activities that are of general interest to the community and providing support services (much like a public utility) to the CoP. As Lieberman (1996) points out, "Network leaders try to create *public spaces* where educators can work together across classrooms, schools, or districts. In locations free of the normal boundaries and cultural constraints of one's own organization position or place, it becomes possible to grow a culture of commitment to a new set of ideas and ideals. Helping to build a culture through activities that keep these ideas visible and integral to the work is an important part of leadership" (pp. 53–4). Through informal online activities and support services, policy makers can develop and obtain feedback on new initiatives, build a professional culture, motivate the use of reformed practice, and gain public understanding of and support for reform (Corcoran & Fuhrman, 1999).

If, as we have argued, the concept of a community of practice is central to effective teacher professional development, the capacity of a state education system to establish and maintain a well-functioning online CoP that represents all TPD stakeholder groups is as important to the sustainability and scalability of systemic reform efforts as the political, pedagogical, and organizational factors on which traditional TPD research has focused. The next research challenge on the horizon for our project is understanding how the Tapped In CoP model can be adapted to meet the needs of education reform at a systemic level. Recognizing that technology is only a small piece of a very complex puzzle, we want to apply what we have learned to help state education agencies build the capacity to sustain the momentum of systemic reform projects and scale them up to reach all teachers in their states.

Acknowledgments

The research presented in this paper was supported by National Science Foundation Grants No. REC-9725528 and CDA-9616585, Sun Microsystems, and SRI International. The findings and conclusions reported here, however, do not necessarily reflect those of the funders. We also thank Edward Geary and Holly Devaul for their trust and perseverance back in the "early days." Finally, we are grateful to Richard Godard, our MOO Wizard, and the Tapped In interns and educator associates who have served as community leaders, evangelists, and resources for their colleagues over the past three years, including: B. J. Berquist, Barbara Chriss, Hunter Gehlbach, Courtney Glazer, Chuck Merritt, Hulda Nystrom, Linda Polin, David Weksler, and Erik Wilson.

References

Becker, H. J. (1999, February). *Internet use by teachers: Conditions of professional use and teacher-directed student use.* Teaching, Learning, and Computing: 1998 National Survey, Report #1. Irvine and Minneapolis: The University of California at Irvine and The University of Minnesota, Center for Research on Information Technology and Organizations.

Brown, J. S., & Duguid, P. (1996). Practice at the periphery: A reply to Steven Tripp. In H. McLellan (Ed.), *Situated learning perspectives* (pp. 169–74). Englewood Cliffs, NJ: Educational Technology.

Brown, J. S., & Gray, E. S. (1995). The people are the company. *Fast Company*, p. 78. Available: www.fastcompany.com/online/01/people.html [November 1995].

Bush, W. S. (1997). *Throwing money at professional development: Some lessons learned.* White paper. Louisville, KY: University of Kentucky.

CEO Forum on Education and Technology. (1999). *The CEO Forum school technology and readiness report, year two. Professional development: A link to better learning.* Washington, DC: CEO Forum on Education and Technology.

Constant, D., Sproull, L., & Kiesler, S. (1997). The kindness of strangers: On the usefulness of electronic weak ties for technical advice. In S. Kiesler (Ed.), *Culture of the Internet* (pp. 303–22). Mahwah, NJ: Lawrence Erlbaum.

Corcoran, T., & Fuhrman, S. (1999). *Going to scale: Building effective infrastructure.* Available: www.cpre.org/Research/ResearchProjectA-3.htm [9 December 2001].

Corcoran, T. B., Shields, P. M., & Zucker, A. A. (1998). *The SSIs and professional development for teachers.* Menlo Park, CA: SRI International.

Cothrel, J., & Williams, R. (1999). On-line communities: Helping them form and grow. *Journal of Knowledge Management, 3*(1), 54–60.

Darling-Hammond, L., & Ball, D. L. (1997). *Teaching for high standards: What policymakers need to know and be able to do* [World Wide Web page]. National Educational Goals Panel. Available: www.negp.gov/Reports/highstds.htm [June 1997].

Derry, S. J., Gance, S., Gance, L. L., & Schlager, M. S. (2000). Toward assessment of knowledge building practices in technology-mediated work group interactions. In S. Lajoie (Ed.), *Computers as cognitive tools II* (pp. 29–68). Mahwah, NJ: Lawrence Erlbaum.

Elmore, R. F. (1996). Getting to scale with good educational practice. *Harvard Educational Review*, 66(1), 1–26.

Hardin, J., & Ziebarth, J. (1996). *Digital technology and its impact on education* [World Wide Web page]. National Center for Supercomputing Applications, University of Illinois at Urbana-Champaign. Available: www.ed.gov/Technology/Futures/hardin.html [9 December 2001].

Hawkins, J. (1996). Dilemmas. In C. Fisher, D. C. Dwyer & K. Yocam (Eds.), *Education and technology*. San Francisco: Jossey-Bass, pp. 35–50.

Lave, J., & Wenger, E. (1991). *Situated learning: Legitimate peripheral practice.* New York: Cambridge University Press.

Lieberman, A. (1996). Creating intentional learning communities. *Educational Leadership*, 54(3), 51–5.

Lieberman, A., & McLaughlin, M. (1992). Networks for educational change: Powerful and problematic. In M. McLaughlin & I. Oberman (Eds.), *Phi Delta Kappan*, 73, pp. 673–77.

(1999). *Professional development in the United States: Policies and practices.* Address presented at International Conference on New Professionalism in Teaching: Teacher Education and Teacher Development in a Changing World, Hong Kong.

Little, J. (1994). Teachers' professional development in a climate of educational reform. *Educational Evaluation and Policy Analysis*, 15(2), 129–51.

Loucks-Horsley, S., Hewson, P. W., Love, N., & Stiles, K. E. (1998). *Designing professional development for teachers of science and mathematics education.* Thousand Oaks, CA: Corwin.

McDiarmid, G. W., David, J. L., Kannapel, P. K., Corcoran, T. B., & Coe, P. (1997). *Professional development under KERA: Meeting the challenge.* Preliminary research findings prepared for The Partnership for Kentucky Schools and The Pritchard Committee for Academic Excellence. Unpublished manuscript.

McLaughlin, M., Mitra, D., & Stokes, L. (1999). *Theory-based change: Going broader, going deeper.* Paper presented at the 1999 PACT meeting, Hong Kong.

National Science Foundation (1997). *Foundations: A monograph for professionals in science, mathematics, and technology education, Vol. 1: The Challenge and Promise of K-8 Science Education Reform.* National Science Foundation Report, NDF 97-76. Washington, DC: Author.

Oldenburg, R. (1997). *The great good place.* New York: Marlowe.

Olson, G. M., Olson, J. S., Carter, M. R., & Storrosten, M. (1992). Small group design meetings: An analysis of collaboration. *Human-Computer Interaction*, 7, 347–74.

PCAST (President's Committee of Advisors on Science and Technology: Panel on Educational Technology). (1997). *Report to the President on the use of technology to strengthen K-12 education in the United States* [World Wide Web page]. Available: www.whitehouse.gov/WH/EOP/OSTP/NSTC/PCAST/k-12ed.html [March 1997].

Pea, R. (1999). New media communications forums for improving education research and practice. In E. Lagemann & L. Shulman (Eds.), *Issues in education research: Problems and possibilities.* San Francisco: Jossey-Bass.

Rényi, J. (1996). *Teachers take charge of their learning: Transforming professional development for student success* [World Wide Web page]. National Foundation for the Improvement of Education. Available: www.nfie.org/publications/takechargefull.htm [9 December 2001].

Schank, P., Fenton, J., Schlager, M., & Fusco, J. (1999). From MOO to MEOW: Domesticating technology for online communities. In C. Hoadley (Ed.), *Proceedings of the Third International Conference on Computer Support for Collaborative Learning* (pp. 518–26). Stanford, CA: CSCL.

Schlager, M., Fusco, J., & Schank, P. (1998/1999). Cornerstones for an on-line community of education professionals. *IEEE Technology and Society Magazine, 17*(4), 15–21, 40.

Schlager, M. S., & Schank, P. (1997). Tapped In: A new on-line community concept for the next generation of Internet technology. In R. Hall, N. Miyake, & N. Enyedy (Eds.), *Proceedings of the Second International Conference on Computer Support for Collaborative Learning* (pp. 231–40). Hilldale, NJ: Lawrence Erlbaum.

Schofield, J. W., Davidson, A., Stocks, J. E., & Futoran, G. (1997). The Internet in school: A case study of educator demand and its precursors. In S. Kiesler (Ed.), *Culture of the Internet* (pp. 361–84). Mahwah, NJ: Lawrence Erlbaum.

Stokes, L., Sato, N., McLaughlin, M., & Talbert, J. (1997). *Theory-based reforms and the problem of change: Contexts that matter for teachers' learning and community.* Stanford, CA: Stanford University, Center for Research on the Context of Teaching.

Wellman, B. (1997). An electronic group is virtually a social network. In S. Kiesler (Ed.), *Culture of the Internet* (pp. 179–205). Mahwah, NJ: Lawrence Erlbaum.

Wenger, E. (1998). *Communities of practice: Learning, meaning, and identity.* Cambridge, UK: Cambridge University Press.

6   Building Social Networks Via Computer Networks

Creating and Sustaining Distributed Learning Communities

Caroline Haythornthwaite

The ideal and widely held belief about communities is that they are composed of people who live close to each other, who freely share companionship, goods, services, and support of all kinds to other members of the community. Although this view still holds our hearts, it is often lamented as an ideal "lost" with the advent of urban life (Burbules, 2000; Fischer, 1982; Wellman, 1999a). However, we still find ourselves as members of communities, tied to others by kinship, friendship, work, and neighborhood. What has changed is our ability to maintain relationships with more far-flung intimates and associates, using the telephone, cars, airplanes, and electronic communication to keep in contact. Communities exist "liberated" from geography and neighborhood (Wellman, 1979). We can define community based on what we do with others, rather than where we live with others in terms of the *social networks* we maintain* (Fischer, 1982; Wellman, 1988, 1999a; Wellman & Gulia, 1999a).

Viewing community as resting on an underlying social network provides us with a way of examining and understanding the basis of computer-networked communities (Wellman et al., 1996) – communities where geographical colocation and face-to-face meetings have been removed as prerequisites for communal ties, where people do not need to meet face to face and yet sustain personal relationships with others within a community context. A social network perspective lets us explore some of the ambiguities of online communities, such as how "community" can be used to refer to both "networks of virtual strangers exchanging ideas and information" and "virtual friends debating the finer points of

---

* This discussion of community and social networks is a summary of that articulated at length by Wellman (1999a) in the introduction to *Networks in the Global Village*, which brings together over thirty years of research in this area.

gender-bending their online personae" (McLaughlin, Osborn & Smith, 1995, p. 93).

By opening up the black box of community and looking inside, we can examine what types of interactions and associations make for a community. We can ask: What types of exchanges – information, aid, social support, companionship, and so forth – sustain a community? How much exchange is needed, how often, and between whom to provide a sense of belonging? Can different types of communities be sustained with different types of exchanges and yet still be considered communities by their members? What types of exchanges support a virtual community, a learning community, or a work community?

Taking a social network perspective to learning, community, and computer-mediated communication opens up a number of potential areas for investigation, but not all can be addressed here.* The emphasis in this chapter is on social network considerations pertaining to information exchange and community membership for computer-supported distributed learners. Key issues and challenges for such environments will be discussed and illustrated with results from a series of social network studies of distance learning classes and data from ongoing longitudinal interviews with students in the same distance program.

This chapter begins with a brief review of the impact of computer-mediated communication (CMC) on interpersonal communication, with attention to its impact on learning communities. Discussion then overviews the social network perspective, explaining how interpersonal exchanges act as the building blocks for distributed online learning communities, followed by illustrative data from social network studies of distance learners.

Computer-Mediated Communication and Learning Communities

Computer-supported learning programs represent a growing trend in academia. These programs support individuals who are distributed geographically from each other and from the institution offering the program. The reach of the Internet has enabled whole universities to

---

* For discussions and reviews of social networks applied to the online context see Garton, Haythornthwaite & Wellman, 1997; Garton & Wellman, 1995; Haythornthwaite, Wellman & Garton, 1998; Rice, 1994; M. A. Smith, 1999; Wellman, 1997; Wellman & Gulia, 1999a.

operate in cyberspace (see Acker, 1995; Noam 1998a, 1998b), as well as whole programs to be offered by traditional universities. CMC is also used as a means of offering individual courses at a distance and of extending traditional courses with online activities and communications (Harasim et al., 1995). A common concern among faculty and students is that fully distributed programs prevent students from experiencing "campus life," and that they may feel alienated from the program, the instructors, and from each other. This concern translates into an ongoing desire to build a sense of community for these students, giving them the sense of belonging to a class that is full of others, as well as to a program, a university, and a profession (Dede, 1996; Kaye, 1995; Haythornthwaite, 1998; Wegerif, 1998).

Concerns about creating community online are fueled by our prevailing notions of community as dependent on colocation and by concerns about the alienating nature of CMC (e.g., Kraut et al., 1998). Because CMC does not convey the full range of communication cues, such as voice tone, body language, dress, and seating arrangements, it has been considered unsuitable or inappropriate for "rich" communications, those that involve negotiation, promote consensus, or contain socioemotional content (e.g., Daft & Lengel, 1986; Fish et al., 1993). Perhaps most damning from a community perspective has been the notion that CMC could not convey "social presence," the feeling of "being there" (Short, Williams & Christie, 1976).

Even liberated from geography, community depends on creating and sustaining strong interpersonal ties, those based on multiple exchanges that include social and emotional content, intimacy, and self-disclosure (Granovetter, 1973, 1982; Marsden & Campbell, 1984; van der Poel, 1993; Walker, Wasserman & Wellman, 1994). How can such ties be maintained through media that support only reduced cues (e.g., text-based media) and are traditionally described as lean and unable to transmit the verbal and nonverbal cues that enhance trust and commitment?

Although there is much research emanating from the "media richness" (Daft & Lengel, 1986) or "reduced cues" (Culnan & Markus, 1987) approach to CMC, after two decades of use we do find lean CMC supporting a range of social and emotional exchanges, with purposes ranging from entertainment and recreation (e.g., Baym 1995, 1997) to information seeking and social support (e.g., Alexander, Peterson & Hollingshead, in press).*

* For reviews of CMC research, see Garton & Wellman, 1995; Haythornthwaite et al., 1998; Lievrouw et al., 2001; McGrath & Hollingshead, 1994; Walther, 1995; Wellman et al., 1996.

CMC communications have become more expressive, with the invention and adoption of emoticons, paralanguage (e.g., common acronyms such as IMHO for "in my humble opinion"), and new vocabulary (e.g., spoof, spam, newbie, hacker; McLaughlin et al., 1995; Marvin, 1995).

CMC capabilities are being reevaluated for their potential to enhance rather than hamper interpersonal contact. A few of the attributes that enhance communication capabilities are asynchronous (any time), remote (any place) communication; multiple addressing facilities; and simultaneous transmission to multiple recipients (Huber, 1990; Rice, 1987; Sproull & Kiesler, 1991). Asynchronous communication can give participants control over when and where they read messages (Rice, 1987; Trevino & Webster, 1992), an important feature for computer-supported distance learners as their increasing distribution across times zones increases difficulties in coming together simultaneously. However, this feature comes with the caveat that message overload may decrease perceptions of control (McLaughlin et al., 1995; Whittaker, 1997). Also, asynchronous communication does not provide the richness of a synchronous conversation during which information can be clarified as necessary. Asynchronous communication may also alter the flow of conversation since messages can be read out of sequence (Rice, 1987).

Multiple addressing and simultaneous transmission have been reported to aid the inclusiveness of individuals in group contexts – an important goal of learning communities. Peripheral players can keep in touch with central activities and continue to communicate even when not colocated (Eveland & Bikson, 1988; Finholt & Sproull, 1990; Harasim et al., 1995; Sproull & Kiesler, 1991). Indeed, communicating via CMC may actually help such peripheral participants because the reduced cues environment may allow them to feel less exposed when asking for information, posting questions, or contributing ideas, thereby encouraging participation (Constant, Kiesler & Sproull, 1996; Finholt & Sproull, 1990; Garton & Wellman, 1995; Hiltz, Johnson & Turoff, 1986; Kiesler & Sproull, 1992). However, this participation also comes with a caveat that this same lack of exposure can lead participants to engage in antisocial behavior, including "flaming" (i.e., the use of extreme and aggressive language; Finholt & Sproull, 1990; Lea et al., 1992; Sproull & Kiesler, 1991), misrepresentation of personal identity (Donath, 1999; Gelder, 1996), and simulated violence against others as in the infamous "rape in cyberspace" (Dibbell, 1996). Online class conversations may have to be managed conversations (Murphy & Collins, 1997).

On this lean and lawless base, people are building communities. They come together in online places and spaces to interact and exchange information, social support, and companionship. Their common place is the chat room, Usenet group, MUD, MOO, or Virtual World they visit.* They develop for themselves an environment that shows many commonalties with offline communities and that are referred to as communities by the participants.[†]

Some key aspects of communities are exhibited online and these include adherence to common goals, membership requirements, hierarchy and roles, shared history, common meeting place, social construction of rules and behaviors, and enactment of rituals (Bruckman, 1998; Fernback, 1999; Jones, 1995, 1998; Kollock & Smith, 1999; McLaughlin et al., 1995; Mynatt et al., 1998). Online communities exhibit common goals in their adherence to topic discussion in Usenet groups (e.g., Baym, 1995), and in their strong commitment to communal goals relating to the purpose and tone of their community (Curtis, 1997; Donath, 1999; King, Grinter & Pickering, 1997; Reid, 1995; Rheingold, 1993). Local rules of behavior are created to identify the goals of the community and may be published as frequently asked questions (FAQ) lists. Community members create their own vocabularies (e.g., Marvin, 1995) and modes of discourse (as in the local flaming style adopted by the Rowdies, described by Sproull & Kiesler, 1991) that are accepted as normal for communication among themselves.

Rules of behavior provide an identity for the group, a shared history that provides a way of knowing how to behave and how to anticipate the behavior of others (Donath, 1999; Mynatt et al., 1998). Correct behavior can also be used as a means of validating the membership qualifications of others (e.g., when language and message content are out of synch with normal discourse in the group, it can signal a deceptive incursion into the group; Baym, 1995; Donath, 1999). Hierarchy and roles have evolved online, including the wizards and Webmasters who manage conflict and can control the presence of others online and trolls and hackers who

---

* MUDs and MOOs are text-based chat environments in which participants can program new features and adopt new personae (see Bruckman, 1998; Curtis, 1997). Virtual worlds are graphic-based chat environments in which the participant is embodied as an avatar that moves in the graphical world in place of the participant's body.

[†] For further discussions and reviews of online work, community, and societies, see Agres, Igbaria, & Edberg, 1998; Dourish, 1998; Haythornthwaite et al., 1998; Gackenbach, 1998; Jones 1995, 1998; Kiesler, 1997; Smith & Kollock, 1999; Sproull & Kiesler, 1991; Wellman et al., 1996.

aim to disrupt communities (Curtis, 1997; Donath, 1999; Gilboa, 1996).*
Additionally, long-term members of communities may adopt the role of
mentors and take it on themselves to introduce "newbies" to local rules
and to chastise them for contravening them (McLaughlin et al., 1995).

As rules of behavior and conduct become known, individuals can invest time and trust into relationships. With trust comes the opportunity
to add emotional content and self-disclosure to their messages, thereby
increasing their commitment to the continuity of their interpersonal online ties, as well as to the continuity of the community as a place for such
exchanges. In this way, their exchanges build social networks that support
and define the community.

Overall, we are presented with an ambiguous picture of whether CMC
provides the appropriate means for building learning communities: reduced cues on the one hand and increased connectivity on the other,
increased participation and inclusiveness but the potential for misrepresentation and antisocial behavior, and reduced communication richness
but committed participants engaged in the rules and behaviors of their online community. Our problem is how to use this ambiguous environment
to promote learning and community. To do this, we need to understand
the types of interactions that support learning and community. From there
we can assess our success in (re)creating communities online and direct
our intervention efforts in the appropriate direction.

We turn now to an introduction to the social network approach to
evaluating communal behavior. The following sections explain the basic
approach and its potential for exploring online learning communities.

Social Network Perspective

Social networks analysts explore the way in which the exchange
of resources between individuals creates connectivity among all members
of a social system. The number and types of resources exchanged, the
direction in which they flow, and how frequently and voluntarily they
flow describe the social structure of the system and define the sustaining
characteristics of the social group or community (Wasserman & Faust,
1994; Wellman & Berkowitz, 1988). An exchange represents a connection
between two individuals (e.g., a line connecting two nodes in a graph). Sets
of exchanges form social networks, connecting many nodes with many

---

* For more on conflict and control, see Carnevale & Probst, 1997; Kollock & Smith, 1996;
Reid, 1999; A. D. Smith, 1999.

lines. The pattern of lines and connections describe the way in which resources flow from one member of the community to another, and among all members of the community (an example is given in Figure 6.1). These exchanges show what types of resources are important for a community and which sustain it and, therefore, which are important to recreate and provide support for in the online environment.*

A basic premise of the social network perspective is that the concept of a group, a community, or other collective can be assessed empirically from behaviors among network members rather than from external criteria (Bates & Peacock, 1989; Monge, 1987). With many people questioning whether online activity can support online communities, it is particularly important to have a means of assessing them without resorting to labeling based on external criteria such as geographic proximity. The criteria for the existence of a group is the presence a specific kind of interaction, or more often a set of interactions, that connects a set of individuals. For example, groups may be shown to exist where pairs work together frequently: working together may include discussing new ideas, formulating plans, allocating work tasks, sharing work products, and sharing in profits from their endeavors. Groups may also emerge based on members coming together in a common meeting ground, whether that is exhibited as coattendance at face-to-face meetings (such as conferences, or board meetings), coenrollment in a class, comembership in an electronic listserv, or coparticipation in a MUD.

The converse of this is that what relations sustain a group or community can also be derived empirically. Thus, when individuals consider themselves to belong to a community, we can examine what types of interactions they engage in to see what defines the community. When people question whether an online community provides the same benefits to individuals as an offline community, we can examine what differences exist in these two settings and see how these affect the nature of each community.

Relations and Ties

Specific kinds of resource exchanges or interpersonal interactions are known as social network *relations*. Relations may entail the exchange of tangibles such as goods and financial aid or intangibles such as small

* For further reading on social networks see: Haythornthwaite, 1996; Nohria & Eccles, 1992; Scott, 1991; Stohl, 1995; Wasserman & Faust, 1994; Wellman, 1997; Wellman & Berkowitz, 1988.

services, information, and social or emotional support. Pairs who maintain one or more relations are said to maintain a *tie*, and such ties may range from weak to strong. Weaker ties are based on few relations: usually instrumental exchanges rather than emotional ones, occurring infrequently and not reciprocated. Stronger ties are based on the maintenance of many relations, including reciprocal relations involving self-disclosure and intimacy (Granovetter, 1973, 1982; Lin & Bian, 1991; Marsden & Campbell, 1984). Recent research also shows that online weak ties are maintained through fewer media, usually those associated with groupwide exchanges, whereas strong ties are maintained through more media (Haythornthwaite, 1999a, 1999b, 2000, 2001; Haythornthwaite & Wellman, 1998). Weak ties tend to be more opportunistic, taking advantage of passive, group-oriented means of communication, whereas strong ties tend to be proactive, seeking out means of contact (Haythornthwaite, 2000).

The advantages of strong and weak ties are fairly well accepted. Strong ties provide timely access to information circulating the network. Those with whom we are strongly tied are more motivated to share information with us. However, since these individuals tend to travel in the same social circles that we do, the information they have may be redundant with that available from others within our close network (Burt, 1992; Granovetter, 1982; Lin & Bian, 1991; McPherson & Smith-Lovin, 1986, 1987; see also Haythornthwaite, 1996; Wellman & Gulia, 1999a). By contrast, those with whom we are weakly tied are likely to travel in different circles from our own, thereby opening up access to new information (Burt, 1992; Granovetter, 1973; for online effects, see Constant et al., 1996; Feldman, 1987; Kiesler & Sproull, 1992; Kollock & Smith, 1996; Pickering & King, 1995). However, our infrequent contact with these others and their lack of motivation to share with us may make for less timely receipt of information.

Delays in receiving information can be a serious impediment for time-limited groups, such as semester-length classes or work task forces. Information may not arrive in time for assignment deadlines. Time-limited groups may also suffer when trying to create strong ties since they may not have sufficient time to build trust and to progress to relations that include social content. This may be exacerbated online as the asynchronous exchanges and the reduced communication modalities delay interpersonal tie formation (Walther, 1995). Therefore, members of such groups may also be limited in the number of others in their network who are sufficiently motivated to share information with them. Thus, time-limited groups may be hampered at both ends of the scale in terms of information exchange, suggesting that specific interventions may be necessary to boot strap exchanges in such groups.

Networks

Relations tie two people – two nodes – in a network. When we connect all the dots in the network by the relations maintained between them, we see a picture of the *whole network*. From this view, we can examine the way in which resources circulate within the network and how individuals are positioned within the network to play central or peripheral roles in the movement of resources. In learning environments, one of the key resources is information. Pictures of whole networks, known as sociograms, can show whether information is circulating to all members of a class, or whether some subsets of class members are only communicating with each other. The way in which resources flow in a learning network has an important impact on each individual's exposure to information, as well as their sense of belonging to a community. We will return to this discussion later.

Networks can also be examined by considering them from the perspective of a focal individual. These personal or *ego-centric networks* provide a view of the many ties that individuals maintain with others. Ego-centric networks studies also probe relationships among those named by the focal individual to assess the range and interconnectedness of the individual's networks (Burt, 1985; Wellman, 1988, 1999a; Wellman et al., 1988; Wellman & Potter, 1999). Viewing networks from this perspective is useful when examining a large population, such as a city neighborhood, and has been used in particular to study personal communities (Fischer, 1982; Wellman, 1999b). Aggregating across all members of a sample gives us a view of the typical ego-centric network of individuals, showing how many others they interact with and about what. From this kind of view, we can explore what makes for an ideal personal network for learners: How many others is too many? Too few? What types of relationships make for good learning and community outcomes? Characteristics such as the size of the personal network and the diversity of its members have important consequences for an individual's access to resources and support.

This section outlined briefly the social network concepts that can be used to examine what constitutes a learning community. The following section looks at what types of relations and ties are likely to be important in learning networks. This is followed by a look at the way in which structures found in whole networks can affect the way in which resources circulate to members of a network.

Relations and Ties in Learning Networks

Among the challenges in supporting learning communities is to identify which types of exchanges matter, and thus which to make a particular effort to support. Supporting learning is often considered as an issue of information delivery (i.e., information flowing from one central individual to all members of a group). This is indeed a social network relation: it involves the delivery of a resource (information) from one member of the social system (the instructor) to all others (the students). Students also maintain relations with instructors: they receive the information that is delivered, they ask questions and receive answers, and they hand in assignments and receive grades. These are the immediately apparent types of exchanges in a learning environment, but other types of exchanges are also important.

Within educational settings, there is a desire to increase the amount of peer-to-peer information exchange. Collaborative learning and computer-supported collaborative learning scholars identify active construction of knowledge, problem articulation, and peer-to-peer communication as integral components in the collaborative learning process (Bruffee, 1993; Dede, 1990; Koschmann, 1996; Harasim et al., 1995). A key to such learning is to have participants interact and share experiences with each other, extending their exposure to new ideas and to different approaches to problem solving. Advocates see collaborative learning as a preparation for a lifelong learning strategy that will serve students well when they reach the workforce (Bruffee, 1993; Dede, 1996; Kaye, 1995) and as teaching individuals the skills necessary to handle analyzing and solving complex problems (Feltovich et al., 1996).

Outside instructional settings, collaborative learning may be the norm, and the model of the single information disseminator may not apply. Learning groups may not be guided by a single individual. Instead, they may learn by sharing information among themselves, building a repertoire of knowledge within the network. This type of collaborative learning is common when product teams set out to create something new, or when scholars seek to expand and build on a complex area of knowledge (Scardemalia & Bereiter, 1996). For these learners, communication among network members matters the most.

Thus, to support these types of learning groups, it is necessary to go beyond consideration of information dissemination to consideration of mutual exchanges among learners, exchanges that are also essential building blocks of communities. The discussions here focus on assessing this peer-to-peer, many-to-many communication.

To explore communication among members of a network, we ask questions that elicit social network data and address the overall question: "Who talks to whom about what?" We already know that communities are not built on instrumental relations alone; therefore, to tap into both learning and community relations, it is important to ask questions that explore both task-oriented and socially oriented relations. Social network questions are phrased to gather data on each person's interactions with each other person in the group (for whole network data) or each person's interactions with others that they name (ego-centric network data). The studies discussed below asked these four questions:

- How often in the last month have you collaborated on class work with [each member of the class]?
- How often in the last month have you received or given information or advice about class work with [each member of the class]?
- How often in the last month have you socialized work with [each member of the class]?
- How often in the last month have you exchanged emotional support (described as support during a minor or major upset) with [each member of the class]?

Although many more specific questions can be asked, often the range of questions must be chosen to fit the time constraints of participants in the study, as was done for these studies.*

Data gathered from questions such as these can be examined to see the extent to which group members are in contact with each other, and what types of relations form the basis of the contact. These exchanges can also be examined to see whether all network members are participating equally or whether some members are more influential in the network than others.

The following sections discuss in more detail what is known from the social networks literature about information exchange, social support, and

---

* See also Burt (1985) regarding the selection of the phrasing for the one question to be asked on the 1985 General Social Survey. That question asked: "From time to time, most people discuss *important matters* with other people. Looking back over the last six months – who are the *people* with whom you discussed matters important to you? Just tell me their first name and initial." (Burt, 1985, p. 119). Follow-up questions were asked concerning the demographic characteristics of the first five people named, and how well each of those people knew each other.

community and from the management and social psychology literature about working groups and the relations they maintain.

Information Exchange Relations

From a network perspective, there are two major considerations regarding information exchange in collaborative learning communities. First, we want network members to share what information they have; therefore, we want to build the kind of environment that fosters that kind of sharing – the "safe" communities described by Bruffee (1993) as important for learning. Sharing, and the acceptance of self-exposure that accompanies asking "dumb" questions, occurs when interpersonal bonds are strong, or as they are strengthening among members of a newly formed group. Second, we want network members to add new information to the pot of ideas circulating the network, information that is likely to come from individuals outside our close circle, those with whom we share a weak tie (Granovetter, 1973).

In supporting these two aspects of information exchange among computer-supported distributed learners, we have a dual focus (1) making members of newly formed groups (i.e., classes) feel comfortable enough to share information and ask questions and (2) keeping information circulating among as many members of the network as possible to increase the different types of information available to network members. These two goals may pull against each other. To feel comfortable sharing information (and perhaps also to manage information load), individuals may form closer ties with only small subsets of class members, thereby limiting the number of others with whom they exchange information. They may also form these closer ties because of class structures such as group assignments, and then may stay with this group for all their information needs during the course. On the other hand, individuals may receive information from many other network members, maintaining only weak ties and not feeling motivated to share what information they have nor able to benefit from others willing to share with them. Either extreme – high information exchange with a small clique of others or low information exchange among many – supports only one form of information exchange. Not only is this likely to have an impact on learning outcomes, but it also has an impact on the ties individuals maintain and therefore on their sense of belonging to a community.

CMC studies highlight some effects that can have an impact on these types of information exchange. As discussed earlier, strong tie formation may be inhibited, or at the very least delayed (Walther, 1995) by the reduced cues of the CMC environment. Learners may consider it inappropriate or difficult to exchange sensitive or personal information, the kind of exchange that is needed to build closer bonds. Weak tie formation may initially be helped by the reach of computer networks, and the reduced social overhead associated with contacting a stranger via CMC, making it easier to approach others for new or different information (Constant et al., 1996; Haythornthwaite et al., 1998). However, research also suggests that groups have more difficulty discussing complex issues via CMC, and they take increased time to reach consensus when using CMC (Fish et al., 1993; Garton & Wellman, 1995; Kiesler & Sproull, 1992). Thus, those trying to work together may have a more difficult time completing information exchange tasks, particularly in learning environments where they are grappling with new, often complex ideas.

Another issue that affects the information environment is the way in which social networks constrain who can communicate with whom (Wasserman & Faust, 1994). For example, in work environments, social networks of hierarchy and information access give managers inside information on organizational activities while keeping line workers out of the loop. So, too, computer networks define interaction networks – "who talks to whom" is constrained by "who is connected to whom." Thus, both social networks *and* computer networks can constrain who can communicate with whom.

Distance learners are more constrained than on-campus students in a number of ways. They are more constrained to communications with members of their own department because they are unlikely to be able to take a course from another unit unless that unit offers courses online and is willing to admit them. They are more constrained to communications with members of their own classes because they cannot meet nonclassmates casually in the computer lab, lunch room, or local pub. Additionally, the features of the computer media made available to distributed learners can constrain the style of interaction they can engage in. For example, providing only asynchronous CMC (e.g., email) prevents the more rapid exchange of ideas and greater social presence perceived with synchronous distance interaction (e.g., chat rooms). Providing recorded sessions may inhibit informal, conversational interactions (e.g., when using Webboards; Haythornthwaite, 2000; Wegerif, 1998). Patterns of discourse such as formal Webboard postings may also become entrenched in a local setting, making it difficult to change the way people interact and further constraining the type of discourse and information exchange deemed acceptable in each locale.

Thus, even though we strive for an open environment, social and computer networks still act to constrain communication, and perhaps more so for distributed learners than for local, on-campus learners. Each constraint limits and channels the kinds of information that reach an individual in these networks, which may in turn limit their exposure to information and the types of interpersonal bonds they can form.

Social Support Relations

Although information exchange is key to learning environments, communities are not built on instrumental exchanges alone. Social support is important in cushioning stress, helping during a crisis, and promoting a "sense of social unity (a 'we' feeling)" (van der Poel, 1993, p. 2). Social support – expressed as companionship, emotional aid, advice, sharing of small goods and services – also promotes individual well-being (Haines & Hurlbert, 1992; Hammer, 1981; van der Poel, 1993; Walker et al., 1994; Wellman & Gulia, 1999b). Thus, when examining a learning community, it is important to explore the extent to which socially supportive relations are maintained among members.

One aspect of social networks that matters in social support is the size of an individual's personal community (i.e., the size of their ego-centric network). The more *others* with whom an individual maintains supportive ties, the more positive the association with measures of happiness, mental health, and well-being (Haines & Hurlbert, 1992; Hammer, 1981; van der Poel, 1993; Walker et al., 1994; Wellman & Gulia, 1999b). Larger, more diverse personal networks contain ties to people who can respond to various types of needs, thereby allowing an individual to find support of the appropriate kind when the need arises (Haines, Hurlbert & Beggs, 1996; Wellman & Gulia, 1999b). Supportive ties may also provide a background level of support that helps carry the individual through crises if they occur, but more generally provide the individual with the sense of there being support available should the need arise (Hammer, 1981). The presence of latent support ties that can be activated if the need arises helps the individual feel supported by his or her personal community.

Within an individual's network of ties, those with whom the individual shares stronger ties and who are more like them (more homophilous) are most likely to provide support than those with whom the individual shares weaker ties and who are less like them (more heterophilous) (Haines et al., 1996; van der Poel, 1993; Walker et al., 1994; Wellman & Wortley, 1989). At the same time, not every person in the network provides every kind of support: different people provide different kinds of resources (Wellman & Gulia, 1999b). There is also evidence that integration with the community, signified by a larger ego-centric network, positively affects the exchange of support among community members (i.e., those who are more embedded in the community are more likely to reach out more voluntarily to others in the community in times of need; Haines et al., 1996; House, 1981).

Since social support is a cornerstone of community, it is necessary to foster such relations, and the strong ties on which they are based, when promoting learning communities. Individuals in learning communities, particularly in new computer-supported learning communities, are faced with an often overwhelming array of new challenges – new media, new rules of behavior, new course materials, new classmates, and new balance of home, work, and school – as well as the loss of familiar means of interaction and learning – face-to-face classroom encounters, rapid real-time dialogue, informal encounters in hallways, and social encounters over coffee, lunch, and the like. The newness and constant learning about the online environment often leaves these students suffering from an "exhaustion of newness" (Haythornthwaite et al., 2000). Without social support, they have difficulty coping. Thus, we find in interviews that many students maintain close ties with a circle of two to four others with whom they stay in touch regularly and who help each other over hard times. Those who do not have such ties when they begin the program express increased satisfaction and happiness when they do eventually make contacts. Moreover, students report that it is not contact with "outsiders" (heterophilous ties) that provides the support they need but contact with others in the program – in their community – who understand and share their experiences in the distance environment (homophilous ties).

The newness of the distance environment fades with familiarity, but it can be a serious impediment for first-term students. New computer-supported learners face extra challenges that students in off-line environments do not. Moreover, these are *relational challenges*. To gain information or social support, they must reach out and contact someone; by their own account, this contact requires extra effort compared to a face-to-face environment. Thus, maintaining each and every relation is more challenging than it would be for on campus students, and students may become parsimonious in the relations they maintain.

By knowing that social support is key to sustaining community, and knowing that it is best received from someone like themselves, administrators and program directors can focus their efforts accordingly to support and encourage this kind of interaction. We can help to bring students together (virtually or otherwise) so that they can develop and sustain close ties with other community members for the duration of their membership in the learning community.

Task Support Relations

Even though a learning community may exist as a network of information sharing and social interaction, it is more common to find it associated with the production of some kind of product. Educational class members complete individual assignments as well as collaborate on projects. Members of learning groups operating in commercial or institutional settings share information to create or implement a particular project or product. Academic collaborators exchange data and information that leads to grant applications and research papers. Members of each of these environments share the need to complete specific tasks, usually within a limited time frame.

Task support relations include planning work, allocating tasks, coordinating joint efforts, reviewing drafts, and negotiating and resolving conflicts (for a more extensive description of work group functions, see McGrath, 1984, 1990, 1991). These more instrumental exchanges are needed to bring projects to conclusion. Online distributed learners need means to accomplish these exchanges as well as means to deliver the end-products (papers, posters, presentations), and they need to receive technical support and training in the technologies used for these exchanges.

These end-products represent the objectives of participants and form part of the reason for the community. Students in programs have the very important goal of obtaining a degree; each course and each assignment is a step toward achieving that goal and joining a profession. Their co-orientation to that goal, and to the near-term objectives that lead to that goal, are further characteristics that support the overall sense of community.

The way in which work assignments structure interactions has important consequences for the social networks that form, and thus on who works with whom, learns from whom, and learns to learn from whom. Classwide discussion provides weak contact with many others. Group projects focus individual attention to a subset of class members, strengthening intrateam ties, but taking time and effort away from cross-class exchanges (Haythornthwaite, 1999a). A social network perspective tells us that work structures constrain relation formation. In learning communities, attention needs to be paid to the way in which assignments structure social interactions and the way in which these structures promote the goals of the community.*

Information exchange, social support, and task support relations are three major categories of interaction that are important for building and sustaining learning communities. How can we see whether such relations are present among our network members? Can we see whether a class is maintaining multiple relations and building stronger interpersonal and intraclass ties? Viewing the whole network of relations among all class members can provide a picture of these interactions, giving us a view of the community processes. The next section demonstrates the kinds of

---

* The emphasis here is on creating and sustaining a learning community; however, it is important to point out that learning groups need not be communities to operate successfully. They may instead exhibit behaviors more like working groups in organizations. A learning network that is more like a working group is poised somewhere between the more long-standing, support-providing network of a community and the instrumental association of a temporary work group. Because working groups are quite often constituted for only a limited amount of time, during which members build working relationships, they may provide good models for how time-limited learning groups also operate.

  Research on groups in social psychology and management shows that working groups demonstrate features that are very similar to those found in communities. Successful work groups, like successful communities, mix task-oriented and socially oriented behaviors in exchanges among members. Work groups have been described by McGrath (1990, 1991) as continuously involved in: *production* (i.e., contributions of the group to its organization), *member support* (i.e., contributions of the group to its members), and *group well-being* (i.e., contributions of the group to its own continued functioning as a social unit) (McGrath & Hollingshead, 1994).

  Work group members, like learning group members, come together knowing little about each other. Over time, they get to know each other, develop their own ways of working together and of using their technologies, before coming to a termination of their joint endeavors (Chidambaram & Bostrom, 1997a, 1997b; DeSanctis & Poole, 1994; Gersick, 1988; McGrath, 1990, 1991). Within the confines of their time constraints, they develop working relationships based on both task and social exchanges, and they gain a sense of belonging to the work group. Feelings of belonging have positive outcomes for work groups. The more individuals feel part of the group, the greater their commitment to group efforts, the greater their cooperation with others, and the greater their satisfaction with group efforts (Argyle, 1991; Chidambaram & Bostrom, 1997a; Gabarro, 1990; McGrath, 1984; Wellman, 1999a).

information that a whole network picture can give us about interactions among learners.

Networks of Learners

Looking at a whole network is like looking at the map of a road system. Figure 6.1 shows the map of the "collaborative work" road system from one class of computer-supported distance learners. This figure shows the social network of who reported working with whom during the term. Pairs who worked together also turned out to be many of the same pairs who exchanged information and advice about class work, particularly near the end of term (data were gathered at three times during the term). Thus, we can look at this sociogram as showing key paths for the exchange of information as well as for who actually worked with whom.

The sociogram shows only those connections that were maintained at least twice a week on average over the term. Weekly synchronous classes

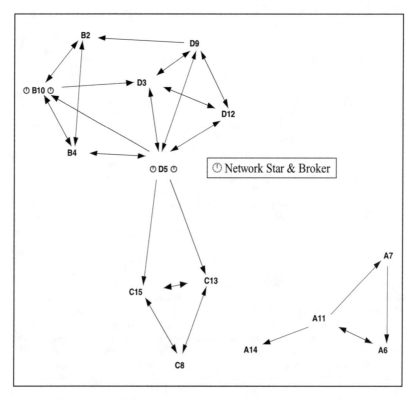

Figure 6.1. Collaborative work for connections that occur more than twice a week.

were conducted via Internet Relay Chat, which most students attended, so this frequency catches those who maintained ties outside class time. Although others might have worked together briefly at some point in the term (and in fact all did in this class), here we are examining those engaged in a more continuous collaboration. This network shows connections that represent the possibility of timely exchange of information (i.e., within three to four days). As mentioned earlier, frequent contact is important in time-limited groups because delays may mean that information does not arrive until after a work deadline has passed. (For further details on the study on this class, see Haythornthwaite, 1998, 1999a, 2001.)

Individual Roles and Positions

Central Players

On road maps, we see many roads leading into large urban centers. So too in social networks, many routes connect central individuals to others, but few connect to members of the periphery. In Figure 6.1, many roads lead to D5, but few branch out to A14. This whole network picture shows how a particular individual (D5) occupies a central position in the network. D5 is the social network star who occupies a key position in the dissemination of information from and to all members of the network. Connections to a more central star can also increase the centrality of other network members. B10 in Figure 6.1 scores high in centrality because of frequent communication with the star D5 and also with D3. As mentioned earlier, social networks can constrain who communicates with whom. Constraints exist even if the structure was not imposed externally; social structures that develop from individual interaction patterns constrain or facilitate information flow. Here, the patterns that have developed mean that information is constrained to pass through D5 to move in a timely manner from one part of the network to another.

When information passes through a key individual on its way from one part of the network to another, that individual can also be identified as a *broker*. Although D5 passes information from one part of the class network to another, brokers can also sit between more distinct groups and bring information from disparate settings into their home network. In online learning environments, individuals who are taking several classes may bring information from one class into another. One familiar kind of broker is the *technological gatekeeper*, or the technological guru, who brokers information circulating in scientific or technical circles to members of their own specialized network (Allen, 1977). Other brokers may place themselves strategically so that they can fill a *structural hole* between two networks (Burt, 1992). Strategic positioning may also mean strategic forwarding of data or information: brokers may delay, edit, embellish, or add interpretation to the information they receive. Collaborative brokers may facilitate information exchange, but competitive brokers may not. In learning environments, we may need to monitor whether group activities promote collaborative activity (e.g., rewarding early results may lead to information hoarding rather than information sharing, thereby working against the notions of collaborative learning).

Peripheral Players

While some individuals are central, others occupy more peripheral positions, remaining relatively isolated in the entire social system. In Figure 6.1, A14 and the other three A-group members are more peripheral in the network than the more highly interconnected B, C, and D group members. An individual who has no connections to others is known as an *isolate*. Although not everyone can be expected to be a star in a network, learning environments that contain isolates need to be concerned that these individuals are neither hearing from nor contributing to the network exchanges. They do not benefit from the community, nor does the community benefit from what they might know. By gathering data on who is communicating with whom, and viewing the network, we can see if some intervention is necessary to increase participation by peripheral participants or nonparticipants.

Cliques

It is apparent in Figure 6.1 that some sets of individuals within the network are more highly interconnected with each other than they are with others. They form subgroups or *cliques* within the network. Cliques have many routes for passing information among themselves, increasing the number of routes that information can take to reach an individual in a timely manner. Four subgroups are visible in Figure 6.1, each of which is a team that worked together over the term on a group project (team membership is indicated by letter prefixes).

Here the external designation of a team does indeed translate into activity among team members, which, although expected, cannot be taken as a given. It is precisely the point of the social network approach to validate that team membership does indeed mean team members working together. It also means finding out what other activities team members engage in that connects them as a team. What other kinds of relations do team members maintain? Can we expect to see the same team configuration for socializing or for emotional support relations (i.e., for relations that are important for building strong, communal ties)?

In the same study, students also reported with whom they exchanged information or advice about class work, socialized, and exchanged emotional support. For this particular class, team membership did influence pairs' collaboration on work and the exchange of information and advice, but it had less influence on patterns of socializing and even less influence on patterns of emotional support. Over time, however, the similarity in who talked to whom across these four relations increased (i.e., as the term progressed, individuals constrained their interactions more and more to communications with their team mates; see Haythornthwaite, 2001). We find that pairs who socialized or exchanged emotional support frequently (once a week or more) are almost always also team mates.*

It is not surprising that, as the end of term and project deadlines approached, individuals narrowed their communication focus to those with whom they are working. However, it does show that the group focus competes with classwide exchanges for students' time and energy. Team projects require task completion, which leads to an increased focus on intrateam communication, which is achieved at the expense of cross-class communication. This observation does not advocate the abandonment of group projects; computer-supported learners are the computer-supported workers of the future, and this type of exercise is important preparation for future endeavors (Dede, 1996). However, it is important to recognize that online learning classes have competing calls on their limited time together, and class structures such as group projects make communication decisions for them on where (and how) they spend their limited time.

Properties of the Whole Network

So far, the discussion of networks has concentrated on internal characteristics: roles, positions, and cliques. We can also look at properties

---

* Nineteen pairs socialize an average of once a week, and only two of these pairs are not team mates; nine pairs exchange emotional support an average of once a week, and all of these are also team mates.

of the network as a whole. For example, we can look at the cohesiveness of the network (i.e., the extent to which class members are interconnected). This can be done by looking at the *centralization* of the network, the extent to which it is organized around a single central individual, and at the *density* of the network (i.e., the extent to which all members of the network are interconnected). To be brief, we will look at density only. (For further information on these and other network measures, see Wasserman & Faust, 1994).

Density is simply the number of connections maintained and expressed as a proportion of the total number of possible connections. In a dense network, all or almost all members of the network are connected to each other, and resources can flow readily from one part of the network to another. If the network connections are more sparse, resources may have to flow from the outer periphery through central individuals before they can reach other sectors of the network, and, in fact, there may be no connection between some parts of the network. For example, in Figure 6.1, resources that C8 possesses cannot reach B2 without passing first through C15 or C13 on the way to D5 who can then forward that information through B4 to B2. This is likely to slow the circulation of information and even its actual transference to the final learner in the chain. Also, Figure 6.1 shows that resources available within the A group will not reach others within the three to four day timeframe shown in this figure. Thus, the denser the network, the more likely every individual in the network will have access to the same information within the same time interval.

In a network of fourteen individuals (as in Figure 6.1), there are ninety-one [(14 × 13)/2] possible connections. The density in Figure 6.1 is 0.24 (22 / 91). On its own, this density tells us that 24 percent of class members collaborate on work at least twice a week. This number can be compared to some theoretical ideal, such as 100 percent for complete connectivity among all class members. If we have data from other, similar classes, we can compare densities across classes to see if this class is doing better or worse in terms of connectivity. Density also gives a way of comparing across relational networks to see what types of interactions connect network members. For example, for the class shown in Figure 6.1, all pairs reported that they collaborated on work at some point during the term (weak ties), although fewer than half worked collaboratively on a weekly basis (stronger ties; see Table 6.1). This class was also more interconnected for collaborative work and exchanging information than for socializing or emotional support.

Table 6.1. *Network Densities*

Frequency of Communication	Collaborative Work	Exchanging Information	Socializing	Emotional Support
At least once during the term	1.00	0.97	0.84	0.78
At least once a week	0.42	0.34	0.21	0.10

Still to be explored is what this array of relations means to members of the network in terms of learning and community outcomes and how this relates to individual's perceptions of the class (some preliminary explorations of this are discussed later). Also still to be explored is what a "normal" amount of collaborative work or emotional support is in such networks. While it is not expected that members of a class will need to exchange emotional support as often as they work on class work, we do not yet know what is too much or too little of each and the consequences for the learning community.

Ego-Centric Views

A drawback of the density measure is that its meaningfulness may vary with the size of the network. When classes are large, densities may be low even though individuals are maintaining appropriately sized personal communities. Therefore, comparing densities across networks must be done with some thought to the overall size of the network. Contact with 20 percent of a 100-person network (twenty others) may be too many, whereas contact with 20 percent of a ten-person network (two others) may be too few. Thus, it may be more appropriate to look at personal networks, as done by many community scholars (i.e., assessing networks from the perspective of a focal individual).

The goal when looking at learners' personal networks is to see how many others they interact with, which kinds of relations and ties they maintain, and how this combination affects their sense of social unity and satisfaction with the learning environment. Again, we are faced with having no baseline data on what makes for a "normal" learning community network. The social support literature already suggests that the larger the personal network, the more support available from that network. However, those networks need to include strong ties. Thus, the first question is whether the online environment can sustain the stronger ties that provide social support and how that is associated with perceptions of community.

In the four classes studied, students do seem able to form strong ties despite their geographical separation from each other (for details see Haythornthwaite, 2000). The typical network of a student from this set consists of thirteen to nineteen ties to others (in classes of fourteen to twenty-three). They maintain strong ties with four others with whom they work collaboratively, exchange information and advice about class work, and socialize and exchange emotional support. They communicate daily with these others, via multiple media. They maintain an average of seven ties that are of intermediate strength, with whom they maintain two to four of the relations. They communicate with these others at least once a week via one to two media and include more emotional support and more media the more frequently they communicate. Weak ties are maintained with the rest of the network, with communication occurring only monthly, and usually relating to class work and communicated via the media used for classes. While this begins to give a baseline from which to compare with other classes, and other communities, more data are needed from different classes to explore this further.

Only three brief questions were asked of these students about their sense of community: did they think the class worked together; did they feel part of the class; and did they feel the class included social interaction. Questions were answered on a five-point scale from never to always. The size of the personal network and the number of others in the top quartile of communication frequency were positively correlated only with answers to the last question regarding social interaction. Although this question did not differentiate between socializing and emotional support, results seem to be in keeping with the social support literature with social interaction received from those with whom students maintained strong ties. It is also interesting to note that the size of an *individual's* network significantly affects that individual's perceptions of how the *whole* network operates. The more an individual hears from others, the more he or she may also hear about the network as a whole, and thus gain a sense of overall interaction. However, perceptions of the group may also be projected based on an individual's own interactions. This relation requires further investigation.

Mediated Support

Thus, we see that distance classmates can form strong ties that include emotional support, as well as maintain weaker ties that may expose them to different types of information. When a learning community is supported via CMC, there is an added challenge of finding the right technology to support the interaction. From the studies of the four classes, one thing that stands out most clearly is that classes need a variety of media, each providing different communication options to compensate for the lack of face-to-face interaction. They also need media that provide options that support both weak and strong ties.

Each of the questions asked of these classes also asked about which media were used for each type of exchange. Patterns of media use suggest that it is not so much which medium was used for which kinds of exchange, but rather which media and how many were used by pairs who maintained different strengths of ties.

In each of the classes, weak ties were sustained most through the class-mandated media, usually Internet Relay Chat for regular, synchronous classes and the Webboard where discussions continued asynchronously over the week. Strong ties required a private means of communication used in addition to other means of communication. The medium of choice was email, used markedly more frequently by those maintaining strong ties than by others (averaging several times weekly to several times a day across the four classes). Moreover, both in these studies and in an earlier one of an academic research group (Haythornthwaite & Wellman, 1998), the more that pairs communicate, the more media they use for those communications. As ties increase in strength, they increase in the number of relations they maintain, the extent to which those relations include emotional support, and the number of media they use to stay in touch.

In conclusion, results suggest the usefulness of taking of social network perspective when making administrative decisions about support for learning communities. Weakly tied pairs are likely to constrain their interactions to class-mandated media, and therefore such media should be chosen so that it supports the desired outcomes for these pairs. Strongly tied pairs find many ways to communicate, but also need many ways to communicate. In particular, they need a private way of communicating so that self-disclosure can occur without proceeding in full view of all learners. By framing community support as a question about support of ties, we reframe the concern from which medium to use for distributed learning communities to how many media, and with what features to provide to support which kinds of ties.

References

Acker, S. R. (Ed.). (1995). Collaborative universities. *Journal of Computer-Mediated Communication*, vol1/issue1/, whole issue. Available: at www.ascusc.org/jcmc/vol4/issue2/.

Agres, C., Igbaria, M., & Edberg, D. (1998). The virtual society: Forces and issues. *The Information Society, 14*(2), whole issue.

Alexander, S. C., Peterson, J. L., & Hollingshead, A. B. (in press). Help is at your keyboard: Support groups on the Internet. In L. Frey (Ed.), *Group communication in context: Study of bona fide groups*. Mahwah, NJ: Lawrence Erlbaum.

Allen, T. J. (1977). *Managing the flow of technology: Technology transfer and the dissemination of technological information within the R&D organization*. Cambridge, MA: The MIT Press.

Argyle, M. (1991). *Cooperation: The basis of sociability* (pp. 115–31). London: Rutledge.

Burbules, N. C. (2000). Does the Internet constitute a global educational community? In N. C. Burbules & C. Torres (Eds.), *Globalization and education: Critical perspectives* (pp. 323–55), New York: Routledge.

Bates, F. L., & Peacock, W. G. (1989). Conceptualizing social structure: The misuse of classification in structural modeling. *American Sociological Review, 54*, 565–77.

Baym, N. K. (1995). The emergence of community in computer-mediated communication. In Steve Jones (Ed.), *CyberSociety: Computer-mediated communication and community* (pp. 138–63). Thousand Oaks: Sage.

(1997). Interpreting soap operas and creating community: Inside an electronic fan culture. In S. Kiesler (Ed.), *Culture of the Internet* (pp. 103–20). Mahwah, NJ: Lawrence Erlbaum.

Bruckman, A. (1998). Community support for constructionist learning. *CSCW: The Journal of Collaborative Computing, 7*, 47–86.

Bruffee, K. A. (1993). *Collaborative learning: Higher education, interdependence, and the authority of knowledge*. Baltimore: John Hopkins University Press.

Burt, R. S. (1985). General social survey network items. *Connections, 8*, 119–23.

(1992). *Structural holes*. Cambridge, MA: Harvard University Press.

Carnevale, P. J., & Probst, T. M. (1997). Conflict on the Internet. In S. Kiesler (Ed.), *Culture of the Internet* (pp. 233–55). Mahwah, NJ: Lawrence Erlbaum.

Chidambaram, L., & Bostrom, R. P. (1997a). Group development (I): A review and synthesis of developmental models. *Group Decision and Negotiation, 6*, 159–87.

(1997b). Group development (II): Implications for GSS research and practice. *Group Decision and Negotiation, 6*(3), 231–54.

Constant, D., Kiesler, S. B., & Sproull, L. S. (1996). The kindness of strangers: The usefulness of electronic weak ties for technical advice. *Organization Science, 7*(2), 119–35.

Culnan, M. J., & Markus, M. L. (1987). Information technologies. In F. M. Jablin, L. L. Putnam, K. H. Roberts & L. W. Porter (Eds.), *Handbook of organizational communication: An interdisciplinary perspective* (pp. 420–43). Newbury Park, CA: Sage.

Curtis, P. (1997). MUDDING: Social phenomena in text-based virtual realities. In S. Kiesler (Ed.), *Culture of the Internet* (pp. 121–42). Mahwah, NJ: Lawrence Erlbaum.

Daft, R. L., & Lengel, R. H. (1986). Organizational information requirements, media richness and structural design. *Management Science, 32*(5), 554–71.

Dede, C. J. (1990). The evolution of distance learning: Technology-mediated interactive learning. *Journal of Research on Computers in Education, 22,* 247–64.

(1996). The evolution of distance education: Emerging technologies and distributed learning. *American Journal of Distance Education, 10*(2), 4–36.

DeSanctis, G., & Poole, M. S. (1994). Capturing the complexity in advanced technology use: Adaptive structuration theory. *Organization Science, 5*(2), 121–47.

Dibbell, J. (1996). Taboo, consensus, and the challenge of democracy in an electronic forum. In R. Kling (Ed.), *Computerization and controversy* (pp. 553–68). San Diego: Academic Press.

Donath, J. S. (1999). Identity and deception in the virtual community. In M. A. Smith & P. Kollock (Eds.), *Communities in cyberspace* (pp. 29–59). New York: Routledge.

Dourish, P. (Ed.) (1998). Interaction and collaboration in MUDs. *Computer Supported Cooperative Work, 7*(1–2), whole issue.

Eveland, J. D., & Bikson, T. K. (1988). Work group structures and computer support: A field experiment. *ACM Transactions on Office Information Systems, 6*(4), 354–79.

Feldman, M. (1987). Electronic mail and weak ties in organizations. *Office: Technology and People, 3,* 83–101.

Feltovich, P. J., Spiro, R. J., Coulson, R. L., & Feltovich, J. (1996). Collaboration within and among minds: Mastering complexity, individually and in groups. In T. Koschmann (Ed.), *CSCL: Theory and practice of an emerging paradigm* (pp. 25–44). Mahwah, NJ: Lawrence Erlbaum.

Fernback, J. (1999). There is a there there: Notes toward a definition of cyberspace. In S. G. Jones (Ed.), *Doing Internet research.* Thousand Oaks, CA: Sage, 203–20.

Finholt, T., & Sproull, L. (1990). Electronic groups at work. *Organization Science, 1*(1), 41–64.

Fischer, C. (1982). *To dwell among friends: Personal networks in town and city.* Chicago: University of Chicago Press.

Fish, R., Kraut, R., Root, R., and Rice, R. (1993). Video as a technology for informal communication. *Communications of the ACM, 36*(1), 48–61.

Gabarro, J. J. (1990). The development of working relationships. In J. Galegher, R. E. Kraut & C. Egido (Eds.), *Intellectual teamwork: Social and technological foundations of cooperative work* (pp. 79–110). Hillsdale, NJ: Lawrence Erlbaum.

Gackenbach, J. (Ed.). (1998). *Psychology of the Internet.* San Diego: Academic Press.

Garton, L., Haythornthwaite, C., & Wellman, B. (1997). Studying online social networks. *Journal of Computer-Mediated Communication, 3*(1). Available: www.ascusc.org/jcmc/vol3/issue1/garton.html.

Garton, L., & Wellman, B. (1995). Social impacts of electronic mail in organizations: A review of the research literature. *Communication Yearbook, 18,* 434–53.

Gelder, L. V. (1996). The strange case of the electronic lover. In R. Kling (Ed.), *Computerization and controversy,* 2nd ed. (pp. 533–46). San Diego: Academic Press.

Gersick, C. J. G. (1988). Time and transition in work teams: Toward a new model of group development. *Academy of Management Journal, 33*(1), 9–41.

Gilboa, N. (1996). Elites, lamers, narcs and whores: Exploring the computer underground. In L. Cherny & E. R. Weise (Eds.), *Wired-women: Gender and new realities in cyberspace* (pp. 98–113). Seattle: Seal Press.

Granovetter, M. S. (1973). The strength of weak ties. *American Journal of Sociology*, *78*, 1360–80.

(1982). The strength of weak ties: A network theory revisited. In P. V. Marsden & N. Lin (Eds.), *Social structure and network analysis* (pp. 105–30). Beverly Hills, CA: Sage.

Haines, V., & Hurlbert, J. (1992). Network range and health. *Journal of Health and Social Behavior, 33*, 254–66.

Haines, V. A., Hurlbert, J. S., and Beggs, J. J. (1996). Exploring the determinants of support provision: Provider characteristics, personal networks, community contexts, and support following life events. *Journal of Health & Social Behavior, 37*(3), 252–64.

Hammer, M. (1981). Social supports, social networks, and schizophrenia. *Schizophrenia Bulletin*, *7*, 45–57.

Harasim, L., Hiltz, S. R., Teles, L., & Turoff, M. (1995). *Learning networks: A field guide to teaching and learning online*. Cambridge, MA: MIT Press.

Haythornthwaite, C. (1996). Social network analysis: An approach and technique for the study of information exchange. *Library and Information Science Research*, *18*, 323–42.

(1998). A social network study of the growth of community among distance learners. *Information Research*, *4*(1). Available: www.shef.ac.uk/~is/publications /infres/paper49.html.

(1999a). Collaborative work networks among distributed learners. *Proceedings of the 32nd Hawaii International Conference on System Sciences*. Los Alamitos, CA: IEEE Computer Society.

(1999b). Networks of information sharing among computer-supported distance learners. In C. Hoadley (Ed.), *Proceedings of the Third International Conference on Computer Support for Collaborative Learning* (pp. 218–22), Stanford, CA: CSCL.

(2000). Online personal networks: Size, composition and media use among distance learners. *New Media and Society*, *2*(2), 195–226.

(2001). Exploring multiplexity: Social network structures in a computer-supported distance learning class. *The Information Society*, *17*(3), 211–26.

Haythornthwaite, C., Kazmer, M. M., Robins, J., & Shoemaker, S. (2000). Community development among distance learners: Temporal and technological dimensions. *Journal of Computer-Mediated Communication*, *6*(1). Available: www.ascusc.org/jcmc/vol6/issue1/haythornthwaite.html.

Haythornthwaite, C., & Wellman, B. (1998). Work, friendship and media use for information exchange in a networked organization. *Journal of the American Society for Information Science*, *46*(12), 1101–14.

Haythornthwaite, C., Wellman, B., & Garton, L. (1998). Work and community via computer-mediated communication. In J. Gackenbach (Ed.), *Psychology of the Internet* (pp.199–226). San Diego: Academic Press.

Hiltz, S. R., Johnson, K., and Turoff, M. (1986). Experiments in group decision making: Communication process and outcome in face-to-face versus computerized conferences. *Human Communication Research*, *13*(2), 225–52.

House, J. S. (1981). *Work stress and social support*. Reading, MA: Addison-Wesley.

Huber G. P. (1990). A theory of the effects of advanced information technologies on organizational design, intelligence, and decision making. In J. Fulk & C. W. Steinfield (Ed.), *Organizations and communication technology* (pp. 237–74). Newbury Park, CA: Sage.

Jones, S. G. (Ed.). (1995). *CyberSociety: Computer-mediated communication and community*. Thousand Oaks, CA: Sage.

(Ed). (1998). *CyberSociety 2.0: Revisiting computer-mediated communication and community*. Thousand Oaks, CA: Sage.

Kaye, A. (1995). Computer supported collaborative learning. In N. Heap, R. Thomas, G. Einon, R. Mason & H. MacKay, *Information technology and society* (pp. 192–210). London: Sage.

Kiesler, S. (Ed.) (1997). *Culture of the Internet*. Mahwah, NJ: Lawrence Erlbaum.

Kiesler, S., & Sproull, L. (1992). Group decision making and communication technology. *Organization Behavior and Human Decision Processes, 52*, 96–123.

King, J. L, Grinter, R. E., & Pickering, J. M. (1997). The rise and fall of Netville: The saga of a cyberspace construction boomtown in the great divide. In S. Kiesler (Ed.), *Culture of the Internet* (pp. 3–33). Mahwah, NJ: Lawrence Erlbaum.

Kollock, P., & Smith, M.A. (1996). Managing the virtual commons: Cooperation and conflict in computer communities. In S. Herring (Ed.), *Computer-mediated communication* (pp. 109–28). Amsterdam: John Benjamins.

(1999). Communities in cyberspace. In M. A. Smith & P. Kollock (Eds.), *Communities in cyberspace* (pp. 3–25). New York: Routledge.

Koschmann, T. (Ed.). (1996). *CSCL: Theory and practice of an emerging paradigm*. Mahwah, NJ: Lawrence Erlbaum.

Kraut, R., Patterson, M., Lundmark, V., Kiesler, S., Mukopadhyay, T., & Scherilis, W. (1998). Internet paradox: A social technology that reduces social involvement and psychological well-being? *American Psychologist, 53*(9), 1017–31.

Lea, M., O'Shea, T., Fung, P., & Spears, R. (1992). "Flaming" in computer-mediated communication: Observations, explanations, implications. In M. Lea (Ed.), *Contexts of computer-mediated communication* (pp. 89–112). New York: Harvester Wheatsheaf.

Lievrouw, L., Bucy, E., Finn, A. T., Frindte, W., Gershon, R., Haythornthwaite, C., Kohler, T., Metz, J. M., & Sundar, S. S. (2001). Current new media research: An overview of communication and technology. *Communication Yearbook, 24*, 271–95.

Lin, N., & Bian, Y. (1991). Getting ahead in urban China. *American Journal of Sociology, 97*(3), 657–88.

Marsden, P. V., & Campbell, K. E. (1984). Measuring tie strength. *Social Forces, 63*, 482–501.

Marvin, L. (1995). Spoof, spam, lurk and lag: the aesthetics of text-based virtual realities. *Journal of Computer-Mediated Communication* Vol. 1, Issue 2. Available: www.ascusc.org/jcmc/vol1/issue2/marrin.html.

McGrath, J. E. (1984). *Groups, interaction and performance*. Englewood Cliffs, NJ: Prentice-Hall.

(1990). Time matters in groups. In J. Galegher, R. E. Kraut & C. Egido (Eds.), *Intellectual teamwork: Social and technological foundations of cooperative work* (pp. 23–61). Hillsdale, NJ: Lawrence Erlbaum.

(1991). Time, interaction and performance (TIP): A theory of groups. *Small Group Research*, 22(2), 147–74.

McGrath, J. E., & Hollingshead, A. B. (1994). *Groups Interacting with Technology*. Beverly Hills, CA: Sage.

McLaughlin, M. L., Osborn, K. K., & Smith, C. B. (1995). Standards of conduct on usenet. In S. G. Jones (Ed.), *CyberSociety: Computer-mediated communication and community* (pp. 90–111). Thousand Oaks, CA: Sage.

McPherson, J. M., & Smith-Lovin, L. (1986). Sex segregation in voluntary associations. *American Sociological Review*, 51(1), 61–79.

(1987). Homophily in voluntary organizations: Status, distance, and the composition of face-to-face groups. *American Sociology Review*, 52, 370–9.

Monge, P. R. (1987). The network level of analysis. In C. R. Berger & S. H. Chaffee (Eds.), *Handbook of communication science* (pp. 239–70). Newbury Park, NJ: Sage.

Murphy, K. L., & Collins, M. P. (1997). Communication conventions in instructional electronic chats. *First Monday*, 2(1). Available: www.firstmonday.dk/issues/isssue2_11/murphy/index.html.

Mynatt, E. D., O'Day, V. L., Adler, A., & Ito, M. (1998). Network communities: Something old, something new, something borrowed. . . . *CSCW*, 7, 123–56.

Noam, E. M. (Ed.). (1998a). CMC and higher education. *Journal of Computer-Mediated Communication*, 4(2), whole issue. Available: www.ascusc.org/jcmc/vol4/issue2/.

(Ed.). (1998b). CMC and higher education. *Journal of Computer-Mediated Communication*, 4(3), whole issue. Available: www.ascusc.org/jcmc/vol4/issue3/.

Nohria, N., & Eccles, R.G. (Eds.). (1992). *Networks and organizations: Structure form, and action*. Boston: Harvard Business School Press.

Pickering, J. M., & King, J. L. (1995). Hardwiring weak ties: Interorganizational computer-mediated communication, occupational communities, and organizational change. *Organization Science*, 6(4), 479–86.

Reid, E. (1995). Virtual worlds: Culture and imagination. In S. G. Jones (Ed.), *CyberSociety: Computer-mediated communication and community* (pp. 164–83). Thousand Oaks, CA: Sage.

(1999). Hierarchy and power: Social control in cyberspace. In M. A. Smith & P. Kollock (Eds.), *Communities in cyberspace* (pp. 107–33). London: Routledge.

Rheingold, H. (1993). *The virtual community: Homesteading on the electronic frontier*. Harper Perennial.

Rice, R. E. (1987). Computer mediated communication and organizational innovation. *Journal of Communication*, 37(4), 65–94.

(1994). Network analysis and computer-mediated communication systems. In S. Wasserman & J. Galaskiewicz (Eds.), *Advances in social network analysis: Research in the social and behavioral sciences* (pp. 167–203). Thousand Oaks, CA: Sage.

Scardamalia, M., & Bereiter, C. (1996). Computer support for knowledge-building communities. In T. Koschmann (Ed.), *CSCL: Theory and practice of an emerging paradigm* (pp. 249–68). Mahwah, NJ: Lawrence Erlbaum.

Scott, J. (1991). *Social network analysis: A handbook*. London: Sage.

Short, J., Williams, E., & Christie, B. (1976). *The social psychology of telecommunications*. London: Wiley.

Smith, A. D. (1999). Problems in conflict management in virtual communities. In M. A. Smith & P. Kollock (Eds.), *Communities in cyberspace* (pp. 134–63). London: Routledge.

Smith, M. A. (1999). Invisible crowds in cyberspace: Mapping the social structure of the Usenet. In M. A. Smith & P. Kollock (Eds.), *Communities in cyberspace* (pp. 195–219). London: Routledge.

Smith, M. A., & Kollock, P. (Eds.). (1999). *Communities in cyberspace*. London: Routledge.

Sproull, L., & Kiesler, S. (1991). *Connections: New ways of working in the networked organization*. Cambridge, MA: The MIT Press.

Stohl, C. (1995). *Organizational communication*. Thousand Oaks, CA: Sage.

Trevino, L. K., & Webster, J. (1992). Flow in computer-mediated communication: Electronic mail and voice mail evaluation and impacts. *Communication Research*, *19*(5), 539–73.

van der Poel, M. (1993). *Personal networks: A rational-choice explanation of their size and composition*. Lisse, Netherlands: Swets & Zeitlinger.

Walker, J., Wasserman, S., & Wellman, B. (1994). Statistical models for social support networks. In S. Wasserman & J. Galaskiewicz (Eds.), *Advances in social network analysis* (pp. 53–78). Thousand Oaks, CA: Sage.

Walther, J. B. (1995). Relational aspects of computer-mediated communication: Experimental observations over time. *Organization Science*, *6*(2), 186–203.

Wasserman, S., & Faust, K. (1994). *Social network analysis*. New York: Cambridge University Press.

Wegerif, R. (1998). The social dimension of asynchronous learning networks. *Journal of Asynchronous Learning Networks*, *2*(1), 34–49. Available: www.aln.org/alnweb/journal/vol2 issue1/wegerif.htm.

Wellman, B. (1979). The community question. *American Journal of Sociology*, *84*, 1201–31.

(1988). Structural analysis: From method and metaphor to theory and substance. In B. Wellman & S. D. Berkowitz (Eds.), *Social structures: A network approach* (pp. 19–61). New York: Cambridge University Press.

(1997). An electronic group is virtually a social network. In S. Kiesler (Ed.), *Cultures of the Internet* (pp.179–205). Mahwah, NJ: Lawrence Erlbaum.

(1999a). The network community: An introduction to networks in the global village. In B. Wellman (Ed.), *Networks in the global village*. Boulder, CO: Westview Press, pp. 1–48.

(Ed.) (1999b). *Networks in the global village*. Boulder, CO: Westview Press.

Wellman, B., & Berkowitz, S. D. (Eds.) (1988). *Social structures: A network approach*. New York: Cambridge University Press.

Wellman, B., Carrington, P., & Hall, A. (1988). Networks as personal communities. In B. Wellman & S. D. Berkowitz (Eds.), *Social structures: A network approach* (pp. 130–84). Cambridge, UK: Cambridge University Press.

Wellman, B., & Gulia, M. (1999a). Net surfers don't ride alone: Virtual communities as communities. In M. Smith & P. Kollock (Eds.), *Communities in cyberspace* (pp. 167–94). London: Routledge.

(1999b). The network basis of social support: A network is more than the sum of its ties. In B. Wellman (Ed.), *Networks in the global village* (pp. 83–118). Boulder, CO: Westview Press.

Wellman, B., & Potter, S. (1999). The elements of personal communities. In B. Wellman (Ed.), *Networks in the global village* (pp. 49–81). Boulder, CO: Westview Press.

Wellman, B., Salaff, J., Dimitrova, D., Garton, L., Gulia, M., & Haythornthwaite, C. (1996). Computer networks as social networks: Collaborative work, telework, and virtual community. *Annual Review of Sociology, 22,* 213–38.

Wellman, B., & Wortley, S. (1989). Brothers' keepers: Situating kinship relations in broader networks of social support. *Sociological Perspectives, 32*(3), 273–306.

Whittaker, S. (1997). Email overload: Exploring personal information management of email. In S. Kiesler (Ed.), *Culture of the Internet* (pp. 277–301). Mahwah, NJ: Lawrence Erlbaum.

7   Mask and Identity

The Hermeneutics of Self-Construction in the Information Age

Dorian Wiszniewski and Richard Coyne

The issue of identity features prominently in discourses about information technology (IT). One conspicuous narrative presented in IT commentary is that the use of the Internet radically changes our perception of who and what we are. Apparently, in anonymous online chat groups you can play charades, wear a mask, and pretend to be of a different age, gender, or appearance (Turkle, 1995; Murray, 1999). It seems that we can accomplish this transformation of identity with great fluidity now. As the Internet and its successors become more pervasive and the technologies become more sophisticated and convincing, then presumably the issue of identity itself comes under review, as do related concepts: that against which we assert our identity (community) and the means by which one's identity is promoted and transformed (education).

We survey the debt owed by contemporary IT narratives and practices to certain intellectual positions as they pertain to identity. This analysis inevitably involves a consideration of change, community, and education. Identity implies continuity in a sense of the self, a constancy behind the ever-changing mask of appearances. In the philosophies of Plato and Aristotle, which dominate in the western tradition, the changing nature of the sensible realm is contrasted with the invariance of the realm of the forms, the place of identity. Whereas we and other things change, through the forces of generation, destruction, locomotion, growth, and diminution (our hair turns grey and disappears, we gather wrinkles, stoop a little, and change our occupation), that which remains constant is our identity – the immutable part of our human being that participates in the realm of the forms. Identity is clearly related to community. The Enlightenment promoted the concept of the individual, the lone identity, who sets herself apart from the collection of other individuals, or amongst whom she has her place, and with whom she may ultimately identify. In as much as we wear a mask, it is to assume a role in the social sphere.

Education can be seen as the change process by which identity is realized, how one finds one's place. Education implicates the transformation of identity. Education, among other things, is a process of building up a sense of identity, generalized as a process of *edification*. Education also makes play on the theme of masking. To learn is to have things revealed, as though the mask of ignorance is removed, but professional education also seems to involve learning to assume a role, putting on and changing masks, and managing our roles on the professional stage. The theme of the mask has appeal in our own field of architectural education. Various aesthetic theories of architecture attempt to come to terms with ornamentation as a mask to the purity of architectural form, in the same way that our changing appearance and circumstance mask the constancy of our identity. More radically, both architecture and education involve play within the space of masking and unmasking – a position, we argue, that finds support from contemporary hermeneutical studies (Gallagher, 1991; Snodgrass & Coyne, 1998) and that steers the discourse away from Platonic idealism and always returns the issue of identity back to practice. We argue that this strategy diffuses many of the claims of information technology as the agent of radical change – IT as harbinger of a radically transformed age and the Internet as the new means of problematizing the issue of identity. In turn, the hermeneutical position provides valuable modes of inquiry into the place of information technology in education.

The Romance with Identity

Certain IT narratives are caught up in the prospect of transcendence from the here and now into the realms of cyberspace, where you can directly interact with data, experience a melding of minds, and participate directly in the unity of all things. As we have explored at length elsewhere (Coyne, 1999), this narrative draws from a transformed Platonism and Neoplatonism, which present continuity and changelessness as belonging to the realm of the ideas, universals, and immutability beyond the sensible world (the realm of the senses and passions). For Plotinus (1948), the abiding aspect of our being resides with the soul, which has its origins in the world of ideas and to which it will return. For Plato, in *Phaedrus*, the soul is a flying chariot restlessly driven by the wild horses of passion steered by the charioteer of reason (Allen, 1966). For the Neoplatonists, the ambition of philosophy and art was to release the soul from the strictures of the sensate body so that it could ascend to its true home in the ideas. To revert to the metaphor of the mask, the embodied, sensual realm of everyday experience acts as a mask to the realm of the soul and the forms.

On the subject of community, Plato's understanding of the polis trades in this implication of a hierarchical progression. The city is made up of citizens of various ranks, headed by the philosopher king, who, by virtue of his access to philosophical contemplation, is able to participate in the ideas and thus govern wisely. For Platonic idealism, what we now call community was understood in terms of our relationship with the ideas (or the good), a social order in which everyone knew their place, or at least that to which they aspire. Each had a role to play. The process of education, as edification, implicates this progression, which is not so much a departure as a return. In being educated, we are exhorted to remember that in which we participated prior to the transient residency of our souls in the sensible realm. The ancient exhortation to "know thyself" requires us to recall our true place in the realm of ideas. There is a moral imperative in edification, a call to temperance, which also implies an unmasking. To build up, for the soul to progress toward the ideas, is also to be open to scrutiny or to uncover the good.

Of course, there are many lessons from Plato on the subjects of society and education. The Socratic method of question and answer suggests that learning involves a restless movement without resolution (through dialectic) (Stewart, 1999), and commentators such as Arendt (1958) have indicated that perhaps there is an ironical strand to Plato, which serves the cause of education as a hermeneutical enterprise well. But a straightforward Neoplatonic idealism (Plato without irony) thrives in the rhetoric of cyberspace, variously transformed, first through the romantics, for whom the soul was displaced by the Enlightenment sense of individuality, self, and personhood. The soul was transformed into the mind of the subject, and its essence was communicated as creative genius, striving for emancipation. This transformation exemplifies what Taylor identifies as the movement from looking outward (to the ideas) to looking inward (the construction of the thinking subject) (Taylor, 1989). The IT age affects a further transformation that elsewhere we discuss under the heading of "technoromanticism," a particular melding of high-tech reductionism and eighteenth-century Neoplatonic romanticism (Coyne, 1999). The mind of the subject is transformed to become information; the essential patterns that make up our being are ultimately transposed into networked computer systems, or putative cyberspace (Moravec, 1988; Dery, 1996). Under romanticism, induction into the digital realm assumes the gravity and significance of the progression to Plato's realm of ideas, as the new real (Heim, 1993).

Idealistic narratives resonate with utopian views of education. Though few educational theorists would accede to the expectation of melding minds in cyberspace, many maintain that the growth of democratizing computer networks provides greater access to education and transformation to a better society (Schneiderman, 1994). Additionally, those in architectural education see cyberspace as a means of liberating the creative spirit. As romantic artists and educators, following Rousseau (1974), sought opportunity to free the creative spirits of their acolytes from the strictures of dull custom, by exercise or practice in dramatically new media, so the cyberspace impresario offers an unfettered digital world in which the imagination may roam freely (Novak, 1991). The digital realm provides the opportunity to strip back the formal masks that conceal the expressive features behind. It also provides opportunities to engage in the child's game of dressing up, assuming different persona, and taking on new identities.

The Experience of Identity

The Internet as a means of expressing one's identity, belonging to a group, promoting an educated and informed citizenry, as expounded so starkly in Hiltz and Turoff's (1994) *Network Nation*, continues the tenets of the eighteenth-century Enlightenment. Against Neoplatonic idealism, we have the sober reflections of empiricists such as Locke and Hume, for whom the final arbitration on matters of identity, community, and the accrual of knowledge is not some appeal to other-worldly ideals, but *experience* – the authority of the senses. Here the metaphor of the mask functions much as it does for romanticism and idealism, except that the imperative is to strip back custom and prejudice (the mask) to reveal reason informed by unencumbered sense impressions.

On the subject of community, Hume (1975) was party to the Enlightenment project (attributable also to Descartes) that started with the concept of the individual and independent-thinking subject. From this basis in subjectivity derives the notion of the collective. For Hume, as members of community, most of us are driven by self interest. We need to be governed by those who are in a position to see their own interest best served by the interest of the group. Bolstered and developed by Enlightenment economic theorists, including Adam Smith and others, this empiricism informs reflections about the Internet on the basis of utility (here defined as a means of maximizing common good), especially the corporate narratives of Gates (1996) and others. For Gates, the Internet will provide a "new world of low-friction, low-overhead capitalism, in which market information will be plentiful and transaction costs low" – "shopper's heaven" (Gates, 1996, p. 181). IT removes the inertia of day-to-day transactions so that we can get closer to what everyone really wants.

For empiricism, the acquisition of knowledge requires the exercise of scientific method, from a position free of prejudice and custom. For Hume's empiricist forebear, Locke (1960), the mind unmasked is a blank slate and devoid of a priori impressions (the idealist claim); the young mind is formed by experience and sense impressions. The blank slate model resurfaces in traditional views of education as a matter of funneling information into otherwise unformed minds, and the Internet and electronic media resurface as systems of conduits for knowledge, exemplified in Gate's enthusiasm for endless flows of information and online encyclopaedias. But empiricism as a philosophy of engagement with experience rather than idealistic speculation informed Dewey's liberal, pragmatic exhortation that we learn by doing, not by a dependence on facts (Dewey, 1916). Elsewhere, we have explored the influence of this liberal empiricism, and its confluence with McLuhan's pragmatism, in the culture of IT design (Coyne, 1995).

In Hume's sensible realism, we have the seeds of a radical position on identity, later taken up by contemporary theorists such as Deleuze (1994). For Hume, what we choose to call personal identity is already fraught with discontinuities. We experience life through a series of perceptions, which for some purposes we choose to bundle together under the rubric of personal identity: "we feign the continued existence of the perceptions of our senses, to remove the interruption, and run into the notion of a *soul*, and *self*, and *substance*, to disguise the variation" (Hume, 1975, p. 302). The concept of identity serves as a disguise, a mask, that presents a unified face to the vagaries of human experience. So Hume would have little patience with contemporary ego psychology (Fromm, 1942), which pursues the psychological project of the integration of self, and Turkle's (1995) idealistic project of reconfigured and reintegrated postmodern identities on the Internet. Neither would the empiricist be impressed by the claims that these discontinuities in identity are the products of information technology. Identity is already chimerical, an idealist fiction.

Critical Identity

Certain IT narratives position themselves critically toward idealist and Enlightenment narratives. Against the utopian narratives of a transformed sense of identity, utopian community, and the dispersal of more and better information, we have the critical polemic of writers such as Barthes, Jameson, and Baudrillard. Contemporary critical theory takes a reformed Marxist line on the Enlightenment project. Revolution is the operative trope for the process of change – change becomes dialectical exchange – raising as its principle objective the dynamic project of resituating the individual in the community. Critical theory abhors the pressure on the individual to conform, but it is also suspicious of the extreme socialist position that presents the primacy of the collective over the individual. Critical education is a liberal and a liberating process by which pupils acquire the facility to challenge and dismantle existing structures of oppression (Freire, 1972).

Critical theory borrows substantially from structuralist language theory (Jameson, 1972). The theme of the mask provides a variation on the theme of the sign. Barthes (1973) provides a political account of everyday things: that drinking wine or beer each signal different social pretensions, as do clothing, costume, and our participation in various kinds of entertainment. Critical theory exhorts us to recognize how the obvious and overt signification can conceal other messages. So we need to look past the congeniality of the Pacific Islander on the cover of a magazine to the history of colonial oppression that this masks. The narrative of critical theory exhorts the removal of the fraud, the mask, that covers over our obsession with consumption and the hegemony of capitalism. The charge of fraud can also be leveled at the digital mask: the enthusiastic rhetoric of cyberspace, utopian visions of progress through information technology (Stallabrass, 1995).

Critical theory draws attention to at least five main ways that our obsessions with electronic communications and their putative communities operate to conceal. First, there is the problem of uneven access. Whatever we think about computer networks as a means of providing opportunity, restoring an informed and active citizenry, overcoming social barriers, and realizing Enlightenment educational objectives, access to networks is uneven. The Internet belongs to highly literate, economically progressive individuals, groups, and nations. Like all new and pervasive technologies, IT is implicated in the reconfiguration of social relations, and, whatever its merits or demerits, those who are not connected are at a disadvantage.

As data become increasingly available to those connected, so it becomes less accessible to those who are outside the network. The network reveals to some but conceals to others. This injustice is concealed by the rhetoric of ubiquitous access.

The second target of critical theory is the deception in the claims commonly made of communications networks. The claims of egalitarian access and the necessity, inevitability, and desirability of growth in computer systems conceals other agendas: the growth of big business, globalization, control, and the preparation of a yet more compliant consumer culture.

Third, the game of computer simulation masks other deceits. For Baudrillard (1988), the deception of conspicuous simulations (Disneyland theme parks, virtual reality, virtual communities, etc.) is that they mask the "unreality" of everyday existence in a consumer culture. They present the imaginary to make us believe that the rest is real. For Barthes, too, we are encouraged to be incensed about conspicuous evils (perhaps violent computer games or pornography on the net), while we are inured to the substantive, pernicious, and more complicated injustices of the whole – the hegemony that requires more careful analysis to identify and deal with. For critical theory, the most pernicious aspect of the (capitalist) mask is that it conceals the fact that there is a mask.

Fourth, there is the critique of the kind of reason promoted by computer logic. Computer systems encourage us to value that which presents itself to us informationally, in terms of propositions – the proposition itself being subject to critique. For Marcuse (1988), propositional logic is an attempt to arrest discussion by pronouncing the truth. Logic, as with all metanarrative systems, is a means of silencing dissent. It masks that which does not fit the logical schema. Insofar as computer systems promote this logic, they are a party to concealing domination under the metanarratives of logic, order, rule, and objective reasoning.

Fifth, for critical theorists, the technology does not stand in isolation as the force for oppression or liberation, but the social system comes under scrutiny. We need to subject the whole information society to analysis: consumers, advertisers, developers, designers, manufacturers, educators, and law makers. And computer networks implicate other technological systems and institutions: the mass media, communications, publishing, and systems of education. The focus on the putative transforming power of computer systems masks the wider picture.

Finally, on the subject of identity, Marcuse embraces Freud's implication that human identity is already and always caught up in struggle – within the "rhythm of liberation and domination" (Marcuse, 1987, p. 67).

Exhortations to find our true identity, and even the pursuit of identity as an issue, masks our engagement with life's struggles and attempts conformity to the status quo. The problem of identity is already an attempt to deflect concern from the social field.

Fluctuating Identity

Critical theory accords substantially with Heidegger's polemic against technological reason and draws from Heidegger in some cases. For Heidegger (1977), we are inescapably technological beings, measuring, attributing causes, looking for utility value, and constructing totalizing knowledge schemas. Also, in keeping with various strands from Romanticism, there is the suggestion that authentic being stands apart from a technological mode of existence. As we shall see, Heidegger also draws attention to the issue of masking and unmasking (concealing and revealing) as providing a way of understanding truth. There are two interrelated strands to Heidegger's contribution on the subject of identity that break with romanticism and inform an engagement with technology.

First, there is Heidegger's (1962) concept of Dasein. Dasein, a noun, is the label Heidegger coins to identify the entity that inquires after its own being. We can regard the term "Dasein" as a placeholder for what the romantic and empiricist traditions would regard as the subject, the agent, the self, an identity. But Heidegger attempts to move away from the Enlightenment schemas of self, personhood, individuality, and subjectivity. The self is displaced by Dasein, the being who is engaged before he or she is reflective. That is, as Dasein, we understand our place most authentically when we are engaged in a task of work, like the mason wielding a mallet or the painter engrossed in making an art work – not when we are reflecting, as did Descartes, the romantics, and empiricists, on our independence as a subject from a world of objects. From a Heideggerian perspective, we do not need to presume an independent-thinking subject, a whole and individual identity, before we encounter what it is to be in the world. We need to understand the nature of this absorbed being, the authentic understanding that comes prior to the constructs of self and identity. Whereas identity suggests an idealistic whole, a continuity, Dasein implicates the practical field of working and doing.

What then is identity according to Heidegger? To participate in identity, or to find one's identity, is to face the present squarely by "emplacing," participating in material circumstances, the "topology of being" (Pöggeler, 1989, p.228). This idea is the main advance of

Heidegger's (1969) revised principle of identity. For Heidegger, partici-pating in what it is to work as a stone mason wielding a mallet, an example of basic technological equipment, produces a more productive philosoph-ical system than the primacy of abstracted reflection (as presented through the idealist philosophy of Descartes). Without succumbing to Hume's pri-ority of subjectivity, or empirical certitude, Dasein resonates with aspects of Hume's concept of the experiential field of interruption and variation that the romantic and empiricist tradition later gathers up under the rubric of "personal identity."

Second, for Heidegger, difference is the essential characteristic of time (or more precisely of temporality): "Dasein is characterized as care through being-ahead-of-oneself and therefore is always not yet something" (Pöggeler, 1989, p. 44). In other words, there is little sense in talking about a thing (a cup, a table, a person) as having an identity (being a whole with essential properties or with an essence) independently of certain unrealized expectations manifested in a context of use. We need to engage with the thing and appreciate the differences it brings to light – to understand it as an entity with an identity. For Heidegger, the empir-ical model of identity assumes the preexistent identity of the object: the thing is the same as itself, an object is in the same category as itself, an object has the same properties as itself, $A = A$. This is a basic scientific principle, the mathematical principle of identity. But Heidegger draws attention to the space between the first and the second A, which brings to light the priority of difference. Science may deal with the incontrovert-ible, but Dasein, as identity, is always in flux: I am never simply the same as myself, I jump out of my own categories, I change attributes from one moment to the next, A does not equal A. For Heidegger, as far as Dasein is concerned, A never equals A, though they certainly belong together.

We can only hope to introduce Heidegger's concepts of identity here. By now it should be apparent that Heidegger looks beyond the traditional idealist, romantic, or empiricist view of identity to disclose more *authentic*, unsettled categories. Heidegger's discourse claims to be antimetaphysi-cal. It seeks to unsettle or problematize idealistic certainties, and it does so with recourse to an appeal to unreflective engagement, just being. In this and other aspects of Heidegger's work, there is accord with the prag-matism of Dewey and James and with certain developments in analytic philosophy, including the work of Ryle (1963) (who reviewed Heidegger's *Being and Time* in the 1920s soon after it was published in German). We have reviewed the relationship between Heidegger, pragmatism, and the appeal of Heidegger in certain computer studies elsewhere (Coyne, 1995).

Heidegger does not specifically deal with concepts of community; however, for him, the notion of community would begin through the question of identity as Dasein. His Dasein is always a being-with. The impetus for Heidegger was a "matter of placing the individual in his-self relation into the totalizing circle of being-with-one-another" (Pöggeler, 1989, p. xvii). His Dasein is always a being involved: "Earth as well as sky, the gods as well as mortals are never by themselves, but rather only together with the others; they are only in the onefold, the dance and round dance of the four, the play of the world" (Pöggeler, 1989, p. 201). This strand of thought is set out by Heidegger's phenomenology and is extended by Gadamer's hermeneutics, which are discussed later.

Education, as acquiring skill, experience, and knowledge, is subsumed by Heidegger's preoccupation with *thinking*. For Heidegger, thinking, authentic thought, involves "letting things be" rather than understanding things as objects, through measurement, qualitative attributes, and categories. Thinking operates in the ambiguity between what is new and what is existing: the space between that which is concealed and what is revealed. Heidegger's concept of thinking borrows from interpretations of pre-Socratic notions of flux and the Hegelian theme of authentic philosophy, or the movement of thought. This amalgam is not merely an individual instantiation but also a whole historical movement: the ways in which being (and human being) discloses itself through different epochal movements. This grand picture accords with concepts of edification rather than education. Education as knowledge acquisition is a secondary concern for Heidegger. But there are implications for education in the pragmatic aspects of Heidegger's thought that concern how the position of Dasein deals with the ambiguities of identity.

Heidegger's distinctions impinge on the role of information technology as a mask. Computer equipment commonly appears to us under one of two marketing strategies. Computers present themselves mutely, as familiar, inconspicuous, or ubiquitous objects, as a variation on the typewriter, television screen, hi-fi, and briefcase – modest mutations of technological equipment already familiar to us (Weiser, 1991). Alternatively, in the hyperbole of computer marketing, they present themselves as instances of the latest technology: responding to the developing literacy of IT and encasing themselves with glamorized materials, transparent plastics, and colorful, luminous finishes, with color-coded command buttons and anthropomorphized forms. They themselves are representations of computerized production, as first generation cyborgs. This duality (ubiquitous computing versus the showy consumer object) re-invokes the ambiguity that is intrinsic to identity – the difference between being and existence, here manifested in terms of the difference between the inconspicuous and the conspicuous. But this duality also invokes the duality that resides in concepts of representation. As a means of representing the latest in technological accomplishment, the computer operates as a mask.

How does the mask operate in Heidegger's schema? Masks conceal; however, they simultaneously reveal. Practical engagement with the masks of IT can ontologically disclose. In the case of constructing a building of stone, as the stone is struck, it discloses itself to the stone mason. Its character and nature is slowly revealed. It may be marble or granite, soft or hard, but in striking it, its nature is touched upon, communicated, and its temporal identity approximated. This is also the case with computers. The newness or unfamiliarity of equipment serves as a mask. Its purpose is concealed, but perhaps gives way to a new discovery. In the right setting, faced with a strange or unfamiliar language or tradition, an incidental distancing, an inducement to do things differently, the computer encourages questions of identity, of experimentation, and of devising strategies by which one gets closer to the issue of identity.

The medium of IT, as a representational format, operates as a sensual masking. In representing building (in CAD and 3D modeling systems), it misses aspects of things, especially those of tactility and embodiment. However, it may also be seen as providing a sensual enframing. As the chisel leaves traces on the stone, so does IT affect the products of its making. For example, the computer operates as a medium of light, allowing architecture to be explored as luminosity. The computer can temporarily sublimate questions of materials to allow other questions to come to the fore. As the transfer of knowledge from IT to production is materially affecting our architectural world, so it is affecting the artefacts of our world. In this way, Heidegger's ontological questions of being raise questions of disclosure and masking germane to IT practice (Coyne, Sudweeks & Haynes, 1996) and to the question of identity and the computer.

Identity Proliferated

Whereas Heidegger's project seems to establish powerful, systematic modes of thinking to counter traditional, idealist positions (on technology, equipment, thought, time, and identify), writers such as Derrida and Deleuze, attempt to radicalize Heidegger's project further in the direction of deconstruction. For the radicals (Caputo, 1987), Heidegger's reflections seem to be predicated on the pursuit of authenticity (the essential being behind the mask), albeit a tortured, highly problematized authenticity. Even though Heidegger writes extensively against totalizing metaphysical schemas, the radicals view Heidegger's commitment to concepts of authenticity, the ontological, and the primordial as metaphysical. The radicals question the notion of authenticity.

We can explain the radical position through a review of the nature of the mask. As we have seen, the romantic might celebrate the mask as a means of assuming different roles, dressing up, or living out a fantasy. Masked balls, carnivals, pageantry, the theater, and costume are the stock in trade of romance. There are places and occasions appropriate to the charade, where we momentarily cast aside the strictures of day-to-day reality, but the mask is always seen as a mask. This is also the case with romantic conceptions of IT. According to Murray (1999), the ability to play with masks, assume new identities, and present oneself through the mask of the avatar, is one of the strengths of the new, emerging narrative forms of cyberspace. We mask our true identity or assume a new identity by make-believe.

A conventional, empiricist view of masking would recognize that, outside the false imagery of the carnival, our experience is also fraught with exposure to superficialities – custom and prejudice. The mask provides a metaphor for the fact that there is something beneath the surface, some truth behind the barrier of our prejudices. In each case, the mask is artifice. The face behind it is the true object.

For critical theory, the mask is constituted by all the ruses of the capitalist system to conceal the hegemony of oppression. More perniciously, the mask conceals the fact that there is a mask.

Heidegger's phenomenology explicitly plays on the theme of masking and covering. The search for "truth" always involves us in the play of revealing and concealing (Heidegger, 1971a). As one thing is revealed so another is concealed, much as a spotlight operates through the relationship between the background field of darkness and the roving concentration of illumination. But the spotlight metaphor is limited. It suggests that there is a truth already there to be revealed by our inquiry. In keeping with empiricism and as developed in Popper's (1972) account of science, the tools of our inquiry often generate the facts, in the sense that observations are already laden with theory. The spotlight is already implicated in what can be seen. It shows things to be stark, silhouetted, and deeply shadowed. For Heidegger, we do not need to presume that there is a truth preexisting our inquiries. Neither are facts simply constructed, as though manufactured by the spotlight. A text or a work of art discloses ontologically in a way more basic than representing truth or creating it. This is

the ontological quest for truth as disclosure. To explain the phenomenological position in terms of the mask, the mask is an artifice, but the face
behind it is subject to the same account. The question of what constitutes
a mask and what is not is subject to the workings of the practical field of
engagement. So Heidegger deflects attention away from the mask to the
context, the situation in which the masking takes place: the masquerade
party, the theater, the dressing-up game, and the practices of getting into
and out of computer role games.

Following on from Heidegger, the radical position probes and distorts
the mask itself. Insofar as it acts as a signifier, the mask deflects the function
of the sign away from the object behind the mask to some other object. So
the mask presents the wearer as a harlequin, a monster, or a clown. But the
object to which the mask refers is also a mask: depictions of monsters and
clowns are artifices that refer to other masked creatures. These, in turn,
are caught up in a series of references to well-known masked creatures and
other mythic characters. The mask participates in this chain of reference,
which turns out not to terminate in some fixed referent. The meaning
of the mask seems to invoke an endless series of references that leaves a
trace. Manipulating the mask metaphor further, the mask bears a series of
imprints from previous maskings. In turn, these leave an impression on
the face. Alternatively, the face is but one of a series of masks. The essential
being behind the mask is shown also to be a mask. This is tantamount to
asserting that there is nothing behind the mask, there is everything behind
the mask, or the mask is everything. This discourse further invokes the
concept of the transparent mask. We see through one mask to another,
and it is in the translucency of their interaction that something is revealed.

For the radical, the mask is a metaphor for the workings of signification, but metaphor also acts as a mask. According to Aristotle, metaphor
is giving a thing a name that belongs to something else, $A = B$. As such,
the mask is prone to all the workings of metaphor, which simply involves
the juxtaposition of two terms. To see a house as a machine (a well-known
architectural metaphor) is to apply the machine mask to the house object.
To see the MUD-role-playing impresario as a wizard is to apply the wizard mask to the computer game controller. But for theorists of metaphor
(Ricoeur, 1977; Black, 1979; Lakoff, 1987), the two terms inform each
other. We see house as machine, but the machine also assumes houselike
properties. After being immersed in IT narratives, it is difficult to think
of mythic creatures – wizards and elves – now without seeing them as a
particular form of computer user. Metaphor also invokes a play between
concepts of the literal and the figurative. In traditional terms, the house is

not literally a machine, the computer user is not literally a wizard, but we still understand the metaphoric association. For Ricoeur, language operates precisely in this space between the truthful and the fanciful, between literal falsity and metaphorical truth. Insofar as the mask participates in the workings of metaphor, it also operates between the literal and the figurative. The Darth Vader mask and the ten-year-old wearing it presents an incongruity, provoking reflections and inquiries comparable to the metaphor of "child as despotic over-lord of mass destruction" and invoking a tangled web of diverse references – the apparatuses of consumer culture, Jungian archetypes, and child psychology. Such is the abstruse and oblique nature of the metaphor, and the mask.

Insofar as education implicates the metaphor of the mask, for the radical, the mask operates as a provocation. It sets up a difference, a distanciation (Gallagher, 1991) between the subject matter and the learner. The role of the educator is also to provide the mask, to draw attention to it, to evoke curiosity as to what lies behind. In Whitehead's (1929) terminology, it is to render the familiar strange, by disguising it as something peculiar, and to dress up the strange in familiar guise. This is a continuous provocation. So, for the architecture student, the familiarity of the house is rendered strange under the guise of the house as a machine. It provokes particular lines of inquiry and controversy. At the same time architectural education can render the strange language of architecture (space, place, threshold, land use, procurement, phenomenology) cosy and comfortable through familiarity and repeated usage. At its best, education involves the careful negotiation along this knife edge between the strange and the familiar: the judicious use of masks.

In accord with this game of the mask, Deleuze and Guattari (1984) present a radical affront to concepts of community. Whereas traditional concepts of community seem to appeal substantially to notions of common ground, integration, and wholeness, for Deleuze and Guattari the operative trope is schizophrenia: the condition of the fragmented, deluded, unstable personality. The psychotic subversive is to be let loose, to develop "action, thought, and desires by proliferation, juxtaposition, and disjunction," in opposition to the process of building structures: "subdivision and pyramidal hierarchization" (Deleuze & Guattari, 1984, p. xiii). The task of "schizoanalysis" is destruction: "a whole scouring of the unconscious, a complete curettage" (p. 311). The conjecture of schizoanalysis presents as an unsettled masking and remasking, a disruption of conventional appearances and roles, a laying bare of the putative unconscious and its repressed conditions. It also serves as means of exposing what is behind the mask of conventional analysis. Deleuze and Guattari's conjecture serves as an example of radical pedagogy. In *Anti-Oedipus: Capitalism and Schizophrenia*, Deleuze and Guattari (1984) assume the role of the provocateur, presenting a series of outrages as a means of provoking not just their readers but also their own thinking. In taking on the role of provocateur, they assume the mask of intellectual trickster.

Radicalizing Change

Radical hermeneutics, as exemplified by Deleuze, picks up the thread of Hume's experientially conditioned problematic of identity. Hume and Heidegger conspire to present a radical position on temporality, granting ontological precedence to the concept of difference, a position that also engenders speculation on being. The problem of identity is presented as the problem of how identity is disclosed at specific points in time. Being discloses itself as a temporal phenomenon.

Heidegger (1969) sets identity as an issue in contrast to difference. For Heidegger, difference precedes identity. That is, we need to understand what difference is before we can come to terms with identity. Heidegger's various phenomenological analyses start with the distinction between being and existence. To talk about Dasein is to address the issue of being. On the other hand, to speak of the self is to deal merely with matters of existence, a convenience for the contingencies of empirical inquiry. Heidegger makes great play of this difference: between the ontological and the ontic, between phenomenological understanding and scientific knowing, between thinking and merely philosophizing. This difference between the ontological and the ontic is not just a major and interesting difference, but it also defines difference itself. As the archetypal difference, it is as different as things can get. All examples of difference, between the properties of this cup and the one next to it, derive from tensions between being and existence, the engaged mode of being that is Dasein, and the analytic reflection that posits a notion of the self.

In relating time to repetition, Deleuze (1994) borrows from Nietzsche's (1977, p. 253) concept of the "Eternal Recurrence of The Same." Deleuze deflects attention from the answer to the question of identity (what is identity?) onto the incessant recurrence of the question itself. Identity is raised as a question time and time again. Repetition is not characterized so much as a repetition of the same circumstances, events or questions through time, but a repetition of the inquiry into identity. The question of identity in past, present, and future time is never settled, even in the traditions of conventional inquiry. In empiricist terms, the question of identity is culturally conditioned. The issue of identity as a problematic is the result of an interpretation reflecting the concerns of the moment. For Deleuze's radical hermeneutic position, the question into identity requires a further reinterpretive act to get closer to the nature of identity. Deleuze places difference central to all inquiry and constructs a critical framework alongside Heidegger's concern for the ontological. Deleuze wishes to undermine the romanticist view that gives authority to the past and glorifies an idealized future. He tries to agitate the stasis in the model of past, present, and future. Deleuze considers the present as repeater, repeater of the question into identity, past as repetition itself, all history being merely an initial inquiry into identity. Future is that which is repeated, the necessary return of the inquiry. In his model, the future is valorized as the "royal repetition" – the moment of time understood from the present, which stands as a constant reminder of the need to inquire after the essence of things but also as a reminder of the central position and corollary of difference. That identity changes, and it is entirely necessary for it to do so.

To summarize, for radical hermeneutics, identity is always in question, rather than being a static idea. Change, or difference, is the central dynamic that conditions identity, rather than a superficial effect. Time is not merely an infinite linear progression of moments but must be considered through a complex critical model that fractures conventional concepts of past, present, and future.

In the traditional account, also known as the romantic and empiricist account, "community" is the term that describes differing individuals coming together and sharing a common ground. The image of an easily accessible technological ground of abundant information presents the users of IT as an idealized community. The ground destabilized by radical hermeneutics and Deleuze's "schizoanalysis" explores the common ground and asks whether a common ground can exist? Derrida (1976) also suggests that the questions raised by looking into the chasms within the broken ground are not exclusive to technologies but are integral to our language systems. The problems of technology are the natural conditions resulting from considering language as a problematic. Embedded in our language lie all prejudices and a priori judgments. Radical hermeneutics from Derrida's position, attempts to re-define the language which defines community, and, as for Deleuze, this requires "playing an open game" of the question into identity by also considering the discursive possibilities for communities and technologies. From the radical position, it is no longer possible to discuss identity in traditional terms. Identity is constantly in flux, the repetition of the question into identity being the only constant. By its very nature, identity is always elusive, and the notion of community follows suit.

For radical hermeneutics, the interrelationship of architecture and IT also become particularly charged on the question of representation, a further issue of the mask. Architecture shares with IT an affinity with the Cartesian language of space. The virtual world of the computer shares the same language as the architectural model (the computer, perspex, or wooden model), and technology is often promoted as able to produce more accurate models, conforming to closer correspondences through the language of Cartesian geometry. We commonly assume that as the technology develops so does the accuracy of the model, ultimately suggesting that the virtual world can transcend and even supplant the physical world. For Deleuze, this world of Cartesian representation is illusory, a mask of deception he seeks to render transparent. A representational model is a simulacrum, a nontruth. Recognizing the nontruth of the model permits the possibility for ontological disclosure. In other words, new typologies of objects, or, in terms of phenomenology, new modes of being, can be revealed. When we reflect on how the thing represented is so unlike the representation, then we can see both the object and its model afresh. So the cardboard model of the building brings to attention folding, cutting, layering, and sharp angles. But the representation and the represented act as the two terms of a metaphor, each informing the other. Each inform the other, just as the model and the building inform. Operating in radical mode, the practitioner and pedagogue can render the mask of the model transparent. This is to recognize that representation deals in metaphor. It is also to play with the identities of the thing and its representation (the object and the model) and the repeated questioning of which is which. For Deleuze, to play with the varying opacities and transparencies of the mask is to join in the dynamic between difference and repetition.

The game of charades that IT invites would be welcomed by radical hermeneutics. The computer can be seen as a learning medium: a testing ground for the active re-edifying process of identity. The dislocation and masking that is characteristic of virtual presence requestions the veracity of specific sensibilities. Identity is already fractured by the abstraction of the qualitative, quantitative, and locational aspects of change. Only the destructive and generative aspects of Aristotle's model of change remain intact. Identity is newly created by the on switch and destroyed by the shut down command. On each occasion of starting up, it is clear that each encounter places identity as a problematic, to be clarified by the active participation in asking questions and engaging in conversation.

Interpreting Identity

Gadamerian hermeneutics attempts to put the radicals in their place. We argue that the radical position is subsumed within the hermeneutical and that to focus on the hermeneutical is to elevate *practice*: a major concern of IT touching on issues of design, use, and context.

Gadamer (1975) progresses Heidegger's phenomenological project on a different trajectory to the radicals, to make explicit that the particular task for the being who inquires after his or her own being is hermeneutical (i.e., engaged in a question of interpretation). For Gadamer, this involves a reflective dimension from the beginning of the inquiry (Gadamer, 1976, p. 45). To understand oneself is not merely to accept an externalized, quasi-common-sense definition of identity, an uncritical acceptance of a particular community's view of what constitutes knowledge, or a preconceived view of what is identifiable but requires an ontological encounter with knowledge. It demands reflection on the processes of acquiring knowledge to make knowledge authentic by truly understanding as a thinking being what is knowable. This sees the core of knowledge as understanding, and Gadamer, like Deleuze, treats understanding as a process of repetition. Deleuze borrows from Gadamer. However, whereas Deleuze focuses specifically on the issue of identity as a subjective concept, Gadamer's concern is for the relationship between understanding and knowledge: "Understanding is not a mere act of reproduction of knowledge . . . rather, understanding is *aware* of the fact that it is indeed an act of repeating" (Gadamer, 1976, p. 45). This is a repeating of the initial inquiry into that which is inquired of, a repeating of the search for authentic knowledge. Hermeneutical inquiry is contingent on the relationship between individual and community. The question into self identity is therefore not simply a question of the interpretation of individual identity but requires the interpretation of the relationship between the individual and communities, and the traditions in which they participate.

According to Gadamer, the special circumstance of the hermeneutical problem appears when there is either no tradition that absorbs one's interpretive practice or when confronted by an alien tradition. This observation leads to the hermeneutical project's particular method of inquiry: the establishment of distance and acknowledging the situatedness of experience. This process of distanciation is promoted through two ontological practices, understood through the metaphors of conversation and play, and characterized by a non-self-conscious dynamic. Through conversation and play, the interpreter inevitably moves to a new position. Ricoeur (1981) analyzes these metaphors under his theory of appropriation – a reciprocal exchange between appropriation and relinquishment, wherein we move from a position that takes an identity initially deemed familiar and subsequently relinquishes it by making it alien through distanciation. After reflection we return, refamiliarized with the identity, not as the same identity, but certainly colored by the initial encounter. Heidegger (1971a) also refers to these processes as appropriation and expropriation. Gadamer refers to them under the theme of play: the "to-and-fro of play" (Gadamer, 1986, p. 23); the complementary nature of the simultaneous underlining of an identity and the abstraction of that identity, the identity played with; and a movement between loss of self and acquisition of self. So Ricoeur, Heidegger, and Gadamer are involved in similar projects of re-interpretation, appealing to processes that involve a fluctuation between de-edification and re-edification.

Gadamer's initial observation and resulting interpretive practices are particularly incisive for educators and students. If education involves acquiring new understanding, a process of "enlightenment," then most interpretive practice must initially be considered as an encounter with the alien. Gadamer's acknowledgment of the "futurity" of Heidegger's Dasein, that is the basic character of projection that befits its temporality, presents the hermeneutical task as raising questions from the encounters between traditions, traditions of history, and traditions as they are encountered through practice – including the romantic, empirical, and hermeneutical traditions.

As a practical hermeneutics, and the writing of this chapter provides an example, the task of hermeneutics is to make clearings for "the bridging of personal or historical distance between minds" (Gadamer, 1976, p. 95). Practical hermeneutics does not seek to "penetrate the masks" which infect public opinion, thereby carrying on the pure traditions of the enlightenment which tries to overcome all prejudices. It sees this objective as a prejudice in itself and merely the application of a new mask. Hermeneutics acknowledges the likelihood of individual practice already being contingent on the practices of community, and therefore already caught up in the process of masking. To extend the metaphor, practical hermeneutics plays the role of jester, as well as king, and participates in the theater of role play: of wearing masks, removing masks, and donning new masks. In this oscillation between a concealing and revealing, one can comprehend practical differences, which brings us closer to the nature of identity and community. The hermeneutical position does not abandon the metaphor of the mask, but it recognizes its role in the master metaphor of the play of tradition.

Practical Implications

We can summarize by drawing attention to several corollaries for information technology on the question of identity. First, the ideological view of continuity and changelessness places IT as the romantic and empiricist tradition's latest representative. Presenting IT as a better tool for the implementation of imperatives – varying from moral, aesthetic, religious, juridical, technological, and representational – this imperative misses the opportunity for IT as a medium to contribute to the dynamic discourse of change in all areas. The computer can act as a provocation, rendering the familiar strange again.

Second, the hermeneutical narrative suggests that we should take up the invitation to play in all seriousness. The putative universal is one of a selection of masks that can be donned, suggesting the possibility of an ironic encounter with universal ideas (freedom, truth, justice), whilst simultaneously offering the same possibility with the alternatives that consequently stand in relief (restraint, error, exclusivity). Why should we give priority to the utopian practice of the emancipated technologically creative spirit (Benedikt, 1991), or the mutant-cyborg-inhabited dystopia of Gibson (1993), or Virilio's (1991) utopia of technological exchange? The appropriateness of whichever mask we choose depends on the reciprocal shift from specific realm to discursive realm, from individual to community. Our obsession with technoromanticism can be countered by a pragmatic playful scepticism. The virtual reality helmet need not be an opaque mask putting the wearer in a condition of blindness.

Third, Dewey's rejection of the Cartesian divide, and relinking of theory and practice as one and the same, underlines an orientation toward effective education. We can see Heidegger's phenomenological task and Gadamer's hermeneutic task as an extension of this pragmatism: the practical engagement in reflective practice from the outset of all inquiry.

Fourth, the reconstitution of community and the individual by dialectical exchange through the critique of domination – as pseudo democracy, exclusivity, technomorality, hyperreality, embeddedness of reason, isolated practice – is, as Deleuze points out, still caught up in causal and ideological practice. Its initial universalization, practically stated as globalization of power structures, in some way is guilty of reification, the very thing it sets out to counter. It assumes a trapped individual from the outset. Because of its global moral imperative, it limits the inquiry, and perhaps limits the opportunity for localized emancipation. The characterizing of individual as slave leaves the possibility of emancipation only by acquiring the costume and armament of the hero.

Fifth, Heidegger's encouragement to investigate the topology of being, points the way for participation in the practice of IT. His notion of temporality with its propensity toward futurity provides an optimistic foundation from which to begin an interpretive inquiry, a theme taken up in IT commentary by Winograd & Flores (1986), Dreyfus (1972, 1990), Borgman (1999), and Coyne (1994, 1998).

Sixth, the fractured identity and the resultant fractured world that the radical hermeneutical critique brings to discourse certainly yields insights, but its in-built scepticism may be accused of leading to an ideological solipsism, which cares little for the communicability, the community, of ideas. To only edify on unstable ground in fragile material renders the world insubstantial and offers a pessimistic view, the view of Virilio (1991), among others.

Finally, the pragmatic model favors the position of a "moderate" hermeneutics (Gallagher, 1991), which always returns the issue of identity back to practice. The pragmatic view acknowledges the prejudices of various practices and seeks to make practice a discourse promoting it in the specific and discursive realms. The discourse acquires accessibility by offering a more playful critique that reveals the prejudicial ground, background, and foreground. With regard to IT, the discourse can be extended by participation in its many games, serious and flippant, and its various apparatuses of conversation – the issues of identity, community, and change remain open always for localized edification, as a result of the play between masking and unmasking.

Acknowledgments

Chistopher Pierce helped us develop the theme of the mask in the context of the design studio. We are indebted to Adrian Snodgrass for introducing the theme of hermeneutics to our understanding of design.

References

Allen, R. E. (1966). *Greek philosophy: Thales to Aristotle*. New York: Free Press.
Arendt, H. (1958). *The human condition*. Chicago: University of Chicago Press.
Barthes, R. (1973). *Mythologies* (A. Lavers, Trans.). London: Paladin.

Baudrillard, J. (1988). Simulacra and simulations. In *Jean Baudrillard: Selected writings* (pp. 166–84). Stanford: Stanford University Press.

Benedikt, M. (1991). *Cyberspace: First steps*. Cambridge, MA: MIT Press.

Black, M. (1979). More about metaphor. In A. Ortony (Ed.), *Metaphor and thought* (pp. 19–43). Cambridge, England: Cambridge University Press.

Borgman, A. (1999). *Holding on to reality: The nature of information at the turn of the millennium*. Chicago: University of Chicago Press.

Caputo, J. D. (1987). *Radical hermeneutics: Repetition, deconstruction, and the hermeneutical project*. Bloomington: Indiana University Press.

Coyne, R. D. (1994). Heidegger and virtual reality: The implications of Heidegger's thinking for computer representations. *Leonardo, 27* (1), 65–73.

    (1995). *Designing information technology in the postmodern age: From method to metaphor*. Cambridge, MA: MIT Press.

    (1998). Cyberspace and Heidegger's pragmatics. *Information technology and people*, Special Issue: Heidegger and Information Technology, *11*(4), 338–50.

    (1999). *Technoromanticism: Digital narrative, holism, and the romance of the real*. Cambridge, MA: MIT Press.

Coyne, R. D., Sudweeks, F., & Haynes, D. (1996). Who needs the Internet? Computer-mediated communication in design firms. *Environment and Planning B: Planning and Design, 23*, 749–70.

Deleuze, G. (1994). *Difference and repetition* (P. Patton, Trans.). London: Athlone Press.

Deleuze, G., & Guattari, F. (1984). *Anti-Oedipus: Capitalism and schizophrenia* (R. Hurley, M. Seem, and H. Lane, Trans.). London: Athlone Press.

Derrida, J. (1976). *Of grammatology* (G. Spivak, Trans.). Baltimore, MD: Johns Hopkins University Press.

Dery, M. (1996). *Escape velocity: Cyberculture at the end of the century*. London: Hodder and Stoughton.

Dewey, J. (1916). *Democracy and education: An introduction to the philosophy of education*. New York: Free Press.

Dreyfus, H. L. (1972). *What computers can't do: The limits of artificial intelligence*. New York: Harper and Row.

    (1990). *Being-in-the-world: A commentary on Heidegger's being and time division I*. Cambridge, MA: MIT Press.

Freire, P. (1972). *Pedagogy of the oppressed* (M. B. Ramos, Trans.). New York: Herder and Herder.

Fromm, E. (1942). *The fear of freedom*. London: Routledge and Kegan Paul.

Gadamer, H.-G. (1975). *Truth and method*. London: Sheed Ward.

    (1976). *Philosophical hermeneutics* (D. E. Linge, Trans.). Berkeley: University of California Press.

    (1986). The relevance of the beautiful: Art as play, symbol, and festival. In R. Bernasconi (Ed.), *The relevance of the beautiful and other essays*. Cambridge, UK: Cambridge University Press, pp. 3–53.

Gallagher, S. (1991). *Hermeneutics and education*. Albany: State University of New York Press.

Gates, B. (1996). *The road ahead*. London: Penguin.

Gibson, W. (1993). *Neuromancer*. London: Harper Collins.

Heidegger, M. (1962). *Being and time* (J. Macquarrie and E. Robinson, Trans.). London: SCM Press.

(1969). *Identity and difference* (J. Stambaugh, Trans.). New York: Harper and Row.

(1971a). The origin of the work of art. In M. Heidegger *Poetry, language, thought* (A. Hofstadter, Trans.) (pp. 15–87). New York: Harper and Row.

(1971b). The thing. In M. Heidegger *Poetry, language, thought* (A. Hofstadter, Trans.) (pp. 165–86). New York: Harper and Row.

(1977). *The question concerning technology and other essays* (W. Lovitt, Trans.). New York: Harper and Row.

Heim, M. (1993). *The metaphysics of virtual reality*. New York: Oxford University Press.

Hiltz, S. R., & Turoff, M. (1994). *The network nation: Human communication via computer*. Cambridge, MA.: MIT Press. (First published in 1978.)

Hume, D. (1975). *Enquiries concerning the human understanding and concerning the principles of morals*. Oxford: Clarendon Press.

Jameson, F. (1972). *The prison-house of language: A critical account of structuralism and Russian formalism*. Princeton, NJ: Princeton University Press.

Lakoff, G. (1987). *Women, fire, and dangerous things: What categories reveal about the mind*. Chicago: University of Chicago Press.

Locke, J. (1960). *An essay concerning human understanding* (A. D. Woozley, Ed.). London: Collins. (First published in 1698.)

Marcuse, H. (1987). *Eros and civilisation: A philosophical inquiry into Freud*. London: Routledge and Kegan Paul.

(1988). *One-dimensional man: Studies in the ideology of advanced industrial society*. London: Routledge.

Moravec, H. (1988). *Mind children: The future of robot and human intelligence*. Cambridge, MA: Harvard University Press.

Murray, J. H. (1999). *Hamlet on the holodeck: The future of narrativity in cyberspace*. Cambridge, MA: MIT Press.

Novak, M. (1991). Liquid architectures in cyberspace. In M. Benedikt (Ed.), *Cyberspace: First steps* (pp. 225–54). Cambridge, MA: MIT Press.

Plotinus. (1948). *The essence of Plotinus: Extracts from the six enneads and Porphyry's life of Plotinus* (G. H. Turnbull, Ed.; S. Mackenna, Trans.). New York: Oxford University Press.

Pöggeler, O. (1989). *Martin Heidegger's path of thinking* (D. Magurshak and S. Barber, Trans.). Atlantic Highlands, NJ: Humanities Press International.

Popper, K. (1972). *Objective knowledge: An evolutionary approach*. London: Oxford University Press.

Ricoeur, P. (1977). *The rule of metaphor* (R. Czerny with K. McLaughlin and J. Costello, Trans.). London: Routledge and Kegan Paul.

(1981). *The conflict of interpretations: Essays in hermeneutics* (D. Ihde, Ed.). Evanston: Northwestern University Press.

Rousseau, J. J. (1974). *Emile* (B. Foxley, Trans.). London: Dent.

Ryle, G. (1963). *Concept of mind*. Harmondsworth: Penguin.

Schneiderman, B. (1994). Education by engagement and construction: A strategic education initiative for a multimedia renewal of American education. In

E. Barrett (Ed.), *Sociomedia: Multimedia, hypermedia, and the social construction of knowledge* (pp. 13–26). Cambridge, MA: MIT Press.

Snodgrass, A., & Coyne, R. D. (1998). Is designing hermeneutical? *Architectural Theory Review, 2*(1), 65–97.

Stallabrass, J. (1995). Empowering technology: The exploration of cyberspace, *New Left Review, 211*: 3–32.

Stewart, S. (1999). *Sir Henry Wotton's* The elements of architecture *and the articulation of justice: A discourse on theory and practice*. Unpublished PhD thesis, University of Sydney, Sydney.

Taylor, C. (1989). *Sources of the self: The making of the modern identity*. New York: Cambridge University Press.

Turkle, S. (1995). *Life on the screen: Identity in the age of the Internet*. London: Weidenfeld and Nicolson.

Virilio, P. (1991). *The aesthetics of disappearance* (P. Beitchman, Trans.). Brooklyn, NY: Semiotext(e).

Weiser, M. (1991). The computer for the 21st century. *Scientific American, 265*(3), 66–75.

Whitehead, A. N. (1929). *The aims of education and other essays*. New York: Macmillan and Company.

Winograd, T., & Flores, F. (1986). *Understanding computers and cognition: A new foundation for design*. Reading, MA.: Addison Wesley.

8 WISE Learning Communities

Design Considerations

Alex J. Cuthbert, Douglas B. Clark, and Marcia C. Linn

In this chapter, we identify design considerations and strategies for creating online learning communities. Learning communities encourage integrated understanding and develop a common set of criteria for evaluating ideas. We report on four distinct learning communities focused on teacher professional development, curriculum authoring, scientific inquiry, and peer review of projects. The examples illustrate the design considerations and strategies that we use to facilitate the transformation and sharing of resources to support integrated understanding within learning communities.

Design considerations are general guidelines for creating effective communities. This chapter illustrates four design considerations for creating successful learning communities:

- Support the actual practices and daily tasks of the participants,
- Collect experiences and represent them in an accessible and equitable manner,
- Provide a framework to guide the learning process,
- Represent the identities of the community members.

We implement these design considerations in our communities using various design strategies. For example, a strategy for representing the identities of community members involves displaying photographs alongside comments in discussions. These design strategies, based on the underlying design considerations, encourage community members to share their ideas, build on each other's views, and refine their own understanding. Our instructional framework, called "scaffolded knowledge integration" (SKI; Linn & Hsi, 2000), inspired our design considerations and guided the learning process in the communities.

In this chapter, we describe how our design considerations and strategies scaffold four teacher and student communities as they exchange resources, develop coherent ideas, and support individual understanding. All four communities use the Web-based Integrated Science Environment (WISE; wise.berkeley.edu) to develop and interact with these resources, which include Web pages, class ideas, and scientific investigations.

WISE, like our design considerations, is informed by the scaffolded knowledge integration framework. WISE emphasizes coherent understanding by supporting participants as they compare, contrast, sort out, and organize their ideas. WISE enables participants to support ideas with evidence and compare alternatives. From a community-building perspective, we illustrate how different strategies can progressively involve members by helping them become resources for other students and teachers.

Background and Rationale

In this chapter, we describe the design of teacher professional development, curriculum authoring, scientific inquiry, and peer review communities that each play decisive roles in achieving the goal of improving science education. We define learning communities as supporting networks of personal relationships that enable the exchange of resources and the development of a common framework for analysis of these resources. Members of the community jointly analyze resources and develop a common set of criteria for evaluating those resources. We define resources as a collection of ideas or interactions that are accessible to community members and can be incorporated into their practice. Communities, with their boundary conditions, niches, and cycles of opportunity, evolve as they organize, transform, and sort resources.

The four communities we describe form an interconnected set, supporting the teaching and learning of science (Barksdale, 1998). We draw on models from ecological systems where locating relevant information has associated costs and benefits (Pirolli & Card, 1995). From this ecological perspective, resources are most useful when they pass through a series of transformations that make them suitable for multiple functions. For curriculum-authoring communities, these transformations occur as project authors locate, organize, and annotate Web sites for inclusion in projects. Well-designed online communities can transform the resources that comprise curriculum materials to make them more successful, useful, and effective for instruction. Naturally, communities can also make unproductive transformations. Our strategies structure relationships in communities, guiding them toward specific pedagogical goals.

Our approach resonates with ideas from cognitive apprenticeship and related frameworks for characterizing community practices (Saxe & Guberman, 1998; Tudge & Rogoff, 1989; Vygotsky, 1978). Cognitive apprenticeship (Collins, Brown & Newman, 1989) calls for innovative participation patterns in communities of practice (see Lave & Wenger, 1992). This synthesis of approaches adds a cognitive dimension to the social learning theories derived from Vygotsky's social–historical perspective on development.

Vygotsky's "zone of proximal development" refers to situations where students can complete certain tasks only with the aid of peers or adults. Even though some pedagogy experts have focused on the zone of proximal development, it is important for community designers to remember that this construct is part of a larger perspective on how learning, development, and membership in communities of practice shift over time. We can design cultures that help students interact with each other and the teacher in ways that lead toward understanding of complex activities such as scientific inquiry. From the cognitive apprenticeship perspective, students are apprentices. Practices and patterns of participation are modeled by the teacher and, in turn, by students and their peers. Students become resources for each other by assuming specific roles, such as summarizer or questioner (Brown, 1992). Other students emulate these roles, appropriating the associated language and perspectives. Students often provide encouragement in the zone of proximal development since they share many common experiences with their peers.

The scaffolded knowledge integration framework is inspired by cognitive apprenticeship and the work of Vygotsky. The framework has four design tenets that jointly encourage students to link and connect their ideas so that they develop more integrated and cohesive ideas. These tenets are (a) to make the process of thinking visible, (b) to make science accessible, (c) to encourage students to learn from each other, and (d) to foster lifelong learning. The scaffolded knowledge integration framework is an integral part of our design considerations for online communities. For example, the need to collect experiences and represent them in an accessible and equitable manner is closely related to making thinking visible and encouraging students to learn from each other. The importance of this framework as well as the design considerations for online communities will become clearer as we present the different examples of communities, associated strategies for making thinking visible, and techniques for representing resources.

The Web-Based Integrated Science Environment

The communities discussed in this paper are all supported through the Web-based Integrated Science Environment (Slotta & Linn, 2000). Following the scaffolded knowledge integration framework, our instructional and design strategies seek to make science accessible for inspection, to make thinking visible, and thereby to help students learn from each other about the process of scientific investigation. WISE stresses the coordination and integration of ideas as well as encouraging different paths for learning. By mixing hands-on learning with online discussions and modeling tools, WISE creates a repertoire of representations that aid students as they become part of a community of learners. These representations also provide supports for teachers and curriculum designers as they collect resources for constructing projects.

The WISE Perspective

WISE activities are designed to feature generative resources and to engage students in connecting and critiquing information rather than absorbing more and more ideas. There is, in fact, little evidence to support the assumption that the instant availability of information will improve the quality of communication (Goldsmith, 1998). In WISE, our primary vehicle for improving curriculum and enhancing communication is iterative refinement based on reflection and analysis. Research into effective teaching and design strategies also informs the design of our learning communities.

WISE employs Internet sites as evidence to support theories, arguments, and design decisions (see Figure 8.1). In many WISE projects, the presence of a shared product or resource grounds discussions, creating the potential for negotiation, clarification, justification, synthesis, and other processes that contribute to knowledge integration (Slotta & Linn, 2000). In addition, developing a common framework for learning helps to focus and guide discussion, contributing to the sense of a shared commitment about pedagogical strategies.

In WISE, the inquiry map in the left-hand frame guides students through the activities and steps that comprise a project. An on-demand guide provides hints and prompts for students, helping them reflect on

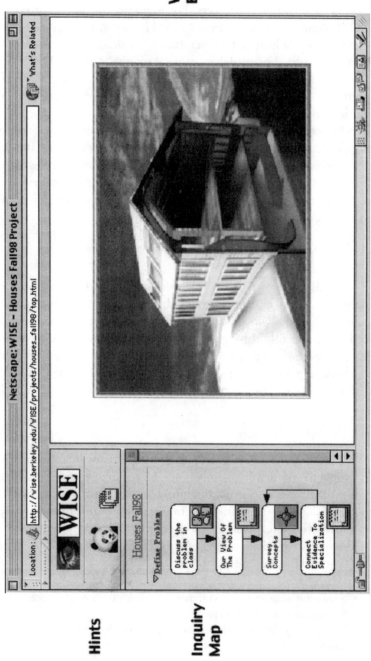

**WISE
Evidence**

Hints

**Inquiry
Map**

Figure 8.1. The Web-based integrated science environment.

their own thinking processes as well as providing procedural guidance. These features support teachers as they learn how to use WISE and students as they complete projects. For example, the WISE project in Figure 8.1 shows an evidence item from "Houses in the Desert" where students learn about heat and temperature while designing a passive solar house for the desert. Theory debate projects such as "How Far Does Light Go?" help students organize evidence in support of different theories and perspectives. A third type of project is a critique project where students critique scientific claims.

To help authoring communities and to capture productive activity structures, we created templates for critique, collaborative debate, and design projects focused on scientific inquiry. Online communities are an integral part of this inquiry process in WISE. For example, teachers learn about effective teaching strategies by participating in a NetCourse that introduces them to WISE's pedagogical framework.

The Role of the Teacher

WISE changes the dynamics and culture of the classroom by freeing the teacher to circulate through the class and interact with groups of students. The built-in guidance scaffolds students so that they can proceed independently through the different projects. Learning to use WISE requires teachers to adopt a new stance toward teaching where they serve more as a guide-on-the-side than as a sage-on-the-stage, standing in front of the class transmitting knowledge.

The Role of Resources

We define resources as a collection of ideas or interactions that are accessible to community members and can be incorporated into their practice. WISE uses resources to scaffold and support interactions. By designing resources to support social interactions, WISE provides models of constructive engagement as well as offering community tools for connecting people working on shared projects. Examples of constructive engagement include, but are not limited to,

- Seeding discussions with comments to illustrate how evidence is used to support different theories;
- Using video clips of student–teacher interactions to anchor discussions about pedagogy;

- Developing templates for activities to guide project authors as they create projects involving theory debate, critique, and design.

Comments in online discussions are viewed as resources because students and teachers can refer to them for guidance. Web sites are another type of resource. Web sites that are potential candidates for use in projects are annotated by project authors, becoming WISE "evidence pages."

Other types of resources include entire curriculum projects, assessment measures, pivotal cases (frequently in digital video format), hints and prompts within projects, and static text such as FAQs or documentation. These resources can be referenced in a variety of ways. Projects (and evidence pages) can be duplicated and modified. Online discussions serve both as historical records of exchanges between community members and as ongoing forums to support authoring groups and professional development classes. Web pages can be cross-referenced in online discussions, linking two categories of resources.

We want resources to be easily accessible to teachers and students. In addition, we want the connections between resources to be represented in a way that leads to knowledge integration. In short, we want to help make the process of thinking visible for students. Given this perspective, our analysis examines how resources are connected and organized in WISE communities. For example, annotated Web sites are substantially different than a set of links to those sites since the annotations may contain information about the credibility, reliability, and usefulness of the site. "Advance organizers" for Web pages help students focus on relevant topics so that they can more effectively use evidence in Web pages to support their arguments. The advance organizer introduces the Web site, focuses attention on a specific part of a site, or highlights a question that students should focus on when reading the material. Students can then take notes on the site and even publish these notes so that other members of the class can see them.

As researchers and designers, we need to understand the types of resources in a community system, how they are represented, and how they can be connected. Many factors influence the ways in which communities exchange and develop resources (Bowker & Star, 2000). The WISE software lets teachers and researchers track how resources circulate through communities, providing insights into the processes of community development. In addition, making the process of critique visible encourages students to reflect upon the credibility, reliability, and usefulness of those resources (one of our primary learning goals for critique activities).

Design Strategies for Teacher Communities

What strategies does WISE use to involve teachers in learning communities? WISE involves teachers in communities for teaching WISE projects, customizing projects, and authoring new projects. Typical access to the WISE teacher communities occurs following a professional development course in which a group of teachers learn how to use WISE; however, some teachers locate the Web site independently.

WISE supports teachers' practice by helping them manage their daily tasks (our first design consideration for online communities). Many teachers use curriculum units as they exist in the project library. As they begin to localize and customize projects, they interact with other teachers who have used the project as well as the project designers (Linn & Slotta, 2000). Eventually, some teachers join or form partnerships with other community members to author new projects (Linn, 2000).

How can we support these communities more effectively? When we talk about authoring partnerships, what is the actual practice we are concerned with in terms of curriculum design? "Design is the arrangement of parts . . . assembling conceptual, strategic, and material components in a pattern which functions to support specific goals" (Mollison, 1990, p. 36). The distinction between conceptual, strategic, and material components is one potentially useful starting point for thinking about curriculum development. In this manner, we can help teachers formulate and reflect on their overall goals, the strategies for achieving them, and, finally, the appropriateness of different resources for building such a project.

The NetCourse is one tool to support teachers using WISE. The NetCourse helps teachers develop a common framework for approaching instruction (our third design consideration for online communities).

The NetCourse

The NetCourse addresses the first design consideration, supporting teachers' actual practice, which in this case involves teaching with WISE. See Figure 8.2.

The NetCourse can be configured so that teachers see only the comments from members of their professional development class. Alternately, discussions can be set-up so that they are accessible to the general public. Teachers that locate the WISE Web site independently have access to these discussions, which serve as social supports including connections to a broader teacher community.

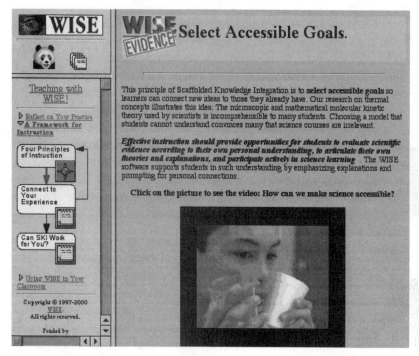

Figure 8.2. The WISE NetCourse.

Our approach provides multiple paths into communities, moving from peripheral participation to more sophisticated involvement over time (Lave & Wenger, 1992). In the following examples, "community" exists only in the sense of teachers having access to a collection of online discussions about their teaching experiences and strategies. Later, as they reflect on their own practice and begin to customize projects, teachers contribute to the community by exchanging ideas with other teachers using similar projects. This approach addresses the fourth design consideration of representing teachers' identities. Contributions can be made anonymously or linked to a profile containing a picture and short background description.

Professional Development Communities

We studied a professional development class of five in-service teachers who used the NetCourse for two days as an introduction to WISE. Participants made a total of thirteen contributions, took four online notes, participated in two short discussions, and used six resources consisting of two annotated Web sites and four video segments associated with the four principles in the SKI framework. While smaller than most classes, the exchanges were representative of the dynamics in the larger classes.

The WISE NetCourse introduced teachers to the pedagogical framework and the technical supports for WISE. Teachers typically participated in the NetCourse as part of their professional development class, moving through the NetCourse as a cohort, posing questions and reflecting on their own teaching experiences. The NetCourse is a WISE project. Teachers become familiar with using WISE as part of this professional development activity.

To illustrate how the community interacted, this example shows a teacher's comment in the NetCourse followed by several replies from other teachers (titles in parentheses):

(Ready for the Challenge:) I am very excited and probably a bit niave [sic] about using the internet in our science lab. Not only am I a novice teacher, but we are just setting up computers in our classroom and starting a computer lab for next fall. I want to learn from this community some good practices for integrating the internet in the science curriculum (and all curriculum). I plan to use it as a research source to stimulate discussions, obtain relevant and topical information for various view points and learn how to evalute [sic] the information that is being read off our screens. My big concern is how to do everything you want to do in such a short amount of time (45 min classes two days a week).

Here are three responses from other teachers:

1. I understand your apprehensions. Take a look at some great things other teachers are doing out there on the web. So much can be done now. Take a look at VISEARTH out of UCSD. It is a great example of computer and WWW use in the science classroom.
2. I don't know if you're familiar with WebQuests or not but these are interactive online adventures for lack of a better term, that are structured to help teachers integrate the Internet into the classroom in meaningful worthwhile ways. For example, here's a webquest on cloning where students are led to review information resources from different perspectives to debate the ethics of cloning: http://powayusd.sdcoe.k12.ca.us/dolly. There is also a site called "WebQuest Collections" at: edweb.sdsu.edu/webquest/webquest collections.htm which is very helpful as well.
3. (Consider a Design or Evaluation Lesson:) I'm with you! I'm always looking for new ways to incorporate technology. I'm a former novice teacher and have used technology in a variety of ways in the classroom. But one thing I have found that students enjoy most is the opportunity to design something of their own whether its [sic] an experiment or multimedia presentation. Other things students have enjoyed involve them critiquing (sp?) the work of others. For example, giving students a couple of websites to peruse and then asking them to select the best or worst. Realizing their opinion has value is a big confidence booster and also helps them develop higher level thinking skills.

These responses include resources because they provide examples of teaching experiences and strategies that have engaged students in activities with specific cognitive outcomes such as "reviewing information resources from different perspectives." These personal accounts illustrate how teachers can learn from each other about teaching strategies.

Recognizing the need to support teachers' actual practices as a way of involving them in a broader community is a critical step in the design of self-sustaining communities (the first design consideration). For example, using the community system to help teachers manage classroom activities creates the potential for increased participation in the community, a simple but powerful strategy for building community. In short, the online tools initially support teachers in managing their classrooms and configuring projects. Later, the systems that provided social supports become the mechanisms through which real collaborations develop and a sense of community emerges.

Authoring Communities

WISE projects are designed by partnerships of teachers, scientists, and pedagogy experts (Linn, 2000). This partnership model involves iterative refinement where research, theory, and classroom experiences inform curriculum design, thereby leveraging the expertise represented by these groups, ensuring scientific validity, and increasing the likelihood that the project will be appropriate for the targeted audience. Project authoring communities are communities that support the creation of new curriculum units. The size of authoring communities is typically small ($N = 3$ to 5), though some groups have involved many more people.

In project-authoring communities, WISE makes authoring accessible in a number of important ways, for example through project templates for critique, theory debate, and design projects. WISE enables community members to learn from each other with collaborative tools that help authoring groups assemble resources for building projects. The collaborative tools include shared white boards, resource libraries, task lists, and online discussions. These tools are intended to help in the initial stages of project development where pedagogical goals and potential evidence pages (Internet sites) are collected, annotated, and organized. The community tools make these resources easily accessible (the second design consideration). A sophisticated set of Web-based project and evidence managers aid authors as they refine their evidence sets and embed them in the activity. The outcome is a WISE project complete with hints, activities, and steps that guide students through the inquiry, critique, or design process.

WISE helps make thinking visible for authoring groups by creating a representation of the project as it emerges. This approach combines the knowledge integration framework tenet of making thinking visible with the goal of creating accessible resources (the second community design consideration). For example, authoring groups can view and modify the steps in a project along with the associated hints and prompts. Besides determining the sequence and type of steps in an activity, the project authors locate the sites that serve as evidence for the project and formulate the hints and prompts that students access while viewing the sites. The authoring communities help manage these resources through Web-based, searchable libraries and project managers. See, for example, Figure 8.3.

Study of Engineering Authoring Community

Authoring groups are complex social systems. Building technical solutions to support their practices required an understanding of how these groups function. We conducted a pilot study in an undergraduate engineering class to better understand the dynamics of authoring groups.

Figure 8.3. Malaria project authoring community.

This pilot study contributed directly to the specification of the design considerations for learning communities. In particular, this study illustrated the importance of supporting the daily tasks of design teams to determine how to help those groups collect and represent resources effectively. By studying four teams of students ($N = 16$) working without technology supports to design multimedia presentations (Cuthbert, 2000), we were able to identify the challenges of creating a shared product and the coping mechanisms that were spontaneously adopted by different groups. This research helped us understand the actual practices of design groups and lead to the specification of the first community design consideration for supporting the actual practices and daily tasks of participants.

We identified several challenges by analyzing the log files from online discussions (see Table 8.1). Note that most of these excerpts are paraphrased from the actual discussions and appear in the order of importance based on frequency counts. The right-hand column labeled "Scaffolded Knowledge Integration Framework" illustrates how these challenges connect to the scaffolded knowledge integration framework.

The pilot study helped reveal the set of supports for the "process of authoring" by identifying the needs of design groups. In turn, to support authoring groups in WISE, we created solutions for managing resources and developing design templates for projects. We also began work on peer review processes such as critiques in online discussions (described later in this chapter). This pilot study provides an example of the first steps in a process of iterative refinement where research informs design. In addition, it shows how design considerations can be specified for authoring communities in general.

How Do Resources Support Communities?

From annotated Web sites to online discussions, resources need to have the potential for being used in practice. First, they need to be persistent and accessible to community members (the second community design consideration). Developing a visible history of interactions and linking those histories to other artifacts such as Web sites or project designs create social supports that guide teachers as they learn how to use WISE (i.e., by making the process of thinking visible). These resources are social supports because they serve as examples of how to incorporate resources into both curriculum material and teaching practice. In many cases, such as online discussions, social information appears alongside the descriptions of teaching episodes, making these resources socially relevant

Table 8.1. *Challenges to Collaborative Groups Working without Technology Supports*

Challenge	Description of Challenge	Scaffolded Knowledge Integration Framework
Arranging Meetings	Difficulty meeting was the foremost problem in all groups.	
Sharing Resources	Resource sharing involves being able to collaborate or share resources such as images or ideas, linking them to specific team members.	Provide social supports.
Organizing Resources	Organizing resources was problematic especially when the group could not meet (e.g., "our main folder is a big mess of pictures and data that needs organization, we are just scrolling to find info, meeting to collaborate on how we were going about collecting resources.").	Make thinking visible.
Visualizing Information	Inability to visualize resources resulted in categories with uneven distribution of content (e.g., not enough information . . . to cover the [planned] categories).	Make thinking visible; develop a repertoire of models.
Reviewing Peer Progress	Lack of a mechanism for feedback from team members affected performance and efficiency of groups.	Learn from others.
Presenting Designs	Templates were crucial to maintaining consistency. Lack of a mechanism for specifying, sharing, and updating templates slowed design process.	Encourage autonomous learning.

for teachers (Hoadley, 1999). In addition, these resources can be used to help teachers customize projects to local classroom conditions.

Making resources accessible and persistent is only a first step in supporting practice. The second step is helping teachers make connections between those resources and their practice by providing examples of how to introduce ideas that connect with learning goals. This connection between design and learning goals is what differentiates learning communities from other types of online communities. Because of this difference, the ways in which community values develop are linked closely to the framework that guides the learning process, in this case knowledge integration.

Often, access to collaborative tools such as online discussions provides social supports but does not create a sense of "community." In most cases, a sense of community does not emerge until teachers, researchers, and scientists begin to assemble instructional materials together in project authoring communities. This shift in focus and practice has the potential to change not only the frequency of interaction between community members but, more importantly, the nature and quality of those interactions. Designing materials together has the potential to create a sense of community and ownership, especially if there is a shared set of goals or common perspectives.

Our current approach is to negotiate the pedagogical goals in online discussions within the authoring communities. The outcome of these discussions is then used to complete the questions in the WISE project manager about prerequisites, goals, and lesson plans. Tying discussions about pedagogical goals to the project authoring system makes these discussions serve a practical purpose. However, to ensure that these discussions are equitable and move toward consensus, someone in the group needs to play the role of synthesizer or summarizer. Understanding these needs and making sure that discussions serve a practical purpose go a long way in sustaining interaction in online discussions both for teachers and students. Further research involving different types of communities is required to develop more effective strategies.

In pursuit of this goal, we now discuss student communities, focusing on how to incorporate online discussions so that they support specific types of relationships and the development of resources for collaborative debate and design.

Design Strategies for Student Communities

How can we encourage students to share ideas in online learning communities so that specific pedagogical goals are addressed? WISE projects have made advances in supporting students by investigating reflection and knowledge integration through science inquiry (Hoadley &

Linn, 2000; Linn & Hsi, 2000). WISE offers innovative strategies for creating personalized electronic discussions that help elicit self-explanation and clarification from students (Cuthbert et al., 2000). As instructional designers and teachers, we need to ask how we can structure relationships within learning communities so that the community members share resources and help refine each other's ideas. Two of the most successful approaches, described in detail in the following sections, involve personally seeded discussions and peer review discussions. In personally seeded discussions, students' scientific explanations become initial comments in the discussion, making thinking visible for students. In peer review discussions, students share research findings in an online question-and-answer session, creating resources that are accessible to the entire class. In both of these types of discussions, the critical resources are the community members and their ideas. The common goal is the refinement of the community members' ideas.

Strategies employed by both types of discussions involve (a) contrasting students' perspectives about the same phenomena and (b) increasing personal relevance by making students responsible for specific areas of knowledge. Contrasting students' perspectives about the same phenomena can encourage students to clarify their own statements while considering the relevance of other students' opinions (Chi et al., 1989; diSessa & Minstrell, 1998). This perspective taking is important because (a) students have trouble supporting their ideas with evidence, (b) students don't have shared criteria for evaluating explanations, and (c) clarification often involves contrasting perspectives and developing a repertoire of models (both difficult processes) (Cuthbert et. al., 2000). By increasing personal relevance around the process of contrasting student perspectives, we create relationships that elicit community members' conceptual resources to refine the community's ideas. An example of this type of relationship is found in personally seeded discussions.

Scientific Inquiry Communities

In this section, we provide an example of a scientific inquiry community with personally seeded discussions. Personally seeded discussions have comments constructed outside the discussion system, which then get inserted as initial seed comments. The discussion develops around the different perspectives represented in the seed comments, ideally through a process of comparison, clarification, and justification (part of our learning goals). To help students develop a repertoire of models, we created software to automatically group students in discussions with peers that have different perspectives. We studied 300 students who were participants in a WISE project called "Probing Your Surroundings."

Research on students' initial conceptions about heat and temperature (Clark, 2001; Lewis, 1996; Linn & Hsi, 2000) helped us identify a set of principles students typically used to describe heat flow and thermal equilibrium. Our Web-based Principle Builder lets students construct scientific principles from this set of predefined phrases (Figure 8.4).

The Principle Builder and seeded discussions support the actual practices and daily tasks of the students, which involve constructing explanations for scientific observations. The advantage of using this structured format is that we can create discussion groups with students who have explained their data using different sets of principles. Students work to clarify and justify their own scientific principles, comparing and contrasting them with other students' principles. Finally, thinking is made "visible" for students as they elaborate upon and justify their ideas.

Students start by making predictions about the temperature of everyday objects around them in the classroom. Then they use thermal probes to investigate the temperature of these objects and to construct principles to describe the patterns encountered. (see Figure 8.5.)

The "Probing" software places students in electronic discussion groups with students who have constructed explanatory principles that are different from their own; the impact of these groups has been great. The student-constructed principles appear as the seed comments in the discussions. The groups critique and discuss these principles, working toward consensus.

This type of structured relationship is very successful. Students entered twice as many comments as previous semesters (when they did not comment on their own and other students' principles). Furthermore, they were much more helpful to one another in the refinement process. Consider an initial principle constructed by a pair of students:

Eventually all objects in the same surround at room temperature remain different temperatures even if an object produces its own heat energy. At this point, the objects are different temperatures and they feel different.

Ideally, we would like students to ask questions that prompt for self-explanation, clarification, and justification. Giving examples that ground

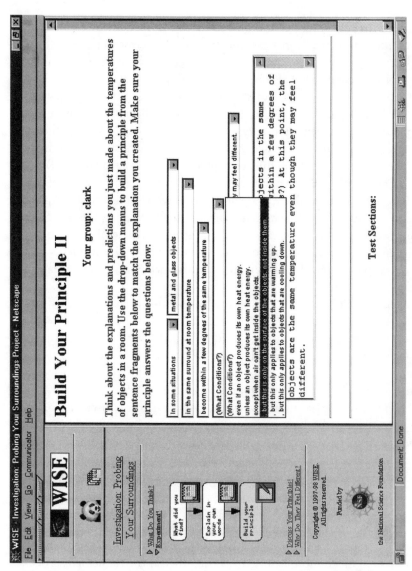

Figure 8.4. Principle Builder used to construct scientific principles that become discussion comments.

232

Figure 8.5. Probing your surroundings.

the discussion, asking for comparisons, and proposing counterexamples seem like reasonable responses that we would want to encourage.

In response to the initial principle, another pair of students asked a question, linked to the specific situation, while providing a counterexample (note that the actual comment was all in capitals):

How come each object would stay at the same temperature being in the same room. Wouldn't the objects gain or loose heat energy depending on the temperature of the room. It is sort of like you are saying that if you put things in the oven for a while they won't get any hotter!

We expect that specific examples coupled with questions will lead to comparison and explanation. In this discussion, a third pair of students responded to the question with a scientific explanation.

The objects would stay the same temperature of the room because they lose heat energy because the room is cooler, or they gain heat energy because the room is hotter than the object.

By having students explain and defend their own principles, we get students not only to take an interest in their own ideas but also to take interest in responding to and critiquing the other ideas in the discussion. The role of the teacher shifts from presenting alternative views to helping students understand those alternatives, ask for clarification, and refine their own ideas. We thereby facilitated a community wherein students were successfully sharing their conceptual resources in the common task of refining their own ideas. In our next example, we will see how different social arrangements and technical designs can encourage cooperation between groups of students.

Peer Review Communities

Peer review and "pin-ups" in architecture typically consist of posting design sketches and having peers and instructors circulate through the studio making comments, asking questions, and offering suggestions. For science instruction, we see forms of peer review occurring spontaneously in classroom communities where different ideas are exchanged and critiqued in a situation that is less formal than posting complete design solutions for review. These question–answer sessions with the entire class can be restructured in online discussions, making ideas visible and stable for students. At the same time, online discussions give students a greater opportunity for participating in an equitable manner (Linn & Hsi, 2000). This strategy balances the need for making resources accessible with the knowledge integration goal of encouraging students to learn from each other.

We provide an example of a peer review community that developed as part of a WISE project called "Desert Houses." The Desert Houses project was the capstone activity for a semester on thermodynamics. Throughout the semester, students learned about thermodynamics from laboratory work and WISE projects including Probing Your Surroundings. We studied 158 students who worked in self-selected pairs for fifty minutes per day for two weeks to design a passive solar desert house that would stay cool in the day and warm at night. Students created their first designs individually in the form of sketches with heat flow arrows for day and night conditions. Over the rest of the activity, they worked in pairs to merge the designs together (see Figure 8.6).

In the first part of the Desert Houses project, student pairs researched one of the house components (either windows, walls, or roofs). As student pairs researched one of these components, they searched for "evidence" on the Internet to develop alternatives and support their design decisions. Then all students participated in an online discussion to explain

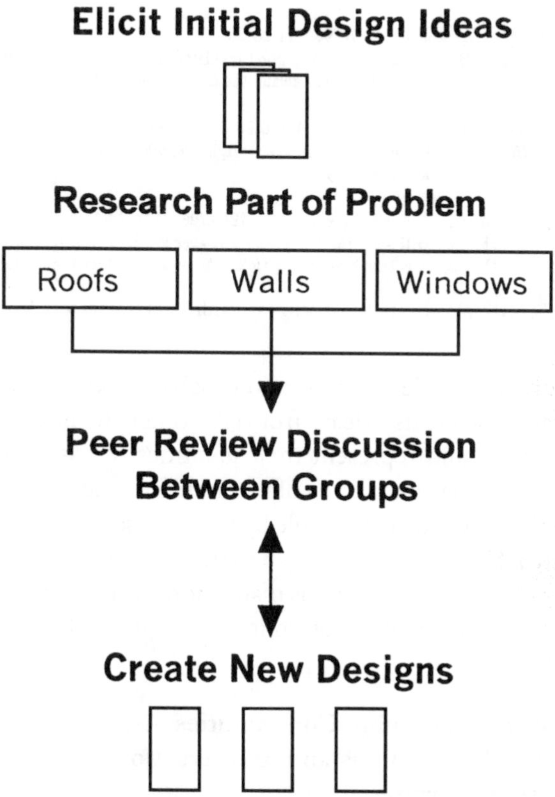

Elicit Initial Design Ideas

Research Part of Problem

Roofs	Walls	Windows

Peer Review Discussion Between Groups

Create New Designs

Figure 8.6. Overview of activities that prepare for the online discussions in the Desert Houses project.

their research findings and critique each other's ideas (see Figure 8.7). Students created a final design using the discussions and evidence they found (the resources) and showing how their laboratory work, scientific principles, and other experiences supported their design decisions.

Our strategy here was to structure and support relationships around the common task of designing a house and refining the community's ideas. To achieve this goal, we focused on developing a shared set of criteria within the classroom community and using those criteria to guide participation and assessment. By having the teacher and community stress the importance of comparing alternatives and supporting ideas with evidence (such as references to laboratory work or scientific principles), we provided teachers and students with a common method for assessing whether comments compare alternatives and justify claims.

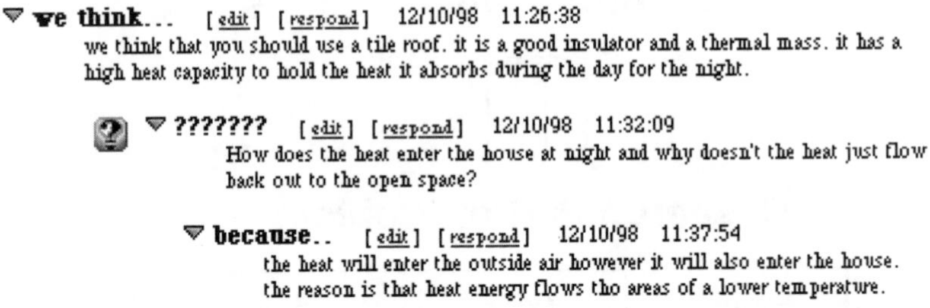

▽ **we think**... [edit] [respond]   12/10/98   11:26:38
we think that you should use a tile roof. it is a good insulator and a thermal mass. it has a high heat capacity to hold the heat it absorbs during the day for the night.

　　▽ **???????** [edit] [respond]   12/10/98   11:32:09
　　　　How does the heat enter the house at night and why doesn't the heat just flow back out to the open space?

　　　　▽ **because**.. [edit] [respond]   12/10/98   11:37:54
　　　　　　the heat will enter the outside air however it will also enter the house. the reason is that heat energy flows tho areas of a lower temperature.

Figure 8.7. Example of a student discussion (with identities removed).

We began with the knowledge integration goals of making thinking visible and encouraging students to learn from each other. To make resources accessible to students and represent their identities, we associated students' identities with their initial area of research (i.e., walls, windows, or roofs). These linkages were made visible by having discussion topics dedicated to each area. Students' comments appeared with an icon indicating their area of research. The science was made more accessible to students because it was interpreted and discussed in the language of their peers.

Lessons from Learning Communities: Assessing Trade-offs between Sustaining Interaction and Supporting Learning

When structuring learning communities, a balance needs to be struck between sustaining interaction and achieving learning goals. For example, even though vague or underspecified questions may lead to increased interaction, the overarching goal is for students to begin to adopt an orientation toward discourse that is based on comparison, critique, and justification. This focus on the nature of interactions as a priority in learning communities shifts the goals and the design considerations for these systems. The prioritization of learning goals falls out of the third community design consideration of providing a framework to guide the learning process. As illustrated in the last section, the learning framework can help in the specification of design strategies.

Achieving Learning Goals

In these WISE projects, we developed three strategies for encouraging students to reflect on the type of comment they were making

Suggest Alternative: "I think white tile the best to use and not aluminum. Aluminum has little R-value and tile has high R-value. Unless you use really good insulation."

Clarification: "Black roofs attract heat and get hotter faster than white roofs because the darker the color the more it absorbs. For example if you went to the beach on a sunny day and you wore a white cap and your mom wore a black one your mom would get hotter faster and would sunburn easier but you would take a much longer time to heat up and sunburn. So if you have a black roof in the desert you are just making it harder to cool down your house."

R Recommendation: "We recommend that the white coating tile for the roof because that reflect the most sunlight and it wouldn't absorving."

Agree/Disagree: "I agree with you completely. The highest r-value in any material in this house would be best. The foam dose have the highest r-value than any other building material. But the foam might be the best solution for your house because the foam would be best if it matches the strategy you are using. If you are using a different strategy than what the foam follows, foam wouldn't be the best material for you to use."

Figure 8.8. Comment types in the first iteration of WISE discussions.

before posting it. First, we prompted students to reflect on their comment by putting it into a category, as shown in Figure 8.8.

We selected these categories based on analyses of previous student discussions, fitting students' comments into these categories and pilot testing them to see if students made comments that did not fit into the categories. Students were able to select a default generic comment type as well.

In addition to prompting students to reflect on their own ideas, using common comment types facilitates the teacher's role in supporting student relationships. Common comment types allow teachers to characterize the overall discussion and determine the degree to which students' comments reflect the classroom criteria. To assist teachers in this task, we developed strategies (techniques and software solutions) that help teachers manage and guide peer review discussions, for example, by grouping all comments by a single student together for grading. Even the simple task of having students specify whether or not they are posting a question can help teachers and students find unanswered questions, thereby sustaining interaction in the community.

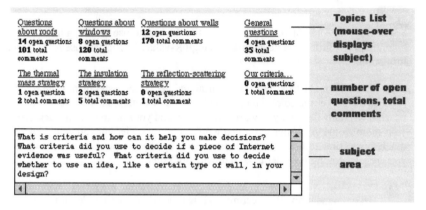

Figure 8.9. Discussion topics aligned with students' research areas.

Using comment types to serve both a pedagogical and an assessment function is an example of creating synergy between social organization and technical designs. The potential for synergy between social organization and technical solutions increases as we build knowledge management systems that support cooperative learning.* This synergy is a natural development of encouraging students to learn from one another by representing linkages between ideas and identities (two community design considerations). For instance, in Desert Houses, the social organization of the project came from the different initial task focuses for the groups (researching windows, walls, or roofs†). The online discussions enabled the groups of students to share ideas, while providing a structure for grouping resources based on their content (windows, walls, roofs). Specifically, each group was responsible for answering questions about its own area of research. A topic was created for each of these areas (note that Figure 8.9 is a snapshot of an on-going set of discussions).

Second, we encouraged reflection by grouping comments under a specific topic to structure the discussions. In previous iterations of the project where comments were not grouped together, students had trouble locating topics. This difficulty resulted in fragmentation, repetition of topics, and clustering of responses around the earliest postings. Our current strategy makes resources in discussions more accessible.

---

* Typically, collaboration is characterized by a shared product across groups, while cooperation has a shared task with distinct solutions developed by each group.
† We also conducted studies comparing an initial task focus on thermodynamics concepts, house components, and complete house designs to investigate how varying the initial conceptual framework affected learning trajectories.

Third, we encouraged reflection by listing the number of unanswered questions (open comments). Newly posted comments and links to the related discussions appear below the topic list in Figure 8.9, helping students see "were the action is."

Sustaining Interaction

These design strategies for encouraging reflection also address two persistent problems in online discussion systems and communities: (a) determining where action is required and (b) locating newly posted comments. In the peer review example, the social organization of the groups and the layout of the discussion system work together to address these problems.

The asynchronous nature of online discussions makes sustaining interaction particularly challenging. Representing ideas in a way that encourages students to build upon each other's ideas has the potential to sustain interaction. However, this goal is extremely hard to achieve in the context of online discussions because related comments can appear within and across discussion topics. It is an open question how to represent these linkages.

Discussion and Next Steps

These investigations illustrate our four design considerations for creating effective online learning communities. We focused on four distinct learning communities involving teacher professional development, curriculum authoring, scientific inquiry, and peer review of projects. We now summarize the strategies related to our four design considerations, refining them to suggest the next steps in developing even more effective strategies.

Support the Actual Practices and Daily Tasks of the Participants

Communities need to support the practices of participants in order to motivate sustained, vibrant interactions. WISE communities support the actual practices and daily tasks of teachers by helping them guide students' learning process through the creation of a visible history of student work. In addition, WISE elicits teachers' ideas and helps them develop curricula through its authoring communities. For students,

WISE communities support learning practices and tasks by making the thinking of their peers visible and by illustrating the process of group inquiry. The examples in this chapter illustrated how thinking was made visible for students through online discussions.

Next Steps

From a knowledge integration perspective, the practice of teaching and learning involves developing a repertoire of models for explaining situations. Community resources and collaborative systems can help students and teachers in their practice by illustrating this repertoire of models. The scaffolded knowledge integration framework provides general guidelines for designing projects and serves as an inspiration for creating design considerations for online communities. However, to refine the details of a WISE project, such as the hints and prompts, linkages between pedagogical goals and curriculum material need to be examined. We need to help curriculum authors create a shared vocabulary for this critique process. From a design perspective, we need to connect these critiques to the appropriate curricular elements. The scaffolded knowledge integration framework can help in this process by focusing project review on lifelong learning goals as opposed to memorization tasks.

Collect Experiences and Represent Them in an Accessible and Equitable Manner

Communities need to maintain a history of experience and to make these accessible to all to promote the process of connecting ideas. WISE communities collect experiences and represent them in an accessible and equitable manner. WISE makes representations accessible so participants can use them in consequential tasks such as arguments and debates.

This chapter outlined several strategies for organizing resources for authoring communities and student communities. For example, linking the prompts for annotating Internet sites to the criteria for evaluating scientific claims is one way to guide students as they search for and collect evidence. Another strategy is to assign students to discussions such that each discussion can be seeded with radically different ideas from the actual students involved in the discussion so that the students compare and contrast their beliefs. Although these two strategies have different goals (helping develop a common set of criteria and developing a repertoire of models), they share the common approach of representing ideas in an equitable manner and support the process of connecting these ideas.

Next Steps

We see three major areas for next steps in terms of collecting and representing experiences to encourage cohesive understanding. First, we need to investigate further the potential of structuring discussions in different ways based on the type of discussion and the associated pedagogical goals. Communities, if viewed as a network of relationships and resources, can be structured to elicit ideas, develop shared understanding, and promote the integration of a diverse set of ideas. Linking these types of pedagogical goals to design strategies is a challenging task because most community members are not accustomed to reflecting on the nature of their contributions. For example, when we talk about online discussions, we need to remember that we engage in many different "types" of discussions. For instance, there are important differences between discussions depending on whether the purpose of the discussion is debate, brainstorming, or peer review. Each of these discussion "types" has a distinct structure and format and, hence, different requirements for setting up, running, and assessing the discussion. As a research community, we are just beginning to understand the potential of these different discussions for learning and community development.

The second major area for further research in terms of collecting and representing experiences involves preventing discussion fragmentation. Fragmentation, characterized by the emergence of overlapping topics in different locations, is a persistent problem in all discussion systems. Organizing discussions into related categories to avoid fragmentation is only partially addressed by the approach of creating separate discussion topics. Search software can automatically cross-index discussions and build lists of active topics and participants, unanswered questions, and even themes, based on semantic analysis. However, metatopics and even the presence of social information do not seem to change the practices of community members beyond helping them locate other members with similar perspectives.

The third major area for further research in terms of collecting and representing experiences involves determining whether intelligent systems or community members should produce representations that connect related ideas. It seems likely that the best solutions will combine these approaches. Having automatic and actively constructed categories (specified by community members) makes it possible to create public and private spaces. Community coordinators (e.g., teachers or curriculum design leaders) can specify a list of public themes. As members post comments, they can be prompted to link their comments to these themes (or software can be used to automate the process). Creating private and public representations balances the need for personal collections of indices into discussions with the need for public categories that help to develop common themes.

Provide a Framework to Guide the Learning Process

For communities to maintain coherence and develop a sense of what is appropriate behavior, it is important that a strong community culture be established with a common set of values and criteria for making contributions (Brown, 1992). Communities need a general framework to help define the mission and vision for the learning process. In our work, the knowledge integration framework characterizes the learning and curriculum design processes. This framework lends a shared focus to teacher professional development discussions, creating the potential to view instruction as a design problem. By a design problem, we mean a problem that has multiple solutions and can be improved by selecting appropriate solutions and testing them in context. Discussion of a shared framework for learning can shift the focus from logistics and prerequisites to pedagogical goals and teaching strategies. For example, professional development communities might discuss how WISE units handle much of the procedural guidance for students, freeing teachers to engage students individually, elicit their ideas, and encourage them to reformulate their ideas by considering other alternatives and supporting their ideas with evidence. This design strategy of off-loading the procedural guidance onto the learning environment shifts the role of the teacher and enables the pursuit of larger learning goals.

Next Steps

Requiring participants to support their ideas with evidence (e.g., Internet sites, references to laboratory work, scientific principles, or everyday experiences) creates a culture where people ask each other for justification and clarification (Linn & Hsi, 2000). As researchers, we can help refine these contribution criteria by investigating how participants adjust their behavior as their peers prompt them to support their ideas with evidence (Cuthbert et al., 2000). How can we investigate how participants adjust their participation patterns? One strategy is to create commonly agreed upon criteria and examine how these criteria are adopted and transformed by community members as they interact with each other.

Represent the Identities of Community Members

Socially relevant information helps participants recognize the coherence of an individual's comments (Hoadley, 1999). Identities can be linked to resources (e.g., based on who contributed or accessed a resource) or displayed separately in a "profiles" section of the community site. Representing people's backgrounds and interests can help develop personal relationships, especially when face-to-face interaction may be limited because of geographical distances in authoring communities. In addition participants' profiles help connect contributions to the overall view of the individual. Simultaneously, we need to provide ways for students and student communities to make contributions without being identified. This design strategy balances gender inequities found in most classroom discussions and creates a safe place for students to express their opinions.

Next Steps

We need ways to represent the identities of community members, to illustrate the refinement of ideas, and to mark departures from past views. One common strategy involves the use of avatars (virtual representations of community members) to provide visual indications of community membership and contribution patterns (see Turkle, 1997, for related literature). Regardless of the strategy, we have found that entering profile information needs to be part of an on-going process linked to use of the community system so that the task of entering descriptors (e.g., background, areas of expertise, and instructional topics) does not deter members. The idea of mutually revealing information (e.g., not being able to see other members' pictures until you have submitted one: see www.adappt.org) is another alternative that can motivate people to complete their profiles. Cross-linking people with similar interests is yet another approach where value is added through the connections that result (Goldberg et al., 1992).

Conclusion

Even though they are different in many respects, teacher and student learning communities both benefit from the four design considerations illustrated here. The strategies derived from these design considerations scaffold members as they exchange resources, develop coherent ideas, and support understanding. Our goal is to develop design considerations and strategies that facilitate the transformation and sharing of resources to support integrated understanding. These design considerations and "next steps" set out a broad research agenda that has the potential to improve science education both in terms of curriculum development and classroom practice.

Acknowledgments

This material is based upon research supported by the National Science Foundation under grants REC 98-73160 and REC 98-05420. Any opinions, findings, and conclusions or recommendations expressed in this publication are those of the authors and do not necessarily reflect the views of the National Science Foundation.

The authors appreciate the help and encouragement of the Web-based Integrated Science Environment (WISE) research group and the Science Controversies Online: Partnerships in Education (SCOPE) research group. In particular, thanks is given to Greg Pitter, who designed the project authoring community interface, and to Jim Slotta, the WISE project director and creator of the NetCourse.

References

Barksdale, J. (1998). Communications technology in dynamic organizational communities. In F. Hesselbein, M. Goldsmith, R. Beckhard & R. F. Schubert (Eds.), *The community of the future*. New York: The Drucker Foundation, pp. 93–100.

Bowker, G. C., & Star, S. L. (2000). *Sorting things out: Classification and its consequences*. Cambridge, MA: MIT Press.

Brown, A. L. (1992). Design experiments: Theoretical and methodological challenges in creating complex interventions in classroom settings. *The Journal of the Learning Sciences, 2*(2), 141–78.

Chi, M. T. H., Lewis, M. W., Reimann, P., & Glaser, R. (1989). Self-explanations: How students study and use examples in learning to solve problems. *Cognitive Science, 13*, 145–82.

Clark, D. (2001). *New representations of student knowledge integration in CLP: Theories or repertoires of ideas?* Paper presented at the annual meetings of the American Educational Research Association, Seattle, WA. Available: www.kie.berkeley.edu/people/dclark.html.

Collins, A., Brown, J. S., & Newman, S. E. (1989). Cognitive apprenticeship: Teaching the craft of reading, writing, and mathematics. In L. B. Resnick (Ed), *Cognition and instruction: Issues and agendas*. Hillsdale, NJ: Lawrence Erlbaum, pp. 155–87.

Cuthbert, A. (2000). *Investigations of cooperative learning and design*. Paper presented at the annual meeting of the American Research Association, New Orleans, LA. Session on Learning from Design Activities: Two Years Later, Janet Kolodner, Chair. Available: wise.berkeley.edu.

Cuthbert, A., Clark, D., Slotta, J., & Jorde, D. (2000). *Helping elicit self-explanation & clarification through personalized electronic discussions*. Paper presented at Annual Meeting of the American Research Association (AERA), New Orleans. Structured session on Strategies for Sustaining Interaction in Online Discussion Forums & Virtual Communities, Tim Koschmann, Chair. Available: www.kie.berkeley.edu/people/alex.

diSessa, A. A., & Minstrell, J. (1998). Cultivating conceptual change with benchmark lessons. In J. G. Greeno & S. Goldman (Eds.), *Thinking practices*. Mahwah, NJ: Lawrence Erlbaum, pp. 155–87.

Florin, F. (1993). Information landscapes. In S. A. Hooper &. K. Hooper (Eds.), *Learning with interactive multimedia: Developing and using multimedia tools in education*. Cupertino, CA: Apple Computer Press.

Frederikson, J. R., & White, B. Y. (1997). Metacognitive facilitation: A method for prompting reflective collaboration. *Proceedings of the Second International Conference on Computer Support for Collaborative Learning (CSCL)*. Toronto. Mahwah, NJ: Lawrence Erlbaum, pp. 53–62.

Goldberg, D., Oki, B., Nichols, D., & Terry, D. B. (1992). Using collaborative filtering to weave an information tapestry. *Communications of the ACM, 35*(12), 61–70.

Goldsmith, M. (1998). Global communications and communities of choice. In F. Hesselbein, M. Goldsmith, R. Beckhard & R. F. Schubert (Eds.), *The community of the future*. New York: The Drucker Foundation, pp. 101–14.

Guindon, R. (1990). Designing the design process: Exploiting opportunistic thoughts. *Human-Computer Interaction, 5*(2–3), 305ff.

Hoadley, C. (1999). *Scaffolding scientific discussion using socially relevant representations in networked multimedia*. Unpublished doctoral dissertation. University of California, Berkeley.

Hoadley, C., & Linn, M. C. (2000). Teaching science through on-line peer discussions: SpeakEasy in the Knowledge Integration Environment. *International Journal of Science Education, 22*(8), 839–58.

Latour, B. (1999). *Pandora's hope: Essays on the reality of science studies*. Cambridge, MA: Harvard University Press.

Lave, J., & Wenger, E. (1992). *Situated learning: Legitimate peripheral participation*. Cambridge, UK: Cambridge University Press.

Lewis, E. (1996). Conceptual change among middle school students studying elementary thermodynamics. *Journal of Science Education and Technology, 5*(1), 3–31.

Linn, M. C. (1995). Designing computer learning environments for engineering and computer science: The Scaffolded Knowledge Integration Framework. *Journal of Science Education and Technology, 4*(2) 103–26.

(2000). Designing the knowledge integration environment: The partnership inquiry process. *International Journal of Science Education, 22*(8), 781–96.

Linn, M. C., & Hsi, S. (2000). *Computers, teachers, peers: Science learning partners.* Mahwah, NJ: Lawrence Erlbaum.

Linn, M. C., & Slotta, J. D. (2000). WISE curriculum projects: Bridging the gap between educational research and classroom customization. *Educational Leadership, 58*(2), 29–33.

Mollison, B. (1990). *Permaculture: A practical guide for a sustainable future.* Washington, DC: Island Press.

Pirolli, P., & Card, S. (1995). *Information foraging in information access environments.* Proceedings of the Conference on Human Factors in Computing Systems, CHI-95. Denver, CO: Association for Computing Machinery. Available: www.acm.org/sigchi/chi95/.

Saxe, G. B., & Guberman, S. R. (1998). Studying mathematics learning in collective activity. *Learning and Instruction, 8*(6), 489–501.

Slotta, J., & Linn, M. C. (2000). How do students make sense of Internet resources in the science classroom? In M. J. Jacobson & R. Kozma (Eds.), *Learning the sciences of the 21st century.* Mahwah, NJ: Lawrence Erlbaum, pp. 193–226.

Tudge, J., & Rogoff, B. (1989). Peer influences on cognitive development: Piagetian and Vygotskian perspectives. In M. H. Bornstein & J. S. Bruner (Eds.), *Interaction in human development.* Hillsdale, NJ: Lawrence Erlbaum, pp. 17–40.

Turkle, S. (1997). Constructions and reconstructions of self in virtual reality: Playing in the MUDs. In S. Kiesler (Ed.), *Culture of the Internet.* Hillsdale, NJ: Lawrence Erlbaum, pp. 143–55.

Vygotsky, L. S. (1978). *Mind in society: The development of higher psychological processes* (M. Cole, V. John-Stenier, S. Scribner & E. Souberman, Trans.). Cambridge, MA: Harvard University Press.

Wellman, B. (1997). An electronic group is virtually a social network. In Sara Kiesler (Ed.), *Culture of the Internet.* Hillsdale, NJ: Lawrence Erlbaum, pp. 179–208.

Part Three

Possibilities for Community

9 Reflexive Modernization and the Emergence of Wired Self-Help

Roger Burrows and Sarah Nettleton

> *In post traditional contexts, we have no choice but to choose how to be and how to act . . . choice has become obligatory.*
>
> – Giddens, 1994a, pp. 75–6

The computer mediated sharing of common interests, experiences, thoughts, and fellowship combined with an ability to access health and welfare information and/or challenge professional monopolies of expertise is becoming ubiquitous. This is especially true in the United States (Denzin, 1998; Ferguson, 1996) but is also increasing on a global scale (Burrows et al., 2000). At the time of writing, the bulk of Internet traffic relating to online self-help, and social support occurs within the almost 20,000 different Usenet news groups. Also important are the 100,000 or so publicly accessible discussion lists. However, given the recent trend for different forms of computer-mediated communication (CMC) to coalesce with Web pages to form more integrated systems of information and online support (offering perhaps Web-based information services alongside integrated provision to join mailing lists, discussion groups, and/or to engage in real-time chat), the virtual geography of wired self-help and social support is in a state of some flux. This chapter asks what sociologists are to make of the emergence of these wired forms of self-help and social support?

We begin with an illustration of the sort of "virtual community care" and support with which we are concerned. Within a well-used U.S.-dominated news group concerned with parenting matters, a thread begins with a posting making a simple request for advice (edited material is indicated by [. . .], otherwise the material here and elsewhere in the chapter is presented as posted):

249

Hi – I'm new to this newsgroup, but I would appreciate any input any of you might have about my 19 mos. old and a case of eczema. I am particularly interested in any home remedies that might relieve his condition. We presently bathe him with Aveeno soap, no wash cloth, and treat outbreaks with a low dose cortisone cream, which I am not thrilled about. He is just realizing how good it feels to scratch, and now I am afraid the real problems will begin. Any advice from a parent experienced with this will be greatly appreciated.

The responses come in thick and fast:

Aveeno soap can get to be expensive – try putting regular (uncooked!) oatmeal in a nylon stocking (pantyhose) and running it under the bath water. And rub it on your little one's skin too in the bath. Check a package of Aveeno bath satchets – it's oatmeal. Using your own is just as effective and much less expensive.

OATMEAL???!?!?! WOW – I had NO IDEA . . . I just learned something! <grin> Thanks for sharing.

My youngest (now 17 months) has excema. I too am concerned about using the hydrocortisone creams, but it is the only thing I've tried that actually takes care of it. We do other things, which help, such as using aqueous cream to wash him (never soap, or other baby bath solutions). I'm hoping that it will go away eventually, because he's absolutely gorgeous in every other way.

I'm just curious, why are you two concerned about cortisone creams? That is definitely what works; is there some issue with them that I'm unaware of? Honest question.

I read on another site that a parent was concerned because these types of creams thin the skin. Whether this is true or not, I'll continue to use the cream to control the outbreaks. Just the thought of putting something as strong-sounding as cortisone cream on his skin bothers me – I'm worried about side effects from long term use. Are there any that you aware of, or do you know that there are no side effects? I don't have much experience with cortisone creams. Anyway, I'm trying to find out how to prevent outbreaks, rather than treat them once they occur.

Our daughter has eczema and uses a prescribed hydrocortisone cream. Under side effects, the accompanying information said that hydrocortisone does thin the skin, making it and the underlying tissue prone to infection. The information said this was a side effect when used over a wide area over a constant period of time. That says to me that you should use it sparingly if possible, but our ped says we should use it aggressively to treat an outbreak because an infection from scratching the skin open is more possible and damaging. We use Cetaphil lotion every day and Aveeno soap every three or four days. Right now our climate is extremely dry and hot, so we're getting more outbreaks lately. I know we should do more about finding the cause (the actual allergy), but for the most part we seem to keep it under control so we're hoping she outgrows it soon. I grew up with the same problem.

What are we to make of these sorts of exchanges, literally millions of which are now occurring daily across the globe? Looking specifically at the United States, sociologist Norman Denzin suggested that the phenomena can be viewed in terms of the elective affinity that exists between two strong impulses at the heart of American culture:

We cannot imagine America without its self-help groups. And, we cannot imagine an America that is not in love with technology. Cyberspace and the recovery movement were meant for each other. (Denzin, 1998: 113)

Although there is obviously something in this observation, the growth of online self-help is not a phenomena restricted solely to the United States. Although the United States has led the way in the development of virtual communities expressly designed to offer self-help and social support, wired welfare is now a global phenomena. As U.S.-dominated systems of wired welfare communicate with locally based systems and structures in other countries, we have seen an increased participation in existing systems of online self-help. In addition, we have witnessed the formation of many new virtual spaces designed to deal with some of the specificities of different national contexts. So, for example, in the United Kingdom we see the emergence of the uk.people. hierarchy of the Usenet (see Smith, 1999, for an introduction to the form and structure of the Usenet). A significant proportion of this hierarchy is dedicated to news groups concerned with various aspects of self-help and social support within a specifically British context; virtual self-help and social support able to deal not just with the particular institutions and structures of the British health and welfare systems but also conducted in a manner perhaps more attuned to British cultural predilections (Burrows et al., 2000).

Whether or not the large number of social actors currently engaging in online self-help and social support are members of legitimate "virtual communities" is, of course, a key area for debate (Baym, 1998; Jones, 1998; Kollock & Smith, 1999; Wellman & Gulia, 1999). But regardless of whatever conceptualization one favors, growing numbers of people across the globe are using email, the Web, mailing and discussion lists, news groups, MUDs, IRC, and other forms of CMC to offer and receive information, advice, and support across a massive range of health and social issues. It is also the case that even larger numbers of individuals are observing (and perhaps being influenced by) these various virtual interactions without ever necessarily actively contributing themselves (Smith, 1999).

So, does this represent something more than just the extension of American cultural impulses to the virtual sphere, or is it symbolic of some broader set of social transformations? Is it the case, as Moursund (1997: 54) contended, that the emergence of virtual communities function to fulfil a deep human need for social support? According to Moursund:

> One reason for [the] enormous interest in social support may have to do with the rapid changes our social landscape is undergoing. Social institutions that have, in the past, helped stabilize our society...appear to be losing influence. People no longer grow up, marry, settle down, and live to old age in the same geographical location, and with increased mobility comes a loss of sense of community.... Things seem to move faster and faster, and we look desperately for something to hold onto, something to connect to.

In order to engage with these sorts of questions, we draw upon the work of two sociologists – Ulrich Beck in Germany and Anthony Giddens in the United Kingdom – who dominated debates in European social and political theory in the 1990s. We outline certain aspects of their work which, we argue, are of direct relevance to understanding the broader social and cultural significance of the emergence of virtual communities in general, and those offering various forms of online self help and social support in particular. We begin by outlining some central features of their theory of *reflexive modernization*. We then outline the relevance of this theory to an understanding of changes in the British welfare regime and seek to show how there is developing a symmetry between the restructuring of the welfare state and the emergence and growth of various forms of computer-mediated communication. We conclude that emerging patterns of Internet use in relation to self-help and social support are not just emblematic but also facilitative of many of the sociocultural shifts that Beck and Giddens identify.

Reflexive Modernization

Although initially working independently, the theoretical and political conclusions that Beck (1992) and Giddens (1991, 1992) came to in the early 1990s concerning the changing dynamics of modern societies, were remarkably similar (see Lupton, 1999, for a clear explanation of some of the differences between their respective positions). Although the conceptual terminology they initially utilized differed somewhat, the extent of their agreement soon became apparent when they came together with Scott Lash to produce a joint text (Beck, Giddens & Lash, 1994). Since this time, they, and others, have produced various books and essays (Beck & Beck-Gernsheim, 1996; Franklin, 1998; Giddens, 1998; O'Brien, Penna & Hay, 1999) elaborating various elements of their approach to understanding contemporary patterns of social change. In 1999, many of these ideas found a truly global audience when Giddens delivered a series of lectures as part of the prestigious annual Reith Lecture series sponsored by the BBC. These lectures were widely broadcast and were also intensively debated on the Internet. In the following few paragraphs, we attempt to summarize some of the key features of their analysis without, we hope, doing too much violence to its various subtleties.

Theories of reflexive modernization attempt to grasp the nature of contemporary social change. Of course, all societies experience change, but what characterizes the contemporary period is "not only the pace of social change [which is] faster than in prior system[s]" but also its "scope and . . . profoundness" (Giddens, 1991, p. 16). Changes in economic life, family life, technology, culture, and so on led many to experience life in the closing decades of the last millennium as a period full of uncertainty, unpredictability, and instability. These experiences add up to more than just *fin-de-millennium* angst; social and economic life is more complex and far less clear-cut than once it was. For the major part of the twentieth century, social traditions combined with economic imperatives meant that the trajectory of many people's lives were relatively predictable. Now these trajectories are far less certain.

Greater uncertainty in people's social and economic lives has been compounded by cultural changes of various sorts. In particular, there has been an immense loss of faith in the discourses of science and technology. All these changes provide the context to the emergence of what Beck (1992) has termed the *risk society*. For Beck (1998, p. 10), "the risk society begins where nature ends." By this he means that we have switched from worrying about what nature does to us to worrying about what we have done to nature. Of course, we can still suffer from the effects of nature such as when earthquakes, floods, or hurricanes occur (although, of course, there is now much uncertainty about whether even these phenomena are in some way or other influenced by human actions), but the point here is that very few areas of the material environment exist that have not been affected by human intervention.

A distinction is often made in the literature between *external* and *manufactured* risks. The former refers to those risks which characterized premodernity, and the latter refers to those risks that are typical of late modernity and occur as a consequence of *human interventions*. Many of these risks have numerous intangibles and are not amenable to actuarial calculation. For example, we cannot assess the levels of risk associated with phenomena such as global warming, the consumption of genetically modified foods, or the introduction of new human immunization programs (the latter two examples we will consider in more detail later). Furthermore, and crucial to our discussion here, the "experts" on these and other subjects cannot agree if risks are associated with them either (Lupton, 1999).

Manufactured risk not only concerns nature – or, as Giddens tellingly puts it in one of his Reith lectures, "what used to be nature" – it penetrates into all other areas of life too: relationships, sex (Giddens, 1992), work, housing (Ford et al., 2001), and so on. Alongside this *end of nature* comes the *end of tradition*; the less we can rely on traditional certainties, the more risks we have to negotiate for ourselves (Beck, 1998, p. 10). More risks engender more decisions and thus more choices. Associated with this end of tradition is a loss of faith in those who have traditionally been regarded as figures in authority such as doctors, fathers, teachers, and scientists. Under conditions of early modernity, scientific knowledge became a kind of traditional authority (scientific expertise would often override our grandmothers advice on the diet of our children, for example). Lay people "took" advice from experts. But now, the more science and technology intrudes into our lives, the more people question it. Thus, lay views of science and expert knowledge more generally are changing. Scientists have, of course, always changed their ideas and disagreed with each other – that is the nature of the development of scientific knowledge, but that was not how lay people viewed it. Now so-called expert or scientific knowledge is under increasing scrutiny. Giddens (1994a) calls this process of ongoing questioning *detraditionalization*.

Beck and Giddens argued that the nature and content of contemporary risk is qualitatively different from that of early modern societies. A distinctive feature of it is the way in which it permeates our psyche, both in terms of how we think about ourselves and how we relate to other people (Nettleton, 1997; Ogden, 1995). Three interrelated conceptualizations, developed by Giddens (1991), neatly capture the key elements of the contemporary experience of risk: reflexivity of the self, lifestyles and life planning, and ontological (in)security. For Giddens, the concept of risk becomes fundamental to the way both lay actors and technical specialists organize the social world...the future is continually drawn into the present by means of the *reflexive* organization of knowledge environments. (1991:3; our emphasis)

A core feature of contemporary risk culture is the need for assessing and calculating the potential risks within our lives. We seek out and are continually presented with information produced by an increasingly diverse array of "experts" on virtually every aspect of our lives: what we eat, how we sleep, our finances, our intimate relationships, our health, our leisure, and so on (Nettleton, 1997). This is typified by the growth of self-help guides, manuals, and other guide for living. The German academic Barbara Duden was struck by this phenomena in relation to health in the United States some years ago:

in a bookstore in Dallas I found about 130 manuals that would teach me "how to be an active partner in my own health." For many years now the self-care-budget in the United States has been growing at three times the rate of all medical expenses combined. (Duden, 1991, p. 20)

For Giddens this is characteristic of the *reflexivity of the self*, "a project carried on amid a profusion of reflexive resources: therapy and self help manuals of all kinds, television programs and magazine articles" (Giddens, 1992, p. 30). Of course, now we would add the myriad virtual resources of cyberspace (Denzin, 1998; Burrows et al., 2000). Thus, we are able to work constantly at and negotiate our notions of the self within the context of an increasing array of options. Giddens went on to suggest that

because of the "openness" of social life today, the pluralisation of contexts of action and diversity of "authorities", *lifestyle* choice is increasingly important in the constitution of self identity and daily activity. Reflexively organized *life-planning*, which normally presumes consideration of risks as filtered thought contact with expert knowledge, becomes a central feature of structuring self-identity. (1991, p. 5; our emphasis)

Thus, Giddens argued, we are increasingly required to make lifestyle choices. Such choices may involve decisions about our longer term life plans such as choosing to buy a particular house, taking out a personal pension, or sending our children to a particular school. This notion of lifestyle choice is fundamentally related to the availability of resources. Furthermore, the lifestyle choices and life planning of some individuals and groups can influence not only their life chances but also the life chances of others. This can have a cumulative effect where the social arrangements are such that we are encouraged to make lifestyle choices and life-planning decisions, which limit the life chances of others. Notions of the contemporary self then are constituted by way of an ongoing project in which people are bound to make lifestyle and life-planning decisions. Such projects are contingent upon the availability of material resources and can often alter and exacerbate social divisions. But lifestyle choices and life planning are not just activities of the better off; they are – to a greater or a lesser extent – made by all members of society.

Giddens linked these notions of risk, reflexivity, and lifestyle planning to a final, and perhaps more familiar, concept, that of *ontological security*. Crudely this refers to emotional security and is based on the notion that one's self identity is linked to one's biography. Hence an ontologically *insecure* individual is, according to this thesis, a person who displays certain characteristics (Giddens, 1991, pp. 53–4): first, they "lack a consistent feeling of biographical continuity"; second, "in an environment full of changes the person is obsessively preoccupied with apprehension of possible risks to his or her existence, and paralyzed in terms of practical action"; and third, "the person fails to develop or sustain trust in his [sic] own self-integrity" and may subject him- or herself to constant self-scrutiny.

In sum, late modern societies are characterized by greater uncertainty, intensified by a lack of faith in modern science and "experts." In their day-to-day lives, people seem to be facing a vast array of decisions based on probabilities rather than certain outcomes. Hence, people are constantly engaged in a process of reflexively organizing evidence and information. In turn, this imperative serves to undermine their ontological or emotional security. In other words, it permeates their psyche.

Reflexive Modernization and the British Welfare State

We outlined elsewhere (Nettleton and Burrows, 1998) the manner in which these ideas might relate to the current restructuring of the British welfare state. Indeed, in the United Kingdom, there is an important sense in which the theory of reflexive modernization has been transformed from a sociological description to something more akin to a political prescription for the restructuring of the welfare state (Giddens, 1994b; 1998). Increasingly, welfare discourse in the United Kingdom under New Labour aims to provide policies with the goal of fostering self-reliance and individual responsibility. Individuals are encouraged to be enterprising and take advice so that they may calculate and negotiate their own risks. American readers may not find anything very startling about this, but, in the context of the British welfare state, this discourse represents a sea change compared to dominant postwar models of social welfare. Most social policy analysts in the United Kingdom now accept the fundamental shift away from a more traditional conception of welfare in the United Kingdom – one based upon a rationally administered state provision coupled with paternalistic professionally determined needs and bureaucratic organizational delivery systems – toward one more characterized by fragmentation, diversity (Carter, 1998), and a range of what Beck (1992) terms processes of individualization.

A more reflexive form of modernity means that the balance between the imperatives of social structure and those of human agency shift. The relative autonomy of agency increases alongside a concomitant decrease in the determining powers of social structures. This change has important implications for the analysis of social policy (Deacon & Mann, 1999) as Beck and Beck-Gernsheim (1996, p. 27) pointed out:

one of the decisive features of individualization processes ... is that they not only permit, but demand an active contribution by individuals ... if they are not to fail individuals must be able to plan for the long term and adapt to change; they must organize and improvise, set goals, recognize obstacles, accept defeats and attempt new starts. They need initiative, tenacity, flexibility.

Flexibility, of course, demands the cultivation of a reflexive monitoring of risks and the ability to alter life plans rapidly. The necessity for such flexibility tends to undermine the stability required to generate ontological security. The clear downside of the development of a flexible, reflexive self is the potential for increased ontological insecurity. Living under conditions of reflexive modernization may lead to a certain liberation of the self. But individualization processes may also erode the social capital necessary for sustaining a viable community life (Putnam, 1995), as more and more people withdraw into the private sphere and become increasingly unable or unwilling to contribute to more collective forms of public provision and participation.

Ironically perhaps, although rapid technological change is often conceptualized as one of the major forces invoking feelings of ontological insecurity, it is also often held up by some as the means by which "community" can be reinvigorated and the welfare state "modernized." Certainly, it is the case that the emergence of the new sets of social relations associated with reflexive modernization have occurred in tandem with dramatic changes in information technologies (ITs). Some writers have recognized the influence of ITs as a means of changing the management of liberal democratic welfare states (Burrows and Loader, 1994), but their potential for facilitating entirely new social relations of welfare delivery (Loader, 1998a) has not been adequately envisaged (Hughes, 1998). So in what ways might the new ITs successfully underpin a new form of welfare state under conditions of reflexive modernization?

Information and Communication Technologies and the British Welfare State

Much has been written about the increasing role of ITs in the provision and delivery of formal welfare services in Britain. Much of the organizational restructuring occurring in the British welfare state can be attributed to the alleged potential of ITs in creating flexible and decentralized organizational forms (Loader, 1998a). The introduction of quasi-market mechanisms in various areas of the British welfare state, for example, is heavily dependent upon the development of highly sophisticated information networks between a range of statutory, voluntary, and private sector agencies. In local government, discussion has focused upon the potential of computer networks in facilitating organizational forms responsive to "customer" demands (Hague & Loader, 1999). Some writers have argued that new forms of social innovation in relation to the delivery of social welfare are developing rapidly. While not including all citizens, most European countries have a high level of telephone connection, and cable companies are rapidly connecting millions of urban households to a range of digital communications services. Together with smart card technology and ever greater access to the Internet, these ITs constitute the physical infrastructure that may provide the setting for a radical renegotiation of the social relations of welfare (Loader, 1998a).

However, of more importance than the application of new ITs within the context of the formal institutions of the welfare state, is the emergence of virtual self-help and social support systems "from below." The formation of "virtual communities of interest" around issues of health and social welfare are representing the prime sites for the working through of processes of reflexive modernization in relation to welfare. Informal systems of computer-mediated self-help are, perhaps, the embryonic social forms that are to become the major arenas for playing out aspects of the new social politics of "defensive engagement" (Ellison, 1997). By way of illustration, we take two quite specific and concrete contemporary debates in the sphere of public health policy that have a high media profile in the United Kingdom: the MMR debate and the GM foods debate.

The MMR Debate

As already indicated, formal welfare is not simply "provided" and uncritically accepted in a late modern context. Inevitably this can create tensions for both the providers and the users of services. Public health is perhaps a good example of this. Doctors, on the basis of medical science, develop policies that they try to implement on the basis of what they perceive to be the collective interest. Take vaccinations for example. During the time we have been writing this chapter, the Chief Medical Officer (CMO) for England publicly reinforced the government view that all children should receive the combined MMR (measles, mumps, and rubella) vaccination. In the UK, general medical practitioners (GPs) receive financial inducements encouraging them to immunize their patients. The CMO's announcement was made amid growing concern among official circles that parents were sometimes reluctant to have their children vaccinated because there was "evidence" that the combined vaccine might have detrimental "side effects." In the face of uncertainties, all parents must ask themselves: Will my child suffer any side effects? Will my child contract the disease if he or she is not immunized? Is my child being offered the vaccination so that my GP can claim his "additional payments"? Such debates have received much media coverage, and so more and more parents have become exposed to these uncertainties, and many will have lost sleep over what course of action to take. For Beck and Giddens, instances such as this make for the day-to-day experience of living in a risk society.

Not surprisingly, these debates have also been much in evidence on the Internet, especially within UK-dominated news groups concerned with parenting and health issues. The following thread illustrates the manner in which such discussions resonate with many of the themes foregrounded by the theory of reflexive modernization. The thread begins with a request for information by a father trying to decide whether to allow his daughter to have the MMR jab:

My nine month old daughter will soon be of the age to have the MMR vaccination jab. I am slightly concerned as I have heard some stories of babies having an adverse reaction to the jab as the three vaccines interact with each other; in some cases allegedly leading to brain damage. Two questions: 1. Are these stories true ? 2. Is it possible to have the three jabs separately over a period of time or do you have to have the MMR?

This posting initiated a long thread from a large number of contributors. What follows is a commentary on some of the contributions informed by some of the insights of the theory of reflexive modernization. One of the first responses follows:

If you have such strong doubts about this, my own personal view would be not to do it, because a mother's instinct is the greatest gift nature gives us.

Whilst it might or might not be true I believe that the MMR was introduced into Britain under a rather dubious route. Perhaps one of the Dr's who use this newsgroup would like to prove me wrong.

The post continues:

One of the reasons vaccination seems so attractive to some, but also causes considerable psychological distress to mothers trying to decide is because we have a Government vaccination target system in place. The high %'s of people going for vaccination is proof of undue pressure on parents.

This initial exchange captures a central feature of the debate. The first post is an example of someone who has picked up upon the controversy surrounding the MMR and how this makes them feel uneasy about making a decision about their own child. The second post illustrates some further themes outlined earlier in our discussion on reflexive modernization: first, that nonscientific evidence may form the basis of rational and informed decisions (i.e., to follow ones "instinct"); second, that those within government circles cannot always be trusted (indeed there *has* been debate about the way that the MMR jab was introduced); and third, that health professionals may not always act on the basis of altruism and may be swayed by economic interests.

The UK government picked up on these debates, and the Department of Health Web site (www.doh.gov.uk/mmr.htm) has a large section on the merits of the MMR jab. It says, "This site gives the facts about research carried out in this area" and argues that the "publicity" surrounding the MMR has meant that "many parents were left understandably unclear about the true risks and benefits: and unclear about what is best for their child's health." But the government site represents just one of many sources of information that people access and weigh up when making their decisions. For example, they may consider alternative solutions. Take the next post for example:

I have a friend who has had all of her children (4) protected using homeopathic vaccinations. Which may sound a bit odd, but then what is the concept behind vaccination anyway? If it's all in her mind, then her mind has produced some very robust happy and healthy children.

The "evidence" here is based on experience and observation. In a further post, this same person added:

There are some things you do and some things you don't. Vaccinating a whole generation of children without the long term research to support the act is one of those things you don't do. Forcing Dr's into a position where they are using strong arm tactics to get numbers up is nothing short of immoral.

Other posts, however, support the case for vaccination:

Whilst many kids will breeze through these diseases without obvious long-term harm, some don't. The risk/benefit ratio is highly stacked in favor of vaccination. If I had kids I would have them vaccinated.

A further twist to the MMR debate is the call by some parents to administer the vaccines separately. For example, having highlighted some of the concerns touched upon in the post cited earlier, this poster wrote:

Some other things I've picked up: Other European countries do individual vaccinations on separate occasions. This makes more sense to me. A vaccination actually gives you a little bit of the disease, and if your immune system is fighting against one disease, it's not a good idea to give it another two to fight against two.

Similarly another person wrote in the same thread:

I've heard it rumored that you can get the individual vaccines yourself and have your child immunized separately. Does anyone know if this is true? I've also heard rumored that your GP can remove you from your list if this happens – but I heard on "You and Yours" [A popular BBC Radio 4 program] about a woman who was struck off her GP's list for arguing with the receptionist, so they can do this almost at whim. There is (or was when the radio program was on) no mechanism for complaint or appeal by patients. This makes me think of the wider picture: are GPs getting paid too much for high hit rates, or penalized financially or otherwise for not following government policy, and is there a conflict of interest here? Can we no longer rely on them for good advice?

The government responded to these concerns by reiterating the "scientific evidence" on their Web site (www.doh.gov.uk/mmr.htm) where they challenged the

media reports about giving MMR vaccine separately. This suggestion was made by one researcher – although not via published papers – is unsupported by any scientific evidence and would expose children to an increased risk of disease while waiting unnecessarily between immunizations.

The various pros and cons of the MMR vaccine are not, of course, of direct relevance to our discussion in this chapter. But what is of interest is the way in which the issue is debated. Parents are not prepared to accept uncritically the views and advice of health professionals or the results of studies which are supported in learned scientific journals. They are keen to seek advice from a range of sources and to listen to the views of other nonprofessionals whose observations are based on experiential "evidence." In this context, it is difficult to feel confident and certain that one is doing one's best for one's children.

We are not suggesting here that the MMR jab issue is being debated in this way *because* of the emergence of virtual communities; indeed, disquiet about its benefits and risks have been debated by patents and practitioners in many other contexts (Rogers & Pilgrim, 1995). However, the issue is indicative of the way in which the Internet and news groups in particular provide a forum that is both emblematic and facilitative of the ever-growing dissenting and critical voices of welfare recipients in the United Kingdom; it is but one of many examples of the *new insecurities*, which characterize late modernity. Ironically, of course, immunization programs are designed to control and eliminate illness and disease, and yet their very existence generates new anxieties under conditions of reflexive modernization. Reflecting on our earlier discussion, we can see how human attempts to control nature (preventing various diseases) have *manufactured* new risks (the side effects of immunizations). In this context, ordinary people are especially wary of those experts whom they see as being involved in generating such risks and so they turn to other forms of self-help or experiential knowledge to assist them in making choices. However, in being confronted with the realization that in a posttraditional world there is no expert arbiter, just a range of different discourses that may be more or less legitimate, it is easy to see how feelings of ontological insecurity can be invoked. What is also striking is the way in which such anxieties are permeating so many areas of our everyday lives and lifestyles. Another topical public health example in the United Kingdom concerns worries about what we eat.

The GM Debate

Anyone who visits a supermarket these days in the United Kingdom would undoubtedly be struck by the ever expanding range of foods and products that are labeled "organic." We can buy anything from *organic* baked beans to *organic* butter, *organic* extra virgin olive oil, and *organic* spinach, tomatoes, and cheese. Food manufacturers and the "big" food retailers such as Sainsbury's and Tesco's are also making play of the fact that they are *not* selling genetically modified (GM) foods. The issue is being debated extensively in the media, and this again has been reflected in the discussions on the net. The food producers, the manufacturers, and the government have lost the trust and confidence of many British consumers. The following exchange is typical and is taken from an ongoing thread within a news group in which the organic and GM debate form the core:

Unscrupulous chemical companies cannot be trusted to be honest as they have ulterior motives, but the same can often be said of 'Green' groups who twist the facts just as successfully to suit their own ends. The result is that the knowledgeable, sane, logical scientific arguments get drowned in a torrent of PR rubbish on the one hand or emotional rubbish on the other. That I think is the most dangerous result of all.

This invoked the following detailed response:

The most dangerous result of all is that these technologies should be introduced without sufficient public debate, and research into possible side effects of these technologies. I think Monsanto [a large corporate GM Seed Producer] and the other biotech companies thought they could introduce GMO's [Genetically Modified Organisms] into the United Kingdom and Europe with as little fuss as seemed to have happened in the US. Given the stance of the UK government and the European Union they were probably right to think so. Yes the pressure groups can get carried away sometimes, but if it wasn't for public pressure and campaigning groups we'd be a lot further down the road to large scale farming of GMO's in Britain. There was an interesting program on Radio 4 this afternoon (File on 4) about government policy towards GMO's. The highlights were:
    1. The HSE [Health and Safety Executive – a UK Government agency] is responsible for overseeing the safety of the GM trials, but 1/3 of trials are not monitored for compliance with safety rules as the plant concerned (Maize) received EU commercial approval before the current regs on GM plants were introduced. 2. Results from the current farm trials won't be all in until 2003, but These Maize plants could potentially be grown commercially from next year as the restriction on their use ends this year. 3. Jack Cunningham (Gov. minister responsible) wouldn't confirm that they would wait until the end of the whole trial before giving clearance for particular plants to be grown commercially. 4. Concerns about the Governments contradictory stance, from bodies like the RSPB [Royal Society for the Protection of Birds], which are in support of the current trials. Lord Sainsbury [a member of the New Labour Government] owns a Biotech Co., and Novartis (large biotech co.) have sponsored a number of Labour Party events. Government factsheets and EU information seem to be very pro GMO's. 5. Number of large food companies are worried about the image of GM food, and looking to cut out

such ingredients – just not worth the hassle. 6. GM/Non-GM food starting to be separated in the US from harvest onwards, some farmers getting less for GM crops than non-GM. 7. Possible trade war looms, as US threatens to go to the GTO over labeling of GM foods. (Yet another example of using the GTO to overcome consumer health concerns – but lets not get into that).

This thread is of interest here not only because it provides some insight into the nature of the online debate, but also because it does set out the various governmental and commercial interests involved in the current debate. There is much public concern about what we are putting into our bodies and intense debate about what we are feeding our children. Much of the debate and public concern, however, is among the middle classes who perhaps have the "luxury" of worrying about the quality of their foods and are most likely to have access to the Internet and information, as well as, crucially, the analytic and material resources to act upon their concerns. Middle-class anxieties are of prime importance in the new social politics of the risk society, and virtual communities are, as we have already noted, one of the prime sites within which these iterative processes of defensive engagement can take place.

Concluding Discussion

This chapter has attempted to view the emergence of wired self-help through the theoretical lens of reflexive modernization. We have concluded that such a lens is helpful in making sense of some of the new global virtual spaces that are opening up. In conclusion, we might point toward four issues that might structure future debate about the role of virtual communities in the context of the politics of social welfare.

First, although the *rise of self-help groups* is not a consequence of wired forms of welfare, the Internet has almost certainly accelerated the spread of such groups. The illustrative threads we have presented represent but a very tiny fraction of the millions of such threads now in constant global production (and, of course, consumption) where topics are debated independently of formal welfare institutions. They provide a medium for sharing and exchanging information and ideas and, as such, form a prime site for the emergence of a new social politics of defensive engagement. However, even though these fora do comprise "groups" or "virtual communities," they are, nevertheless, the result of a collection of contributions from *individuals* and the scope and opportunity for any politics of collective resistance may be limited. As Williams (1989) pointed out, self-help groups are the descendants of an uneasy relationship between two ideologies of individualism and collectivism, in which individualism is the dominant partner. It would appear that the format and nature of virtual groups are essentially about self-help rather than collective help in that individuals seek out information and support or offer individualized responses to other participants.

A second, but strongly related issue, is the salience and privileging of *personal experience and lay knowledge over "expert" knowledge* within online self-help. As was clear from our discussion of the illustrative MMR jab debate, advice from orthodox experts is not accepted uncritically, and parents gathered information and advice from a range of sources. As we have seen, according to Giddens, this is a key feature of reflexive modernity:

Modern life is a complex affair and there are many "filter-back" processes whereby technical knowledge, in one shape or another, is re-appropriated by lay persons and routinely applied in the course of their day-to-day activities. [...] Processes of re-appropriation relate to all aspects of social life – for example medical treatments, child rearing, or sexual pleasure. (Giddens 1991, p. 146)

In a posttraditional society, traditional authority (such as the medical expert) is being replaced by multiple sources of authority. Clearly the Internet dramatically expands the array of information sources on virtually (excuse the pun) every aspect of people's lives. But we have little understanding of how and when people turn to the Internet for information and support and the relative weight they give to the sources of help they access. Virtual communities offering online self-help undoubtedly do provide important sources of information and social support (Burrows et al., 2000). However, as the preceding discussion illustrates, they can also provide so much information and so many different perspectives on an issue that, rather than assisting in the reflexive management of risk, they can also induce anxiety. People are better informed, but this does not mean that they are any more able to make the choices that they must make (Williams & Popay, 1994).

Third, we must recognize that reflexive modernization provides a rather positive reading of the meaning, functioning, and significance of virtual communities. Reflexive modernization presumes an active model of citizenship, which sits easily with a vision of the Internet as a "lean to" technology – a technology with which people have to engage and interact and in which they must be proactive in their participation. However, as the primary mode of Internet access shifts away from PCs towards digital TV over the next few years another model of Internet use may emerge. Is there danger in the Internet becoming more of a "lean back" technology engagement, and thus a more passive experience? Individuals will become primarily consumers rather than producers. It is already thought that for every active participant on news groups, for example, there are many more "lurkers" – people who read posts but never make a contribution. Some research suggests a ratio of 1:20 (Smith, 1999). For some of these lurkers, the information, advice, and support being given may well offer positive benefit. However, there is also the possibility that publicly accessible systems of wired welfare – with their multitude of daily narratives of hope and despair – are being treated as a form of voyeuristic entertainment and, as such, simply represent yet another expression of the depressing *Oprahfication* of popular culture.

Of course, modes of engagement with the technology are strongly socially patterned (Loader, 1998b), and it is already becoming clear that the better equipped (virtual?) middle classes are best placed to understand and engage with the technology in ways that advantage them even further. This leads us to our final observation that, like traditional forms of welfare, wired welfare may tend to offer strategic advantages to a middle class who has the time, the reflexivity, the inclination, and the resources to exploit it. The manner in which Ellison has expressed this concern in general can, we think, be seen even more acutely if one just focuses on the emerging social politics of the virtual life:

citizenship in late modernity is best understood as a reflexive condition of defensive engagement involving new processes of social and political interaction . . . [in which there are] . . . To paraphrase Beck . . . "reflexivity winners and losers". Some groups will be more adept than others in adjusting to more fluid social and political forms, constructing and reconstructing solidarities which further a variety of claims across space and time according to the dictates of social change. (Ellison, 1997, p. 114)

Acknowledgments

The work reported here is being funded by the British ESRC (award number L132251029) under the auspices of its Virtual Society? Programme. Full details of the project can be found on the project website at www.york.ac.uk/res/vcc. Thanks are due to our co-workers on this project: Nicholas Pleace, Brian Loader, and Steve Muncer.

References

Baym, N. (1998). The emergence of on-line community. In S. Jones (Ed.), *Cybersociety 2.0*. London: Sage, pp. 35–68.
Beck, U. (1992). *Risk society*. London: Sage.

(1998). Politics of risk society. In J. Franklin (Ed.), *The politics of risk society*. Oxford: Polity, pp. 9–22.

Beck, U., & Beck-Gernsheim, E. (1996). Individualization and precarious freedoms. In P. Heelas, S. Lash & P. Morris (Eds.), *Detraditionalization*. London: Blackwell, pp. 47–63.

Beck, U., Giddens, A., & Lash, S. (1994). *Reflexive modernization*. Cambridge: Polity.

Burrows, R., & Loader, B. (Eds). (1994). *Towards a post Fordist welfare state?* London: Routledge.

Burrows, R., Nettleton, S., Pleace, N., Loader, B., & Muncer, S. (2000). Virtual community care? Social policy and the emergence of computer mediated social support. *Information, Communication and Society, 3*, 1, 95–121.

Carter, J. (Ed). (1998). *Postmodernity and the fragmentation of welfare*. London: Routledge.

Deacon, A., & Mann, K. (1999). Agency, modernity and social policy. *Journal of Social Policy, 28*(3), 413–35.

Denzin, N. (1998). In search of the inner child: Co-dependency and gender in a cyberspace community. In G. Bendelow & S. Williams (Eds.), *Emotions in social life*. London: Routledge, pp. 97–119.

Duden, B. (1991). *The woman beneath the skin*. Cambridge: Harvard University Press.

Ellison, N. (1997). Towards a new social politics: Citizenship and reflexivity in late modernity. *Sociology, 31*(4), 697–717.

Ferguson, T. (1996). *Health on-line*. Reading, MA: Addison Welsey.

Ford, J. (1998). *Risks: Home ownership and job insecurity*. London: Shelter.

Franklin, J. (Ed). (1998). *The politics of risk society*. Oxford: Polity.

Giddens, A. (1991). *Modernity and self-identity*. Oxford: Polity.

(1992). *The transformation of intimacy*. Oxford: Polity.

(1994a). Living in a Post-traditional society. In U. Beck, A. Giddens & S. Lash (Eds.), *Reflexive modernization*. Cambridge: Polity, pp. 56–109.

(1994b). *Beyond left and right*. Oxford: Polity.

(1998). Risk society: The context of British politics. In J. Franklin (Ed.), *The politics of risk society*. Oxford: Polity, pp. 23–34.

Hague, B., & Loader, B. (Eds). (1999). *Digital democracy*. London: Routledge.

Hughes, G. (Ed.) (1998). *Imagining welfare futures*. London: Routledge.

Jones, S. (1998). Information, Internet and community: Notes towards an understanding of community in the information age. In S. Jones (Ed.), *Cybersociety 2.0*. London: Sage, pp. 1–32.

Kollock, P., & Smith, M. A. (1999). Communities in cyberspace. In M. A. Smith & P. Kollock (Eds.), *Communities in cyberspace*. London: Routledge.

Loader, B. (1998a). Welfare direct. In J. Carter (Ed.), *Postmodernity and the fragmentation of welfare*. London: Routledge.

(Ed). (1998b). *Cyberspace divide*. London: Routledge.

Lupton, D. (1999). *Risk*. London: Routledge.

Moursund, J. (1997). SANCTUARY: Social support on the Internet. In J. Behar (Ed.), *Mapping cyberspace*. Oakdale, NY: Dowling College Press, pp. 53–78.

Nettleton, S. (1997). Governing the risky self: How to become healthy, wealthy and wise. In A. Peterson & R. Bunton (Eds), *Foucault, health and medicine*. London: Routledge, pp. 101–29.

Nettleton, S., & Burrows, R. (1998). Individualisation processes and social policy. In J. Carter (Ed.), *Postmodernity and the fragmentation of welfare*. London: Routledge, pp. 153–67.

O'Brien, M., Penna, S., & Hay, C. (Eds). (1999). *Theorising modernity: Reflexivity, environment and Identity in Giddens' social theory*. London: Longman.

Ogden, J. (1995). Psychosocial theory and the creation of the risky self. *Social science and medicine, 40*(3), 409–15.

Putnam, R. (1995). Bowling alone: America's declining social capital. *Journal of Democracy, 6*, 65–78.

Rogers, A., and Pilgrim, D. (1995). The risk of resistance: Perspectives on the mass childhood immunisation programme. In J. Gabe (Ed.), *Medicine, health risk*. Oxford: Blackwell, pp. 73–89.

Smith, M. (1999). Invisible crowds in cyberspace: Mapping the social structure of the usenet. In M. A. Smith & P. Kollock (Eds.), *Communities in cyberspace*. London: Routledge, pp. 195–219.

Wellman, B., & Gulia, M. (1999). Virtual communities as communities: Net surfers don't ride alone. In M. A. Smith and P. Kollock (Eds.), *Communities in cyberspace*. London: Routledge, pp. 167–94.

Williams, G. (1989). Hope for the humblest? The role of self help in chronic illness: The case of anklosing spondylitis. *Sociology of Health and Illness, 11*(2), 135–59.

Williams, G., & Popay, J. (1994). Lay knowledge and the privileging of experience. In J. Gabe, D. Kelleher & G. Williams (Eds.), *Challenging medicine*. London: Routledge, pp. 99–114.

10 Understanding the Life Cycles of Network-Based Learning Communities

James Levin and Raoul Cervantes

More than half of the classrooms in the United States are wired to the Internet, and the number of classrooms connected is rapidly increasing (NCES, 1999). As this network infrastructure is put in place, teachers and learners can form and participate in network-based learning communities. But for these communities to function in productive ways, we need to better understand how these communities are formed, grow, function in some mature steady state, and decline and terminate. A better understanding of this "life cycle" allows teachers and learners to better function in these network-based learning communities and permits the development of institutional structures that more appropriately support learning and teaching in these new media.

In this chapter, we review studies of network-based learning communities, especially those communities formed around collaborative projects, and present evidence for systematic patterns of change in these communities over time. Such communities are born, undergo growth, reach a level of mature functioning, and then undergo decline and cease to function. Like biological organisms, this life cycle can be truncated when the community is not properly supported or when external factors intervene in some traumatic way. We describe the life cycle of network-based communities by examining in depth an extended case study of a network-based learning activity. We conclude with a discussion of the kinds of support needed to encourage the growth and mature functioning of productive network-based learning communities.

Review

There have been a number of pioneering efforts to explicate the nature of network-based learning communities. Three have described a

269

specific time sequence that network-based projects typically experience. These include Levin et al.'s (1992) and Waugh, Levin & Smith's (1994a, 1994b) description of six stages of organizing network-based instructional interactions, Riel's (1993) five steps in a Learning Circle (forming the Learning Circle, planning the Learning Circle projects, exchanging work on the projects, creating the publication, and evaluating the process), and Harris's (1995) eight steps in organizing telecollaborative projects (choose the curricular goal(s), choose the activity's structure, explore examples of other online projects, determine the details of your project, invite telecollaborators, form the telecollaborative group, communicate, and create closure).

How many "stages" are there in the life cycle of network-based community? In the case study to be described here, it is clear that there is a continuum of development without discrete boundaries, where activity in one stage flows into another. The critical issue is the concept of a life cycle, with the named stages as a convenience for keeping track of the different sections of an otherwise continuously changing process. The issue of whether there are six stages, five stages, or eight stages may turn out to be less important than the idea that learning communities go through a life cycle, and that the nature of the interaction early on can be quite different from the nature of the interaction later.

For learners and teachers to engage productively in these activities, it is important to understand the ways that these activities systematically unfold over time. An understanding of the lifecycle of network-based communities can lead to more productive learning by communities of learners distributed across the world. This understanding can help create powerful learning environments for diverse sets of learners in ways that may help people become better able to deal with the challenges of today and tomorrow.

Network activity is episodic, unfolding over time through a series of different phases. The exact list of steps or stages specified varies, but there is generally some sort of initiation phase, a phase in which the educational activity is carried out, and then some sort of wrap-up phase. Following Levin et al. (1992), this study examines six stages in the network project life cycle: proposal, refinement, organization, pursuit, wrap-up, and publication.

Levin et al. (1992) described the proposal stage of a network activity life cycle as follows:

[T]he first stage of the life cycle occurs when the idea for the activity is proposed to the network, usually appearing as a message on a network-wide bulletin board.... For some of these messages, teachers and students across the network respond, and the activity moves on to the next stage. However, for many of these proposed activities, this is also the end of their life cycle.

They described the Refinement stage as follows:

[I]nterested people generally exchange electronic mail to refine the idea. Messages suggesting changes or extensions to the project are interchanged, initially by sending messages to the original proposer. Often the proposers will then set up a "conference" (an electronic mailing list) of those interested.

The organizational stage is described as follows:

[M]essages are exchanged with proposed time schedules, with detailed descriptions of planned procedures, and sometimes even the exchange of software tools.

They described the pursuit stage as follows:

The next stage of the activity life cycle is when the planned activity is actually carried out. The messages exchanged during this stage may contain reports of data collected or descriptions of problems that are encountered during the activity. Sometimes there are messages from some of the participating sites that inquire about the missing reports from the other sites (an indirect complaint). At other times there will be apologies for delays, and promises of actions to be carried out in the near future.

The wrap-up stage is described as follows:

[T]ypically, the person who proposed the activity would send out a message thanking the participants for their contribution. For those activities viewed by the participants as successful, there are often congratulatory messages as well, and sometimes promises of future participation.

They described the publication stage messages as

aimed at people who haven't shared the context of carrying out the project. The publication messages, however, are important, because they can then serve as the starting point for anyone who wants to participate in the project the next time that it is conducted.

The episodic nature of educational network interactions is important for several reasons. Since the nature of the interaction in these different phases varies, the roles that participants in the activity need to play differ as well. Unless participants are aware of the ways in which these interactions unfold, they may be disappointed in their expectations about the timing or nature of interactions. In addition, knowing about the nature of these network processes allows the participants to integrate them more effectively with the other educational activities in which they are engaged.

One of the ways that educational network interactions differ from other comparable face-to-face interactions is that the network interactions can be stretched out over time. Riel describes a network interaction as a "group conversation carried over electronic mail in slow motion" (Riel, 1993). This time elongation is surprising to novices, who see electronic networks as enabling communication at the "speed of light." Compensating, at least partially, for this is the fact that networks allow one to participate in several such interactions at the same time. Even though a given learning activity is stretched out in time, the same group of learners can participate in many such activities over the same time period.

Stapleton (1991) conducted a study of eighteen different network-based projects in order to map out the stages that they went through. He found that the further along a project reached before ending, the more successful it was judged by the participants. In cases where a project was proposed but never received responses, the proposer was left very unsatisfied, and very little learning occurred. Even for projects that were initiated and conducted, the participants judged the project as less successful if there was no closure on the project than if there was closure. Because projects are stretched out over such a long time, participants often have the impression that not much has happened until they write or read a "wrap-up" summary of the project. At that point, they then realize that quite a bit of learning occurred, stretched out over weeks or months of the project's duration.

Following up on this research, Cervantes (1993) conducted an in-depth study of one network-based project, the Zero-g World Design Project (or Zero-g Project), to explore these processes in detail and to describe the relation of network activity to face-to-face classroom activity. This project was conducted during the 1991–2 school year. Many of the precollege participants used the FrEdMail network, a low-cost electronic network with email and electronic bulletin board features that allowed precollege schools to participate in educational network activities before the Internet was widely available to them.

The Zero-g Project – An Extended Case Study

The Zero-g Project was a year-long project in which participants designed activities for a zero-g environment, such as exists in the space shuttle or in current space stations. Zero-g Project activities included the

Collision Course Challenge, in which students generated solutions for a problem involving two people on a collision course in zero-g; the Design Challenge, in which students addressed the problems of recreation and food in zero-g; the School Design Challenge, in which students designed a school for zero-g; and the Five Same and Different Challenge, in which students proposed five differences and similarities between conventional and zero-g schools.

The designers and coordinators of the Zero-g Project attempted to create functional learning environments to provide a wide range of instructional opportunities for the participants in this study. The Zero-g Project and the activities it generated then provided a context for mediation. Within this context, experts assisted novices to achieve goals specified by the project.

Proposal Stage

The message marking the proposal stage of the Zero-g Project was posted on an electronic bulletin board in the summer prior to the school year in which the project was conducted. The project director sent the proposal message, which provided a context and purpose for the project, its goals, the diversity of participants, and applications for instructional settings.

The following message excerpt informs potential participants of the context and purpose of the project:

> There are orbiting space stations like SkyLab and the Soviet Solyut, in which people live "in freefall", where things don't fall when dropped. Eventually there will be orbiting cities, which unlike most science fiction visions, may also exist in such "zero-g" environments.
>
> In this network-based design project, students and teachers will select an aspect of our everyday life and consider how it would have to be redesigned to function in a zero-g environment. The participants in this project will be constructing a consistent overall design for a large-scale orbiting zero-g space station.

This opening sentence introduces ideas that were central to the Zero-g Project. First, the project directed participants to create designs for space station environments, like *SkyLab*. And second, the fact that people lived in "freefall," where objects did not fall, was central to the participants' thinking throughout the project and provided a constant constraint for participants when solving problems and creating designs. These two concepts included in the proposal message influenced work throughout the entire project.

This section of the message also relates the notion of zero-g to a potential real-world condition. The concepts of gravity and zero-g are made less abstract by situating them in the context of environments where people will live. This notion that zero-g is a condition that affects people and objects in life-supporting environments also influenced work throughout the course of the project.

A crucial component of the proposal message is the statement of project goals. The message focuses on project goals in the task of designing or redesigning aspects of everyday life to be consistent with zero-g conditions. The linking of everyday life aspects to the novel environment of a space station gives the participants a point of reference and requires them to use what they know and work with it. Throughout the project, which eventually issued a variety of problems and challenges to the participants, tackling everyday aspects of life in zero-g remained consistent. This project has its parallels in the Cognition and Technology group at Vanderbilt's Jasper Project, but it differs from that project by engaging learners in interaction with other people from both within the educational system and outside, instead of just engaging learners in a synthetically constructed learning environment.

To achieve continued and successful participation in the Zero-g Project, participants, particularly teachers, required a range of resources. The project director anticipated this and included information on resources in the proposal:

Outside expertise will be available, including university and NASA experts. To help students and teachers to start thinking about life in a zero-g environment, we will loan anyone requesting it with a short videotape of SkyLab astronauts functioning in "freefall". We will also draw upon the reports of American astronauts and Soviet Cosmonauts of life in zero-g.

This section of the proposal mentions the participation of experts and availability of resources for use in the classroom. It also sets up the future interactions online by naming the players and proposing information to be shared. These resources were crucial to the project and proved influential throughout. The teachers in this study had limited knowledge of life-supporting space environments and had never taught in this particular content area. All of them expressed reliance on outside experts to assist in providing knowledge to be used by their students and by the teachers themselves.

The videotape offered in the message proved to be useful to the participants in this study throughout the project and was perhaps the most robust and useful single teaching tool. By viewing the video, the participants learned about the physical appearance of space environments and how objects and people are affected by zero-g.

Teachers involved in this study expressed concern about how the Zero-g Project would support their curriculum. This concern was also expressed by teachers who responded to the proposal message. The following message excerpt addresses this issue:

> This project can provide an extended network experience for students and teachers that cut across a wide range of curricular areas: science, social studies writing, problem solving, mathematics, art and design.

At first glance, the Zero-g Project gives the impression of a narrowly defined science project. However, as the project director stated in this message, the project engaged students in a range of skills and knowledge domains, giving the teacher the flexibility to focus on pertinent areas.

By definition, the proposal stage occurs when the network project is introduced to the potential participants, primarily through a network message. The proposal stage, although consisting of a single message, is critical to any project. Only some proposals attract participants and continue on to the following life cycle stages (Levin et al., 1992). The Zero-g Proposal message initiated a project that extended through all the life cycle stages. Also, the initiatives in this message – goals, purposes, resources, and curriculum relevance – affected project work through the entire lifespan of the project.

Of central importance for the success of a proposed project is the readiness of participants to engage in the project. Of the many teachers who volunteered to participate in the Zero-g Project, four were selected for intensive study. All four teachers had some instructional telecommunications experience. The high school teacher, with the most experience among the four, had taken a course in networking at the university and had participated in network projects for four years. The second-grade teacher also had taken a course in telecommunications, had one-year's experience with network projects, and had been a systems operator of a K–12 electronic network for a year. Our research team worked with the fifth-grade teacher the year prior to this study, participating in a network project. The middle school teacher had taken a course in instructional telecommunications seven years prior to this study, participating in an email pen-pal project at that time, but had not used telecommunications since then with her students. Even though they expressed uncertainties about the likelihood of success in their interviews, these doubts did not outweigh their motivation and beliefs that the project would clearly benefit their students.

Refinement Stage

For several weeks after the project director posted the Zero-g Project proposal message, interested teachers and other network users sent messages inquiring about the project. A primary concern was whether the project was appropriate for the teachers' students, as this message states:

I am interested in learning more about the Zero G project. Is this something that you would like to have high school students participate in?

The following message expressed a similar concern, inquiring whether their participation could be a useful contribution to the project:

Since this is a topic that is unfamiliar to my class and to myself, would we be valuable contributors?

The project director made clear that the Zero-g Project was not limited to experts or even science classes, but that it was appropriate for participants who possessed a wide range of interests and abilities. This message excerpt, in particular, underscores this point:

Since very few folks have spent very much time in zero-g, we're all "novices" at this.

The project director was attempting to recruit not just teachers and students but also experts working in business or government institutions. Because collaboration between outside experts and teachers and students was new to most of the participants, their roles were a matter of uncertainty. This message exchange, between a NASA scientist and the project director, reflects this concern:

> *NASA scientist message*: I am interested in learning more about the
> project. The time that I would have available will be very limited.
> Lockheed at JSC is involved in many projects for the space station
> along these lines. Although I work primarily with the shuttle I have
> done a few things for the space station, such as testing candidate soaps
> for use in the space station shower. I'm not sure what I would be able
> to contribute to the project, but I am willing to try to help.
>
> *Project director reply*: Great to hear of your interest. I'll append the
> tentative timeline for the project. Do you want me to add you to the

electronic mailing list? Then you can follow what's happening and if you see something interesting feel free to jump in. When I see something that might be interesting for you, I'll send it your way.

This message exchange illustrates qualities of the Zero-g Project that may have appealed to experts working in fields outside education who have been concerned about their role, expectations, and demands of their time. The project director assures the NASA researcher that any commitment would be voluntary, collaborative, low pressure, and flexible.

In the four classrooms that were part of our study, the communication concerning the Zero-g Project during the refinement stage was conducted through email, as well as over the phone and in person. Two considerations were crucial for the teachers in our study: (1) Would they be able to carry out technical tasks using their available computer equipment? (2) How would they integrate the Zero-g Project into their curriculum?

Of these concerns, the curriculum integration issue was resolved with each teacher incorporating the Zero-g Project into their existing curriculum and teaching practices. As stated by the project director, the project could be applied to language arts, science, social studies, or computer literacy. Although this was true, what emerged fairly early into the project was that the participation in the project would spread into knowledge areas outside of their curriculum. For example, in the middle school computer literacy class, students were required to address the issue of the nature of gravity, what caused it, and if it could be produced artificially.

The problems of technical expertise and equipment were addressed throughout the project as difficulties arose. Prior to the project, the teachers were reassured that they would have full support of our research team, including troubleshooting, training, software, and equipment.

In the refinement stage of the Zero-g Project, the project director's role was to clarify the demands of the participants, emphasize their possible contributions, and offer what support, if any, is available. The potential participants decide whether the project benefits their students and is appropriate in their respective situations. The commitments that were crucial to the success and completion of the projects were declared in the refinement stage.

Organization Stage

The refinement, organization, and pursuit stages overlapped in time during the lifespan of the Zero-g Project. During the course of the project, participants joined and left, new challenges and activities were proposed, and participants sent messages containing their designs, questions, and solutions to problems. Although this overlap was evident, there was an intensified effort to plan procedures, establish a timeline, and distribute resources in August and early September, prior to the beginning of the school year. A message sent by the project director on August 30th detailed a timeline and procedures for the entire school year. In the initial plan stated in this message, in September, participants would view the zero-g videotape and send their solutions to a problem of what two people in zero-g who were moving toward each other could do to avoid colliding with each other. In October, participants would select a challenge from a list of design challenges. In November, they would submit a progress report, and in December they would post a final design that would be evaluated by a group of experts. From January to April, this process would be repeated with the addition that participants would generate their own design challenges. In May, participants would integrate their design challenges into a single report which would be submitted to NASA.

Throughout the school year, specific design challenges and activities were posted on the network. In October, participants received specific design challenges and were asked to choose either a food problem or a recreation problem. On February 26, the project director posted another message, outlining procedures for another challenge in which students would describe a typical day in zero-g. This message also asked participants to design a school, addressing the differences they noted in a zero-g environment. Finally, on March 4, the project director posted another message, asking participants to list five differences and similarities between zero-g and gravity environments.

Once the teachers decided to commit to the Zero-g Project, they began making arrangements in their respective instructional situations to carry out technical requirements. Each teacher required at least one computer, a modem, and a phone line to carry out the project with their students. Combining resources from their classroom equipment and funds, their schools, district, and the research team, the equipment was obtained. Computer facilities and online access varied across classrooms, with the middle and high school having a computer for each student but only one phone line in their computer lab. The elementary school classes shared one or two computers among twenty to thirty students and performed online tasks outside their classroom.

Each site also received technical support including training, software, and, in some cases, hardware from our research team. This support was essential, both to the initial and continued commitment of the teachers in this study. The second-grade teacher said about support from the research team:

The support from the University has been wonderful, I couldn't have done it without them, because they loaned me a lot of the equipment first, without any questions asked, they just loaned it to me, every time something happens I call them and they know what to do.

During the organization stage, which for the teachers occurred immediately prior to the school year, instructional logistics were planned. At this time, teachers determined how often class time would be devoted to network activity, where the work would occur, what tasks the students would perform, and what social groupings would perform those tasks.

Pursuit Stage

In our study, the pursuit stage was observed to be the most active both inside the classrooms and on the network. Both network and classroom activity were organized round the goals and tasks set forth in messages in the proposal and organization stages of the project. The focus of the network messages during the pursuit stage served to carry out the project challenges. As mentioned in the description of the pursuit stage, other messages involved management, logistics, and relationships between participants during the course of the project.

Messages addressing the challenges in the project can be grouped into six categories: (1) designs and solutions, (2) feedback to designs and solutions, (3) questions, (4) replies to questions, (5) discussions, and (6) referring to resources.

In the classrooms we observed, students spent the greatest proportion of time engaged in tasks devoted to design challenges set forth in the Zero-g Project. This message excerpt sent by the fifth-grade students includes solutions they generated in order to address the Collision Course Challenge:

We are writing this message about zero-g. we had a class descussion. The problem was you and your friend are running down the hall when the gavity stops and you and your friend are on a collision course.
What would you do?
1. You could get a grip on the lockers and pull your way down to your classroom and push off into your classroom.

2. I would "swim" (do breaststroke) to the ceiling and stay there until he (or she) floated by and keep hoping the gravaty would come back.
3. I would flap my arms like a bird and I will go up.

These students interpreted the problems as a school in zero-g, rather than a space station. This context shaped their first solution, in which students would grab on to school lockers. The second and third answers illustrated a common misconception found in participant's messages, that people could propel themselves in zero-g through swimming or flying motions.

In response to the Collision Course Challenge, one of the middle school students created a game to be played in a zero-g setting. This game is typical of many of the student designs, in that human movement in zero-g needed to be incorporated in the game design. The students learned, over the course of the project, that moving from one point to another in zero-g, required the individual to push off a stationary object, aiming in the intended direction. This game design addresses this problem.

Floater Ball

There would be a circular room big enough for two people to float around in. The object of the game is to hit a ping pongtype of ball with padles, (that has a computer chip in it) so as to hit targets marked on the walls of the room (they are about 3 inches in diameter). The targets would be placed once every square foot. While the players would be trying to accomplish this the room and them would be floating around at the same time.

They would also push off of the walls. But once the players would hit the target, the target would turn a different color. And in the end, the player that had hit the most targets would win. (the computer would keep track of points.)

This student's design addresses two issues addressed in the Recreation Design Challenge. First, participants were asked to consider how people would control their movement in zero-g. Game logistics, including the physical setting, equipment, and rules also needed to be addressed. These elements of the game would later be studied by experts and other participants when critiquing the design.

The third challenge in the Zero-g Project asked students to consider how everyday life would be different in a zero-g environment and to write a short story based on the theme, "A Day in Zero-g." A middle school student wrote:

Saturday we'd be floating in the air when we wake up. You couldn't take a shower. It would be more difficult to get dressed. It would be tough to deliver papers. It would be a lot harder to play basketball. The movie theatre would be different, everyone would be floating around. It would be fun to go bike riding. It would be tougher to eat. The snow wouldn't come down to the ground. It would be hard to watch T.V. It would be difficult going to bed at night.

A fourth challenge sent to the Zero-g Project asked students to identify five similarities and differences between normal gravity and zero-g environments, particularly school and instructional environments. The participants who tackled this project sent responses similar to the following message excerpt sent by a group of second-grade students:

Same:
1. Both schools would have rules.
2. Students would study the same subjects.
3. The schedule in both schools would be about the same.
4. Students would still learn.
5. There would still need to be some form of transportation between the living quarters and the school.

Different:
1. Desks and chairs would have to be bolted to the floor.
2. Things would float around in a zero-gravity school.
3. If you had a class pet, you would have design a different type of cage for it.
4. The restrooms would have to be different.
5. Disposing of waste would be very different.

The Five Same and Different Challenge was the last problem-solving activity in the pursuit stage. The second-grade class sent their solutions in April, and the middle school students sent their messages in mid May, near the end of the school term. The Day in Zero-g and the Five Same and Different Challenges were particularly effective in allowing students to apply their knowledge of zero-g gained in the previous challenges to situations familiar to them. These everyday situations, including going to school, getting dressed, showering, and attending classes, provided opportunities for students to test their personal theories of how zero-g affects the motion of objects and people. In the second-grade and middle school classes, which participated in these challenges, students completed their work with fewer obstacles and interruptions than with the previous activities.

Analysis of the Pursuit of Challenges

Qualitative analysis of the pursuit of the four challenges in the Zero-g Project revealed a common set of steps. These pursuit steps include orientation, problem solving, writing and graphic construction, sending messages, feedback from net participants, network discussions, class discussions of feedback and network discussions, and written responses to feedback and network discussions.

Orientation

The orientation phase introduces the topic to the students, cultivates background knowledge, and asserts or interprets the problem or task.

Before beginning work on the Zero-g Project at each of the four sites studied, students and teachers viewed the freefall video prepared for the project, followed by a discussion or question-and-answer session. Teachers asked students to think about living in zero-g and the problems people would encounter. The video included no verbal commentary and offered no explanations about living in zero-g. The video motivated questions from teachers and students on how people went to the toilet, slept, ate, and controlled their movement. These questions provided a basis for the challenges to follow and reoccurred during the course of the project.

To introduce the challenges to the students, teachers either read or paraphrased the challenge description in the message sent by the project director. After the teacher described the challenge and clarified its goal, she led the class in a discussion of the task and the particular aspect or problems of a zero-g environment addressed by the task. When introducing the project to the students, teachers explained that the work they produced for the project would be considered by NASA scientists and possibly be used in the future. In addition, the teacher explained the network community and how messages were sent and received.

If some messages that addressed issues relating to the challenge had already been posted on the network, as in the case of the middle school that joined the Zero-g Project at mid-year, the teacher stimulated discussion by reading these to the students or by paraphrasing their contents.

Problem Solving and Expression

For each challenge, each site spent some amount of time considering the problem, generating solutions, and expressing that solution in verbal and graphic forms. Although there was variation across sites and within each site depending upon the challenge, an identifiable sequence in the way the task was engaged emerged. After the orientation stage, students engaged in brainstorming and problem solving. They carried out their work in small groups for the most part, although they also worked in small groups, in dyads, as a whole class, and as individuals. The process often entailed a series of subtasks including discussion, writing, writing conferences, and revision. However, the particular subtasks varied across and within classes depending upon the skills of the students, the complexity and difficulty of the task, and the time required and available for the task. Some students brainstormed and composed simultaneously; in other instances, students discussed for hours, wrote, discussed their written work, and then composed a final draft. In some instances, written work served as the basis for further discussion, brainstorming, and problem solving. A message was then typed on the computer. This was a separate stage in the elementary school classes where one computer served twenty students. In the middle school and high school, where there was a one-to-one student-to-computer ratio, this took place while students discussed the challenge.

During the problem solving and expression stage, the teachers faced most difficulties, particularly with time pressures. One problem was that students, when tackling the design challenge, typically faced at least one impasse, which would stall their work for two or three class periods. This impasse would often require the assistance of the teacher or one of the adults working with the class. Another obstacle was caused by the shortage of computers for typing messages. In the second-grade classroom, several class periods were required for students to type their messages on a single computer. In the fifth-grade class the teacher, frustrated by computer problems and delays, typed some of the designs on her home computer. The elementary school teachers expressed the most anxiety over time pressures, reporting that they were neglecting other curriculum areas, and felt they lagged behind other project participants.

One episode illustrates their concerns about time. The fifth-grade teacher decided to end her class's participation in the Zero-g Project after they had completed the Design Challenge. In fact, she decided not to send all her students designs to the other Zero-g Project participants. When asked about this, she commented, "I don't have the expertise to upload the files, and I don't see anymore things being sent to Zero-g." One of the authors then offered to send the text files for her and her students. The teacher declined the offer, saying that it was "late in the year, and I haven't finished other curriculum units."

Discussion of Network Messages

During the pursuit stage at each site, students and teachers read and discussed network messages. This review occurred during the pursuit stage, often after the teacher found time to download a batch of messages. The messages served a number of purposes: they were models for student designs, a basis for discussing the characteristics of a zero-g environment, and feedback for student work. In several cases, when time was available, students read the feedback from other network participants and proceeded through the problem solving and expression stage reported earlier.

In the second-grade and middle school classes, a few students wanted to continue working on the project after other students had stopped. One second-grade student enjoyed writing stories in a zero-g setting. A middle school student continued a discussion with one of the professors over the nature of gravity and life in outer space. This scenario was typical of the final phase of the pursuit stage. In the classrooms we observed, the final phase came to a close gradually, as students moved on to other interests and teachers decided to address other curriculum areas.

Network Messages during the Pursuit Stage

Two patterns of message exchange were observed during the course of the Zero-g Project. The more common pattern involved an initial message, typically a question or a student-generated design or solution (which itself was a response to the original proposal message), followed by one or two responses, giving feedback or offering information. In this type of exchange, there were no replies from participants, responding to the original exchange. The exchange did not lead to an extended network discussion or debate. The two message excerpts reported here exemplify this type of exchange in which a high school student asked for feedback for her idea of using a conveyer belt to move in zero-g. The project director replies to her suggestion, after which no other participants responded to the exchange.

> *Student message:* I am a High School student at Central High School in Champaign, IL. I was thinking about the problems astronauts have if they get stuck in the middle of a hall and can't move. I wondered if it would be possible to have a conveyor belt running down the hallway on the wall with handles. That way the astronauts won't get suspended

in mid air with nothing to push off of or grab on to. I would like a response to this idea.

Response to message: The idea of a conveyer belt in the middle of a hall is sort of like a ski tow rope. But I'm not sure why it needs to be moving. As long as the astronauts can push off on it, they don't need to be pulled along, since they'll keep moving once they push off of it. If it were moving, it would be hard for the astronauts to also use it to stop.

The second type of exchange was much less typical. It began with a student question or design and continued with responses that either offered information or feedback or sought to engage each other in an extended discussion or debate. The latter type of response occurred twice during the course of the Zero-g Project, once at the beginning of the project and again near midyear.

The following message excerpts exemplify this type of extended exchange. The exchange was initiated by a message from a high school student, suggesting the use of magnetic shoes:

Message from student 1: I would like to see if magnets would work in space if you put them in shoes. We are working on ways to move around in the halls of a zero gravity space station. Please let me know if you have done any work with magnets in space.

This message received several message responses that commented on the practicality and efficacy of using magnetic shoes on spacecraft as a means of compensating for lack of gravity. Excerpts from two of these responses are reported next.

Message from a NASA scientist: In theory magnetic shoes will work, however, there are a few problems that need to be considered.

First, the space station will be constructed mostly out of aluminum alloys. In order for magnets to work thin metal plates would have to be installed wherever people will be putting their feet.

Second, in space people like to float around. Zero-g is a fun place to work. While floating crewmembers would have to be very careful to keep their magnetic shoes away from things like magnetic disks and sensitive equipment.

Message from a computer science university professor: Magnets will work identically in space as they do down here. The real issue is how much force does the magnet need to apply to you to keep you in place (more or less) yet will be weak enough that you can move around. Such a magnet might be large (but I don't really know).

Here are some thoughts though

1) Use an electro-magnet on the shoe. Then if you just want to float, you could turn it off. Partially avoids problems with stray magnetic fields as well.

Following this exchange, another high school student responded by inquiring about a means to block the force of magnets in zero-g, rendering them harmless to sensitive equipment.

Student message 2: What if there was a way to block the magnetic flow of the shoes when you didn't want the magnetizm. A possibility is lead barriers on the shoes.

This message received a few responses commenting on the ability of lead to block magnetic force and described experiments that the student could conduct to arrive at a solution to his question. One of these responses is reported here.

That's a neat idea about blocking the magnetic flow of the shoes with lead. I'm not sure whether lead will do the trick, but we could find out by using magnets and a compass. Normally magnets affect compasses, so you can take the material you want to test and put it in-between a magnet and a compass to see if it has any blocking effect.

The discussion concludes when one of the online expert participants, a university professor, questions whether magnets would be an optimal solution:

I've been following the discussion and suddenly I began to wonder why you got interested in magnets in the first place? If it is the "stickiness" that would enable traction and allow for walking/positioning, have you considered velcro tape? Small spots of strategically placed velcro tape and "fuzzy" shoes might do what you had in mind and might be much lighter and avoid the problems associated with spurious magnetic fields.

This set of messages illustrates flexibility of identifying problems. The discussion branches from whether magnetic shoes would work, to the feasibility of using magnets on spacecraft, and finally to finding alternatives to magnetic shoes, identifying their function and providing an alternative.

Also the discussion and points of view are distributed among several participants, including students. Participants whose background knowledge differs will find some aspects of problems more salient and critical than others. This gives the student more flexibility to choose the problem he or she wishes to address. In the case reported here, the student decided to experiment for himself whether lead would block magnetic force. This set of messages illustrates how the network community provided rich possibilities for problem solving and learning.

The Network Classroom Interface

What can we say about the relationship between work in the classrooms and activity on the network during the pursuit stage? The overall relationship may be best described as a network of loosely coupled communities, each committed to similar goals, but ultimately achieving those goals largely independently. Each class worked toward reaching their own designs and solutions to zero-g challenges. However, during the problem-solving process, participants both contributed and added to the network resources. Participants posted questions and designs on the network, then, sometimes during the same online session, downloaded questions, designs, and feedback from other participants.

The pace and intensity of activity over the network and inside the classrooms was dissimilar. When engaged in problem-solving discussions or composing their designs, classroom work was at its highest intensity. Network activity only intensified when a message stimulated discussion or debate as in the case of the discussion about wearing magnetic shoes. These peaks in network activity seemed asynchronous with classroom activity.

Activity Lifecycle

Among the Zero-g Project challenges, the Design Challenge proved the most difficult, required the most time, and resulted in more complex social activity than the other challenges. At the four sites we studied, particularly where small groups collaborated on the designs, a distinctive pattern of activity was observed. This pattern consisted of five stages: (1) group and task assignment, (2) initiating problem solving, (3) group discord and work obstacles, (4) reorganization, and (5) revival.

Once groups were formed and the teacher informed them of their goal, to design either recreation or food facilities for a zero-g environment, the students tackled the problem. Activity in the initial stages varied among groups; some students brainstormed ideas, but others pondered the problem in silence.

After a period of time, ranging from minutes to days, the group entered a group discord and obstacle stage, facing both social and problem-solving obstacles. Group members disagreed on a game design or the details of a design. In the fifth-grade class, the students initially decided to design a tennis game in which participants would roller skate on tracks. As students began to disagree on the design of the game, they started to divide and move in different locations. At one point, we suggested that they could consider using the properties of zero-g, rather than trying to overcome them. Immediately the group generated ideas for a new game. One of the students was offended that his roller tennis game was discarded and quit the group. He then worked individually designing a new game. The remaining students divided into two groups, one working on basketball and another on a different tennis game.

This pattern, where students encountered task obstacles that coincided with social turbulence, was observed at all sites in various forms. In some cases, students decided to leave their group to work individually. In the high school computer club, students entered into an argument that was never resolved. Eventually the students abandoned the project and gave their ideas to the teacher who completed the design. In the second-grade class, it was common for one or two students of a larger group to take over the design task, while the remaining students ceased active participation. This is the reorganization stage.

Once new social groupings were reformed, the students entered the revival stage, resuming work on the design. However, after reorganization, there were fewer problems, and the design was completed. In the fifth-grade class, each of the groups designing games completed their designs over a period of several classes. Although problems were encountered, they did not lead to group discord and were worked out in a short period of time.

Student learning was affected by the different challenges over the life cycle of the Zero-g Project. Each challenge confronted students with similar problems and the application of conceptual knowledge in various contexts. The different challenges allowed students to discuss and write through a variety of genres including lists, narratives, and expository discourse. Over time, the solving of similar problems in different contexts allowed students to apply knowledge gained in earlier challenges to problems posed in later challenges. The most common example of this was the tendency for students to equate zero-g conditions with that of water. In earlier challenges, students often wrote that people could swim or float in zero-g and that objects would "float up" if released. Through discussions and feedback from other network participants, students began to understand that zero-g conditions were quite different from that of water. They wrote less about swimming and floatation and devised other means of control of movement in zero-g.

Wrap-up Stage

Following the pursuit stage, there comes a time when the participants end their project work. The end is often indicated through the exchange of messages containing expressions of gratitude, or a semiformal announcement that their work is finished.

All the wrap-up messages in the Zero-g Project expressed gratitude for being included in the project. One message expressed an intention to be more involved in the future. The second-grade class included a summary report, which was more applicable to the publication stage because it was an attachment to the wrap-up message. The project director's message offered thanks to the participants; he also suggested that students view the freefall video once again so that they might recognize how much their understanding of the concepts discussed during the course of the project had changed.

Wrap-up activities took place inside the classrooms. These were sometimes reported on the network, but at other times they were not. Among the four sites studied, there were two patterns of wrap-up activities. One type involved reflective activities in which students returned to ideas previously encountered during the project, discussed concepts, and presented their work. The other type was a teacher wrap-up.

The second-grade and fifth-grade classes spent the greatest amount of time engaged in wrap-up activities. As the second-grade students were finishing their final Zero-g Project challenge in mid May, the class composed a good-bye letter to the project participants. In late May, after the students' project work was completed, the second-grade class viewed the freefall video again and attempted to explain motion in zero-g using the knowledge they had gained.

The fifth-grade class participated in wrap-up activities, but, unlike the second-grade class, their work was confined to their school setting and did not end up being communicated on the network. Instead, the students presented their zero-g designs to other fifth graders in the school. As reported for the second-grade class, this activity also involved reflective thinking and discussion of the students' work and the concepts they encountered during the course of the project.

Unlike the elementary school classes, the middle school and high school students did not participate in reflective wrap-up activities. Wrap-up activity occurred primarily among the teachers. For the middle school teacher, wrap-up involved making sure that all of the students had completed their work and had sent it over the network. The high school teacher collected her students' ideas, composed a recreation design her-self, and sent it to the network.

Publication Stage

For many project participants, the wrap-up stage signals the con-clusion to their work and obligations. However, network projects hold the potential for value to nonparticipating individuals and institutions. Dis-tribution of knowledge gained through the project activity to a wider audience is the function of the publication stage. The publication stage of the Zero-g Project included electronic postings and conference pre-sentation. The thesis of one of the authors of this chapter was posted on the World Wide Web soon after completion of the project. The thesis included a detailed history of the project, email messages, and analysis of interviews, observations, and completed work. In addition, accounts of the project have been presented to educators and scholars at research conferences and workshops.

Discussion

As we can see from the analysis of four schools participating in the year-long Zero-g Project, network-based educational activities undergo a life cycle, starting out with some preactivities (proposal, refinement, organization), continuing through the activity's mature state (pursuit), and then through its postactivity (wrap-up, publication). Furthermore, this life cycle is recapitulated within the overall life cycle of a project, at both micro and macro levels.

There are several reasons why it is useful to know about the life cycle of network-based learning activities. First, an understanding of life cycles helps the participants understand their multiple roles in a network activity, which change as the activity proceeds through its life cycle. The role of the project's leader in the Zero-g Project, for example, was quite different in the preliminary stages than in the mature functioning stage and different again in the closing stages.

The case of the Zero-g Project highlights the importance of active, effective moderators to initiate and sustain the interaction in a networked learning community. The construct of mediation in learning has been a central construct in sociohistorical theories of learning (Vygotsky, 1978). This construct takes on a new appearance in network-based learning en-vironment and, thus, helps us better understand its importance even in more familiar face-to-face learning environments. Interaction in networks tends to stretch out over time, which also makes the importance of mediation and mediators easier to see. Most failures of attempts to build successful network learning environments are due to the lack of appropriate mediation at the appropriate times in the unfolding process of a network learning interaction.

From this analysis of network activity life cycles, it is possible to identify essential elements of mediation. Levin (1999) embedded these into a Web-based interactive guide for people interested in creating and implementing network-based educational activities.

It is helpful to know about the life cycle of network-based learning communities so that systemic support for the projects can be embedded in the institutional structures within which these activities occur. For example, Riel (1993) used this kind of lifecycle knowledge to build "learning circles," systemic organizational frameworks that proved sustainable and scaleable across many years.

Knowledge about the life cycle of network-based learning communities can help teachers, administrators, and learners integrate their involvement in these communities with their involvement in other concurrent educational activities, leading to a more powerful overall environment for learning.

Acknowledgments

This material is based upon work supported by the National Science Foundation under Grant No. RED-9253423. The government has certain rights in this material. Any opinions, findings, and conclusions or recommendations expressed in this material are those of the authors and do not necessarily reflect the views of the National Science Foundation. We would like to thank all the teachers, students, and others who participated in the Zero-g World Design Project.

References

Cervantes, R. G. (1993). *Every message tells a story: A situated evaluation of the instructional use of computer networking.* Unpublished doctoral dissertation, University of Illinois, Urbana-Champaign.

Harris, J. (1995). Organizing and facilitating telecollaborative projects. *The Computing Teacher, 22*(5), 66–9.

Levin, J. A. (1999). Educational network project planning guide [World Wide Web page]. Available: lrs.ed.uiuc.edu/network-project-guide/ [19 November 2001].

Levin, J., Waugh, M., Chung, H., & Miyake, N. (1992). The structure and process of learning in electronic networks. *Interactive Learning Environments, 2*(1), 3–13.

NCES (National Center for Education Statistics). (1999). *Internet access in public schools and classrooms: 1994–98* [World Wide Web page]. U.S. Department of Education. Available: nces.ed.gov/pubsearch/pubsinfo.asp?pubid=1999017 [19 November 2001].

Riel, M. (1993). *Learning Circles: Virtual communities for elementary and secondary schools.* Available: lrs.ed.uiuc.edu/guidelines/Riel-93.html [19 November 2001].

Stapleton, C. E. (1991). *Analysis of successful educational activities on a distributed electronic network.* Unpublished doctoral dissertation, Champaign, IL: University of Illinois.

Vygotsky, L. S. (1978). *Mind in society: The development of higher psychological processes.* Cambridge, MA: Harvard University Press.

Waugh, M. L., Levin, J. A., & Smith, K. (1994a). Organizing electronic network-based instructional interactions: Part 1: Successful strategies and tactics. *The Computing Teacher, 21*(5), 21–2.

(1994b). Organizing electronic network-based instructional interactions: Part 2: Interpersonal strategies. *The Computing Teacher, 21*(6), 48–50.

11   Learning in Cyberspace

An Educational View of Virtual Community

D. Jason Nolan and Joel Weiss

Learning is the creation of knowledge through the transformation of experience and transcends the particular institutional context that society has reserved for that purpose (Cayley, 1992; Illich, 1970; Kolb, 1984). It is also important not to confuse learning exclusively with school knowledge, for knowledge comes in many forms and for different purposes (Barnes, 1988; Dewey, 1938). Using Kolb's view on learning, if we substitute a particular type of change for transformation then change becomes a condition for learning. People participate in learning settings from birth onward. They move from setting to setting such as the home, playground, school, service groups, and church, and over the years add work settings and other leisure activities. Our interests center around creating and conducting inquiry on such learning environments. This particular focus includes both formal school settings, nonschool settings (museums, science centers, public spaces, and the Internet), and the points of intersection between these environments. These interests combine work in both real and virtual, online and off-line spaces. Understanding the nexus of learning and community relies upon an analysis of each context, so as to ascertain the expectations of participants and the task demands of the environment. We accordingly recognize the diversity of virtual environments, and also the interconnections that exist between online and off-line communities. What connects communities, virtual or otherwise, are the possibilities offered for learning; it is not just "school-based" or specifically an educational institution's private preserve. It is no stretch of the imagination for us to include the Internet as a learning site.

The term "virtual community" has become so widespread in its use that there is a tendency to conflate all social activity into a single concept and ignore the diversity of virtual contexts. Another challenge is characterized by the debate about whether online groups can be termed "communities" at all. This debate focuses on the relationship between online and off-line communities. For Baym (1998), two issues should be considered in such a debate: "does online community really serve as a substitute for off-line community in any meaningful way?" and "what occurs online that leads some people to experience them as communities in the first place?" (pp. 37–8). There is also the challenge concerning the possible inter-connections of "learning" and "change," an issue that will become more obvious throughout the chapter. In considering learning in virtual com-munities, several issues or aspects must be considered regarding a learner's background in such a setting. For instance, his role within the community, his participating style (e.g., active participant or lurker), the structure of pedagogy associated with the space, resources for structuring the com-munity, and, of course, what is to be learned all play an important role.

These issues suggest dimensions that Rheingold could not have antic-ipated when he suggested a definition of virtual community that predated the emergence of the World Wide Web in 1994 and the explosion of public involvement that followed; "*Virtual communities* are social aggre-gations that emerge from the Net when enough people carry on . . . public discussions long enough, with sufficient human feeling, to form webs of personal relationships in cyberspace" (Rheingold, 1993, p. 5; italics in original). But, where do these virtual communities begin? Does virtual community begin when the first online birthday party is celebrated, or the first funeral (Rheingold, 1993; Fowler, 1996)? Does virtual commu-nity become fully formed at a specific point in time from the collective efforts of a group? Or are the roots found at a deeper level? Perhaps com-munity finds its genesis in the intentionality and dedication of pioneering individuals who forge the first elements into a shape that we later see as a community. Understanding the location of change and learning that is found in virtual communities requires an exploration of what it means to learn and effect change in these spaces.

Learning and perhaps community itself is a process that goes on, or is formed at, the intersection of the social organization of an environment and the activities expected and conducted by participants in a particular setting. In considering the virtual learning community, we have been in-fluenced by the views of others; such as Moore's (1981) notions of the pedagogy of experience, Baym's (1998) criteria on the events or experi-ences that lead to a sense of community, and, more generally, Ostrom's views on community public spaces (Ostrom, 1990). In this chapter, we use some of their ideas to inquire into the various learning settings found in a virtual community.

Community

Baym (1998) studied task-oriented uses for Computer Mediated Communication (CMC) and suggested that it is difficult to predict CMC patterns due to the complexities of interactions among five factors: external contexts, temporal structure of the group, system infrastructure, group purposes, and participant characteristics (pp. 39–40). She suggested that an understanding of a virtual *style* can be achieved by describing these interactions:

> participants strategically exploit the resources and rules those structures offer. The result is a dynamic set of systematic social meanings that enables participants to imagine themselves as a community. Most significant are the emergence of group specific forms of expression, identities, relationships, and normative conventions. (Baym, 1998, pp. 39–40)

She could easily have described the ingredients for a learning setting.

A community, in reality or as a concept, is a form of a common pool resource (CPR) (Ostrom, 1990). A CPR is traditionally thought of as a natural commons, such as public land used for grazing, as described by Hardin (1968) in his famous essay "The Tragedy of the Commons," or as any other natural resource held in common beyond individual ownership. And there is support for the notion that concepts such as democracy, knowledge, language, spiritualism and even "cyberspace" are examples of CPRs. A socially constructed community also falls under this label of CPR when it is a collectively controlled space whose success or failure rests on the individual members' willingness to subsume individual gain for collective well-being, as well as the well-being of the resource that is the community. Ostrom described numerous models for the management of CPRs, but she asserted that no single model can be used to cover the variety of CPR contexts. This observation extends to the variety of communities that can exist in real life and online. She, however, described a number of key factors important in the success of a community, which Kollock (1998) believed are relevant to online, as well as to real-world communities. Some of these criteria follow: (a) group boundaries are clearly defined; (b) the implementation of rules governing the use of collective goods are well matched to local needs and conditions; (c) most individuals affected by these rules can participate in modifying the rules; (d) the right of community members to devise their own rules is respected by external authorities; (e) a system for monitoring members' behavior exists, undertaken by the community members themselves; (f) a graduated system of sanctions is used; and (g) community members have access to easily accessible ways to resolve conflict. Of course, we are using the word "resource" in the broadest sense, including human resources with all that implies in the creative sense.

Curriculum of Community

Embedded in this description are various perspectives of the educational ingredients of community. There is a real sense of mutually constructing a sense of space, that Morgan suggests as a "range of practices which produce the site as vehicle for the performance of life" (Morgan, 1998, p. 5). How do we connect these ideas on community with learning? Communities are socially constructed entities (i.e., social organizations). According to Moore (1981), learning is the process that goes on at the intersection of the social organization of an environment (setting, context) and the mental works performed by its participants. His ideas were developed within the example of student interns in work/study communities and focused upon cognitive tasks required of the work setting. Working within a framework of situated cognition (Rogoff & Lave, 1984), Moore raised the issue of how a neophyte comes to participate in the social stocks of knowledge in the community. The broader question is, How do members of a community encounter, engage, master, use, and transform the knowledge-in-use in the community. Knowledge distribution in a community helps to identify different roles. In a virtual community this translates to creator, member, keeper of the infrastructure, and the like. A community has certain purposes for its existence, and Moore translated these purposes as the tasks expected within the setting. Each community is organized in specific ways for establishing, accomplishing, and processing the expectations or tasks. To understand the ways in which learning might occur in a virtual community, it seems necessary to depict the kinds of tasks, expectations, indeed learning required to accomplish the tasks. We also need to understand the dynamics of the social means employed to create, accomplish, and process what is required to maintain community.

It is our view that the study of virtual community has not been inclusive enough to address the issue of what it takes to *be* a learning community. We take on the task of clarifying this view by offering an exploration of some curriculum issues involved in identifying community in cyberspace. We deliberately focus on curriculum as a means of expanding an understanding of what it takes to create a learning community. The term "curriculum" is ordinarily viewed in the context of school community.

Indeed, the origins of the term are derived from *currere*, circling the course or track. From its beginning, the curriculum has had two meanings, one conceptual and the other structural. The structural meaning of running a course has a literal connotation, and that has been taken to mean a program or course of study. This conception is static; however, we agree with Schwab (1969, 1971) that curriculum also represents the dynamic interactions necessary for learning not just in schools, but in any setting. These interactions are themselves learning moments: individuals interact with forms of pedagogy in a particular milieu to bring about change. Curriculum, therefore, can be purposeful or unplanned; it can be transparent or opaque to those involved. And identifying educational aspects of community in cyberspace needs to account for the curriculum features of community.

But curriculum is more than an abstract term; it suggests structure for locating learning moments. We suggest that there are several locations for learning in virtual communities. There is the location associated with first initiating and then maintaining the locus of interaction, what we consider to be the Curriculum of Initiation and Governance. This location requires that an individual or individuals make the decision to create and then maintain a virtual site or location (Collins & Berge, 1997). For some individuals, it may be the first time that they have undertaken the responsibility for such a location by adopting the role as a list moderator, Webmaster, IRC chat facilitator, or MOO wizard. Even with prior experiences as a participant in such a space, it is necessary to collect information about, and make decisions on, choosing and implementing software, determining the purpose and governmentality (Foucault, 1991) of the accepted and anticipated interactions and netiquette. It is also important to invite others to participate in the environment that has been created.

The second location, the Curriculum of Access, is associated with accessing and becoming socialized to virtual community itself. The kinds of learning that take place here include the requirements of becoming a member: learning about the site, how to access it, and the rules that govern membership. Finally, there is the Curriculum of Membership, which relates the actual engagements in the community, the purposes for which the site was constructed, and the gains people expect from it. Such purposes may be expressly for learning in the conventional sense, as found in computer-supported cooperative work environments where a range of cognitive knowledge, skills, and processes are the usual purposes for such groups. However, there may be affective learnings as well. Groups more associated with social purposes are nevertheless sites for acquiring information, feeling a sense of community, as well as potential learnings associated with participating in a virtual place. Part of membership in a community is a recognition of when it is appropriate to opt out of the group or decide against further participation. An individual might decide, for a variety of reasons, to join other sites or to drop out for a time from involvement in a community. We also recognize that, in any curricular moment, learners may play a variety of roles and may participate in various ways, from active to passive. One of the features of virtual communities in which attendance is passive is the presence of lurkers. To lurkers, learning may be a covert act, and the only observable manifestation that a lurker may value is the experience of continued affiliation.

Four Examples of Online Community – KS, Project Achieve, MOOkti, Serbia.web

This chapter explores virtual community in a manner rooted in the Canadian cultural experience. We use descriptions of four diverse examples from our studies on virtual communities to orient the frameworks of this discussion. Our examples include school-based online communities such as Project Achieve, a project-based virtual learning environment funded by Canada's Schoolnet (moo.schoolnet.ca) whose intention is project-based collaborative learning for students and educators to create virtual learning settings, and MOOkti (achieve.utoronto.ca/:9696), an eight year-old polysynchronous* virtual environment for relocalizing teacher's pedagogy within virtual learning environments. We contrast these collaborative virtual environments (CVEs) with research into two

---

* Polysynchronous is a term coined to describe the nature of MOOs where communication is an embedded combination of both synchronous and asynchronous communication (Davie & Nolan, 1999; Nolan, 1998). An IRC chat group is completely synchronous. Users communicate in real time, and there is usually no record kept of the communication unless one member personally creates a transcript of the interaction as a log. Asynchronous communication refers to the what happens on bulletin boards and via email where a message is composed and transmitted to another individual or group. In a MOO, communication can be synchronous or asynchronous, but it can also be a combination of both. A conversation can be encoded into an object for others to read. MOO objects can be programmed to listen to conversations between members and generate responses that become part of the MOO-space itself for other participants to listen to later. Additionally, a conversational interaction may take the form of direct synchronous speech *and* the comanipulation of MOO objects. It is possible to talk with another person, hand her virtual objects for her to look at, coprogram MOO objects, and record the conversation for a third party to read later. This type of polysynchrony is particular to MOO-type environments, but it reflects the direction that collaborative virtual environments are anticipated to follow in the future.

out-of-school communities: the Kind_Spirits (KS) email discussion group constructed around the author Lucy Maud Montgomery, author of *Anne of Green Gables* (Nolan, Lawrence & Kajihara, 1998), and a group of communities prominently involved on the world stage of late collectively described as Serbia.web.

The four examples allow us to understand the sense of location and expectations that each group creates for itself as a way of expressing community. We ordered the cases so that the two deliberately developed for social purposes: KS and Serbia.web form one grouping, and those more specifically focused on knowledge acquisition – MOOkti and Achieve – follow. We distinguish these examples by what we consider to be original purposes for framing community, either social or educational. Although the original purposes may differ, each of these examples represent groups that are social in origin and represent learning contexts.*

Social and Cultural Communities

KS-listserve

The Kindred Spirits email discussion list (Kind_Spirits@upei.ca) is an example of a virtual community. KS members are looking for a particular cultural situation with which they identify, one that is embodied in the works and life of Lucy Maud Montgomery (LMM), author of more than twenty-two books including *Anne of Green Gables*. This list has a definite genesis and development predicated on the desire of individuals to join together as a group for a social and cultural purpose (Nolan et al., 1998). KS came into existence when list cofounder Jeff Lawrence discovered a letter by Louise Bruck in the magazine *Kindred Spirits* while traveling in Prince Edward Island, Canada, in the fall of 1994:

Dear Kindred Spirits;
I asked myself today, if Maud were here today would she be cruising the information Highway? The answer is yes! I know she would love to have been able to write to all of her friends and acquaintances via a computer terminal . . . I am trying to grow PEI in my backyard. I would love to talk to anyone of any age . . .
My Internet address is: KindSpirit@aol.com
I hope I will be hearing from many, many Kindred Spirits soon, I will be waiting anxiously at my terminal. (Bruck, 1994)

---

* Some observers, such as Wellman and Gulia (1996) make a distinction between online social organizations that are viewed as virtual communities and computer-supported cooperative work environments.

This was the genesis of the Curriculum of Initiation. Both Bruck and Lawrence were looking to create or construct a space, which later became a community according to its members. They were looking to participate in a social environment reflecting the world LMM wrote about. This community seemed to develop following real-life community patterns described by a founder as pioneer, village, and town phases, which reflect Van Gennep's three phases (separation, transition, and incorporation) of "the rites of passage" important in the development of online communities, as in real ones (Nolan et al., 1998; Tomas, 1991).

Of particular importance in the development of the KS community was its cultural and social focus on a particular writer's life and works. LMM lived much of her life in and wrote about community experience in rural Prince Edward Island. KS list members identify with LMM and her characters and seek to capture in their lives and online interaction the spirit they read about in her works, as well as the mood and essence of the real-world locations they visit in PEI. LMM characters such as the famous Anne Shirley were also striving to be part of and understand their own community, and list members often refer to LMM's characters for support. As Laura Robinson (1999) notes, "Montgomery shows individuals who successfully manage to achieve a level of community acceptance and individual freedom; however, she clearly suggests that clan and community are constructs." The feeling of community that LMM constructed in her novels, based on her life and recollections of life in PEI, energizes this group of kindred spirits. Like the orphan Anne who moves from the mainland to construct her new life on the island of PEI, what they want is a home of their own full of like-minded kindred spirits, and they often echo Anne's words, "I love Green Gables already, and I never loved any place before. No place ever seemed like home" (Montgomery, 1908). KS members are *looking* for people who are kindred spirits in their love for the works, life, and culture of LMM and then construct a community based on this love online. This represents the major purpose for the Curriculum of Membership.

And like LMM's fictional and real worlds, the KS list is a public space. Anyone can join the KS list and participate in the manner they see fit. There are few boundaries or limits to the focus of discussion except that they relate to the important themes of KS members.* These include LMM

* There are several important Web sites for KS and LMM: Lucy Maud Montgomery Institute, www.upei.ca/~lmmi; Anne of Green Gables Encyclopedia, www.hom.kc.rr.com/grelingertb/anne/; PEI Government Page on Montgomery, www.gov.pe.ca/lucy/; Kindred

and her works, life in PEI, and elements of KS members' lives that reflect the themes and interests found in LMM. Discussion of 'Island' politics, kindred events, and any modern issue that might have interested someone like LMM herself are found in the postings to the list. Events involving cats, particularly loved by LMM, are perennial favorites, as are Kindred Teas held across North America and face-to-face meetings of various list members.

Sometimes list members complain about the boundaries and limitations that the list imposes on itself. Some members want to remain wedded to the original purpose of the list to focus on LMM's life and works, but others are more engaged in the tangential discussions that take up events in their own personal lives in relation to LMM. However, it is the fact that whatever goes on in the list hovers in a halo around LMM and her life in a loose yet discernable narrative of communal discourse, distinguishes this list from others, and is likely only repeated in lists focusing on similarly compelling authors who describe and have lived in a world their fans wish to embrace.

The KS list has a documented lineage and history that allows us to observe the growth and flourishing of this community and the specific events that brought it from a meeting of two individuals to a stable community of over 450 members. Lawrence brought the list into existence as a frontier act of homesteading with homemade email list software constructed in his spare time as a graduate student. The etiquette of the list was quickly encoded in a FAQ, or Frequently Asked Questions, file that appeared within four months of the first posting. This file signified KS's movement into a village phase of its existence with codified rules of conduct and documentation of its founding. And within the first nine months, the list community had grown beyond the control of a single graduate student, and list members negotiated its movement to the University of PEI's Lucy Maud Montgomery Institute (LMMI; www.pei.ca/~lmmi), using the industrial strength list moderation software found in many large volume email lists. Under the administration of LMMI, the list quickly grew to the status of a small town.

These three phases of pioneer-frontier, village, and town metaphorically reflect not only the number of participants but also the formal and organizational structure of the community, and the variety of interests

Spirits Society of Hamilton, www.interlog.com/~dalvay/KSSOH/; and Little More Montgomery: LMM in Ontario, www.yukazine.com/lmm/e/ (English) and http://www. yukazine.com/lmm/j/ (Japanese).

and topics taken up by its members. The pioneers were wedded to specific needs and goals just to survive as a group. The discourse was a combination of negotiation of how to administer the list and discussion of specific literary topics. The village formed at a point when the community was already coming into conflict over the direction the list would take, with the inclusion of personal and tangential topics, and some of the founders had already been bypassed in the administration of the community. Those involved in the Curriculum of Initiation including governance were supplanted by others who controlled governance issues. The final movement to the town phase represented a formal external administration of the list. LMMI hosts the list but does not take a central role in the discourse of the community. The LMMI list moderator dealt mainly with issues of protocol and governance, particularly when issues arose with respect to the use of copyright material and trademarks that would put the list administrators in conflict with the corporation that controlled the LMM estate. By this time, the original members had lost all control over the direction the list took, and most of them had left the group, retiring to a newly formed moderated email discussion for LMM scholarship (LMM-l@listserv.utoronto.ca) founded by most of the original list members and academics who were not interested in the vibrant, diverse community's cyclical topics.

KS is an example of a virtual community that was formed by, for, and with people captivated by a literary author's work and life. The initiator was knowledgeable about the technology of cyberspace, though the increased sophistication in the expansion of the site came about through affiliation with a university institute. The example illustrates how a community that began with a generally agreed-upon purpose expanded to a complex group of special interests, which ultimately led to a splintering-off of the original members into other forums. The initial Curriculum of Membership changed over time and then split to accommodate the diverse agendas.

Our next example was initiated by individuals because of personal interest in enabling expatriates access to both informational and personal resources related to ethnic identity. Through IRL (In Real Life) circumstances, the site expanded into a more complex network of communication sources that allowed for expanded and diverse access. Unlike KS, which splintered somewhat because of a change in direction or focus, Serbia.web expanded because of increased membership and increased need both to receive information and to vent emotional concerns.

*Serbia.web**

The various online media that make up the collective discussion on Serbia and issues important to diasporic Serbs represent an example of a particular kind of online community. And there has been a great deal of attention given to diasporic community involvement in CMC environments, centering on the "Wars of the Yugoslav Succession," which locates the online experiences of various diaspora from the region in a growing postnational cultural experience (Stubbs, 1998, 1999). It is both ethnic and cultural, and most importantly it is an online manifestation of a community that transcends the boundaries of both real-life and virtual manifestations. Serbia.web represents an example of a virtual community that manifests itself across various online technologies such as Web pages, Java-chat, IRC, and email discussion lists. Like the KS group, it is founded on an external cultural experience. Additionally, this community has grown in ways unanticipated by its founders as a result of external events and influences.

One instance of this Serbian-speaking virtual grouping started in late 1995 around a Toronto-based Web site dedicated to Serbian-related issues. The original Web site included multiple tools for communication – a Java chat room (averaging fifteen participants) and a bulletin board, covering various topics (music, film, politics, travel). An important factor is the selective sample that this group represented. Participants are usually recent immigrants, mostly since 1991, living throughout the world, but particularly in Canada, the United States, West Europe, and Australia. There is a high degree of computer literacy among members, perhaps because of the educational requirements necessary to immigrate

---

* Serbia.web is a generalized pseudonym for a variety of virtual community locations operating for those interested in Serbian culture, language, and related issues. The information we are using has been provided by a person actively studying the Serbian online community. These data include information from public statements made in several of the communities, Web sites, and email conversations with others. Both authors appreciate the contributions from this individual, and we respect the wish of this individual for anonymity, due to the recent international tensions surrounding events in that part of the world. We respect the challenges undertaken by this person to conduct this ongoing research and particularly for highlighting the fact that community and research into online community is not merely the description and study of nurturing and supportive environments. These locations of community are often dynamic forms of conflict as well as political struggle that reflect, if not mirror, the real-life environments from which the online groups find their members. Though the online Serbian community may be itself undertaking an important struggle for identity and cultural expression, this struggle is not without its own inherent challenges and dangers.

to the West. Therefore, the Curriculum of Access has less of a problem then might occur with other groups.

Observation of this group began in June 1997 at which time there were about thirty regular members in the Java chat room, which by the fall of 1997 moved to an Internet Relay Chat (IRC) channel because of increased participation. The Serbian-speaking IRC channel was hosted on a large primarily English-speaking server. The number of Serbian-speaking participants communicating online grew rapidly, such that by early 1998 several new channels opened. Observations that formed this paper started in one of the subchannels from its beginning.

The participants of the Serbian virtual community developed several stable subgroups, but the members of almost every subgroup are also regular participants in the community gathered around the prime channel. The possibilities of IRC software allow the simultaneous participation on the several channels located on the same server. This type of multi-membership gives an opportunity for a participant to communicate with a large group of members of the various subgroups and to get an idea of a sense of the identity of each particular subgroup.

In late March 1999, and especially during the time of the NATO bombings in April, the number of the participants in every Serbian-speaking IRC chat room increased fantastically – averaging over 300 to 400 active participants, up from an average of fifteen to thirty. Statistics placed the original Web site in the top 1,000 Web sites on the Internet by number of hits (www.alexa.com). The logged public conversation from the chat channels showed that participants were frequently referring to the topics and messages from the conferencing board or different Web sites dealing with the conflict issues, and the moderators requested that participants should discuss certain topics on newly opened chat channels on the same IRC server specifically dedicated to NATO-bombing issues.

After April 1999, all Serbian-speaking channels were transferred to a new server primarily intended for Serbian-speaking participants.* During the conflict, IRC was used as a tool for information exchange between the participants living in Yugoslavia and those living in the diaspora caring about what was happening in their homeland, representing a shift in the Curriculum of Membership. Usually, the validity of information about Yugoslavia from IRC communication tended to be checked and verified on other Web-sites dealing with the conflict issues, so misinformation

---

* It is interesting to note that there are several Bosnian–Muslim chat channels as well on this Serbian run server. Participants on them speak and write the same language as Serbs from Bosnia, which is slightly different from Serbian language used by Serbs from Serbia.

appeared to be less of a problem than anticipated. There was a strong sense that the network of available tools (Web sites, conferencing board, and IRC) were firmly interconnected and in some sense inseparable, necessary to get a clear picture of how the virtual community functioned during the conflict.

What was discovered from conversations with owners of different subchannels is that the most important thing for keeping a channel alive is recruitment of participants, especially those with stable membership in the community. There is a form of trade between users, as channel-operator status is a reward for those populating newly opened channels regularly, enabling the channel to get permanent status. This is an example of how characteristics of membership of the community are used as criteria for ensuring continuity of governance. This important step allows the channel owner to gain protection for the channel against being taken over by someone else while she is otherwise occupied and not online. An example of the ingredients for Curriculum of Governance can be found on the computer conferencing board, where a discussion group was opened and dedicated to IRC chat channel (channel prime). The participants are trying to negotiate the rules of maintenance by asking the channel operators about their actions and regulations.

There are different ways for potential members to find out about the site. Usually they find it by Web-surfing where an individual finds the Web site with detailed explanations about how to use IRC and then find the particular IRC-server with the Serbian-speaking chat channel (channel prime). After a while, when that Web surfer gets more knowledgeable about how to use IRC software, it is easy to choose the different Serbian-speaking subgroups connected on the same IRC server. So, the Curriculum of Access requires the ability to find a site, translate the information, and gain experience in order to select appropriate communities. This curriculum starts with learning the basic software. The process of learning specific IRC software depends upon the user's previous knowledge with such software and experiences with computers. Some users could choose to read help files, ask somebody who is more knowledgeable, either through IRL or virtually, or work through a trial-and-error process.

It could almost be said that the experience of Serbia.web is somewhat mundane, concerned with the same collective and individual matters that all online communities are faced with – that is, if it were not for the Kosovo crisis. The quantum leap in activity in and around the online community reflected the chaotic and kinetic nature of the real-world events playing themselves out. Real-life and death consequences were being taken up in a manner that just is not seen in communities such as KS. The real *need* for a verification of information from a variety of sources, and the bringing together of a variety of experiences and information from members of the community, was necessary to develop the most coherent picture possible of what was actually going on half a world away.

From one informal conversation, we found out that a particular individual started to come on IRC channel prime at the time of conflict. He said that, "chatting with those abroad, despite being ephemeral, helped me to feel a kind of hope" (translated from Serbian). Once the bombing ceased, the activity level decreased somewhat, but it has since maintained itself at a level much higher than before the conflict, a recognition of how communities coalesce around times of threat or stress to their members, and that the threads of a community may often go farther and deeper than is easily discernible on the surface.

Educational Communities

The second set of virtual communities were formed with explicit educational purposes in mind. These communities often have an institutional base for the various curricula locations. They often have particular groups in mind as potential community members and may have specific purposes that compromise the Curriculum of Membership. The first example, MOOkti was initiated with a specific learning agenda for a graduate student group, but the orientation and community membership changed almost immediately. The other environment, Achieve, represents a shift in orientation to finding a community of learners who are dedicated to creating their own small virtual communities to initiate and carry out specific problem-tasks. What might distinguish communities formed for educational, as opposed to social, purposes is the element of control by educators as to whether their students have a choice in participating. In other words, the interaction is either educator-based or learner-initiated.

MOOkti

MOOkti MOO* (achieve.utoronto.ca/:9696) is a social and educational space similar to other CVEs in that it has an intended purpose and

---

* "MOOs are an emerging form of educational computer-mediated communication, a text-based polysynchronous collaborative virtual learning environment that allows users to design and program models of people, places and things, and share them with others" (Nolan, 1998). MOO stands for MUD Object Oriented, and describes a server, database, and

theme but no limitations or conditions for participation or interaction. When MOOkti was started in the spring of 1995, by one individual, it was envisioned as a place where educators and education students at the Ontario Institute for Studies in Education of the University of Toronto (OISE/UT) could learn about virtual environments. However, rather than make this space an isolated "classroom" or research space, it was opened to anyone on the Internet to join or visit, and as many diverse activities as possible were included. The intention was to create a public space that would provide the OISE/UT real-life community with the opportunity to experience a selection of the diverse possibilities found elsewhere on the Internet.

As it turned out, the most active members were not OISE/UT members, but rather the external participants who used MOOkti as one of their virtual homes. At various times, MOOkti hosted Icelandic educators who wished to learn about MOOs in education, members of the Jewish community who created a small resource center, undergraduate environmental studies classes, ad hoc groups of young people on the net who just liked to hang out, and a small group of MOO programmers who experimented and developed the MOO server and software.

These external groups were originally intended almost as window dressing to provide the intended audience with diverse experiences. The MOO founder intended this external group to fulfill the role of "populating the space with interesting people" in order to make the environment appear enticing. One study underway into the intended audience of MOOkti found that the nature of the educational professional community itself inhibited sustained and active participation in the MOOkti community. The intended learning activities of the space did occur through various classes conducted in MOOkti, but the community that did finally develop through the participation of the external members was more predicated on the external members' own needs, interests, and criteria. The community that developed successfully subverted the intended purpose of MOOkti to their own needs and uses, and MOOkti only survives through their interests and efforts. This experience represents a fulfillment of Ostrom's view of a community being able to modify the rules of a space to match their own needs and experiences, a redefinition of the space according to their own rules respected by external authorities. This

programming language. MUD is an acronym that can have many meanings: Multi-User Dungeon/Dimension/Dimensional/Domain/Discourse (Aarseth, 1997; Curtis, 1992; Curtis & Nichols, 1993; Turkle, 1995, 1998).

represents an unintended outcome of the Curriculum of Initiation and Governance.

MOOkti's genesis resulted in the desire of an individual student, Jason Nolan, at OISE/UT to try to create a community of educators similar to other professional virtual communities such as MediaMOO or LinguaMOO (www.cc.gatech.edu/fac/Amy.Bruckman/MediaMOO, lingua.utdallas.edu; see Bruckman & Jensen, this volume). Nolan is a teacher and graduate student with some technical experience but with none of the programming or UNIX experience required to run the sophisticated MOO server and database software. Working alone for a number of months, he engaged in trial-and-error experiments in running the software on various computers at OISE/UT trying to find a home capable of supporting the software and intended user base. Unable to obtain guaranteed access to a computer capable of sustaining the project, he finally was able to obtain the loan of a server from IBM, Canada, and over the 1994–5 winter holidays, the server was delivered and installed, bringing MOOkti (at this time called MOOoise) online.

Almost immediately it became evident that governing the environment required more skill and experience than he was capable of, and a search began for volunteers able to coadminister MOOkti. Nolan searched the Internet for documentation, FAQs, and help files on how to run his MOO. He also communicated with others who ran MOOs around the world through an email discussion list called MOO-COWS (moo-cows@the-b.org), gaining important information on how to select a group of administrators able to help out. After the first request, a number of applicants offered to join the project. After a few conflicts and false starts, a small MOOkti administration committee was in place consisting of members with experience on a variety of MOOs around the world (BayMOO, Weyrmount, Eden, Sprawl, EnviroMOO, MooWP).

Nolan learned that there was a specific sequence of learning steps already in place for the administration of these types of virtual environments that could be adopted and quickly put into place, and that most experienced MOO programmers had already undergone extensive apprenticeships elsewhere (elseMOO in MOO-speak). The MOO community had its own software, discourse, and extensive document archives – a complete learning environment in itself – which an individual needs to be aware of to successfully develop a MOO. It was only after the required information necessary to develop and maintain the MOO infrastructure was absorbed, understood, and put into practice that MOOkti was ready and able to invite and respond to participants. But even before MOOkti had formally opened, a small community of the administrators had already developed, and this social core became a template for interaction that new members could learn from or ignore, but this primary level of community clearly influenced the way in which new members manifested their own experiences in the environment. Community that developed on the larger scale was dependent on and reflected this original community. This development addresses important events in learning the Curriculum of Initiation and Governance. The founder put himself through the phases of initiation, pushing the process of constructing the site as far as he could alone in order to understand better how the technology worked by itself, before stepping out and looking for help and codevelopers from the greater MOO community.

Project Achieve

In contrast to the informal and primarily social space of the KS list, or the diverse technical, educational, and casual communities of MOOkti, Project Achieve (moo.schoolnet.ca) intends a form of community that is located solely in an educational culture. The external context is not necessarily communal, in the usual sense, but rather various and diverse. Achieve is a more artificial and intentional construction than the other environments discussed in this chapter. It finds its genesis in discussions between Canada's Schoolnet/Industry Canada, a branch of the Canadian government, and educators with the specific goal of creating an environment for Canadian youth and educators aimed at project-based learning intended to promote intentionality and task dedication as a vehicle for learning. The system infrastructure is not so much constructed by the users, but is built by them upon a structure provided by the project developers in concert with a government organization. The virtual space is not a casual public space where people can just hang out, but a space where projects are planned, developed, and implemented with the support of project staff. As such, it is a private space open to public participation. Though it is open to guests, it is intended to generate a series of small group projects that are not explicitly interrelated. Participants need not interact with others who are pursuing different projects, and only individuals who are part of specific projects are permitted to be members. So, if Achieve is successful, it will be a metacommunity constructed from a set of very small subcommunities.

The various purposes of the projects and the various participant characteristics are also not synchronous; instead, thay are based upon differing goals and interests of the specific projects. There are specific boundaries to participation in Achieve, but unlike other virtual environments there is not a specific social or cultural theme of the space beyond that of the project-based nature of the space. Any project that can be developed by prospective members is acceptable. It is about the culture of learning. Current projects and projects under development include various writer's workshops, environmental education simulations, cross-cultural projects linking Canadian and Macedonian students and Icelandic and Canadian students, and a project for students who wish to learn to program and manage virtual reality environments. There is even a proposal to create a virtual Green Gables simulation. The limitation of the Achieve virtual space comes with the requirement for participants to be actively involved in a specific project, so there is a question as to whether a sense of community for the Achieve space as a whole will develop at all. However, it is hoped that community will develop between members of specific projects through communal learning about how to program and construct virtual spaces, and the sharing of the products of their projects with each other. This is already occurring, even at this early stage of the project, four months old at the time of writing this chapter.

The genesis of Achieve is particular and unlike other MOOs or CVEs that the authors have experienced. The project was initiated by Schoolnet administrators who were attempting to find an alternative environment for Schoolnet users. Schoolnet had it's own CVE, SchoolNetMoo, that was successful as a social space but did not take up the learning purposes that SchoolNet envisioned. They were looking for an environment with more specific pedagogical aims and structure, and they looked to MOOkti as a successful model of a learning environment. But rather than merely try to recreate what had been done, interested MOOkti members wanted to start over and use what they had learned in the creation of a new model of CVE that was more focused on learning. They realized that many CVEs ended up as casual social spaces and that only a few members of CVEs actually engaged in any systematic attempts to construct environments that were useful learning tools. Primarily, issues of intentionality and task dedication were perceived as characteristics found in the best users of CVEs, and they hoped that the construction of an environment specifically dedicated to project-based learning might provide a guided opportunity for developing these skills and attitudes in learners.

The way in which the Curriculum of Access manifests itself in Achieve is particular. Whereas most CVEs, especially MOOs, attract users and get them online by mere invitation, and then often provide minimal support,

Achieve planners chose to solicit participants directly by posting descriptions of the project on specific learning and education sites. They are then targeting the audience of learners whom they think will find the project most interesting. Additionally, the project is designed such that a large percentage of the resources are spent on a full-time online staff whose primary purpose is facilitating interactions; holding your hand, as it were, while you take your first steps through a virtual landscape. When you visit Achieve, the odds are that you will find someone there who will communicate with you about your project. Intentionally populating cyberspace with people, rather than merely setting up a space and expecting visitors to work it out among themselves is a somewhat novel situation. Most online environments do not have active paid facilitators who are trained in education and experienced users of the environment. The goal is to shift the somewhat vertical learning curve of CVEs into something more easily encountered.

In order to provide this *personalized* facilitation, Achieve restricts participation or access by putting a requirement on the user. As mentioned previously, all members must be actively involved in a project, and members are responsible for planning and implementing the projects. This requirement of intentionality and task dedication placed on the participants means that that the restriction can be seen as a function of what the participants bring with them in terms of personal willingness to undertake and complete projects, or the situational interest generated by the site itself being able to motivate the participants.

It remains to be seen how successful Achieve will be at motivating participants and creating the kind of situational interest considered necessary for project-based learning to succeed (Hidi & Berndorff, 1998). But by front-end loading of Achieve with project design heuristics and models, and examples of projects, it is hoped that participants will form their own learning environments according to their own interests and needs. If the project is successful, participants other than the founders of Achieve will form a sufficiently cohesive sense of community and that they will be able to take control over the environment at the end of the three years of the funded project.

Commentary on Examples

These examples represent just a few of the myriad virtual communities that are in existence at any particular point in time. Although each community is different in some ways from others, we believe that there are similarities across all. First, they are all, more or less, learning communities. Whether purposeful or not, these are contexts in which different degrees and types of learning are necessary. They may vary as to what their purposes are, from social to political to educational, even for comfort and emotional support. There are limits to membership in certain communities stemming from personal understanding of language; as an example, neither of us could become members of Serbia.web because we are not familiar with the language.

What information is required in each community? There are different tasks in each, and there is a need to understand something of the nature of the tasks themselves, how they get established and accomplished and processed to see how the community is successful or not successful. All the communities have shifting purposes; before the war, Serbia.web was a global community tool that necessarily framed a real community in order to maintain community. During the war, there was intensive interaction leading to a different sense of community than before. But how different is the community now than before the war? Ongoing research will provide answers to these questions in the Serbia.web community.

Nolan et al. (1998) described the shifting purposes and goals of the KS community along the linear development of the community from pioneer to mature community, followed by a repetition of issues as new members join and take an active part in the community. New groups of members continually revisit questions and issues relating to the direction of the list, coming to their own conclusions that often reflect new orientations or values for the list. The most dynamic shift was from the original intention of the list to focus directly on the life and works of LMM. Very quickly, new members embarked on a series of TANs, or tangential discussions of personal issues that only vaguely reflected on LMM, such as personal events with pets, real-life meetings, and social conflicts among list members.

Because of the polysynchronous nature of Achieve and MOOkti, there is very little collective discussion of issues that involve all, or even a majority of, members. Like a real community, too much is going on for any one issue to involve all members, and only those involved with administering the site are engaged in the metadiscussion of the direction the environment will take. Rather, individual members and subcommunities carry on among themselves and only seek recourse to the site administration team on a case-by-case basis. Individuals wishing to take a more active role in the administration regularly move up the hierarchy and take on administration roles, but this is not mandatory, and the administration team can be largely ignored by individual members if they wish.

All these types of community do not require a long-term commitment to function, but they require continuity among membership, and a mechanism to pass control on to new members. This is one of the features that differentiates them from the real. It is more difficult in IRL communities. If you shift your role in an IRL community, you may have to move out to stop interacting with it. In these virtual communities, it is easier to move out, or reposition yourself in relation to the community. It is much easier to move from the status of passive lurker to active participant to a position of power and control in the site. This feature is consistent for all the environments we have described.

However, individual mobility in relation to a community is slightly different with Achieve and MOOkti. These virtual environments are polysynchronous and constructivist, based on MOO technology. With MOOs, anything that can be described can be created, and they are best described as places in which participants create virtual representations' of people, places, and things and share them with others' (Nolan, 1998). In MOOs, such as Achieve and MOOkti, individuals create and leave behind artifacts or objects in the space when they are not present, or if they have left the community. With email discussion lists such as KS, individuals may leave records behind that are searchable, but these archives are somewhat external spaces to the community itself; they are records of the community rather than active elements within it. The multitechnology-dependent Serbia.web community keeps no records of interaction or archives, due to the primarily synchronous nature of the IRC and Java chat environments and the limited archival resources of their email discussion lists. The only way to participate in a community and not leave any artifacts is to have never posted, or to be a lurker. The act of delurking is the act of participating directly in the community. On a MOO there is a record of joining and leaving, but there is not on a list or IRC.

In the KS email list, the primary locus of learning may appear to focus around sharing knowledge and information about the author and her works, but the tacit learning is *learning about each other.* Achieve, on the other hand, is more focused on how to learn with others in virtual spaces. MOOkti's intended focus, about how to extend teaching and learning into online and virtual environments, was subverted by members into a casual social community where the primary social focus entailed learning about the virtual environment itself and how polysynchronous learning and community takes place. But with Serbia.web, the important learning was directed to learning about what was going on in the outside world. Although all the communities we describe required participants to learn how to interact and communicate within the community, only MOOkti had this kind of learning as its initial primary goal.

Learning the Social Construction of Interaction

In each of our examples, certain criteria are needed to define and describe community learning in terms of who is involved, technical aspects, and the front-end loading of the site with interesting people or topics. Baym's notions of external context, temporal structure, getting in, and formal membership manifest differences in control, structure, and forms of learning that can and do take place. Where does the learning take place and how do we justify our claims? The various mechanisms of interaction – joining, leaving, participating, lurking, and researching – are all locations of learning that reflect on issues of participation in and control of the community. These issues are ones that we are considering in our exploration of the curricula of virtual community.

Curriculum of Initiation and Governance

Virtual communities tend to have a definable moment of initiation, unlike some IRL communities in which genesis may be open to historical interpretation. Somebody or somebodies must locate a space for starting the community. There is the Curriculum of Initiation, which requires learning about the type of communication, location, and software necessary to allow others to participate. Initiators of any online environment need technical information that varies according to the complexity of the envisioned community. It would be necessary to find a server and software necessary for initiation as well as for development of the site or sites (Web pages, etc.) that would be publicly accessible. Who is responsible for running the software and making it available in the form that potential community members can access? A common problem faced by educators, or those responsible for creating a learning setting, is how to provide information and activities that accommodate a range of learner's backgrounds. If the procedure for joining the community requires sophisticated technical knowledge, then this may set limits as to who may join the community.

After a community site is launched, there are curricular issues associated with ensuring that there is continuity associated with the community. Ensuring this continuity would include monitoring the discourse for netiquette and context, depending on the purpose of the community.

A netiquette has evolved and spawned its own vocabulary of terms ('net, spam, ROTFL, LOL, IRL, ping of death, bot, etc.); it is unique to particular communities and the Internet community as a whole. Over time, the maintenance of the community site may transfer from initiators to others, or a shared sense of control may develop. The individuals who become a part of the maintenance of an environment may graduate from membership to control through a variety of criteria. For example, in MOOkti, there was a structured hierarchical Curriculum of Governance that allowed individuals to assume more responsibility as their proficiency in working with the environment increased, with a number of members gaining administration status over time. And in Serbia.web, community members were chosen to be channel operators because of their track record for stability, good netiquette, and the like. The channel operators communicate with each other about problems encountered, not just netiquette, but what topics are appropriate for a channel.

Curriculum of Access

Individuals come to cyberspace with a variety of experiences, from novice to expert. A certain level of sophistication is required to find virtual communities. Some arrive at locations through *surfing* and may encounter an "unintended experience," while others have a preordained sense of expectation and deliberately look for a specific location. Once at a site, generally a Web page, individuals need information to gain admittance to a community. Information about appropriate software and mechanisms of access provides a context for learning. Some bring past experience with technical know-how and/or exposure to a similar situation whereas others require more elaborate communication for accessing and successfully using the software.

Curriculum of Community Membership

Virtual communities exist for specific purposes, and require members as the raison d'être of their existence. Potential members have to know or have to learn how to find sites, access software, and be a member in good standing. Learning the netiquette for a community is an experiential process; for a novice it probably requires a certain amount of lurking to get a feel for acceptable behavior, and, even for more experienced individuals, a certain amount of 'watching and listening' is probably preferable. Individuals, and those in the group, quickly learn what is acceptable or what is not; the extreme penalty for noncompliance being to be dropped from the list or site (booted, banned, newted, toaded, etc.). Individuals make decisions to join a community to suit their needs, whether it be for specific information, participation in certain activities, or other reasons, including curiosity. The community setting has to be seen by a member as being worthwhile for them.

Analyzing the Various Curricula of Virtual Community

We have suggested that an analysis of the curriculum components of a virtual community might allow us to understand how learning is an integral feature. We have labeled the different locations for learning as the Curriculum of Initiation and Governance, the Curriculum of Access, and the Curriculum of Membership. Some questions that might form a research agenda for analyzing learning in these locations might include:

Curriculum of Initiation and Governance

- Who initiates?
- Why does initiation occur?
- What knowledge and skills are necessary to start?
- How is this knowledge obtained?
- Who is able to obtain it?
- What are the processes involved?
- How is continuity determined?
- How are protocols of netiquette constructed and instituted?
- How are social norms regulated?
- How do members change roles?

Curriculum of Access

- How do potential community members locate a site?
- What software is necessary for access?
- How is information made available?
- What knowledge and skills are necessary for access?
- How are these represented?
- How are they obtained?

Curriculum of Membership

- What are the requirements of membership?
- How do community members interact online?
- Do community members interact IRL?
- Are these two types of interaction different?

- How do members enable their own purposes to be served within a community?
- What are the indicators of success, failure, or stagnation?

These questions are a thin representation of the complexities of understanding learning in such curricula. How to chronicle the past backgrounds and achievements of those responsible for creating the learning settings and the kinds of pedagogies necessary for different possibilities for learners is a challenge. Accordingly, the various ways of representation have to reflect the diverse potential of learners.

To truly understand how each virtual community is a learning community, we have suggested that knowing the history and the descriptive features allows us to determine the various learnings that are necessary for initiation, maintenance, and indeed success. Our examples demonstrate quite disparate learning settings, but all require certain tasks and knowledge and skills necessary and sufficient for success. Of course, there is the knowledge and skills associated with technology of cyberspace, but there also has to be an agenda that will interest others to form a community.

KS and Serbia.web both offer examples of communities formed through intentionality of either creating a culture (KS) or maintaining one (Serbia.web). Each required interest on the part of one or several individuals making a decision about initiating, and finding the appropriate technical features for it to happen. The same could be said for MOOkti and Achieve, since each required intentionality to create a community for the culture of learning. Each community has mechanisms for governing the community site and creating ways for both attracting and maintaining community membership. It would appear that there is a culture of learning and learning in culture.

Back to the Beginning

One of the key difficulties people have in considering or accepting the existence of virtual communities comes from their location in cyberspace, a term coined by William Gibson in his 1984 virtual dystopia *Neuromancer*. Part of this problem is created by the lack of a clear notion of what the location, or *space*, is, both real and virtual. We talk about spaces, social space, mental space, cultural space, and public and private spaces as if there were a clear communal understanding of what these spaces are and what they mean to us. This lack of a canonical sense of what *space* is off-line makes it even more difficult to understand or accept how community can exist online when there is no physical location to which to attach itself. There may have been a collective notion of what a space was in the past, but this notion is not part of the modern fragmented world. Consider French philosopher Henri Lefebvre's notions from *The Production of Space*, where he observes, "Yet did there not at one time, between the sixteenth century (the Renaissance – and the Renaissance city) and the nineteenth century, exist a code at once architectural, urbanistic and political, constituting a language common to country people and towns people, to the authorities and artists – a code which allowed space not only to be 'read' but also to be constructed?" (Lefebvre, 1974, p. 7). This notion of there existing at some definite point in time a consistent notion of location and space, one that has been disrupted in the development of modern culture, suggests that only a multifaceted notion of community can exist in the modern world, online or off. And more particularly the notion that the *space* in which a community exists is a construction, regardless of whether it is a real or virtual location involved.

The construction of these new virtual spaces may be a technological utopian act, what Lefebvre calls a "science of space" that is in part "a technological utopia . . . within the framework of the real – the framework of the existing mode of production" (Lefebvre, 1974, pp. 8–9). This may be a description of what virtual reality may represent. However, Lefebvre was not in a position to include observations of the rich explosion of online communities that have cropped up in the past five years, since the World Wide Web invaded popular consciousness. At this time, access to the Web became less of a luxury for academics and corporations, and more accessible from the home, library, and in some cases laundromat and cafe. But it is through thinkers like Lefebvre that we can gain support for the question of whether virtual community exists as part of our modern, and postmodern, struggle to understand what community and community space itself is (Cicognani, 1998).

The fact that we no longer have an agreed-upon communal understanding of the real world around us makes it is very difficult to develop a communal understanding of what virtual spaces represent. This results in a suspicion in some and an unquestioning acceptance of the notion of virtual community in others. The whole of cyberspace *is* a community, much the same way as envisioning the whole of our planet as one community. The difference between the two is obvious: people make conscious decisions to inhabit cyberspace. These decisions have educational consequences in the way we structure the learning moments. Like any other human invention, a virtual community has the capacity for structuring educative or miseducative experiences (Dewey, 1938). The lessons that we learn are not just about technique or academic knowledge, but they extend to the moral and spiritual domains as well. The choices that we make about what is important and how it should be represented are values that serve to locate curriculum actions.

References

Aarseth, E. (1997). *Cybertext: Perspectives on ergodic literature.* Baltimore: Johns Hopkins.

Barnes, D. (1988). Knowledge as action. *The word for teaching is learning.* Portsmouth, NH: Heinemann Educational Books.

Baym, N. (1998 (1995)). The emergence of on-line community. In S. Jones (Ed.), *CyberSociety 2.0: Revisiting computer-mediated communication and community* (pp. 35–68). Thousand Oaks, CA: Sage.

Bruck, L. (1994). Dear kindred spirits. *Kindred Spirits*, Summer, p. 5.

Cayley, D. (1992). *Ivan Illich: In conversation.* Toronto: Anansi.

Cicognani, A. (1998). On the linguistic nature of cyberspace and virtual communities. *Virtual Reality, 3*, 16–24.

Collins, M. P., & Berge, Z. L. (1997). *Moderating on-line electronic discussion groups.* Paper presented at the 1997 American Educational Research Association (AREA) Meeting, Chicago, IL.

Curtis, P. (1992). Mudding: Social phenomena in text-based virtual realities. *Intertrek, 3*(3), 26–34.

Curtis, P., & Nichols, D. (1993). *MUDs grow up: Social virtual reality in the real world.* Paper presented at the Third International Conference on Cyberspace, Austin, TX.

Davie, L., & Nolan, J. (1999). *Doing learning: Building constructionist skills for educators, or; theatre of metaphor: Skills constructing for building educators.* Paper presented at the TCC, Maui, Hawaii. Available: noisey.oise.utoronto.ca/projcool/conferences/doing.html.

Dewey, J. (1938). *Education and experience.* New York: Macmillan.

Foucault, M. (1991). Governmentality. In G. Burchell, C. Gordon & P. Miller (Eds.), *The Foucault effect: Studies in governmental rationality.* Hertfordshire: Harvester Wheatsheaf, pp. 87–104.

Fowler, S. B. (1996). *Recycling in cyberspace: A case study for identity and community.* Paper presented at the annual meeting of the Midwest Modern Language Association, Minneapolis, MN.

Gibson, W. (1984). *Neuromancer.* New York: Ace Books.

Hardin, G. (1968). The tragedy of the commons. *Science, 162*, 1243–8.

Hidi, S., & Berndorff, D. (1998). Situational interest and learning. In L. Hoffman, A. Krapp, K. A. Renninger & J. Baumert (Eds.), *Interest and learning: Proceedings of the Seeon Conference on interest and gender* (pp. 74–90). Kiel, Germany: IPN.

Illich, I. (1970). *Deschooling society.* New York: Harper & Row.

Kolb, D. (1984). *Experiential learning.* Toronto: Prentice-Hall.

Kollock, P. (1998). Design principles for online communities. *PC Update*, *15*(5), 58–60.

Lefebvre, H. (1974). *The production of space* (D. Nicholson-Smith, Trans.). Oxford, UK: Blackwell.

Montgomery, L. M. (1908). *Anne of Green Gables*. Boston: Page.

Moore, D. (1981). Discovering the pedagogy of experience. *Harvard Educational Review*, *51*(2), 286–300.

Morgan, R. (1998). *From the groves of academe to square feet: Social space and schooling* (pp. 1–30). Invited Lecture: Social and Cultural Studies Faculty Seminar Series, Department of Curriculum. Teaching and Learning, OISE/UT.

Nolan, J. (1998). *Educators in MOOkti: A polysynchronous collaborative virtual learning environment*. Available: achieve.utoronto.ca/jason.mookti.html.

Nolan, J., Lawrence, J., & Kajihara, Y. (1998). Montgomery's Island in the net: Metaphor and community on the Kindred Spirit's e-mail list. *Canadian Children's Literature*, *24*(3/4), 64–77.

Ostrom, E. (1990). *Governing the commons: The evolution of institutions for collective action*. New York: Cambridge University Press.

Rheingold, H. (1993). *The virtual community: Homesteading on the electronic frontier*. Reading, MA: HarperPerennial.

Robinson, L. (1999). A born Canadian: Community and the individual in *Anne of Green Gables* and *A Tangled Web*. In I. Gammel & E. Epperly (Eds.), *L. M. Montgomery and Canadian Culture* (pp. 19–30). Toronto: University of Toronto Press.

Rogoff, B., & Lave, J. (1984). Everyday cognition. In B. Rogoff & J. Lave (Eds.), *Everyday cognition: Its development in social context*. Cambridge, MA: Harvard, pp. 1–8.

Schwab, J. J. (1969). The practical: A language for curriculum. *School Review*, 1–23. (1971). The practical: Arts of eclectic. *School Review*, 493–542.

Stubbs, P. (1998). Conflict and co-operation in the virtual community: eMail and the wars of the Yugoslav succession. *Sociological Research Online*, *3*(3). Available: www.socresonline.org.uk 3/3/7.html.

(1999). Virtual diaspora?: Imagining Croatia on-line. *Sociological Research Online*, *4*(2). Available: www.socresonline.org.uk/4/2/stubbs.html.

Tomas, D. (1991). Old rituals for new space: Rites de passage and William Gibson's cultural model of cyberspace. In M. Benedikt (Ed.), *Cyberspace: First steps*. Cambridge MA.: MIT Press, pp. 31–47.

Turkle, S. (1995). *Life on the screen*. New York: Schuster. (1998). Foreword: All MOOs are educational – The Experience of "walking through the self." In C. Haynes, & J. R. Holmvek (Eds.), *High wired on the design, use and theory of educational MOOs*. Ann Arbor: University of Michigan Press, pp. ix–xix, 167–94.

Wellman, B., & Gulia, M. (1996). Net surfers don't ride alone: Virtual communities as communities. In P. K. Smith & M. Smith (Eds.), *Communities in cyberspace*. Berkeley: University of California Press, pp. 167–94.

12 Finding the Ties That Bind

Tools in Support of a Knowledge-Building Community

Christopher Hoadley and Roy D. Pea

Finding a professional connection with a colleague seems like a simple task but can devour hours of time. An anecdote illustrates why this is hard. A researcher whom we will call David got a call with a question about research on interactive toys. David had some experience in that area and immediately recalled several people who did similar work, but who didn't quite fit the bill of this request. He vaguely remembered someone he had heard about who did do that sort of work – the researcher was a Canadian woman who had recently won an award for women in computer science. He thought but wasn't sure that the woman was from western Canada. With these recollections in mind, he set about trying to find her.

First, he tried searching based on the topic. He began with a Web search on the topic area but found far too many results. He tried narrowing his search but had no luck. He tried a number of refinements, including searching on words related to the award, and so on. After spending nearly half an hour, he decided to try a different strategy.

This time, David tried to find the researcher through his social network. He began by asking a co-worker down the hall. A short conversation didn't yield any leads. Continuing down the hall, he asked another colleague. Again, the colleague didn't know the person he was seeking, but this person did suggest another related researcher who might know the mystery woman's identity. David knew that the related person (let us call her Renee) worked in Los Angeles and had written a book that he thought had cited the mystery person. David tried to find the book. When a quick glance through his own library did not yield a copy, he tried to look the book up on the Internet through searching, this time armed with an author, institution, and an approximate title. Ten to 20 minutes later, not having found the book, he moved to searching for the author's home page, hoping for a link to the publication, a phone number so he could call Renee, or a link to the home page of the Canadian researcher. Again, quick searches yielded no results. Not finding Renee's home page through a search engine, David tried a less direct approach. He started at the home page of the Los Angeles university in an attempt to drill down to Renee's home page directly. Lost in the vast Web site of the institution, he eventually aborted this attempt.

After pursuing a number of dead-end search strategies, he gave up on Renee entirely. He finally did discover the mystery researcher by a brute-force search, starting with the home pages of several universities in western Canada and eventually stumbling on the right person by sifting through a number of computer science department Web pages. This search odyssey lasted hours before David finally reached his goal.

This example is important for two reasons. First, it demonstrates the high cost of finding and making connections to people. In this case, finding the collaborator took much longer than the collaboration, which consisted of a brief conversation and skimming one of the Canadian's articles. Second, it shows how social context is interwoven with finding information. David wanted some information, but he did not search for information in the traditional library sense. Rather, he searched for a person that he knew could help him. The specific information he sought was impossible to find directly, so he had to find its author, the mystery woman in western Canada. As Harold "Doc" Edgerton, the inventor of the strobe light and one of the century's most prominent engineers, once explained, when he wanted to find something out, first he would ask around to see whether anybody knew the answer, then he would try it out in the lab himself, and only then would he try looking the information up in a book or library (Edgerton, personal communication, 1989). The social connection to knowledge is often the most expedient.

Even when finding information through a social network may be the best way, it is by no means an easy way. Finding this woman was difficult. The topic of interactive toys was not really helpful in locating her, but seemingly irrelevant contextual information was – her gender, geographic location, and an award she had won. The Internet's vast information did contain exactly what David needed – contact information for the researcher, her profile, even some of her work. But traditional search engines did nothing to help connect her to David.

This chapter describes how we came to use technology in support of pre-collaboration activities like finding social and topical information, instead of the more traditional role of supporting communication during a collaboration. Our problem is an example of the more general problem of *knowledge networking*: how to get knowledge to those members of a community who need it. Often, when considering what collaborators need, we think of technology to support interaction directly, such as fancy telecommunications systems or "shared workspaces" in the computer. David would have been served much better by a way to find the researcher than by any traditional groupware to help him talk to her.

In the following sections, we will describe some of the general aspects of the problems associated with building collaborative technologies for knowledge networking. We discuss some findings from examining the knowledge-sharing practices of a group of scholars. Finally, we describe our experiences in implementing a knowledge-networking tool with a nascent, distributed community of educational technology users, researchers, and businesspeople called CILT. The Center for Innovative Learning Technologies (CILT) is funded by the U.S. National Science Foundation to foster a productive knowledge-building community among learning technology researchers and stakeholders. We explore the development of technologies for CILT as a case study of what is involved in creating technologies to support knowledge building.

Conceptualizing a Learning Community

Why collaborate? Humans need to coordinate in joint action to achieve tasks larger than any one person could accomplish. In addition, we communicate to express ourselves, to transmit information, and to learn. Through the processes of acculturation, knowledge and culture are perpetuated and transformed as we interact, define new problems, and take on new challenges. People generally highlight collaboration as good and are interested in creating tools to support it. But what is good collaboration? By examining some models of knowledge and organizations, we can get insight into what types of collaboration we might want to support with technology.

Models of Collaboration

In the world of business studies of organizational behavior, the processes of collective action have been simplified into a number of models. The hierarchical model of Taylor was concerned primarily with a top-down control structure in which commands propagated downward from management to labor, purportedly dividing and delegating the tasks of the organization for efficient, coordinated action (Fischer, 1999).

Knowledge in this model is generally simplified to the issue of information transmission – when somebody needs to know something, you tell it to him or her. This model dominated in the early twentieth century, and the collaboration technologies we have inherited from it support the goal of information transmission: telephones, radio, loudspeakers, and the ever-present photocopier all support transmission of information (see especially Pea & Gomez, 1992).

Over time, this model proved ineffective. Flatter organizational structures, team-based work groups, and information management techniques began to emerge. Organizational knowledge was highlighted as an important type of institutional capital. In this more complex model, information transmission gave way to information management. Large organizations, such as companies, developed management information systems (MIS) departments whose job it was to collect, process, and route information to the right people. In this model, there were two ways to bring the right knowledge to bear on a problem: one was to move the people who knew the right things, assembling project teams with ready-made expertise; the other was to codify the information needed and use information technologies to help people find what they were looking for. This model yielded our standard view of corporate training and centralized information technologies for organizations. Technologies, in this case, were less communicative and more data oriented. The technologies used included relational databases, automatically generated statistics and reports, and codified sources of information such as manuals, corporate training documents, and the like. A few innovative applications attempted to do automatic knowledge management by means of techniques such as data mining or automatic information capture.

However, this model also has been proven ineffective. Corporate training cannot keep up with changing skill requirements, and MIS departments have a hard time ensuring access to the right kinds of information. Furthermore, there has been a growing awareness that information does not necessarily lead to knowledge. Until information has been comprehended and interpreted to the point that it can be applied to a situation, it is not knowledge. Decentralization became de rigueur, and the idea of the "learning organization" (Garratt, 1987) was born. In this model, individuals are constantly learning new skills and working to discover and propagate knowledge. We define a knowledge-building community as a community with a shared goal of individual learning and knowledge transfer within the group.

How does knowledge move around in organizations? A famous study of photocopier repair technicians (Orr, 1990) demonstrated that story-telling in social, water-cooler settings was the main way expertise was being passed around. Not only did this social network help the technicians in a community of practice uncover and transmit information, but as the technicians applied the stories in their own repair work, the knowledge in the organization increased (Brown & Duguid, 1991). Individuals were constantly transforming information into knowledge and knowledge into outcomes (in this case, repaired copiers) through their social interactions.

The copier study provides an excellent example of the kinds of reasons why learning is an important function of collaboration. The copier repair people did not really need to collaborate to coordinate their actions; a dispatch system could easily have been rigged up that did not require the repair people to talk to each other. Nor was collecting and routing information a primary benefit; the individual copier repair people primarily invented repair techniques on their service calls, and a system could have been put in place to capture that information impersonally. (Indeed, the U.S. military attempts to capture all processes and make them explicit in manuals, although these explicit process instructions rarely capture what really occurs. This approach is fundamentally flawed, in part because it ignores the constructive nature of understanding and learning (see Hutchins, 1995). No, the primary benefit of this community was how the technicians could learn from one another, increasing their knowledge, thereby enabling the company to solve more copier problems for more people in less time. Getting others to know what one person had figured out augmented the overall knowledge in the community and improved every repairperson's ability to fix copiers. Figuring out a tough copier problem was of some benefit, but sharing that knowledge with others was the real success. One term for this type of community is a "knowledge-building community" (Scardamalia & Bereiter, 1994), where individuals are committed to sharing information for the purpose of building understanding (knowledge) in all the participants. This knowledge-building activity benefits not only individuals but also groups (Pea, 1992). One example of a type of knowledge-building community that has existed for many centuries is the scholarly community, where sharing information (via publishing) and boosting overall knowledge (through teaching) are as important as the creation of new information for oneself (through research).

A fascinating project at the University of Waterloo's Electronic Library has been devoted to documenting the history of scholarly societies.* These historians highlight how the sharing and publication of scholarly knowledge emerged from the scholarly societies formed starting in the fourteenth century. Their chronology documents how until the nineteenth century, scholarly societies were generally of broad scope (e.g., all sciences, all arts, or both) and geographically based. Afterward, increasingly specialized scholarly societies came into being. They highlight the seminal publication in 1938 by Ornstein of her book on the role of scientific societies in the seventeenth century (Ornstein & Cohn, 1938). In this work, Ornstein documented that the goal of these early societies (such as Accademia del Cimento of Florence or the Royal Society) was generally to promote research by providing a place for researchers to meet one another and discuss or even carry out research. This same knowledge-building function, and its affiliated objectives of finding people and collaborating with them, follows to the present day.

Today we find tools that provide not only access to information but access to people. Access to people includes referral technologies for help-on-demand; "customer relationship management software" that aims to help phone operators interact with customers in a consistent way; and participatory news services like the now-famous "slashdot.org" Web site, with news articles and discussion intertwined throughout the site. These technologies help us find not only information but also knowledge by connecting us to people and not just facts.

How Can Technology Help a Learning Community?

Given a model of a learning community as a community that builds knowledge in all its participants through collaboration, how do we support such a community? Certainly, many collaborations are dysfunctional and actually prevent learning through encouraging "groupthink" or by disadvantaging some participants (Linn & Burbules, 1993). Can we help make effective collaboration easier through technology?

It is often observed that a community of practice is embedded in and overlaps with other communities of practice, or CoPs (Lave & Wenger, 1991; Wenger, 1999). CoPs are diverse in nature, and, like organisms in ecological niches, they originate, evolve, and may become extinct. Individuals play membership roles in many different communities. Different

---

* www.lib.uwaterloo.ca/society/overview.html

kinds of communities (e.g., a theatre group, K–12 mathematics education researchers) provide different identifiable roles, thus providing diverse routes into becoming a member of a given CoP.

Members often share work, lifestyles, activities, and identity badges such as ways of speaking and clothing, and these members are interconnected in that they contribute to co-constructing what aspects of activity and choice define a sense of membership. It is an inherent part of communities of practice that members carry out what might be called tacit or indigenous assessments – gauging one another according to the perceived appropriateness of talk, activity, lifestyle, competence, commitment, and other realms of behavior or being.

Part of the process of learning within communities of practice is described by Lave and Wenger (1991) as *legitimate peripheral participation* (LPP), a relationship that individual learners have to the activities of established communities of practice when they act with the goal of increasing their sense of membership in and acceptance by these communities. LPP is "a way of gaining access to sources for understanding through growing involvement." In their development of this view, Lave and Wenger do much to explicate "the relations between newcomers and old-timers, and about activities, identities, artifacts and communities of knowledge and practice."

Lave and Wenger's analysis of CoPs indicates the importance of learning by membership. Learning energy is devoted to becoming a member of a community of practice, and what is learned is how to be a member. Consider what this might imply for knowledge-building communities: since the community is oriented toward the production and dissemination of knowledge, the process of joining the community involves learning how to become committed to these goals in a way that the community values. In short, learning how to learn is the price of entry into a knowledge-building community.

The realization that learning is an inherent property of an effective, knowledgeable organization suggests that technologies for learning and technologies for collaboration may be one and the same. The realization that learning results when people participate in a community of practice has already been documented in social science research studies of apprenticeship systems (Lave & Wenger, 1991), and collaborative learning has been widely proposed as an important pedagogical technique (Cohen, 1994; Webb, 1995).

When attempting to design technology, it is important to remember the triad of components of activity (e.g., Kuutti & Bannon, 1993). This triad is based on Russian activity theory (Bedny'i & Meister, 1997). In every situation, there are tools, activities, and people. These three elements are interdependent. A change to one element affects the others. When a new tool is introduced, people and their activities change to accommodate it. For instance, a piece of bookkeeping software might be introduced into a company. Initially, people will try to use the system to replicate their prior bookkeeping practices (new forms for old functions). Differences in how the software does things and the prior system will most likely chafe the users. Over time, people begin to change, learning the new possibilities of the software and adapting their practices (activities) to take advantage of its benefits and work around its shortcomings.

Technologies can thus change the practices of the people in an organization profoundly. For instance, studies of the introduction of email into companies revealed that underlying power structures in the organization were changed – in some cases, drastically (Francik et al., 1991). These technologies have an impact by changing not only what is possible in the organization but also what is easy (and hard). In the email study, the power structures changed because it became easier for people to communicate with others outside their work group (including those in upper levels of the employee hierarchy). It had previously also been possible to communicate across departmental lines, but email made it vastly easier and thus encouraged people to do so.

One example of a technology that supports but does not supplant student communication is Computer-Supported Intentional Learning Environments (CSILE) (Cohen, 1995; Scardamalia & Bereiter, 1992; Scardamalia et al., 1989), in which students collaborate to co-construct a shared database of knowledge. The system allows students to flag ideas in ways that invite social interaction, such as "My theory for now is . . ." or "What I need to know now is . . . ." This technology was successfully used to change classroom culture with elementary school students, yielding an atmosphere in which students took more responsibility for forming and answering their own questions, and in addition learned at least as well as with traditional didactic methods (Scardamalia & Bereiter, 1991). These University of Toronto-based researchers continue these activities today with the Knowledge Forum, a commercially available knowledge-building software system for communities (Hewitt & Scardamalia, 1999).

Studies on another collaboration tool called SpeakEasy revealed that the interactive and social nature of using the tool was far more important for learning than the information that was exchanged (Hoadley, 1999; Hoadley & Linn, 2000). In this tool, students were able to learn from peers online through a structured discussion tool without having access to any expert information. Their learning was related most closely to the interactivity of the online medium and relatively unrelated to the information they encountered in the discussion. This is a surprising finding, which emphasizes the importance of establishing a social context oriented toward learning. It also suggests that technologies should be designed with at least as much attention to social context as to the information presented within. For instance, when using SpeakEasy in a middle school science class, the inclusion of features such as an anonymity option *erased* the typical significant gender differences in student participation and learning (Hoadley, 1999; Hsi & Hoadley, 1997). Such dramatic effects from technology indicate that we can indeed build tools that help form and sustain more effective learning communities.

Knowledge Networking for Learning Communities

We have described different models of organizational collaboration and learning and suggested that an effective learning community is a knowledge-building community of practice, one in which members of the community interact to help collaboratively other individuals and the group to increase their knowledge. This interaction is in contrast to mere information management, which ignores the role of social interaction in helping individuals find and come to understand information, thereby transforming it into knowledge. We have characterized in a general sense how technological tools can help support knowledge building by influencing people and their activities. In contrast to knowledge management tools or information management tools, where the focus is on helping to route information, knowledge-networking tools help foster all the constituent activities that increase knowledge building. These activities include not only information capture and transmission but also the establishment of social relationships in which people can collaboratively construct understanding. In the next section, we describe how some of these steps have been carried out in helping to foster a new learning community called CILT.

The CILT Community

The Center for Innovative Learning Technologies, or CILT (pronounced "silt"), is an attempt to engineer a learning community among people who work with learning and educational technologies.

Although this is a burgeoning area of work, with billions of dollars being spent annually on research, development, and deployment of technology in education, there are few effective mechanisms for getting information about what types of research and development have been done in the area. Several situations contribute to this problem. First, there is and has traditionally been a divide between (usually academic) researchers and practitioners and industry (Kozma, 1996; Office of Technology Assessment, 1988). This ongoing problem has been recognized by the U.S. federal government at the highest levels, as in the PCAST report (President's Committee of Advisors on Science and Technology, 1997). Teachers are generally in contact with academic experts only during their preservice training. In-service professional development attempts to update the teachers' skills and knowledge with the latest research, but this training is typically limited to a few days per year. A second related issue is that technology, in general, and educational technology research and development, in particular, is changing rapidly. With the typical shelf life of an educational technology hovering around three to five years, an incredible amount of information must be read simply to keep up with the changes in the field. A third difficulty is the multidisciplinary nature of research and development in this area. Even among academics, researchers might be housed in departments as diverse as psychology, computer science, education, sociology, communications, and media. Indeed, many educational technologists are housed in the department of the discipline they are teaching (math, science, English, foreign language, etc.) and have no connection to a general educational technology community. These diverse researchers tend to frequent different conferences, read and publish in different journals or trade publications, and have no way of collaborating with each other.

The results are disappointing. Although much research on learning and technology has been carried out for more than twenty years, it is nearly impossible to answer the simple question, "What do we know about what technologies work for learning?" (President's Committee of Advisors on Science and Technology, 1997). The field of learning technology has been accused of a lack of cumulativity, an irrelevance to everyday practitioners (technology developers and teachers), obsolescence compared with the rapid advances in technology, and a disconnectedness that prevents anybody from finding useful information even if it does already exist.

CILT has been designed to address these challenges as a distributed center for fostering collaboration, research, and dissemination in learning technologies (Pea et al., 1999). The CILT organization was founded by four nonprofit and educational institutions (SRI International, the University of California at Berkeley, Vanderbilt University, and the Concord Consortium) in cooperation with industry and school partners. CILT's slogan, "Uniting people, technology, and powerful ideas for learning," reflects one of its main goals – helping to ensure collaboration and effective transfer of knowledge among members of a community of practice devoted to improving scientific understanding of and ongoing practices with learning technologies. In short, CILT is a knowledge-networking organization that is attempting to form a learning community of researchers, developers, and practitioners from academia, government, industry, and education.

CILT was formed in late 1997 to foster a learning community and has identified and tested a number of strategies since then. These strategies have included hosting workshops and conferences, awarding small grants to help new collaborators seek funding for joint research and development, sponsoring a postdoctoral program for training new professionals, and providing technologies to support collaboration. This last goal – of providing technologies to support the community – is the focus of the remainder of this chapter. The efforts to address this goal led us to the surprising conclusion that the best collaborative software is not any sort of traditional groupware but rather a ubiquitous collaborative infrastructure.

Initial Failures

Initially, CILT attempted to support collaboration through traditional "community" software tools on its Web site. These included a number of leading commercial and research products for collaboration. Several Web-based discussion systems were tried (such as Allaire Corporation's Forums and Berkeley's COOL system), as were more unusual technologies, such as Digital Knowledge Assets' intelligent-agent-based collaborative workspaces, SRI's URLex URL exchange program, Vanderbilt University's Webliographer URL bulletin board, and Vanderbilt's LTSeek daily news publishing system. With the exception of LTSeek, each of these technologies failed to attract a significant user base. When motivated groups tried to use them for directed collaborative activities, they quickly reverted to their prior collaboration technologies, including telephone conferences and email mailing lists. Although there are many possible explanations, the most likely is that these tools did not support the users' workflow or collaborative needs. These "bolt-on" technologies (EDUCOM Review Staff, 1996) were tried out for the problems at issue without attending to the range of issues presented later. It was at this time, in 1998, that we began the development of CILTKN (CILT Knowledge Network, pronounced silt-kay-en), a knowledge-networking technology, for this community. We now discuss our experiences in this design process.

Later, we describe the process of designing the CILTKN in terms of eight areas of activity. Although these areas of work can be seen as stages to be completed in order, in our case they were loosely overlapping. Six areas have been at least initially addressed in our design and implementation phase, and two more areas are under investigation in our evaluation and redesign phase.

Designing and Implementing the CILTKN

Defining the Learning Community

In our case, much of the work of defining the learning community and its goals had been already accomplished through the writing of the initial grant proposal for CILT and the following discussions about how CILT would operate. The perceived challenges of the field – lack of cumulativity, lack of connection between research and practice, obsolescence, and disciplinary isolation – drove the goals and activities of CILT. The CILT leadership team set the following as CILT's goals: identifying areas of high potential for research and development, supporting rapid innovation, stimulating collaborative development in the selected areas, fostering interdisciplinary research and dissemination, and helping train new professionals in the field of learning technology research (Pea et al., 1999). CILT was envisioned as a learning community in which researchers, teachers, developers, and policy makers would collaborate to share and build knowledge about learning, education, and technology.

Examining Existing Practices

Our initial failures were a strong motivation to examine existing practices in the audience we were trying to reach. Certainly, participating in online CILT discussions was not part of examining existing practice, so we went back to the drawing board and tried to enlist friends and colleagues to tell us what they really did need. We realized that the audiences of teachers, researchers, and businesspeople were probably different; given this fact, we decided initially to focus on researchers, both because they were the bulk of CILT's membership and because we felt that they, as professional constructors of knowledge, would form a good base on which to build.

Information Needs. Our first step in trying to uncover latent information needs was to ask people at CILT's workshops, engaging hundreds of researchers and other participants, what they hoped CILT would provide. It became clear that an important part of cumulativity was simply information about the learning technology community, for the community. We began holding brainstorms with researchers at the four CILT institutions on what types of information might be useful. We, as the designers, narrowed their suggestions into a smaller list. In addition to wanting information about the CILT organization, people wanted very basic information, such as:

> Who else is involved in learning technology research?
> How do I contact them?
> What do they work on?
> What institutions are doing work in this area?
> What are the important research results?
> How can I get up to speed in this area?
> How can I share or post information on
>   ... a job opening I have?
>   ... an upcoming conference?
> and so on.

The respondents seemed entirely capable of establishing collaborations and carrying them out, if only they had a better handle on whom to collaborate with. As the example with David points out, social collaboration often begins with information finding. It seemed that people needed a little more information than what was readily available to begin collaborating. Therefore, we shifted our focus from supporting online collaboration directly to people's precollaboration information needs.

We translated these information needs into information types that addressed the needs. The kinds of information people seemed to need included:

> **People.** Names, interests, and contact information for people in the field.
> **Projects.** Descriptions and pointers to more information on research projects, implementation projects, or other work being done in the field.

> **Places.** University departments or labs, K–12 schools, or other places where substantial activity (research, development, implementation related to educational technology) is taking place.
>
> **Papers.** Research results or bibliographic pointers to research results in learning technology.
>
> **Syllabi.** Course syllabi or reading lists to get people up to speed on learning technology. This also might help people decide what research papers were foundational or important in the field.
>
> **Collaboration notices.** "Classified ads" or similar types of notices for items like jobs, conferences, etc., typically distributed through email lists.

Once we identified these types of information, we began to look at how people currently arrived at the information.

Sharing Practices. "I can't imagine losing my date planner; I keep my whole life in there!" Following this idea that people tended to keep important information in a single place, we began to survey and interview professional researchers about the information types listed earlier. We asked where they acquired the information, where they kept it, how they used it, and how they shared it (if they shared it at all). Two surveys of an approximately fifty-person research department touched on researchers, clerical staff, students, and teachers. Participants were rewarded for returning surveys with candy bars, yielding a very high participation rate (over 75 percent).

The surveys revealed several important facts. First, there was no predominant system for keeping most types of information. Second, most people had organizational systems for their personal and professional information that they felt were woefully inadequate. Yet, people did generally manage to function perfectly well with their current systems, even if using them did take a substantial amount of time. (For instance, the time it was reported to take to format a bibliography to a paper was anywhere from a few hours to several days. Though people were largely citing papers they had read and could remember readily, the details of citations were difficult to find.) Third, people rarely shared these types of information; when they did, they would either type them into an email message or photocopy them. A few exceptions cropped up where a coherent system for sharing existed: many people used their email program's ability to store email addresses, and people generally shared their own contact information in the form of business cards or electronic signature files appended to their outgoing email. But when it came time to find information, people were back in the quandary David encountered in the opening section. Basic information about people in this "community" was nearly impossible to find. This fact was serving as a substantial damper on activities that would help establish it as a knowledge-building community. An excerpt from one year's findings in Table 12.1 shows primary means of storing information types. People could list more than one primary means (e.g., if they used both a personal digital assistant, or PDA, and a desktop program in tandem). Note the wide variety of systems.

Identifying Potential Improvements

By interviewing our audience, we were able to identify a number of issues that seemed addressable with technology. Some were areas that required no technical innovation, only a good implementation. Others were (and are) ongoing technical research areas in computer science and human-computer interaction.

Heterogeneity of Formats. The most obvious problem was that there was no simple way to exchange information with others because the information was rarely in a format that could be used directly by another person. One obvious distinction was between people who kept their information in digital form vs. people who kept their information off-line, in a paper-based format. Over and over, ease of use was the determining factor for each individual. Several people would keep telephone contact information on a well-worn piece of paper, folded to the size of a business card and kept in a wallet. Others, especially those for whom searching was important, would keep contact information online in some sort of personal information management software. Even those who did, however, could not readily exchange information because of the wide variety of incompatible file formats. In the first survey, there were nine formats for digital contact information in one department. Only two people used the corporate standard software that had been site licensed (Netscape Communicator). Although it might have been possible to export and import data in text formats, this practice was nearly unheard of, and the general perception was that such actions required technical gurus and arcane knowledge to make the process work. Even within paper-based formats, there were no standards. For instance, only two people used a physical Rolodex system for phone numbers, even though this was a common paper-based standard at one time.

Table 12.1. *Primary Locations of Information by Type*

		Phone Numbers	Postal Addresses	Email Addresses	Events	Papers
Barely Digital						
Text files	Barely digital	1	1			2
		1	**1**	**0**	**0**	**2**
Browser						
Explorer	Browser					
Netscape	Browser	1	1	2	2	2
		1	**1**	**2**	**2**	**2**
Database						
Contact	Database	2	2	1	1	
EndNote	Database					2
FileMaker	Database	1	2	4		
Touchbase	Database	1	1			
		4	**5**	**5**	**1**	**2**
Mail Program						
Emailer	Mail program			3		
Eudora	Mail program	1	1	8		
Mulberry	Mail program			1		
Outlook	Mail program	1	1	2	1	
Pine	Mail program			1		
QuickMail	Mail program			1		
		2	**2**	**16**	**1**	**0**
Paper						
Address book	Paper	4	4	2	1	
Anywhere	Paper					1
Date planner	Paper	2	2	1	4	
Desk calendar	Paper				4	
Filing cabinet	Paper					2
Notebooks	Paper		1			1
Paper	Paper	1	1		2	
Piles	Paper					1
Post-Its	Paper	1	1	1	3	1
Rolodex	Paper	2	4	2		
Wall calendar	Paper				1	
Wallet	Paper	2	2	1		

Table 12.1. (*cont'd*)

		Phone Numbers	Postal Addresses	Email Addresses	Events	Papers
Whiteboard	Paper				1	
		12	**15**	**7**	**16**	**6**
PDA						
HP95	PDA	1			1	
Newton	PDA	1	1		1	
Pilot	PDA	6	6	3	6	
Watch	PDA				1	
		8	**7**	**3**	**9**	**0**
Rummage						
Business cards	Rummage	2	2	2		
Email	Rummage	2	2	4	2	1
Old papers	Rummage					6
		4	**4**	**6**	**2**	**7**
Net						
Tapped In	Net	1	1	1	1	1
Web servers	Net	1	1			2
		2	**2**	**1**	**1**	**3**
	TOTAL	**34**	**37**	**40**	**32**	**22**

Lack of Structure in the Data. Much of the information people stored was not well structured. For instance, when storing bibliographic information online, people typically would glean needed references from the ends of word processing files scattered around their hard drives. Since full-text search of files on desktop computers is only now beginning to be standard, many people would need to open many documents manually to search for a particular reference. Once they found it, it often needed to be reformatted – for instance, from an American Psychological Association style format into an Association for Computing Machinery format. In this case, there was no substitute for human intervention – the reference would have to be retyped. Likewise, many people knew that they could find contact information in signatures at the end of email messages, but a lack of structure in this data prevented importing it into their own contact manager; again, retyping was necessary.

Different Solutions to the Rummaging Problem. Another barrier to sharing information that suggested technological intervention was the wide variety of organizational styles people employed in keeping professional information. It was apparent from the interviews that people engaged, to varying degrees, in what we term "rummaging." Rummaging is searching through loosely organized information when it is needed. Think of it this way: a person may be very organized, cataloging and filing every piece of information in a comprehensive organizational scheme. This up-front effort yields very short search times when the information needs to be retrieved. Libraries use this strategy, for instance. On the other hand, this effort is wasted if the time saved retrieving the information doesn't balance out the costs of creating and maintaining the scheme. Many respondents reported using lightweight organizational schemes such as chronological filing or piling of documents, "clumping" by topic, and the like. These schemes yield longer search times, but if the person refers back to the material infrequently, the person has a net saving of effort.

The difficulty in sharing arises when people fall on different ends of the organize-now/rummage-later continuum. People who rummage may not feel comfortable letting others do the work of retrieval by looking through their materials, and someone who organizes ahead of time may not understand why rummaging is necessary in the first place. The work done by the organized person doesn't really help when he or she sends information along to a rummager, since the rummager's system doesn't have a way to preserve the work done by the first person. Thus, these differences can serve as a barrier to information sharing.

The Diner's Dilemma (Incentives). A fourth difficulty in any collaborative situation is the problem of incentives. As noted by Glance and Huberman in their paper on the Diner's Dilemma (Glance & Huberman, 1994), individual needs often compete directly with group needs. This competition can yield a worse outcome for everybody when people are not willing to give up a little for the greater good. The Diner's Dilemma situation is easy to grasp. Imagine going out to dinner with a group of people; nobody has discussed in advance whether the bill will be divided equally or calculated exactly. The diner must decide whether to order the hot dog, lowering his or her bill, or gamble on an even split and order lobster, with the cost being borne by his or her fellow diners.

Is the effort of putting information out for the community worth it to me? In the case of sharing information with a knowledge-building community, that is the fundamental question. If everyone participates, the community benefits (as do all the individuals in it). But if some people contribute while others merely consume their efforts, the costs of sharing information are unfairly carried. This situation can lead people to act protectively, expending as little energy as possible. In this case, everyone loses. We realized that whatever system we set up not only had to take into account the group's well-being but also had to be enticing enough to individuals to nudge them into sharing their data.

Social Metacognition (Know-who, Not Know-how). The final difficulty we noted has already been brought up: how do you know whom to talk to? In the case of a learning community, knowing people in the social network is at least as important as having a lot of information at your fingertips. We realized that "know-who" was just as important as "know-how" or "know-what" (Kahn, 1999). Research on how novices comprehend a discipline has shown that social cues can facilitate understanding of the discipline and that sustained social interactions over time likewise facilitate learning (Hoadley, 1999; Hoadley & Enyedy, 1999; Hoadley & Linn, 2000).

Finding Ways Technology Can Help

Working from the list of areas ripe for improvement, we expected the following technologies to help establish collaboration.

Standard online database technologies make quick work of storing information in an easily searchable format, making it available over networks. The fact that use of the World Wide Web is nearly ubiquitous among CILT's audience suggested using this technology for dissemination.

Although no unique standards existed for the types of information we were interested in, several technologies did exist to provide information in a variety of formats, and some formats were more easily exchanged than others. A careful study of each information type helped us uncover the best existing formats (e.g., vCards or LDAP servers for contact information) or technologies to support multiple formats (such as the ReferenceWebPublisher software), which allows Web download of bibliographic references in the three most common formats (ProCite, Reference Manager, and EndNote). Technologies (such as Corex's CardScan software and hardware) that allow users to take unstructured or differently structured information readily and convert it into a common, structured data format also seemed promising.

To help ensure that the data would be easily shared, we began work on the development of Very Low Threshold Interfaces (VLTIs). The idea was that if information could be accessed in a very quick manner without disrupting workflow, then users would have fewer disincentives to contribute and would be more likely to use the information. As the databases were enriched with more and better information, individuals would have more and more incentives to participate in maintaining and using them. We identified several desktop technologies that seemed promising for quickly finding information, such as Apple Computer's Apple Data Detectors and Sherlock technologies, which allow selected text in any application to be parsed and fed to search engines without launching an Internet browser.

Finally, we realized that tools for "know-who" would be important in our system. We envisioned that the use of recommender engines (Greer et al., 1997) and innovative visualizations of social information (Kautz, Selman & Shah, 1997) would help individuals find one another and view information about learning technology research in the social context of the community.

Designing and Building the Tool

We began designing the CILTKN tool to help people connect and share information. Since our budget did not permit development of all the features we had designed, we started small, with most of the data types we had identified but few of the advanced features, such as online synchronization with desktop databases or recommender systems.

Currently, the CILTKN software (see Figures 12.1–12.3) is up and running at kn.cilt.org/ and has several thousand active users. Information available in the network includes People (contact information for researchers, teachers, and businesspeople), Pedagogy (course syllabi for undergraduate and graduate courses in learning technology from premier institutions), Papers (bibliographic information for important papers in the field of learning technology), Personals (requests for collaboration), and Places (labs or organizations that study learning and technology). Two kinds of information can be downloaded directly into people's desktop software: contact information, through the vCard format, and bibliographic information, through ReferenceWebPublisher. A partnership

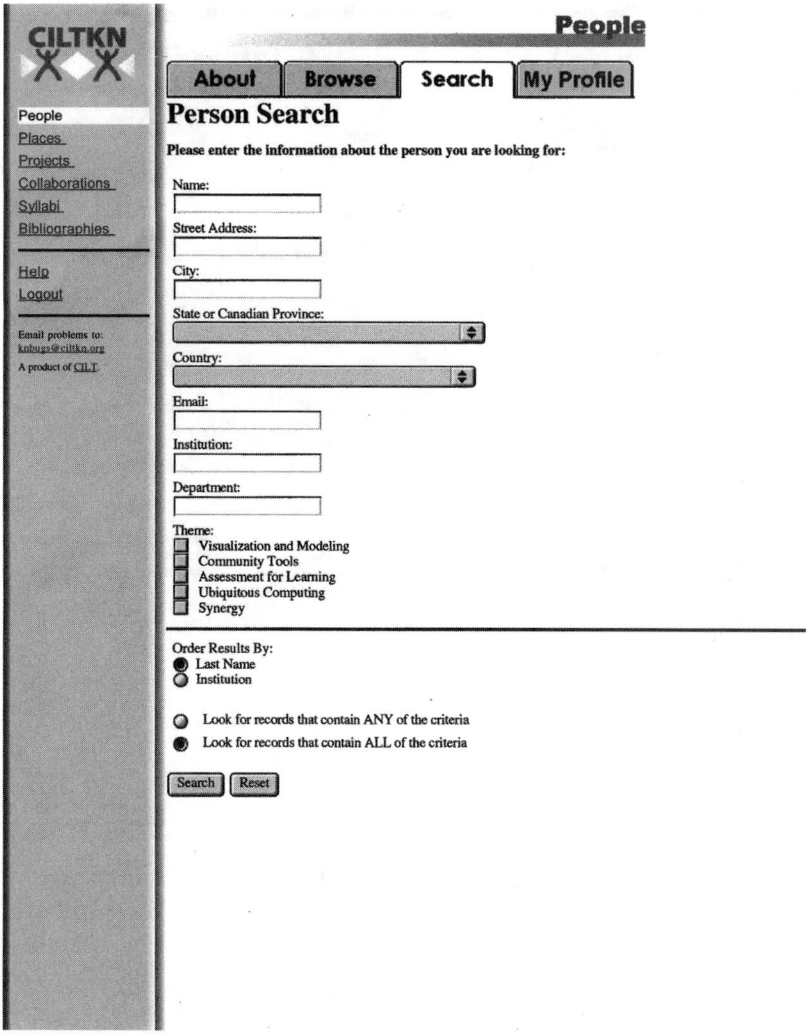

Figure 12.1. CILTKN opening screen.

with AT&T Research has allowed us to use ReferralWeb (a dynamic visualization tool) to show connections between researchers in learning technology, as evidenced by coauthorship of papers. A demo is available at www.research.att.com/~kautz/referralweb/ (note that the demo requires using an IBM-compatible computer). Each type of information can be searched, browsed, and contributed by members of CILT.

CILTKN is 8319 members from 88 countries and growing!	Log In
Visit	Username:
Visit our network as a guest	Password:
Join	Login ☐ Save my name and password on my computer
Click here to join our network. Membership is free.	**Help**
Three reasons to join:	If you have forgotten your password, click here. If you are having trouble logging in or registering, send email to knbugs@ciltkn.org.
1. Save time - find what and who you're looking for 2. Connect - collaborate with other people 3. Advocate - share your knowledge with the field and the world	**CILTKN email** Free to members; login for more info.

Welcome from the Director
Welcome to the CILT Knowledge Network, or CILTKN (pronounced silt-kay-en). CILTKN is the premier source for information for, by, and about the learning technology research and development community. Course syllabi, bibliographic references, and a who's who in technologies for learning are all inside. I personally invite you to sign up and look around, whether you are a teacher, researcher, policymaker, developer, businessperson, or anyone interested in how computers can support learning. Make use of our resources, find a collaborator, or contribute information for others to use. Comments? Contact me at tophe @ ciltkn.org or at +1 (650) 859-2860.
Join the Network!
--Dr. Christopher Hoadley, Director, CILTKN

CILTKN is a product of CILT, the Center for Innovative Learning Technologies, cosponsored by the National Science Foundation, Intel, and others.

CILTKN in the News! CILTKN has been recommended as a resource by educators around the world, from New York to Germany, from Indiana to Hong Kong. See what others are saying about us!

This server hardware was donated by **Intel**. Please send bugs to knbugs@ciltkn.org.

Figure 12.2. Searching the CILTKN.

Cultivating a Community of Use

Fostering participation in CILTKN has taken several forms. First, we began laying groundwork by soliciting material. Some was collected from traditional sources, such as library or Web searching, but most was collected by personal appeal to members of the authors' social networks. Syllabi, in particular, had to be solicited from individual instructors since often they were not publicly available. By "passing the plate" for references and syllabi, searching for projects and places, and pre-entering hundreds of CILT members' contact information, we built a solid start to having databases that could describe the community.

The system was opened for public use at the CILT99 conference (April– May 1999). All attendees were encouraged to register themselves,

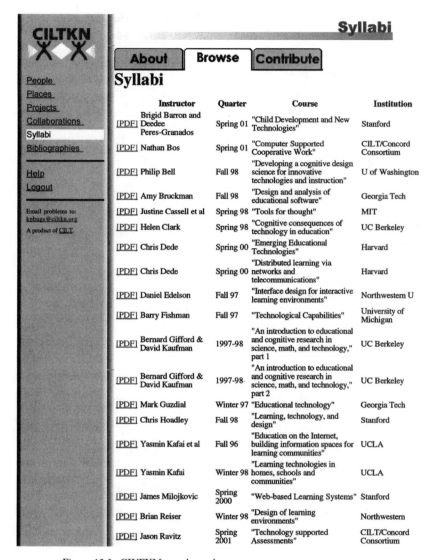

Figure 12.3. CILTKN search results.

and a subset of the databases (People, Syllabi, and Papers) were available for use and testing. Over the following months, additional data types were added, and the system was advertised through conference presentations and mailing lists.

One of the most powerful techniques we used to encourage appropriation of the tool was to employ CILTKN at the source of some of the knowledge-building activities already taking place within the community. For instance, CILTKN was used to collect submissions for the Computer Supported Collaborative Learning 1999 conference and also for a contest sponsored by CILT in late 1999 for educational applications of hand-held computers. Since people could also join CILT by simply checking a box, this encouraged more people to sign up. The use of CILTKN for conference submission allowed the capture of bibliographic information on papers as they were published. It even helped with maintenance of the databases, as current users were asked to confirm and update their contact information. We plan further integration of CILTKN with the learning technology research community by using CILTKN to support registration in two of the field's professional organizations, the American Educational Research Association's Special Interest Groups in Advanced Technologies for Learning (ATL) and Education in Science and Technology (EST).

Last, but not least, personal reminders and social interactions outside the tool remain one of the most effective means to encourage participation. Invitations to participate in CILTKN always go out under the project leader's name (Hoadley) and often lead to brief conversations that serve to remind potential users of CILTKN that they are joining not just a mailing list but a community.

Future Plans: Assessing Our Success

As mentioned earlier, CILTKN is already in use. Over 7,500 CILT members and over 10,000 others use the system now. Most users return more than once, indicating that the tool is perceived to be useful. Our plan is to complete the design cycle by examining tool use and assessing its strengths and weaknesses.

Examining Tool Use

We have only a murky picture of how CILTKN is being used. Only recently did we begin to track individual users over time. We do know that several thousand unique users visit the site each month, and that these users span many countries and include not only university researchers but also people from the education, government, nonprofit, and for-profit sectors. In fact, the most frequent users of the system (apart from CILT's leadership team) are nonresearchers. We would like to conduct user interviews and possibly field observations to judge the impact

CILTKN is having on daily workflow and to document the ways in which CILTKN is being used.

Evaluation

Although we don't have detailed analyses or surveys, anecdotal information suggests that the tool is succeeding at some of its goals. At least three people have reported that CILT is their first place to search for contact information after their personal address book, outranking even the search engines. This information suggests that people are easier to find on CILTKN than anywhere else (and, hopefully, using it will remove a barrier that previously existed for finding collaborators in this field). Several university instructors have used CILTKN in their undergraduate and graduate courses, pointing students to it for more information or even structuring student projects around the tool. We take this use as evidence of the kind of training CILT hopes to foster. At least two groups applying for one of CILT's minigrants used CILTKN to do a background literature review before submitting their proposals to CILT. Also, we have a report that one officer of an international professional society in computer science used the syllabi in CILTKN to begin learning about educational technology. These incidents support the idea that CILT is fostering the kind of cumulativity and dissemination of results we had wished for.

We are beginning to operationalize measures of the learning community we hope to achieve. By defining our goals precisely enough to measure them, we hope to demonstrate real benefits from CILTKN and help guide further development by better characterizing how the tool is shaping the people and activities around it. Although CILTKN may not cure all the ills of learning technology researchers, we feel we have successfully demonstrated that, with care and attention, a learning community might be engineered where there really wasn't one before. By heeding all facets of creating a learning community, from definition of a learning community to evaluation, we came up with an innovative type of collaborative software that wasn't about supporting communication but about supporting a community and its need for information in a social context.

Pieces of the Puzzle

If our end goal is solving the puzzle of how to support learning communities, a number of questions must be considered. We reflect on the eight areas of inquiry we encountered in this project that may help achieve our goals: defining learning communities, examining existing practice, identifying potential changes to improve practice, finding ways that technology might effect these changes, designing and building the technology, advocating the technology and cultivating a community of use, understanding the consequences of the technology, and, finally, evaluating the community with respect to the original goal. If one were to attempt to change a particular community, one might view these as eight stages that occur more or less linearly (or cyclically). Although researchers are pursuing these eight areas of inquiry in a number of settings, finding a case where all eight are present is quite unusual. Each area is essential to understanding fully how knowledge-networking technologies might help build learning communities, and each draws on a different research paradigm. Each of the eight types of inquiry is a type of research. As we step through these areas, we call attention to existing research paradigms that address each type of inquiry.

Defining Learning Communities

The notion of a learning community is not clearly understood. Indeed, this volume is a testament to the complexity of the question "What defines a learning community?" Even seemingly simple terms such as "collaborative learning," "shared goals," and "joint action" are hotly debated. The choice of definition is vital. Almost any group of individuals who interact might be called a community, and certainly people change and learn in some fashion as a result of every life experience, as we have indicated in our earlier discussion of the community-of-practice concept. Yet we need to be selective about what we hold up as exemplars of learning communities and how we recognize a community as a learning or knowledge-building community.

This volume contains a number of important efforts to define learning communities. In addition, others have discussed different definitions and indicators of learning communities. Organizational behaviorists identify the learning organization as important (Garratt, 1987) but offer few concrete measures of learning or of an organization as community. Woodruff (1999) describes some features that distinguish learning communities in terms of cohesion. Hsi (1997), following Pea (1993), defined learning communities as communities in which participants construct productive discussions (with productive discussions defined in terms of inclusiveness, knowledge integration processes, etc.). Scardamalia and Bereiter (1991) propose individual agency as an important feature of a learning community. Research is still needed to examine on a range of scales the different types of communities that exist and to characterize which ones may fairly be called learning communities. Continued philosophical and empirical inquiry is needed to define the nature of a learning community.

Examining Existing Practices

Before attempting to intervene with respect to a system to improve it, one generally characterizes its current state. Learning communities are no exception. Fieldwork could help pin down the existing state of affairs. Anthropologists, sociologists, and other social scientists study current work, home, and school environments for some of the characteristics that concern us – learning, both individual and group; collaboration, competition, and other forms of interaction; and the use of tools and their impact on the overall culture. This is often done by using ethnographic techniques, such as with our copier repair example (Orr, 1990), and is advocated for informing system design (Kling, 1991). This type of descriptive research is required to set the stage for principled interventions.

Identifying Potential Improvements

After a group has been characterized, and in some cases before, one can begin to identify areas that might be improved with respect to collective intelligence. This type of study is often the realm of industrial or process engineers or of management consultants. A careful examination of the groups and comparison with other collaborative groups often yields suggestions for how collaboration or knowledge sharing and knowledge building could be improved, for example, by "increasing communication between division X and site Y." It might be tempting to presume that these suggestions could simply be signed into marching orders, leaving the problem solved; however, identifying areas for improvement is not the same as discovering how to initiate reforms. Management experts frequently grapple with how to create a more learning-oriented organization (Cashman & Stroll, 1989; Davenport & Prusak, 1998). Although drawing implications from existing practices is far from an exact science, it is empirically informed by work on best practices drawn from studying many institutions.

Finding Ways Technology Can Help

Technology is too often thrown at problems with an attitude that it can solve any problem. This view, of course, is naïve. Much of the field of human–computer interaction is concerned with measuring how technologies change people and their behaviors and theorizing how this interaction might be generalized or predicted. Because the technology affects the group only through its impact on individual people, supporting a community often means encouraging individuals to behave in a more group-oriented fashion. However, a user is unlikely to adopt tools that do not support his or her goals at least as well as other alternatives. So "win–win" situations in which technology can enhance the community while minimizing costs to the individual user must be ferreted out. Ehn's and Bødker's (Bødker, 1991; Ehn, 1989) work on participatory design illustrates research strategies for this goal. Like identifying improvements, this area of inquiry can benefit from best-practices research. It can also benefit from theories of human–computer interaction (cognitive, sociocultural, or otherwise), which predict the impact of technology on human systems.

Designing and Building Technologies

This aspect of changing a community through technology is perhaps the most visible – the actual design and creation of the technology tools. Design involves the balancing of the many constraints and multiple goals of the situation with the technological techniques available. Designers frequently have experience with what types of tools "work" in particular kinds of settings and must use their intuition, experience, and information that can be gathered (e.g., from user testing) to evolve a software or hardware design to fit the situation. Building the technology is another task, one that may be more difficult, given the designer's need to test and iterate the design. Typically, the design process is intimately tied to the advocacy of the intervention and cultivation of the community of users (Kling, 1991; Kyng, 1991). This phase can be driven by empirical research on design and engineering methodologies, and, indeed, many design methodologies have research methodologies (e.g., laboratory-based user testing) embedded within them.

Cultivating a Community of Use

A great deal of energy is needed to take a tool, introduce it to a community, and nurture it through adoption or, as we prefer to designate it, "appropriation" (Newman, Griffin & Cole, 1989; Pea, 1992). Tool users come to appropriate a tool by establishing its fit with their work practices or changing their work practices to accommodate special properties of the tool as they come to perceive them. Community-oriented tools, in particular, need nurturing for such appropriation to take place, as do the communities they are intended to help (see, for instance, the description in this volume of the Math Forum). The proponents of the technology must help users overcome initial hurdles to appropriation. They then must help the community and the tool reach a productive equilibrium, which may include the development of very new practices or ways of working. Creating this culture of use is an important person-to-person task that goes beyond simply taking a technology and "throwing it over the wall" to the intended user community. It follows the aphorism that "Use is design" – that design does not end with what the technical designers have created but continues in what the user community makes of the tool in context. There is no one label for this class of activity, but it is practiced by technology coordinators, community facilitators, reformers, and community "champions" who help advocate use of the tool and participation in the community. It is a form of "reciprocal evolution" of technology, work practice, and basic research (Allen, 1993). We term it "cultivating a community of use." It is especially helpful if this participatory design process includes individuals who already have authority or power in the community, such as school administrators in the case of schools or, in business, managers and executives or, in some cases, unions. Although facilitating use of a tool may not initially seem like research, in fact research on collaborative tools cannot easily be separated from "community support." By definition, a research intervention requires the researchers to intervene in some way, and in this field the researchers are thus either directly or indirectly responsible for bringing the tool into the community. In developmental psychology, this type of activity has been practiced by "participant observers" (Becker & Geer, 1969a, 1969b; Trow, 1969); in anthropology, it derives from the ways observers participate in the cultures they study (Burgess, 1984; Charmaz, 1983). In tool design, it derives from the ways the tools are brought into the communities of study by the researchers or their agents. This type of action-oriented research is an essential component of studying technologies to support learning communities, and is perhaps the least well understood of the areas of inquiry.

Understanding Technology's Consequences

How is the technology used, and what effects is it having on the community it is being used in? These questions are often best answered by those in the thick of the matter, the users and participants. Again, anthropologists, ethnographers, and, to some extent, advocates study this question, as do media researchers. Many studies on email, for instance, study the outcomes as the tool has become more and more a part of organizational culture, even if the researchers themselves were not involved in the development of the software or the decision to use it in an organization (Perin, 1991; Reil & Levin, 1990). Participating in the community support (discussed earlier) almost always yields information on adoption and institutional change, although these may be studied separately (Orlikowski, 1992).

Evaluation

The last piece of the puzzle is formal documentation of what has happened and whether or not the technology, the community, and the individuals are successful. Obviously, success varies depending on the goals against which one wishes to measure it. In the case of learning communities, individuals might be assessed for learning, or groups of students might be assessed on their group skills for problem solving in the learning domain. Entire communities might be evaluated on their size and the amount of participation, the degree to which members of the community help other members, or the net quality of the community's output (such as advances in a field made by a research community). A tool's success could be gauged by changes in these individual or group measures, or by looking at the tool's use directly: by investigating whether the tool is appropriated, by asking users how they use the tool and whether they find it helpful, or by cataloging anecdotes of how the tool changes the community and individuals (Gay & Bennington, 1999).

Summary

The development of knowledge-building or learning communities is a complex, multifaceted task. By examining users like David, we came to understand that our goals for a learning community would not be addressed by any "magic bullet" technology solution. Instead, we undertook a lengthy design process that started with self-examination and self-definition and still continues today with community support, assessment, and evaluation. The challenges we faced are similar to those in other community-building efforts, and we have attempted to extract the intrinsic types of work required to engineer technologies to support an online community. Many of these areas of inquiry would exist even if we were not using technology to support our users, but they are all the more important when we consider designing software to support their needs. By now, the reader has probably noticed the wide variety of skills to be brought to the problem, from computer science and design to management and grassroots community building to social science research. To be successful at supporting learning communities, we need to address all the questions here in a multidisciplinary way that not only involves research on existing practices and definition of the goals for the community but also supports design and implementation with community support, technologies that map to the users' needs, and reflection on community and individual outcomes.

References

Allen, C. (1993). Reciprocal evolution as a strategy for integrating basic research, design, and studies of work practice. In D. Shuler and A. Namioka (Eds.), *Participatory design* (pp. 239–53). Hillsdale, NJ: lawrence Erlbaum Associates.

Becker, H. S., & Geer, B. (1969a). "Participant observation and interviewing": A rejoinder. In G. J. McCall & J. L. Simmons (Eds.), *Issues in participant observation* (pp. 338–41). Reading, MA: Addison-Wesley.

(1969b). Participant observation and interviewing: A comparison. In G. J. McCall & J. L. Simmons (Eds.), *Issues in participant observation* (pp. 322–31). Reading, MA: Addison-Wesley.

Bedny'i, G. Z., & Meister, D. (1997). *The Russian theory of activity: Current applications to design and learning.* Mahwah, NJ: Lawrence Erlbaum.

Bødker, S. (1991). *Through the interface: A human activity approach to user interface design.* Hillsdale, NJ: Lawrence Erlbaum.

Brown, J. S., & Duguid, P. (1991). Organizational learning and communities-of-practice: Toward a unified view of working, learning, and innovation. *Organization Science, 2*(1), 40–57.

Burgess, R. G. (1984). Multiple strategies in field research. In R. G. Burgess (Ed.), *In the field* (pp. 143–65). Winchester, MA: Allen & Unwin.

Cashman, P. M., & Stroll, D. (1989). Developing the management systems of the 1990s: The role of collaborative work. In M. H. Olson (Ed.), *Technological support for work group collaboration* (pp. 129–46). Hillsdale, NJ: Lawrence Erlbaum.

Charmaz, K. (1983). The grounded theory method: An explication and interpretation. In R. M. Emerson (Ed.), *Contemporary field research: A collection of readings* (pp. 109–26). Boston: Little, Brown, and Co.

Cohen, A. (1995). *Mediated collaborative learning – How CSILE supports a shift from knowledge in the head to knowledge in the world.* Paper presented at the Annual Meeting of the American Educational Research Association, San Francisco.

Cohen, E. G. (1994). Restructuring the classroom: Conditions for productive small groups. *Review of Educational Research, 64*(1), 1–35.

Davenport, T. H., & Prusak, L. (1998). *Working knowledge: How organizations manage what they know.* Boston: Harvard Business School Press.

EDUCOM Review Staff. (1996). Bernie Gifford on changing the educational technical landscape, *EDUCOM Review, 31*(4), 14–19.

Ehn, P. (1989). *Work-oriented design of computer artifacts.* Stockholm: Arbetslivscentrum.

Fischer, G. (1999). Lifelong learning – More than training. In R. Mizoguchi & P. A. M. Kommers (Eds.), *International Journal of Continuing Engineering Education and Life-Long Learning,* special issue on Intelligent Systems/Tools in Training and Life-Long Learning, pp. 265–94; Vol. II, No 3/4, Olney, Bucks, UK: Inderscience Publishers.

Francik, E., Rudman, S. E., Cooper, D., & Levine, S. (1991). Putting innovation to work – Adoption strategies for multimedia communication systems. *Communications of the ACM, 34*(12), 52–63.

Garratt, B. (1987). *The learning organization: And the need for directors who think.* Aldershot, Hampshire, England: Ashgate.

Gay, G., & Bennington, T. L. (Eds.). (1999). *Information technologies in evaluation: Social, moral, epistemological, and practical implications,* New Directions for Evaluation #84. San Francisco: Jossey-Bass.

Glance, N. S., & Huberman, B. A. (1994). The dynamics of social dilemmas. *Scientific American, 270*(3), 76–81.

Greer, J., McCalla, G., Kumar, V., Collins, J., & Meagher, P. (1997). *Facilitating collaborative learning in distributed organizations.* Paper presented at the Computer Support for Collaborative Learning 97 Conference, Toronto.

Hewitt, J., & Scardamalia, M. (1999). *Knowledge forum: A next-generation discourse environment.* Paper presented at the Annual Meeting of the American Educational Research Association, Montreal, Canada.

Hoadley, C. M. (1999). *Scaffolding scientific discussion using socially relevant representations in networked multimedia.* Unpublished Ph.D. dissertation, University of California, Berkeley, CA.

Hoadley, C. M., & Enyedy, N. (1999). Between information and collaboration: Middle spaces in computer media for learning. In C. M. Hoadley & J. Roschelle (Eds.), *CSCL '99: Proceedings of Computer Supported Collaborative Learning 1999.* (pp. 242–250). Hillsdale, NJ: Lawrence Erlbaum.

Hoadley, C. M., & Linn, M. C. (2000). Teaching science through on-line, peer discussions: SpeakEasy in the Knowledge Integration Environment. *International Journal of Science Education, 22*(8), 839–57.

Hsi, S. H. (1997). *Facilitating knowledge integration in science through electronic discussion: The Multimedia Forum Kiosk.* Unpublished Ph.D. dissertation, University of California, Berkeley.

Hsi, S. H., & Hoadley, C. M. (1997). Productive discussion in science: Gender equity through electronic discourse. *Journal of Science Education and Technology, 6*(1), 23–6.

Hutchins, E. (1995). *Cognition in the wild.* Cambridge, MA: MIT Press.

Kahn, T. M. (1999). *Social "know-who" for building virtual communities: It's both what you know and who you know that count* [World Wide Web page]. EOE (Educational Object Economy) Feature of the Week. Available: www.designworlds.com/ articles/KnowWho.html [1 November 1999].

Kautz, H., Selman, B., & Shah, M. (1997). The hidden web. *AI Magazine, 18*(2), 27–36.

Kling, R. (1991). Cooperation, coordination, and control in computer-supported work. *Communications of the ACM, 34*(12), 83–8.

Kozma, R. (1996). *Increasing the impact of advanced technology on the education market* (Technical Report). Menlo Park, CA: Center for Technology in Learning, SRI International.

Kuutti, K., & Bannon, L. J. (1993). *Searching for unity among diversity: Exploring the "interface" concept.* In Proceedings of the International Computer Human Interaction Conference (Inter CHI) '93 (pp. 263–268). New York: ACM Press.

Kyng, M. (1991). Designing for cooperation: Cooperating in design. *Communications of the ACM, 34*(12), 64–73.

Lave, J., & Wenger, E. (1991). *Situated learning: Legitimate peripheral participation.* New York: Cambridge University Press.

Linn, M. C., & Burbules, N. C. (1993). Construction of knowledge and group learning. In K. G. Tobin (Ed.), *The practice of constructivism in science education* (pp. 91–119). Washington, DC: American Association for the Advancement of Science (AAAS) Press.

Newman, D., Griffin, P., & Cole, M. (1989). *The construction zone: Working for cognitive change in school.* New York: Cambridge University Press.

Office of Technology Assessment. (1988). *Power On! New tools for teaching and learning* (GPO Stock No. 052-003-01125-5, ERIC number ED295677). Washington, DC: U.S. Government Printing Office.

Orlikowski, W. J. (1992). *Learning from notes: Organizational issues in groupware implementation.* Paper presented at the Computer-Supported Cooperative Work Conference, Toronto, Canada.

Ornstein, M., & Cohn, A. E. (1938). *The role of scientific societies in the seventeenth century.* Chicago: The University of Chicago Press.

Orr, J. E. (1990). Sharing knowledge, celebrating identity: Community memory in a service culture. In D. Middleton & D. Edwards (Eds.), *Collective remembering* (pp. 169–89). Newbury Park, CA: Sage.

Pea, R. (1992). Augmenting the discourse of learning with computer-based learning environments. In E. De Corte, M. Linn, H. Mandl & L. Verschaffel (Eds.), *Computer-based learning environments and problem solving.* New York: Springer-Verlag, pp. 313–43.

Pea, R. D. (1993). Seeing what we build together: Distributed multimedia learning environments for transformative communications. *Journal of the Learning Sciences, 3*(3), 285–99.

Pea, R., & Gomez, L. (1992). Distributed multimedia learning environments: Why and how? *Interactive Learning Environments, 2,* 73–109.

Pea, R. D., Tinker, R., Linn, M. C., Means, B., Bransford, J., Roschelle, J., Hsi, S., Brophy, S., & Songer, N. (1999). Toward a learning technologies knowledge network. *Educational Technology Research and Development, 47*(2), 19–38.

Perin, C. (1991). Electronic social fields in bureaucracies. *Communications of the ACM, 34*(12), 75–82.

President's Committee of Advisors on Science and Technology (PCAST). (1997). *Report to the President on the use of technology to strengthen K–12 education in the United States.* Washington, DC: Executive Office of the President of the United States.

Reil, M., & Levin, J. (1990). Building electronic communities: Success and failure in computer networking. *Instructional Science, 19*, 145–69.

Scardamalia, M., & Bereiter, C. (1991). Higher levels of agency for children in knowledge building: A challenge for the design of new knowledge media. *Journal of the Learning Sciences, 1*(1), 37–68.

(1992). An architecture for collaborative knowledge-building. In E. De Corte, M. C. Linn, H. Mandl, & L. Verschaffel (Eds.), *Computer-based learning environments and problem solving*. Berlin: Springer-Verlag.

(1994). Computer support for knowledge-building communities. *Journal of the Learning Sciences, 3*(3), 265–83.

Scardamalia, M., Bereiter, C., McLean, R. S., Swallow, J., & Woodruff, E. (1989). Computer-supported intentional learning environments. *Journal of Educational Computing Research, 6*(1), 55–68.

Trow, M. (1969). Comment on "Participant observation and interviewing: A comparison." In G. J. McCall & J. L. Simmons (Eds.), *Issues in participant observation* (pp. 331–8). Reading, MA: Addison-Wesley.

Webb, N. (1995). Constructive activity and learning in collaborative small groups. *Journal of Educational Psychology, 87*(3), 406–23.

Wenger, E. (1999). *Communities of practice*. New York: Cambridge University Press.

Woodruff, E. E. (1999). *Concerning the cohesive nature of CSCL communities*. In C. M. Hoadley & J. Roschelle (Eds.), Proceedings of Computer Supported Collaborative Learning '99 Conference (pp. 677–80). Mahwah, NJ: Lawrence Erlbaum Associates.

Afterword

Building Our Knowledge of Virtual Community: Some Responses

David Hakken

The generic conventions of an afterword to a printed collection provide an author of the afterword with substantial freedom but also considerable responsibility. Not having been involved in the conception of the project or selection of the contributors, the author has relatively little stake in the outcome. Constrained only by those general rules of scholarly etiquette, the author can more or less say anything. By the same token, however, readers can presume that what the author says is indeed what he or she thinks!

In the light of these considerations, please permit me a few words of situating. I started thinking seriously about education, automated information technology (AIT), and change in general social dynamics like community a long time ago. In the early 1970s, I was a staff person for a new left U.S. organization, New University Conference (NUC). As described in my book, *Cyborgs@Cyberspace?* (Hakken, 1999), NUC's interest in this topic was political, prompted by concern for the de-skilling impact of computerized teaching machines on teachers' work and whether this might lead to greater militancy. I have continued to think about these intersections, as an educational anthropologist (who did a dissertation on workers' education in Sheffield, England); an ethnographer of technology and social change at levels from the local to the global; a consultant on numerous social programs, including the evaluation of several educational initiatives; and a college professor teaching about community more consistently than anything else for twenty-three years, using a variety of technical tools to do so.

I, thus, had already thought quite a bit about their topics before reading the chapters in *Building Virtual Communities: Learning and Change in Cyberspace*. What, then, do I think of it, as a whole as well as the individual chapters assembled? First, I think these topics are both timely and very important. The renewed attention to community is a strong example of how the current research agenda of social science is strongly influenced, if not quite driven, by the interaction of applying new technologies and the reproductive dynamics of "already existing" social formations. A most remarkable feature of this site of interaction, one noted by National Science Foundation Director Rita Caldwell, is the yawning gap between the information we generate and the paltry use we make of it to influence social reproduction.

As the chapters in *Building Virtual Communities* attest, it is very important to figure out how to make good use of information, and therefore of AITs. They, along with much other work (e.g., Stoll, 1996; Brown & Dugiud, 2000) certainly provide examples of how *not* to use new information systems in education. Despite this experience, these technologies have assumed a place near the center of education practice, not unlike their centrality to the economic reproduction of global capitalism. This is just one of the reasons why closing the information/use gap is becoming central to the agenda of educational institutions. Like the writers in this volume, many of those trying to bridge the gap have turned to social science for help. This has spawned a new arena of applied work, around notions like "the learning organization" and "knowledge management" in formal organizations, on the one hand, and "online communities" and "communities of practice" in less formal networks, on the other.

Building Virtual Communities brings together sustained studies of learning, community, and technology. It reflects both the potentials and the shortcomings of educationist/social scientist/technologist interaction on this applied terrain. For those tasked with developing effective AITed learning environments, there is much here of value. The chapters constitute such an excellent point of entry into the thinking of those designing and implementing such programs that I am tempted to turn my afterword into a "practical lessons learned" piece.

To do so, however, would be to ignore the theoretical ambitions of both editors and writers. (Nor would it be easy to cope with the methodological and stylistic diversity of the pieces.) As the chapters make equally clear, education (in both formal and informal aspects) also constitutes an excellent terrain on which to approach more theoretical issues. This work bears importantly on the cyberspace hypothesis, the fundamental issue to which all such work is ultimately related. This hypothesis is the idea that ours is a time of fundamental, technology-induced social transformation. The majority of chapters provide real help in answering the question are the issues confronted and practices developed by the educationist using automated information technology so different or new as to support the notion of fundamental change?

An equally valuable contribution of the volume for me is the way several of the authors take evaluation seriously. Over the last 30 years, a great deal of social policy has promoted computer-based educational technologies. Because this policy has been implemented substantially in public and not-for-profit sectors, the people doing it have not been able to use "the bottom line" of the private sector to justify their efforts and thereby avoid hard thinking. Of course, there is an unfortunate tendency of public/voluntary organizations to make policy in the deliberate absence of information about results, not to demand proper evaluation of what has been done, of whether goals were met and other consequences transpired. Such an approach to policy development marginalizes evaluation. Nonetheless, several of these authors have refused to treat evaluation as merely just some silly administrative requirement to be complied with formally and ignored substantively. Evaluation is, but is not only, helpful for "midcourse correction." Like any good research, good evaluation is also a prod to more theoretical work.

Thus, a fundamental strength of *Building Virtual Communities* is the detail it contains about knowledge/educational technology implementation efforts, especially about diverse implementation strategies. Moreover, although they clearly exercised very different analytic approaches, the writers were generally responsive to the editors' request to orient their descriptions toward the broader social problematics at the intersection of learning, community, and new technology. This response was not too difficult, given that, in general, the projects they describe are consciously informed by what technologists now called "social informatics" (Bowker, et al., 1997). That is, they presume that getting the social right is just as important to building good educational technology as is getting the technical right.

Taken as a whole, the value of the volume for thinking about such general issues is increased because it frames education broadly. Schools and the formal aspects of schooling are just one aspect of a larger moment in social reproduction, one that I like to call 'knowledge networking' (KNing). I am particularly pleased by the volume's implicit recognition that KNing among researchers and teachers is as important to the broad sweep of education as is the actual teaching of students by teachers. The pedagogical turn to Constructivism has been a helpful antidote to passive theories of student learning. While generally a good thing, however, Constructivism has tended to obscure the still useful distinction that can be made between the initial creation/further development (reproduction) of knowledge and its later sharing with students. While Constructivists justly stress that learning involves the active reconstruction of knowledge by each collection of students, this knowledge is not the same as new knowledge co-constructed (e.g., in research) or actively extended (as in scholarly networking) via KNing. The difficulties that arise from ignoring these distinctions parallel those of participatory action research or so-called new ethnography, in which process or narrative concerns (respectively) too easily displace the hard effort needed to figure out what has been learned or discovered that is actually new.

Consequently, I will in this afterword relate to the book theoretically, evaluating it in terms of the intellectual issues that preoccupy (or should preoccupy) its writers. I see these as:

1. Can strategies designed to evoke "community" be used legitimately as means to "engineer" the social dimension of dispersed learning/knowledge networking?
2. How effective are these strategies? What are the consequences for networking aimed at knowledge learning, both positive and negative, of deploying them?
3. What kinds of theorizations make sense in analyzing what happens when a concerted effort is made to introduce an automated information technology supportive of knowledge networking in a "holistic" way – that is, via designed anticipations of the social contexts/consequences of the intervention? More specifically, Does it make sense to use the term "virtual community," or just "community," to describe this?
4. What do these efforts suggest about a potentially important change in community more generally as new information technologies are introduced, now and in the future? Is all the talk about "virtual community" just so much hot air, or is it indicative of something more significant about change in a basic moment in social formation reproduction?

1. Diverse "Community" Strategies for the Social Design of Dispersed, AITed Learning

Perhaps the basic lesson of this collection is that "community" can be addressed via technology at a number of levels and to distinct aspects of the knowledge networking continuum. Most of the pieces focus on cases in a way that illustrates this point nicely. Davidson and Shofield describe a "sharing" intervention, a strategy to draw out shared gender identity as a way to leverage community among students. What was interesting in this case was the extent to which its success depended upon cross status (teacher/student) gender solidarity, including a large element of performed teacher non-expertise.

The strategy employed in the case Davidson and Shofield studied involved a community highly placed; indeed, it is conceivable that its success also depended upon the simultaneous, visible marginalization of the male students in the environment. Levin and Cervantes offer a case more typical of the uses of AIT in educational "sharing" KNing – creation of collaborations involving students and teachers in a shared space (that of the 'Zero-g' Project) that is not a shared place.

Focusing less on sharing knowledge and more on its reproduction, the case addressed by Renninger and Shumar involves fostering community as much among teachers via collectivizing specific content expertise in math as among teachers and students. Cuthbert, Clark, and Linn describe a parallel effort among science teachers, and these teachers and their students. Schlager, Fusco, and Schank describe technology efforts to operate community more exclusively on the general level of teacher professional development. Hunter's case involves two efforts to promote the use of AIT via mobilization of a "community of schools," if you will. Her case again has the salutary effect of highlighting the dependence of online communities on "real-life" geographic communities: the ones that, in the United States at least, have to fund "ed tech" in the long run. Here, reproduction of knowledge is appropriately placed in close analytic proximity to another institutional form of social reproduction. Nolan and Weiss are also concerned with peer-to-peer activities, but of a more informal sort. In tracing the path from Kindred Spirits to Serbia.net, they show how an educational reproduction function was, to an extent, displaced by "purer" community through identity formation.

Bruckman's and Jensen's case, that of MediaMOO, shifts attention toward creating new knowledge. Their study was an effort to promote new understandings of both pedagogy and technology by creating community among teachers and technology researchers. A similar situation is addressed by Hoadley and Pea, whose CILT tool is designed to facilitate knowledge coproduction among learning technology researchers and stake holders. Burrows and Nettleton consider interventions operating in a domain similarly spanning knowledge creation and reproduction. In their wired self-help networks, however, the relations between formal researchers and what we might call "experientialists" emerge as much more problematic.

In these ways, the volume illustrates the diverse ways in which "community" and related concepts can be mobilized to address the social dimensions of learning technologies. It also illustrates how social dynamics labeled "community" can complicate such interventions and thus need to be considered carefully in program design. On the one hand, it seems reasonable to use these findings to conclude that similar conceptual tools might usefully help address the social dimensions of other forms of automated technology. On the other, the extent to which a somewhat opportunistic use of "community" as a gloss for "the social" also has costs is an issue I return to below.

2. The Effectiveness of Community-Oriented Educational Technology Development

Almost all the interventions described in this collection can be usefully thought of as "demonstration" or "proof-of-concept" efforts. That is, resources were made available to show that something that sounds good could actually be made to work.

One benefit of demonstrations is that they often help locate potential problem areas. Thus, efforts to foster gender community via technology to help girls should be concerned about how to do this without inadvertently disadvantaging boys. Several of the cases (e.g., Levin and Cervantes as well as Bruckman and Jensen) underline the importance to KNing of very active, even activist leadership forms of moderation. Similarly, several (e.g., Renninger and Shumar) point out the severe consequences of the still-all-too-frequent technical failures. Hunter's case serves as a salutary reminder that ed tech is not a simple, high-speed road to educational reform. To move beyond demonstration to the reality of fundamentally changed practice, one needs to change institutions, and this means careful, long-term, coordinated pressure.

I also believe that some lessons about effectiveness can be drawn that differ somewhat from those that some of the writers would draw. Bruckman and Jensen, for example, outlined several revisions for reviving MediaMOO. One would involve a distributed architecture, thereby allowing the loci of most intensive networking to go off by themselves, converting MediaMOO into more of an umbrella than an action research project. Similarly, they would promote survival of the MOO by substituting a new goal. The original goal, that of a general community of communication tech researchers and teachers, would be displaced by a new goal, a narrower community for those at the early stages of the "life cycle" of the technology/education professional. Although the first revision would seem to substitute the illusion of virtual community for its reality, the second would harness the technology to a different purpose. In neither case is the new situation argued for, so one is left with the sense that the underlying goal here is survival of the program. I am not arguing that Bruckman and Jensen have surrendered to survivalism, but I am saying that the new approaches need additional justification. Its absence could be used to argue that MediaMOO has become just one of many demonstration projects whose raison d'être would appear to be merely self-perpetuation.

To avoid this problem, demonstration projects must generate new knowledge or reproduce existing knowledge in some new way. A similar problem is manifest in the argument of Cuthbert, Clark, and Linn. Early on, they state that each of their efforts, including peer review community development, "play decisive roles in achieving the goal of improving science education" (p. 216) However, the chapter only addresses how design criteria were implemented, offering neither evidence of improved science education nor how each effort was decisive to this result. Again, readers are left with the impression that they are being asked to assume that mere implementation of the design is itself sufficient indication of improvement and of the effectiveness of design.

It is a good thing to try to draw lessons from the experience of demonstration projects. In both of these cases, however, the pursuit of "lessons" has drawn the writers into drawing dubious inferences, or claiming more than they should.

Interestingly, demonstrations are the kinds of activities that pass for "research" in engineering and technology fields like computer science or informatics. Here, too, success at showing that a system *can* be deployed is often mistaken for evidence that it *should* be; the "If we build it, they will come" syndrome is characteristic of efforts like the "information superhighway" (and maybe the e-rate?). There remains an important distinction, however, between showing that something is feasible and determining if it is effective. I believe the latter should still be the ultimate goal of applied study of interventions. You might be able to make it work in one situation, but will it work in others? To what extent does relative success in one context depend upon its special characteristics, its newness or attention grabbing qualities (i.e., Hawthorne effects)?

These cases make it clear that if one wishes to do deplaced, AITed KNing, one should pay attention to the social dimensions of an intervention. "Community" can be a good moniker under which to do this. There remain larger, more difficult questions that must be confronted by those who would advocate for more deplaced AITed KNing, however.

Despite the obvious efforts of these writers to take demonstration evaluation seriously, it is difficult to use this collection to move beyond
"demonstrableness" to address larger issue of comparative effectiveness.
For example, under what conditions should one choose deplaced KNing,
as opposed to placed? I count myself with these authors as someone
who takes evaluation seriously, but conspicuous by its absence from this
collection is any comparative study of placed vs. deplaced or "hybrid"
community-facilitated KNing. I would guess, of course, that this absence
has more to do with the irresolute commitment of funders to thorough
evaluation than to any decision by our editors.

One could also ask if there is any basis here for prioritizing attention to
KNing among students, among teachers, among researchers, or among
the various possible permutations of these roles. Should one try to address
KNing in more than one, even all of them, in each program? As indicated
earlier, failure to fund work that addresses these broader questions follows
from the penchant of policy makers to prefer to make policy ignorant of
whether some intervention is likely to work. As long as this remains the
case, AITed learning, and attempts to "engineer" community to support
it, will be derivative activity, dependent upon the overflow of technology
development funding.

It is also arguable that, with the bursting of the "dot.com" bubble
and the decline of e-business, surviving arenas of AIT application like
education may enjoy even more "funny money." I would caution that this
would not be dependable in the long run. Thus, this issue of comparative
effectiveness remains one where those of us doing the work described
here can influence our own destiny, by asking such questions ourselves.
It is imperative that we take advantage of opportunities, like a collective
volume, to construct and address a shared agenda. Our editors are to be
commended for initiating the process, but it needs to be taken further.

3. The Theoretical Value of "Virtual Community" for Deplaced KNing

Of central concern to all the chapters is an effort to theorize
the social dimensions of deplaced AITed KNing. Much of the theorizing
effectively addresses the question: what kinds of theorizations make sense
in analyzing what happens when a concerted effort is made to introduce
a technology supportive of knowledge networking in a "holistic" way –
that is, to try to anticipate and address the social contexts/consequences
of the intervention? More specifically, does it make sense to use the

term "virtual community," or just "community," to describe what takes place?

On this issue, the chapters offer a widely divergent array of approaches. Even though several chapters address the utility of community as a concept, some refuse to use it at all. Of those that do, widely different conceptions are used, many of which are undertheorized. Some refuse to define it but use it analytically anyway.

These diverse practices occur despite our editors' efforts to provide a framework for thinking about community, as well as making the case for the relevance of the notion virtual community. The diversity makes the volume less helpful than it might be. Of course, there are significant differences among the writers, of both national and disciplinary sorts, which hugely complicate the effort to do their own displaced KNing. Still, the volume would be stronger if more effort had gone into persuading the writers to justify their use of terms in a more coherent manner. For example, some of the following questions could be addressed at the beginning of each piece. Do you find the notion "virtual community" of value in thinking about your work? Why or why not? If not, what alternative conceptualizations would you argue for, and why?

Conceptual clarity is crucial with regard to community. I personally find it in the following manner. In my experience in the United States and in Europe, when speaking English, "natives" use community in three distinguishable, albeit often overlapping, ways, to refer to

1. Smallish geo-political units like villages, town, and cities;
2. Distinguishable-because-relatively-more-dense sets of social relationships or networked patterns of social interaction (e.g., "workplace community" can be, variously, those aspects of workplace interaction that go beyond the minimum level of necessary socializing, or a workplace that is characterizable as being strikingly sociable); and
3. The existence among some of shared qualities, implying notions like "identity" or "solidarity" (e.g., "the community of believers").

As in the chapters here, claims that "community" is not descriptively relevant often turn on one or more of these three dimensions being missing. Properly informed natives would, I think, find this practice hypercritical. At the same time, the total conceptual ambit of these three uses is vast, so vast that, if the term were to be used when any of the three were present, it's use would tell us very little.

How then do we deal with "community," let alone its even more plastic offspring, "virtual community?" Like the editors, I take my cue from

Anthony Cohen (1985), who suggests that we can approach community from a "performance" perspective. He observes that "natives" regularly evoke community when they wish to place emphasis on what is shared by a particular bunch of people (whether they are in the same place or same network or "have" the same identity, irrespective of place). In this regard, to perform community is to stress implicitly what is *not* shared with those not in the bunch. As such a boundary construction activity, community is highly political.

Deplaced AITed KNing is a new activity for many students, teachers, researchers, and those others implicated in but outside the formal educational institutions relevant to any particular intervention. It takes effort to involve oneself in a new activity. One's willingness to put in the effort depends upon many things, but clearly one important element is being convinced that others, too, will put in the requisite effort. Thus, it makes sense that those involved in trying to promote new activity will plan and implement the occasional performance of community. Whatever the awkwardness that might, for the moment, attend the deliberate ignoring of that which separates us, the unity of purpose implied by collective performance of community is a good way to indicate "buy in," "ownership," or whatever pop biz phrase you prefer. I would go so far as to assert that, over time, the absence of any performance of community will tend to be interpreted by natives as lack of sufficient general commitment, an absence that justifies abandoning their own involvement. In sum, *it is highly likely that deliberate (engineered) community performance will be a necessary component of any deplaced AITed KNing effort.*

Now add the fact that we are most used to performances of community in face-to-face contexts. Community performance at a distance has to be imagined, with all that this implies for increasing possibly-to-be-encountered incommensurabilities. We can with some justice refer to such efforts as engineering virtual community. As these chapters attest, *it is also highly likely that engineering the necessary virtual community turns out to be hard.*

Still, since any effective deplaced AITed KNing intervention must of necessity promote virtual community of the sort outlined, it is reasonable to require it. It also makes sense to then ask, what virtual community engineering works, and what doesn't? Although these chapters don't offer a ready answer, the collection does give some hints. Several chapters indicate that people participate most easily when they see an immediate payoff or benefit, while efforts to promote more fulsome performances of community (e.g., "generalized reciprocity") are less likely to be successful, at least if they occur in the beginning. This fits closely with Mimi Ito's characterization (2001) of the "networked localities" being collectively constructed around online activities similar to the self-help groups or Serbia.net. Ito does see online behaviors analogous to "in real life" community, but these online behaviors have a more tenuous, less reliable tone. Together, this collection and Ito indicate that *it is likely that more substantive performances of community are harder to evoke online, and those performances that are evoked may be less substantive.*

If these three "findings" are correct, they indicate a real problem for those ready to jettison "bricks-and-mortar" forms of educational institutionalization. This is another reason why I tend to be skeptical of any displaced AITed KNing initiative that is "technology pushed" rather than a response to a real, felt need.

One can also think about displaced AITed KNing in social network terms, in terms of "natural," "linear program" "life cycle," seeing it as an occasion to consider interesting perennial philosophical questions and the like. These suggestions are just a few of the other alternatives for theorizing the community dimension of displaced AITed KNing offered by these writers. I find them less helpful in regard to the necessary tackling of virtual community than the approach I have briefly outlined.

4. Is Community Changing?

Does the character of community change as it "goes virtual?" When we "metaanalyze" these interventions and their theorizations, looking at the social dynamics emerging around the cases, do they suggest significant social change, especially in the way related entities like "communities" and "identities" get created, reproduced, and shared?

These chapters illustrate one clear, rather mundane, but not trivial, sense in which technologically based change is real. Humans already practiced various forms of "community-at-a-distance" before computing. Benedict Anderson outlined one striking example, that engendered by national newspapers, in *Imagined Communities* (1991). To sustain displaced AITed KNing, more performing of community-at-a-distance is necessary. If displaced AITed forms of KNing are to displace face-to-face, nontechnology and/or other than AIed technology forms, we must get better at performing community-at-a-distance. These chapters illustrate that groups of people can be cajoled into doing it, but it is hard, and it is even harder to sustain.

More generally, these chapters do not justify concluding that some fundamental shift is taking place in the role of community in the reproduction of contemporary social formations. They can be read as demonstrating that an important shift is probably necessary if KNing is to be shifted from places and mediated by automated information technology, but there is nothing here to suggest that such a shift is occurring already or is even inevitable. If one wants to argue that such a shift is likely, one must do it on the basis of other, more general social dynamics than those theorized here.

Having spoken in limited favor of theorizing deplaced AITed KNing in terms of virtual community, let me end by pointing out an additional limitation of this theoretical framing. Most of the readers of this volume will have grown up in cultures that privilege science by treating it as the most central form of KNing. For a long time, KNing in science has often been deplaced; much of the activity takes place at universities, research centers, corporations, and studies at some considerable distance from each other.

The preceding analysis would suggest that the presence of some forms of community performance, some celebrations of unity – Festschriften, banquets, awards that have large elements of collective self-congratulation, and so on – is predictable. I would assert that more important to scientific KNing, however, is the considerable performance of *non-*, even *anti-*community – conflict over ideas, competition, back-stabbing, sabotage, and so on. Thus, the metaphor, "the scientific community," is largely misleading. As science, technology, and society scholarship demonstrates, this metaphor generally distorts the actual construction of science. What science requires, in addition to institutions that support performance of Cohenian community, are institutions that simultane-ously promote and successfully manage conflict. It especially requires mechanisms to support often conflictual metadiscussion of the criteria by which the kinds of data and arguments to be found telling are to be judged.

In short, any deplaced AITed KNing in science must find ways to accomplish these other functions, as well as to perform community. The notion of "virtual community" helps us see one aspect of what deplaced AITed KNing involves, but there are also other, even more important, aspects to be engineered. I believe an important prerequisite to this change is fostering a critical theoretical perspective on the "revolutionist" rhetoric employed in discussions of education and knowledge (see Hakken, 1999, chapter 7).

The actual engineering requires a fundamental rethink of the stan-dard reductionist approach to knowledge taken in computer science. Fortunately, there are alternative discourses in the broader practice of informatics on which to base the design of such systems. The new anthropology of knowledge, and newer, anti-essentialist perspectives on epistemology in philosophy, provide complementary and necessary elements for the creation of really effective products to support deplaced AITed KNing.

The chapters in *Building Virtual Communities* are characteristic of this alternative approach. I found them of substantial help in my efforts to specify a unified program in my current work (*The Knowledgescapes of Cyberspace*). They are an excellent point of entry into the thinking of those designing and implementing effective AITed learning environments; and they provide real help in addressing the issues of learning and change in cyberspace.

References

Anderson, B. R. O. G. (1991). *Imagined communities: Reflections on the origin and spread of nationalism*. London New York: Verso.

Bowker, G. C., Star, S. L., Turner, W. & Gasser, L. (1997). Introduction. In G. C. Bowker, S. L. Star, W. Turner, & L. Gasser (Eds.), *Social science, technical systems, and cooperative work: Beyond the great divide* (pp. x–xxiii). Mahwah, NJ: Lawrence Erlbaum.

Brown, J. S., & Duguid, P. (2000). *The social life of information*. Boston: Harvard Business School Press.

Cohen, A. P. (1985). *The symbolic construction of community*. Chichester, NY: E. Horwood and Tavistock.

Hakken, D. (1999). *Cyborgs@cyberspace?: An ethnographer looks to the future*. New York: Routledge.

Ito, M. (2001). *Networked localities* [World Wide Web page]. Available: www.itofisher.com/PEOPLE/mito/.

Stoll, C. (1996). *Silicon snake oil: Second thoughts on the information highway*. New York: Doubleday.

Afterword

Building, Buying, or Being There: Imagining Online Community

Steven G. Jones

If one were to read *Building Virtual Communities* for its references alone it would be a valuable book. We have accumulated a considerable body of literature that examines and theorizes online community, and this book does a marvelous job of pushing forward and extending the conversation about their manifestation and maintenance.

But the tensions they manifest and maintain can still be heard as a murmur beneath that conversation. Do we "build" virtual communities, or do they occur on their own, "organically"? Are they "imagined" or "real"? Is online community a new form of encounter with others, or is it a variation on the theme of a (siren) song? We know the virtual cannot (at least, not yet) be *entirely* disassociated from the "real" (Jones, 1998). And our research into online social phenomena is routinely escaping that trap of dissociation. Less and less of it may be critiqued in ways that Wellman and Gulia (1999) critiqued earlier Internet research that

Treats the Internet as an isolated social phenomenon without taking into account how interactions on the Net fit with other aspects of people's lives. The Net is only one of many ways in which the same people may interact. It is not a separate reality. (p. 334)

But as our study of the online and off-line worlds we create continues to grow, let us also increase our sensitivity to the ways that we are creating the articulations between online and off-line. It has been argued elsewhere (Jones & Kucker, 2000) that early research on Internetworking was targeted in such a fashion as to abstract users from the contexts within which they encountered and participated in online communities. Whether online community is built or organic, we "imagine communities" as we write our essays and research reports just as they are imagined when one codes software for threaded discussions, builds MOOs, and the

368

like. Just as we imagine communities, we imagine users and contexts of use (one may argue that we do both simultaneously).

I would like to propose, however, that our imagination, particularly when it is grounded (in the academic and colloquial sense) in scholarly idioms, is at least a little too rational. Much as comparative studies of online versus face-to-face communities tend to foreground rationality in the context of media choice (Wellman et al., 1996), so too the stories we tell about our perceptions and interpretations of online communities tend toward the explanatory, prescriptive, and sometimes exhortatory.

As Internet research, particularly in communication studies, has drifted toward forms of uses and gratifications research, it has increasingly reinforced the idea prevalent in early studies of Computer-Mediated Communication (CMC) that individuals will make a rational choice among available communication media based on consideration of how well each available medium matches the task (Daft & Lengel, 1986; Daft, Lengel & Trevino, 1987; Webster & Trevino, 1995). On the one hand, I believe that we are largely rational and do make thoughtful decisions about the ways we communicate; however, I am also of the opinion that we should create a new term, "e-rational choice," to designate the way choices are made online. Internet use is influenced by more than rational choices made in consideration of message content and the situation or task at hand; use is also influenced by social forces and symbolic cues, which may seem largely irrational, trivial, or lacking consideration (see Schmitz & Fulk, 1991). Think, for instance, of the symbolic value, the stylishness, if you will, of using a new gadget, compared to using a desktop phone or an old computer. Many times the choices that are made about use of a technology of communication have less to do with communication and more to do with fashion, status, or communication to those *present* (rather than to the one at a distance on account of whom the technology, one may believe, is engaged).

The same is likely true of community – the ones to which we belong are not only varied by type (e.g., geographical, electronic, interest) but also vary by choice. Those choices are often irrational, inscrutable, and irreducible to the narratives we write as we seek to understand and explain social behavior. What's more, the sociological study of community (particularly as it has been adopted for use by those studying online community) has closely hewed to western notions of community, likely because those are notions with which CMC scholars are most familiar. And it is in the western world that the Internet has seen its initial phase of development – though whether the west will continue to lead it in future is not certain.

The history of online community has not necessarily been one of rational, linear developments. Indeed, once we have had sufficient time to assay it, we will, I believe, find that an interesting tension was continually at the core of its growth. Its earliest manifestations vary from the accidental (PLATO) to the deliberate (the WELL). Its later manifestations can be placed almost anywhere on that spectrum. But its roots, nevertheless, are rather deep within the 1960s. In his account of the development of the WELL, the "Whole Earth 'Lectronic Link" (Rheingold, 1994), Rheingold sums up the intimate connection between online community and the countercultural rhetoric and beliefs of the 1960s. Rheingold writes,

I was still toting around my 1969 edition of the *Whole Earth Catalog* when I read an article about a new computer service that Whole Earth publisher Stewart Brand and his gang were starting in the spring of 1985. (p. 38)

He goes on to note that "the WELL is rooted in the San Francisco Bay area and in two separate cultural revolutions that took place there," one being "the Haight-Ashbury counterculture" and the other being "the tip-rudder people who steer the movements and disciplines that steer society" (pp. 39–40). From hence, to paint in broad strokes, sprang *Wired*, the "digerati," and most of our notions of what online community "should" be like. The vision was Brand's, Rheingold says, and had three goals:

1. To facilitate communication among interesting people in the Bay area,
2. To provide sophisticated conferencing at a low price,
3. To bring email to the masses.

The model of a "salon" was frequently invoked (and still forms a part of the rhetoric of online community, not only thanks to Salon.com), but most interesting is a comment Rheingold attributes to Matthew McClure, the WELL's first director: "We needed a collection of shills who could draw the suckers into the tents" (p. 42).

I mention that not to criticize McClure, nor to impugn the motives of the WELL's founders, but rather to point out that it was at least fifteen years ago that one can find clear evidence of a problem that still plagues those who seek to create communities online: communities must have *members* who want to *remain* members. On-line or off-line, we are ourselves conflicted – as Carey points out, "Americans are for ever building a 'city on a hill' and then promptly planning to get out of town to avoid the authority and constraint of their creations" (2000, pp. 88–9). It is simplistic to say that his remark points out the obvious, that communities are dynamic, evolutionary things. The true insight he gives is that, in the

United States at least, communities are very much constructed no matter how organic they may seem. In the same essay in which he makes this remark, he underscores the roots of Innis's work in the Chicago School of Sociology (1964). He mines an observation by Hovland, "that in the United States communication is a substitute for tradition. In the absence of a shared inherited culture, communication had to accomplish the tasks of social creation and integration that were elsewhere the more automatic by-products of tradition" (p. 87). When it comes to online community, the only thing close to an inherited culture is what little history there is of the WELL, PLATO, and other early gatherings of users. There is not tradition, at least not as we know it, and there will not be for some time to come (if ever), because online our histories do not intertwine as they do off-line.

The history that we have of online communities is thus greatly important, but it is hardly begun. Rheingold's book is a good step, as is Hafner's "The WELL: A Story of Love, Death and Real Life in the Seminal Online Community" (2001). Neither, though, makes enough of the connections the WELL had to the personal computer's development, to mainstream computing. One particularly notable connection in that regard is between the WELL, SRI International, and Valee, who in 1982 published a book titled *The Network Revolution* and explained the "Grapevine Alternative" to networking in the Digital Society. The WELL continues to exert a powerful grip on the rhetoric and imagination of those hoping to find community online and those seeking to create it.

Another important connection to be made is that the *Whole Earth Catalog*, intentionally or not, marked the beginning of more or less overt attempts *by the counterculture* to capitalize on the counterculture (as opposed to, say, mainstream culture's attempt to capitalize on it, best illustrated by CBS Records's advertising copy in a 1968 issue of *Rolling Stone* stating that "The Man can't bust our music" or its later "The revolutionaries are on CBS" slogan). Calhoun has termed this period as the beginning of the "apolitical counterculture" (1998, p. 377), and trenchantly noted that the term "virtual community" as applied by Rheingold in relation to the WELL is "an overstatement" (p. 383).

The apolitical counterculture's expansion along with the suspension of disbelief concerning the hyperbolic use of "community" in relation to online social relations has resulted in what we might term "commercial community." Its most clear manifestation can be found in the preface to one of the most influential books in e-commerce, Hagel and Armstrong's *Net Gain* (1997). It begins:

Our interest in virtual communities has evolved over many years ... it began in the late 1980s, when we observed the emergence and growth of The Well [sic]. The second impetus for this book came from our work with clients ... [v]irtual communities provided a powerful context for [exploiting new market opportunities] and were therefore more than just an interesting social phenomenon. In fact, they were the kernel of a fundamentally new business model. (pp. ix – x)

Now, I have a hard time restraining myself (given my unease with their use of my own work) from firing back that the communities that matter to me most, and I think matter most to others, are *not* business models. What matters, however, is not simply that the twin engines of advertising and marketing research have found ready fuel for their demographic and psychographic explorations by appropriating concepts of community. What matters is that communities have a cost; in fact, any construction, real or symbolic, has a cost. To build a community, even a virtual one, has costs associated not just with machines and software but also with time, attention, inclusion, and exclusion. The mix of community and value is not only heady but also mutually dependent. It is when value is measured primarily in terms of capital that the mix becomes unstable. The communities that seem to thrive best are the ones that allow multiple values, set by members "between the lines" of the words that are expressed, and not the ones that quantify value.

This leads me to three points. First, scholars are still too focused on *ourselves* and insufficiently attentive to the ways in which others value and define community. Second, while looking for how community is "made," we overlook its ever-presence. And, third, while trying to find community, we fail to look for its disappearance.

Those engaged in using community models for e-commerce make a mistake similar to the one scholars perpetuate. In an October 13 *CNet* story headlined "Portals revamp sites for minorities," the reporter wrote:

But the community model has hardly panned out for all comers, especially among the numerous portal sites that have sprung up to cater to ethnic American audiences. Rather than seamlessly exploiting a niche, these players are still tinkering with their formulas in a bid to find one that works.

"You can't just give [consumers] a site and say, 'This is an Asian hub, come to me,'" said Forrester Research analyst Ekaterina Walsh. "After you take into account income, technology, age, and motivation of life, ethnic background doesn't matter." (Hu, 1999)

The story contains a subhead calling online ethnic communities "An obvious gold mine." The assumption is that people will find ties that bind, no matter what, no matter where. This assumption is patently ridiculous but shows us one of the consequences of the WELL's influence. I agree that there is no such thing as a "community of disinterest," but I would also like to point out that reliance on the notion of a "community of interest" as a means of theorizing about why people "gather" online is hardly sufficient. People as much enjoy spending time with others who are *unlike* them as with those who are like them. We do indeed find ties with most anyone, but whether they bind is another matter.

Scholars concerned with social aspects of the Internet and CMC have centralized "connection" in their research, arguing that human-connecting computer networks are by nature social networks (Jones, 1995; Wellman et al., 1996). They also emphasize context, both that surrounding and encompassed within these media. The former refers more to the physical environment and user demographics existing outside the enveloped media, and the latter attends to the notion of "social space," which is created and re-created in the course of technologically mediated interactions. What is unclear in both cases is whether connection matters, and, if it does, how it matters to those who are connecting. When does community "happen"?

Much can be learned about its formation from studies of disasters, natural and man-made. Having lived in Oklahoma for some years, I saw first-hand the ways in which communities could pull together after tornado and flood. I saw the ways an entire city and state bonded after the Oklahoma City bombing. I am sure we have all heard such stories about any number and kind of other disasters. But what happens to community when the crisis is over? Let me put that another way. While I have come across studies of community formation during and after crisis, I have yet to find much written about what happens to community after the homes are rebuilt, or after people move away, when, basically, the event that brought people together is long gone. What happens on a daily basis, what happens on the anniversaries, where does community "go" when it goes away, may it come back, and why? What are the obligations of scholars, should they do more than find what they are looking for, pack up, and leave?

Wellman's work on communities and social support can again give us insight, as can studies of community and disaster. It is particularly important to attend to studies of community attachment (Sampson, 1988; O'Brien, Hassinger & Dersham, 1994). Though this body of work is based on studies of offline communities, it has consistently shown that length of residence in a community is directly correlated to strength of attachment to it, regardless of how one measures attachment (by way of interpersonal ties, participation, or trust).

It behooves us to continue work on community attachment in the realm of online social interaction. But we should also be cognizant of the ways that a medium may influence attachment, and so I have been working with colleagues to find ways to explore the addition of "medium" as a variable in community attachment measures.

It is important, too, to note that scholars become attached to communities. I believe we should ask about the degree and nature of scholarly engagement. Though there are compelling reasons to maintain critical distance, it is disingenuous to claim doing so as a reason for avoiding contact with a community, online or off. Much is made of "ethnography" as a means of discovering the nature and norms of particular social formations, but it is rare in the study of online community to find anything other than textual analysis. We should ask what the study of online community would look like if it proceeded from a critical ethnography. Nightingale's (1993) masterful critique of ethnographic audience research gives insight:

> The description of work as "ethnographic" describes its research techniques rather than its research strategy. The use of participant observation, observation, interviews, group interviews, personal documents are all included among the naturalistic techniques of ethnography. [Typically studies of online community] do not set out to provide an account of an "other" culture . . . in many of them the only contact with [an] "other culture" is an interview or the reading of a [text]. Indeed the senses in which [users] can be seen as an "other culture" are also tenuous. The relationship between researcher and researched is foregrounded as problematic once the term "ethnography" is used to describe it . . . the very use of the term acts as a reminder of the differences (of class, education, religion, gender, age etc.) between them, differences which are often unacknowledged. Transcripts of interview, accounts of interaction, are substituted for descriptive detail. What occurs, then, in the absence of rigorous ethnographic observation and description, when the techniques of ethnography are divorced from ethnographic process, is a co-opting of the interviewee's experience of the text by the researcher, and its use as authority for the researcher's point of view . . . and demonstrates no sensitivity to the power relations or to the cultural differences which operate when the data is obtained. (pp. 152–3)

Three things should be clear. One, we have not done enough ethnographic work in CMC research and in studies of online community. Two, we have little history of the social formations one may encounter online. Three, scholars bring with them perspectives on community. The essays collected in this volume set us on the path toward expanding our views and knowledge precisely in these three areas. They also illustrate the need to transcend the etic/emic dualism one initially encounters when pursuing ethnographic approaches to the study of online social behavior. Enough has been said and written about "The Matrix" (both the film and the concept from William Gibson), but it does bear repeating that we are woven into webs of meaning and organization. The first step toward transcendence, as shown throughout this book, is acknowledgment of our assumptions and critique of our own subjectivities as we study and write about community. To do less would be to foster the colonization of imagination and rhetoric, to engage unreflexively in basically colonial practice, and to participate in the corrupt valuation of invaluable social possibilities.

References

Calhoun, C. (1998). Community without propinquity revisited: Communications technology and the transformation of the urban public sphere. *Sociological Inquiry, 68*(3), 373–97.

Carey, J. (2000). Innis 'in' Chicago: Hope as the sire of discovery. In C. R. Acland & W. J. Buxton (Eds.), *Harold Innis in the new century* (pp. 81–104). Montreal: McGill Queens University Press.

Daft, R. L., & Lengel, R. H. (1986). Organizational information requirements, media richness, and structural design. *Management Science, 32*(5), 554–71.

Daft, R. L., Lengel, R. H., & Trevino, L. K. (1987). Message equivocality, media selection, and manager performance: Implications for information systems. *MIS Quarterly, 11*, 355–68.

Hafner, K. (2001). *The WELL*. New York: Carroll & Graf.

Hagel, J., & Armstrong, A. (1997). *Net gain*. Boston: Harvard Business School Press.

Hu, J. (1999, October 13). Portals revamp sites for minorities. *CNet News*.

Innis, H. (1964). *The bias of communication*. Toronto: University of Toronto Press.

Jones, S. (1995). *Cybersociety*. Newbury Park, CA: Sage.

    (1998). *Cybersociety 2.0*. Newbury Park, CA: Sage.

Jones, S., & Kucker, S. (2000). Computers, the Internet, and virtual cultures. In J. Lull (Ed.), *Culture in the communication age*, (pp. 212–25). London: Routledge.

Nightingale, V. (1993). What's "ethnographic" about ethnographic audience research? In J. Frow, J. and M. Morris (Eds.), *Australian cultural studies: A reader* (pp. 149–61). Urbana: University of Illinois Press.

O'Brien, D. J., Hassinger, E. W., & Dersham, L. (1994). Community attachment and depression among residents in two rural midwestern communities. *Rural Sociology, 59*, 255–65.

Rheingold, H. (1994). *The virtual community*. London: Minerva.

Sampson, R. J. (1988). Local friendship ties and community attachment in mass society. *American Sociological Review, 53*, 766–79.

Schmitz, J., & Fulk, J. (1991). Organizational colleagues, media richness, and electronic mail. *Communication Research, 18*, 487–523.

Vallee, J. (1982). *The network revolution*. Berkeley, CA: And/Or Press.

Webster, K., & Trevino, L. K. (1995). Rational and social theories as complemetary explanations of communication media choices: Two policy-capturing studies. *Academy of Management Journal, 38*, 1544–72.

Wellman, B., and Gulia, M. (1999). Net-surfers don't ride alone. In B. Wellman, (Ed.), *Networks in the global village* (pp. 331–66). Boulder, CO: Westview Press.

Wellman, B., Salaff, J., Dimitrova, D., Garton, L., Gulia, M., & Haythornthwaite, C. (1996). Computer networks as social networks: Collaborative work, tele-work, and virtual community. *Annual Review of Sociology, 22*, 213–38.

Index

Continued from the front of the book